D1561559

CAMBRIDGE STUDIES

IN ENGLISH LEGAL HISTORY

LAW, POLITICS AND THE CHURCH OF ENGLAND

Stephen Lushington's long career as judge, Privy Councillor, political reformer and anti-slavery campaigner involved him in many of the great political and legal controversies of the nineteenth century. He was adviser to Lady Byron during her separation from Lord Byron and defended Queen Caroline during her trial for adultery. In *Law, Politics and the Church of England* Stephen Waddams examines both cases as well as the records of the Consistory Court of the Diocese of London, to shed important new light on matrimonial and family law during the period immediately preceding the modern era of divorce courts.

As Admiralty judge Lushington dealt with such central political issues as the control of neutral shipping by the British navy during the Crimean War. He also played a crucial part in the ecclesiastical controversies that agitated the Church of England in the mid-nineteenth century. He was required to make decisions on the most controversial political and theological questions of his time in an era of radical change. *Law, Politics and the Church of England* considers afresh the relations between these three fundamental aspects of nineteenth-century life, and makes a major contribution not only to the legal history of the period but to the study of Regency and Victorian England in general.

CAMBRIDGE STUDIES
IN ENGLISH LEGAL HISTORY

Edited by

J. H. BAKER
Fellow of St Catharine's College, Cambridge

Recent series titles include

The Law of Treason in England in the Later Middle Ages
J. G. BELLAMY

William Sheppard, Cromwell's Law Reformer
NANCY L. MATTHEWS

The English Judiciary in the Age of Glanvill and Bracton *c*.1176–1239
RALPH V. TURNER

Pettyfoggers and Vipers of the Commonwealth
The 'Lower Branch' of the Legal Profession in Early Modern England
CHRISTOPHER W. BROOKS

Sir William Scott, Lord Stowell
Judge of the High Court of Admiralty, 1798–1828
HENRY J. BOURGUIGNON

Sir Henry Maine
A Study in Victorian Jurisprudence
R. C. J. COCKS

Roman Canon Law in Reformation England
R. H. HELMHOLZ

Fundamental Authority in Late Medieval English Law
NORMAN DOE

LAW, POLITICS AND THE
CHURCH OF ENGLAND

Portrait of Lushington, aged 80, by W. Holman Hunt.

LAW, POLITICS AND THE CHURCH OF ENGLAND

THE CAREER OF
STEPHEN LUSHINGTON 1782–1873

S. M. WADDAMS

Professor of Law
University of Toronto

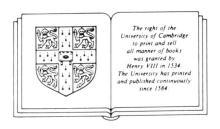

The right of the
University of Cambridge
to print and sell
all manner of books
was granted by
Henry VIII in 1534.
The University has printed
and published continuously
since 1584.

CAMBRIDGE UNIVERSITY PRESS
Cambridge
New York Port Chester
Melbourne Sydney

Published by the Press Syndicate of the University of Cambridge
The Pitt Building, Trumpington Street, Cambridge CB2 1RP
40 West 20th Street, New York, NY 10011–4211, USA
10 Stamford Road, Oakleigh, Victoria 3166, Australia

First published 1992

Printed in Great Britain by Redwood Press Limited, Melksham, Wiltshire

A catalogue record for this book is available from the British Library

Library of Congress cataloguing in publication data applied for

KD
631
. L87
W33
1992

ISBN 0 521 413710 hardback

RB

CONTENTS

List of illustrations	*page*	ix
Preface		xi
Law reports and abbreviations		xv
Parliamentary records		xviii
Table of cases		xix

1	ESTABLISHMENT AND REFORM	1
2	ANTI-SLAVERY	63
3	LADY BYRON'S SEPARATION	100
4	THE DEFENCE OF QUEEN CAROLINE	135
5	THE CONSISTORY COURT	160
	The business of the court	160
	Matrimonial law	172
	Probate of wills	189
6	THE ADMIRALTY COURT	194
	Salvage	194
	Prize law	219
	The *Banda and Kirwee booty* case	230
7	THE PRIVY COUNCIL	238
8	CHURCH RATES	249
9	THE HIGH CHURCH	270
	Gorham	271
	Denison	280
	Liddell	288
	Poole	297
10	THE BROAD CHURCH	303
	The Hampden controversy	303
	Heath	308
	Essays and Reviews	310

APPENDIX   348
    Commissions of which Lushington was a member   348
    Parliamentary committees of which Lushington
       was a member   349
Bibliography   350
    Manuscript sources   350
    Printed sources   351
    Theses   364
Index   365

ILLUSTRATIONS

Frontispiece Portrait of Lushington, aged 80, by W. Holman
Hunt. Reproduced by kind permission of the National
Portrait Gallery, London

1 Aquatint view of the court room at Doctors' Commons,
   after Rowlandson, from *The Microcosm of London*
   (Ackermann, London, 1809)   *page* 11

2 Stipple engraving of Lushington, aged 42, by W. Holl after
   A. Wivell. Reproduced by kind permission of the Pierpont
   Morgan Library, New York. MA55   23

3 The Anti-slavery Convention of 1840, by B. R. Haydon.
   Reproduced by kind permission of the National Portrait
   Gallery, London   82

4 The trial of Queen Caroline in the House of Lords, by
   G. Hayter (1820). Reproduced by kind permission of the
   National Portrait Gallery, London   137

5 Photograph of Lushington with his family on the lawn at
   Ockham, *c*.1870   345

PREFACE

This is a study of the career of Dr Stephen Lushington, and of its links with law, religion, and politics. Lushington was, as Admiralty Court judge and Privy Councillor, one of the senior secular judges in England; he presided over the principal diocesan court, and subsequently became the senior English ecclesiastical court judge; as a Whig Member of Parliament, he was an active participant in political reform. Lushington's career spans a period of radical change, in which many features were laid down of what we now perceive as the essential basis of society. At the beginning of his career, the structure of the courts had changed little since mediaeval times; the ecclesiastical courts lost their secular jurisdiction during Lushington's lifetime, and the first Judicature Act, often taken as the divide between the age of reform and the modern era, was passed in the year of his death. His own branch of the profession, the civil law, was abolished in his lifetime, partly as the result of his own political activities, and just as he came to preside over it. Family law changed, during this period, out of recognition. Lushington was the principal matrimonial law judge under the old system, and a member of the commission that brought in the new one, which is the basis of modern family law. We can hardly conceive of the study of law without law reports, but until the beginning of the nineteenth century, there were no published reports of judicial decisions in the ecclesiastical and admiralty courts; Lushington's last decisions in those courts are reported in the first volumes of the modern series of *Law Reports*. Ecclesiastically, it was an age of revolution, in which the Church of England was transformed from an integral, and seemingly inextricable, aspect of the civil polity, into something much closer to a voluntary society. Politically, it was the age of reform, that changed fundamentally the structure of government. Lushington's career touched on almost all the basic institutions of his society at a crucial period in their evolution.

The first chapter of this study summarizes Lushington's career, including most of his political activities, a separate chapter, however, being devoted to the most important of all his reform causes, antislavery. During his career as an advocate, Lushington acted in the two most notorious matrimonial disputes of his era, those of Lady Byron and Queen Caroline, to which the two succeeding chapters are devoted. The remainder of this study is of his career as a judge.

Assessment of a judicial career requires an examination of the relevant law with sufficient detail to support any conclusions that may be drawn about the significance of the judge's decisions or attitudes. This presents a difficulty, for an examination, in sufficient detail, of the law affecting every decision in a long career would be impracticable, even if it were within the limits of the writer's competence and the reader's patience. On the other hand, there is a danger that the selection of a few cases only, particularly sensational cases, will be unrepresentative. In this study, I have attempted to meet this difficulty by examining all Lushington's reported decisions in each of three separate areas: matrimonial law, salvage law, and the ecclesiastical cases related to the changing role of the Church of England.

The matrimonial law decisions are selected partly because of their link with the two cases mentioned (those of Lady Byron and Queen Caroline) in which Lushington played a key role as advocate, and partly because my study has extended to the matrimonial cause papers. The cases have also a wider significance, because they reflect judicial attitudes in the principal matrimonial court in the period immediately preceding the Matrimonial Causes Act of 1857. One can readily grasp the essence of a matrimonial dispute, and the issues seem to be familiar. There is, however, a danger here, for so radically have attitudes altered on these questions in the years following 1857, that a constant reminder is needed that Lushington's decisions are to be evaluated in the social and legal context of his time.

The attraction of salvage law, as an illustration of Lushington's work in the Admiralty Court, is that it is a fairly distinct, and perhaps the least technical, area of maritime law. Again, the questions at issue are readily grasped. Prize law, which is loosely related to salvage law, is included because Lushington's prize decisions during the Crimean War illustrate very forcefully one aspect of the relation, in his mind, between law and politics, and because a remarkable decision, at the end of his career, on the law of booty (closely related to prize law) offers an extended reflection on the nature of the judicial function.

The role of the Church of England changed radically during Lushington's time. Such a profound change in a basic social institution necessarily had legal as well as religious and political aspects, and it was not by accident that there occurred, in the middle third of the nineteenth century, a number of critically important disputes on matters of ecclesiastical law. Lushington, more than any other judge, bore the legal weight of these disputes. His decisions are of importance not only in understanding the legal side of these controversies, but also in understanding Lushington's own view of the relation among what, to him, were essentially interrelated aspects of the civil order.

In the course of searching for documents relating to Lushington's career, I came across the Consistory Court cause papers, most of which are in the Greater London Record Office. Many of the bundles of papers appeared never to have been opened, and some were enclosed in envelopes closed with the original seal of the court. I realized that I had an opportunity here to bring to light some important and interesting documents which, though available to the public, had never been systematically examined. In one respect, therefore, I have gone a little beyond what might be strictly required in a study of a single career. I have examined every bundle of matrimonial cause papers (though I have not read every document) in causes instituted during Lushington's tenure as judge (1828–57), and I have presented, in the chapter on the Consistory Court, aspects of my findings that I hope will be of use to those interested in the history of matrimonial law.

I was also very fortunate in gaining access to a collection of papers not available to the public. This is the collection that I have called the 'Lushington Family Papers', consisting mostly of letters from Lushington to his daughters and sister-in-law, but including also a few documents, of a very miscellaneous nature, that must have belonged to Lushington at the date of his death. There is evidence that he destroyed documents before his death, and his sister-in-law, to whom he left all his papers by his will, may have destroyed others. Those that remain may have survived by accident or, in some cases, may have been preserved by Lushington for special reasons, which I have suggested in two or three instances.

I have been most fortunate in the generous assistance that I have received from many persons and institutions in pursuing my research. Members of the Lushington family have made available to me documents and other information without which this study would have been much impoverished. I am especially grateful to Stephen Lushington, Dr Lushington's great-great-grandson. The archivist of the Greater London Record Office was extremely helpful in facilitating access to the Consistory Court cause papers. The archivist of the Lambeth Palace Library was also most helpful. I acknowledge, with thanks, permission of the Earl of Lytton to quote from the Lovelace Papers. I am very grateful to All Souls College, Oxford, for a visiting fellowship, to the Social Sciences and Humanities Research Council of Canada for financial support, and to the University of Toronto for research leave and for encouragement and support. Several persons have read earlier versions of the script, or parts of it, and have made very useful comments. I am particularly grateful to S. Anderson, J. M. Beattie, P. Brode, I. Brownlie, D. J. Carter, J. B. Conacher, R. Coombe, M. L. Friedland, D. M. Gaythwaite, R. Giulietti, G. Marston, J. Phillips, R. J. Sharpe, C. G. Riggs, M. A. Waldron, and J. D. Walsh.

LAW REPORTS AND ABBREVIATIONS

(Dates indicate the approximate run of the series)

AC	*Law Reports, Appeal Cases* (1891–present)
Ad & E	Adolphus and Ellis (ER 110–13), 1834–40
Add	Addams, *Ecclesiastical Reports* (ER 162), 1822–6
Bligh NS	Bligh, *House of Lords Reports*, New Series (ER 4–6), 1827–37
Br & F	G. C. Broderick and W. H. Fremantle, *A Collection of the Judgments of the Judicial Committee of the Privy Council in Ecclesiastical Cases relating to Doctrine and Discipline*, London, John Murray, 1865, 1840–64
Br & Lush	Browning and (Vernon) Lushington, *Admiralty Reports* (ER 167), 1855–7
Brooke	W. G. Brooke, *Six Judgments of the Judicial Committee of the Privy Council in Ecclesiastical Cases, 1850–72*, London, H. S. King & Co., 1872
Curt	Curteis, *Ecclesiastical Reports* (ER 163), 1834–44
Deane	Deane and Swabey, *Ecclesiastical Reports* (ER 164) 1855–7
Dow	Dow, *House of Lords Cases* (ER 3), 1812–13
Dow & Cl	Dow and Clark, *House of Lords Cases* (ER 6) 1827–32
El & El	Ellis and Ellis, *Queen's Bench Reports* (ER 120–1), 1858–61
ER	*English Reports* (reprint, published 1900–30)
Hagg	Haggard, *Admiralty Reports* (ER 166) 1822–8
Hagg Con	Haggard, *Consistorial Reports* (ER 161) 1789–1821
Hagg Ecc	Haggard, *Ecclesiastical Reports* (ER 162) 1827–33
HLC	Clark, *House of Lords Cases* (ER 9–11) 1847–66

JP	*Justice of the Peace*, 1837–present
Jac	*Jacob's Chancery Reports* (ER 37) 1821–22
Jur	*The Jurist*, 1837–54
Jur NS	*The Jurist*, New Series, 1855–66
KB	*Law Reports*, King's Bench, 1901–52
LJ Ad	*Law Journal Reports*, New Series, Admiralty, 1865–75
LJ Ecc	*Law Journal Reports*, New Series, Ecclesiastical, 1866–75
LJPMA	*Law Journal Reports*, New Series, Probate, Matrimonial and Admiralty, 1860–5
LJQB	*Law Journal Reports*, New Series, Queen's Bench, 1831–1946
LQR	*Law Quarterly Review*
LRA&E	*Law Reports*, Admiralty and Ecclesiastical, 1865–75
LRPC	*Law Reports*, Privy Council, 1865–75
LRQB	*Law Reports*, Queen's Bench, 1865–75
LT	*Law Times Reports*, New Series, 1859–1947
LT (OS)	*Law Times*, 1843–59
Lush	(Vernon) Lushington, *Admiralty Reports* (ER 167) 1859–62
Moo IA	Moore, *Indian Appeal Cases*, Privy Council (ER 18–20) 1836–72
Moo PC	Moore, *Privy Council Cases* (ER 12–15) 1836–62
Moo PCNS	Moore, *Privy Council Cases*, New Series (ER 15–17) 1862–73
New Rep	*New Reports*, 1862–5
Not Cas	*Notes of Cases in the Ecclesiastical and Maritime Courts*, 1841–50
P	*Law Reports*, Probate Divorce and Admiralty, 1891–1971
Phill Ecc	Phillimore, *Ecclesiastical Reports* (ER 161) 1809–21
Pritch Dig	*Pritchard's Digest of Admiralty and Maritime Law*, London, Butterworth, 3rd edn, 1887
QB	*Law Reports*, Queen's Bench, 1891–1901, 1952–present
Rob Ecc	Robertson, *Ecclesiastical Reports* (ER 163) 1844–53
Russ & M	Russell and Mylne, *Chancery Reports* (ER 39) 1829–31
Sim	Simons, *Chancery Reports* (ER 57–60) 1826–50

Sp	Spinks, *Admiralty Reports* (ER 164) 1853–6
Sp PC	Spinks, *Prize Cases* (ER 164) 1854–6
St Tr	Howell, *State Trials*, 1163–1820
Swab	Swabey, *Admiralty Reports* (ER 166) 1855–6
Sw & Tr	Swabey and Tristram, *Matrimonial and Probate Cases* (ER 164) 1858–65
UCCP	*Upper Canada Common Pleas Reports*, 1850–82
UCQB	*Upper Canada Queen's Bench Reports*, 1844–81
Ves	Vesey (Junior), *Chancery Reports* (ER 30–4) 1789–1817
W Rep	*Weekly Reporter*, 1852–1906
W Rob	Robinson, *Admiralty Reports* (ER 166) 1838–52

PARLIAMENTARY RECORDS

HC Journal	House of Commons Journal
HL Sess Pap	House of Lords Sessional Papers
Hansard	Hansard's Parliamentary Debates, First series (1803–20), second series (1820–30), third series (1830–91)
Mirror of Parliament	(1828–1841)
PP	Parliamentary Papers

TABLE OF CASES

Africa, The, 218
Albatross, The, 208
Albion, The, 195, 209, 210
Aletheia, The, 205
Alfen, The, 203
Aline and Fanny, The, 223, 226, 227
Alpha, The, 197
Amalia, The, 7
Andalusia, The, 203, 218
Andrew Wilson, The, 206
Angle *v.* Angle, 180
Annapolis, The, 217
Anon. (1855), 181
Anon. (1857), 186
Ardaseer Cursetjee *v.* Perozeboye, *see*
     Cursetjee
Armonia, The, 213
Arthur, The, 212, 215
Astley *v.* Astley, 181
Atlas, The, 212, 213
Attorney-General for New South Wales
     v. Bertrand, 246
Aurora, The, 197, 203

B—n *v.* B—n, 184, 185, 239
B—n *v.* M—e, 239
Baboo Janokey Doss *v.* Bindabun Doss,
     243
Baker *v.* Thorogood, 255–6
Baltica, The, 223–4
Banda and Kirwee booty case, 230–7
Bank of Bengal *v.* Radakissen Mitter,
     241
Bank of Australasia *v.* Breillat, 242
Barefoot, The, 211
Bartley, The, 208, 217
Batavier, The, 207
Bateman *v.* Ross, 104
Benedict, The, 223, 226
Bengal, Government of *v.* Mussumat
     Shurruffutoonnissa, 247

Betsey, The, 215
Black Prince, The, 7
Black Sea, The, 215
Blunt *v.* Park Lane Hotel, 172
Braintree cases, *see* Veley
Bramwell *v.* Bramwell, 187
Britain, The, 216
British Empire, The, 213, 215
Bruere *v.* Bruere, 182
Bunwaree Lal *v.* Maharajay Hetnerai
     Sing, 246
Burder *v.* Veley, *see* Veley
Burder *v.* Heath, *see* Heath

Campbell *v.* Campbell, 180, 186
Canova, The, 214
Cape Packet, The, 212
Capella, Cargo ex, 202
Carrier Dove, The, 202
Cato, The, 215–16
Chambers *v.* Wood, 240–1
Chancellor, The, 208
Charles Adolph, The, 199, 204
Charlotte, The, 202
Chesnutt *v.* Chesnutt, 177
Chick *v.* Ramsdale, 171
Chieftain, The, 217
Ciocci *v.* Ciocci, 177
Clarence, The, 7
Clyde, The, 7
Cocksedge *v.* Cocksedge, 178, 187
Colenso case, *see* Natal
Collett *v.* Collett, 185
Colombine, The, 216
Columbus, The, 7
Commodore, The, 208
Cooper, *v.* Bockett, 241
Corneby *v.* Gibbons, 192
Coromandel, The, 218
Croft *v.* Croft, 186

Croker *v.* Hertford, 192
Crus V, The, 215
Cuba, The, 206
Cumberland, The, 204, 212
Cursetjee *v.* Perozeboye, 175, 245

D'Aguilar *v.* D'Aguilar, 104
D—e *v.* A—g, 175
Davidson *v.* Davidson, 176, 187
deBlaquiere *v.* deBlaquiere, 168
DeManneville *v.* Demanneville, 105
Denison case, *see* Ditcher
Deveron, The, 205
Dillon *v.* Dillon, 176, 187
Ditcher *v.* Denison, 280–8
Dormer *v.* Williams, 184
Dosseitei, The, 211
Dysart *v.* Dysart, 163, 175–7, 187–8

E.U., The, 210, 217
Earl Grey, The, 208
Earl of Eglinton, The, 219
Edward Hawkins, The, 217
Egerton *v.* Brownlow, 195
Eleonora, The, 212
Elise, The, 197
Eliza, The, 205
Elizabeth, The, 212
Emma, The, 198
Emu, The, 196, 207
Enchantress, The, 215–16
Endeavour, The, 208
Essays and Reviews case, 239, 242,
   310–47
Evans *v.* Evans (1790), 103–4, 177
Evans *v.* Evans (1843), 177

Falkland Islands Co. *v.* R., 246
Favorite, The, 209
Felix, The, 208
Fendall *v.* Wilson, *see Essays and
   Reviews*
Fielden, The, 197
Firefly, The, 215–16
Flamank *v.* Simpson, 296
Fleece, The, 211
Florence, The, 217
Fortuna, The, 225
Franciska, The, 222–3, 226
Fraser *v.* Fraser, 179
Furlonger *v.* Furlonger, 174, 177
Fusilier, The, 202, 217

G—s *v.* T—e, 185

Galatea, The, 215
Gaudern *v.* Selby, 259–65
Gazelle, The, 7
General Palmer, The, 203, 218
Genessee, The, 203, 210
Ghirdharee Sing *v.* Koolalul Sing, 244
Gloria de Maria, The, 208
Glory, The, 206, 211
Gorham *v.* Bishop of Exeter, 271–80,
   285–7, 315, 318, 331
Gosling *v.* Veley, *see* Veley
Gough *v.* Jones, 269
Graces, The, 199, 213
Graves *v.* Graves, 176, 180
Greenhill *v.* Greenhill, 183

Haidee, The, 197
Harmer *v.* Harmer, 182
Harriett, The, 197, 206, 210, 218
Harriott, The, 197–8
Harris *v.* Harris, 104, 179
Harrison *v.* Harrison, 239
Hawkes *v.* Hawkes, 183
Heath *v.* Burder, 308–10, 316, 320,
   334, 336–8, 343
Hebe, The, 7, 210, 215
Hedwig, The, 196, 208
Helen & George, The, 215–16
Henry, The, 213–15, 219
Hopewell, The, 197, 208
Houthandel, The, 200, 210
Hudson *v.* Parker, 192

Inca, The, 212, 218
Industrie, The, 225
Inflexible, The, 7
Iodine, The, 207, 209
Ionian Ships, The, 223
Ironmaster, The, 7

James Dixon, The, 200
Jan Hendrik, The, 218
Jarman *v.* Bagster, 170
Johannes Christoph, The, 197, 209
Johannes, The, 217–18
John, The, 209
Jonge Andries, The, 214–5
Julia, The, 202

Katharina, Cargo ex, 227
Kenrick *v.* Kenrick, 177
King *v.* King, 187
Kingalock, The, 205, 214
Kingston, Duchess of, Case of, 162

Lady Katherine Barham, The, 212
Lambert *v.* Lambert, 186
Leda, The, 209
Legatus, The, 206
Leucade, The, 223–5, 227
Little Joe, The, 205, 208
Lively, The, 205
Lockwood, The, 201, 217
Lockwood *v.* Lockwood, 181
Louisa, The, 209, 213, 216
Lushington *v.* Sewell, 63

M *v.* H, 185
Magdalen, The, 209–10, 212
Maharajah Moheshur Sing *v.* Bengal
    Government, 244
Maria das Dores, 204
Martha, The, 198, 203, 211
Martin Luther, The, 203
Martin *v.* Machonochie, 296
Mary Pleasants, The, 197, 218
Mary, The, 217
Medora, The, 197, 199, 202
Messenger, The, 206
Miles *v.* Chilton, 182
Minerva, The, 199, 203
Minnehaha, The, 212
Mitchell *v.* Mitchell, 182
Monkswearmouth, The, 203
Moore *v.* Moore, 103
Morgan *v.* Morgan, 179
Morse *v.* Morse, 186
Mortimer *v.* Mortimer, 105
Mudhoo Soodun Sundial *v.* Suroop
    Chunder Sirkar Chaudry, 247
Mullings *v.* Trinder, 210

N—r *v.* M—e, 184–5
Natal, Bishop of, Re, 339
Nautilus, The, 208
Neeld *v.* Neeld, 103, 175, 177
Neptune, The, 197, 200, 202, 206, 210
Nicolai Heinrich, The, 196, 205
Nicolina, The, 197
Nimrod, The, 200
Nina, The, 223
No, The, 199
Norma, The, 206
North and Little *v.* Dickson, 171

Ocean Bride, The, 226
Ocean, The, 196, 209
Orbona, The, 194–5, 199
Ostsee, The, 225

Otto Herman, The, 203, 206, 218

Panaghia Rhonda, The, 224, 227
Paris, The, 199, 207
Peace, The, 197
Pensacola, The, 213, 216
Pericles, The, 215
Perla, The, 204, 212
Persia, The, 208, 212
Phantom, The, 216
Phillips *v.* Phillips, 177, 179, 186
Pickwick, The, 210
Poole *v.* Bishop of London, 297–302
Pride of Canada, The, 216
Primus, The, 224
Prince of Wales, The, 197
Princess Alice, The, 200, 207
Princess Helena, The, 203
Purissima Concepcion, The, 196, 205

Queen, The, 207

R. *v.* Joykissen Mookerjee, 245–6
R. *v.* Hicklin, 298
R. *v.* Eduljee Byramjee, 245
R. *v.* Archbishop of Canterbury, 298
R. *v.* Greenhill, 183
Rajasthan, The, 218
Ranger, The, 200, 208
Rapid, The, 226
Ray *v.* Sherwood, 183
Red Rover, The, 208
Repulse, The, 216
Resultatet, The, 197–8, 213, 215–16
Rosalie, The, 209–10
Rosehaugh, The, 197
Russell *v.* Russell, 102, 178

S *v* E, 184
Salisbury, Bishop of, *v.* Williams, *see*
    Essays and Reviews
Samuel, The, 206, 211
Santipore, The, 203, 210
Sarah, The, 208
Saratoga, The, 215
Saunders *v.* Saunders, 178
Scindia, The, 202
Scrivener *v.* Scrivener, 178
Sergeant *v.* Sergeant, 186
Shannon, The, 207
Shelley *v.* Westbrook, 105
Sheppard *v.* Bennett, 283
Silver Bullion, 196, 213, 216, 218
Simmons *v.* Simmons, 180

Table of cases

Sir Ralph Abercrombie, The, 205
Slave, Grace, The, 73
Smith *v*. Keats, 250
Smith *v*. Billington, 269
Snow *v*. Snow, 180
Speed, The, 200
Spirit of the Age, The, 203, 208
Srimut Moottoo Vijaya Raghanadha
  Gowery Vallabha Peria Woodia
  Taver *v*. Rany Anga Moottoo
  Natchiar, 244
St Nicholas, The, 210
Stone *v*. Stone, 178, 183
Swan, The, 209
Swindin, In bonis, 193
Syrian, The, 218–19

Theodore, The, 215
Thomson *v*. Hall, 192
Towan, The, 199
Trevannion *v*. Trevannion, 186
Tritonia, The, 196
True Blue, The, 202, 215–16
Turton *v*. Turton, 179, 180, 185, 187

U—n *v*. F—s, 184
Undaunted, The, 209, 217–18

Veley *v*. Gosling, 170, 250
Veley *v*. Burder, 170, 250, 259–62
Vrede, The, 202

Walker *v*. Walker, 168
Wallscourt *v*. Wallscourt, 176
Watt, The, 203, 209
Wear Packet, The, 211
Weatherley *v*. Weatherley, 187
Wellesley *v*. Wellesley, 106
Westerton *v*. Liddell, 261, 284–5,
  288–97
White Star, The, 215
Wilhelmine, The, 196–7, 201, 208
William & John, The, 209
William Brandt Jr, The, 214
William Hannington, The, 209
William Lushington, The, 213
William, The, 206–7
Williams *v*. Bishop of Salisbury, *see
  Essays and Reviews*
Wilson *v*. Fendall, *see Essays and
  Reviews*
Wood *v*. Goodlake, 240

Zemindar of Ramnad *v*. Zemindar of
  Yettia-Pooram, 243
Zephyrus, The, 217

1

ESTABLISHMENT AND REFORM

Stephen Lushington was born in 1782, the second son of a director of the East India Company, who was made a baronet when Stephen was nine. He was educated at Eton, and Christ Church, Oxford, where he took degrees in civil law. The state of civil-law education at Oxford at this time was such that what law was learned there was learned by private study. The duties of the Professor of Civil Law had 'dwindled down to a mere sinecure'. The examinations were formal, 'or more correctly speaking "merely nominal"'. After an interval of twelve years from the date of matriculation, for the degree of Doctor of Civil Law, 'the student was supposed to have completed his legal studies'.[1] Lushington matriculated in 1797, at the age of fifteen, and graduated BA in 1802, MA in 1806, BCL in 1807, and DCL in 1808.[2]

Having competed unsuccessfully in 1800 for a fellowship at All Souls College, Lushington was elected in 1801 and held the fellowship until 1821, resigning it on his marriage as was then required.[3] His use of the College declined after 1808, but he was there for some time in each year.[4] He advised the College in 1819 on its response to a hostile publication.[5] He presented the College, in 1808, with a silver salt cellar, and, in 1822, with two silver entrée dishes, bearing a jocular inscription to the effect that, in 1820, 'he fell, alas, into

[1] Report from the Select Committee on Legal Education, PP 1846, x, 1, iii–iv.
[2] *Alumni Oxonienses: the members of the University of Oxford, 1715–1886* (Oxford, 1888), 883.
[3] He resigned and was re-elected in November 1807. All Souls College, Warden's MS 50.
[4] All Souls College, Steward's Books, 1802–21. A letter to Lady Byron of 5 April 1816 is dated from All Souls College. Lovelace-Byron Papers, Bodleian Library, Oxford, 132/141.
[5] [G. J. W. Agar Ellis, later Baron Dover] *A few observations on All Souls College, Oxford* (1819). References to Lushington's advice are in the All Souls College Archives CTM 404/373, 374.

matrimony: farewell, and be warned'.[6] Many references to Lushington in the biographies, memoirs, and letters of the period show that he remained throughout his life a congenial companion, and a good anecdotist.[7] He was described, at the age of seventy-seven, by a visitor to the village where he had his country house, as 'the freshest and heartiest as well as the kindest of old gentlemen',[8] and at the age of eighty, by the artist who painted his portrait, as 'a dear old fellow – as clear and quick in wit as the youngest man in the company, and with the gravest possible judgment in all his remarks and manners.'[9]

Lushington's marriage appears to have been a happy one, though there is some evidence to suggest that his devotion to work imposed burdens on his wife.[10] She was Sarah Grace Carr, a close friend of one of Lushington's most illustrious clients, Lady Byron,[11] though whether that friendship was the cause of her meeting Lushington is unknown. She died, in 1837, after a harrowing illness, and it is evident from Lushington's letters at the time and afterwards that he was deeply moved by her suffering and death.[12] There were ten children, of whom one became a senior Indian civil servant,[13] another

---

[6] All Souls College, Benefactors' Book. The inscription is: Gratissimo animo omnium animarum collegio dedit Stephen Lushington LL.D., viginti annos socius peractus, in matrimonium eheu cecidit. valete et cavete. anno 1821'.

[7] A. J. C. Hare (ed.), *The Life and Letters of Maria Edgeworth* (London, 1894), 638; C. Colvin (ed.), *Maria Edgeworth: Letters from England, 1813–1844* (Oxford, 1971), 306–7, 311–12; Lord J. Russell (ed.), *Memoirs, Journals, and Correspondence of Thomas Moore* (London, 1853–6), iii, 260; M. A. [Mrs H.] Ward, *A Writer's Recollections* (1918), 160; Lord E. Fitzmaurice, *Life of Granville George Leveson Gower*, (London, 1905), i, 163–4; W. Gaunt, *The Pre-Raphaelite Tragedy*, rev. edn (1975), 88; W. Holman Hunt, *Pre-Raphaelitism and the Pre-Raphaelite Brotherhood* (London, 1905), ii, 219–22; D. C. Taylor, *People of Cobham: the Pyports Connection* (Buckingham, 1985), 62; letter to editor, *The Times*, 22 Jan. 1873, 5f.

[8] By F. D. Maurice (the eminent theologian), doing temporary parish duty at Ockham, F. Maurice, *The Life of Frederick Denison Maurice, chiefly told in his own letters* (London, 1884, 4th edn, 1885), ii, 354.

[9] W. Holman Hunt to Thomas Combe, 28 Sept. 1862, John Rylands University Library, Manchester, Eng MS 1213/14.

[10] *Maria Edgeworth's Letters from England*, 490. See also pp. 83–4, below.

[11] See chapter 3, below.

[12] Lushington to Frances Carr, 29 Sept. 1837, 20 Sept. 1838, and 1 Aug. 1839, Lushington Family Papers (letters to sister-in-law, ten days, and one year after the death, and two years after the diagnosis of the fatal illness); Buxton Papers, Rhodes House Library, Oxford, 4/387 (private prayer, by Buxton, for Lushington, 16 Sept. 1838); Priscilla Johnston to her uncle, 27 Sept. 1837, Gurney Papers, Friends House Library, 1/306 ('in a most feeling and afflicted state').

[13] Edward Harbord Lushington, b. 1822; see *Guy's Hospital Gazette*, 5 Dec. 1896, 548.

a county court judge,[14] and another Permanent Under-Secretary in the Home Office.[15]

The career first contemplated for Stephen Lushington was political. In 1804, his mother wrote letters to Lord Melville,[16] attempting to secure for him a government appointment, saying, 'for many months back his head has run upon nothing but politics'.[17] Her style of writing may not have assisted her cause: 'Oh how my little proud soul recoils at that word [petition]! but my love for my darling Boy urges me on.' In an annotation on the copy of this letter, Lady Lushington indicated that she had met Melville, who had '*said* all that was polite & friendly, other *civil letters* have passed but nothing done'.[18] But later, something was almost done. Lushington's son, writing in 1855, gave this account:

No one knows better than he [Stephen Lushington] how precarious is subsistence & work in the Political Below-Stairs; he himself was offered by Mr Windham in *1806* (was it) the Undersecretaryship of State, but some noble lord in the Cabinet objected to it, & my father was not appointed; & I have often heard him congratulate himself on his rejection, for 'Perhaps I should have ended my days long ago in some miserable colony or other, & then where wd you have been, my children?'[19]

Lushington did enter Parliament in 1806 on the nomination of Lord Suffield,[20] as MP for Yarmouth, but lost Lord Suffield's support by asserting an independence to which his patron considered him not to be entitled, and, in 1808, he was induced to resign his seat.[21] He spoke in Parliament against the slave trade,[22] against the withholding from

---

14 Vernon Lushington, 1832–1912; see Taylor, *People of Cobham*, 62–3.
15 Sir Godfrey Lushington (Vernon's twin), 1832–1907; *DNB*.
16 Henry Dundas, Viscount Melville, 1742–1811, member of Parliament, 1774–1802, First Lord of the Admiralty, 1804–5.
17 Lady Lushington to Lord Melville, 3 May 1804 (copy), Lushington Family Papers.
18 Lady Lushington to Lord Melville, 19 Nov. 1804, Lushington Family Papers. Annotation dated 7 Jan. 1805.
19 Vernon Lushington to R. M. Milnes [later Baron Houghton] n.d. but internal references show 1855, Houghton Papers, Trinity College, Cambridge, 15/113. William Windham, Secretary for War and the Colonies in 1806, described Lushington as 'very much a friend of mine', R. G. Thorne, *The House of Commons 1790–1820* (London, 1986) *History of Parliament*, iv, 470.
20 Sir Harbord Harbord, first Baron Suffield (died 1810).
21 B. D. Hayes, 'Politics in Norfolk', unpublished PhD thesis (Cambridge, 1957), 113, 117, 381; Thorne, *House of Commons 1790–1820*, 470–1. In an election speech in 1832, Lushington said that he had been promised political favours in return for opposing Catholic emancipation, but that he had resisted the temptation; *The Times*, 29 Oct. 1832, 3d.
22 See chapter 2, below.

France (at war with England) of a medicinal drug,[23] and against what
he saw as cases of official wrongdoing.[24] He favoured Catholic relief,
not a popular cause at the time, and he later described how he was
attacked, and almost thrown into a river, by an anti-Catholic mob.[25]
Politics were still to play an important part in his life, as will be seen,
but the profession to which he turned, in 1808, was that of civil law.[26]

Until 1858, the civil law was an independent branch of the English
legal profession. Its practitioners were advocates and proctors, corresponding to barristers and solicitors, respectively. The advocates all
held doctors' degrees from Oxford or Cambridge, and, for this reason,
their society was known as Doctors' Commons.[27] Doctors' Commons
was the name also of the buildings, close to St Paul's Cathedral, where
were the offices of the advocates and proctors, the registry of wills, a
library, dining hall, and court room.[28]

The civilians possessed a monopoly in the practice of ecclesiastical
and admiralty law, a conjunction that is explained by the links of
canon law and admiralty law to Roman law.[29] The union of such
diverse subjects has amused Dickens and others,[30] but the more
striking feature of the civilian practice, compared with modern judicial practice, is the high degree of specialization. The court room
was used in turn for sessions of the three principal ecclesiastical
courts, and of the Admiralty Court.

The ecclesiastical courts had jurisdiction over a number of matters
that had, by the nineteenth century, long lost their original connexion
with the affairs of the Church. The most important of these matters
were matrimonial disputes, and the probate of wills. The courts also
asserted a jurisdiction to punish lay persons for certain kinds of
misconduct, principally some sorts of defamation, and unseemly

---

[23] Hansard, x, 728 (24 Feb. 1808), 1169 (16 Mar.).

[24] Hansard, x, 452 (11 Feb. 1808), 1038 (15 Mar.).

[25] Hansard, 2d ser., xx, 909 (9 Mar. 1829), *Morning Chronicle*, 12 Dec. 1834, 3a.

[26] He was also called to the bar, and became a bencher of his Inn (Inner Temple) in
1840, and Treasurer in 1851.

[27] See G. D. Squibb, *Doctors' Commons, a History of the College of Advocates and
Doctors of Law* (Oxford, 1977); Ecclesiastical Courts Commission, PP 1831–2,
xxiv, 13–14.

[28] A plan appears in Squibb, *Doctors' Commons*, 68, and prints at frontispiece, and pp.
70, 72.

[29] W. S. Holdsworth, *History of English Law* (London, 1924), iv, 230–1.

[30] C. Dickens, *David Copperfield* (London, 1850), ch. 23. A. P. Herbert, *Holy
Deadlock* (New York, 1934), 109, referring, in a phrase often quoted, to the
jurisdiction of the indirect successor of Doctors' Commons, the Probate Divorce and
Admiralty Division of the High Court, as one of 'Wills, wives and wrecks'.

conduct ('brawling') on church premises.[31] The courts also enforced
a tax, called church rate, payable by all residents of a parish for
the maintenance of the parish church.[32] All these jurisdictions
were increasingly anomalous in a secular, liberal, and pluralistic
society, and, between 1855 and 1868, they were abolished or removed
from the jurisdiction of the ecclesiastical courts. Lushington's political views tended to support these reforms, and played a significant
role in bringing about the demise of his own profession. The loss
of the probate business made the end inevitable, and, in 1858, steps
were taken that caused the effective dissolution of Doctors'
Commons.[33]

The profession was small, with an average of about one advocate
admitted each year, in the early years of the nineteenth century, some
of whom never practised.[34] The active practitioners, at any one time,
numbered only about five or six.[35] Lushington was admitted in
1808,[36] and practised in all areas of the civil law:[37] he became the
president of Doctors' Commons (Dean of the Arches) in 1858,[38] but
that year marked the effective end of the society, and so it came about
that Lushington attained the office only to preside over a
dissolution.[39]

The chief ecclesiastical courts were the Consistory Court of the
Diocese of London, of which Lushington was judge from 1828 to
1858, the Prerogative Court of the Province of Canterbury, the principal probate court, in which Lushington sat occasionally as a surrogate, and the Court of Arches, the provincial appeal court, and the

---

[31] Pp. 170–1, below.   [32] See chapter 8, below.
[33] See Squibb, *Doctors' Commons*, 105–6. The Society did not legally cease to exist until the death of the last member, in 1912.
[34] Squibb, *Doctors' Commons*, appendix III.
[35] Select Committee on Admiralty Courts etc., PP 1833, vii, 379, 426 (Lushington's evidence). The Law List of 1824 indicates twenty-six advocates; that of 1844, twenty-four.
[36] Register of Doctors' Commons, Lambeth Palace Library, DC 1, 126.
[37] His opinions on a variety of ecclesiastical, testamentary, and matrimonial matters are preserved in the Public Record Office: PRO DC 30/28, 13 and 14.
[38] Minute Book of Doctors' Commons, Lambeth Palace Library, DC 2, 1 June 1858, Squibb, *Doctors' Commons*, 117.
[39] The Minute Book of Doctors' Commons, Lambeth Palace Library, DC 2, indicates that Lushington presided at ten meetings between 1858 and 1865, signing the minutes of the first seven. He was not present at the last meeting recorded, in July 1865, at the house of Dr Lee, the principal opponent of dissolution. See Squibb, *Doctors' Commons*, 107–8.

highest English ecclesiastical court, of which Lushington was judge from 1858 to 1867.

The London Consistory Court was the most important matrimonial court in England, and matrimonial causes formed the bulk of its business. The courts had no power to dissolve marriages, this being possible, until 1858, only by Act of Parliament. Nevertheless, the ecclesiastical court had very significant powers, in particular the power to grant a divorce *a mensa et thoro* (from board and bed), which had the effect of a judicial separation, and the power to compel payment of alimony by a husband for the support of his wife. A divorce granted in favour of the wife entitled her to live apart from her husband, and obliged him to support her. If granted at the suit of the husband, it relieved him of his obligation to provide his wife with either a home or support. The court had power also to grant specific relief (restitution of conjugal rights), in the form of an order compelling a wife to return to her husband, or compelling a husband to receive back his wife. Lushington's practice involved him in two notorious divorce cases, one consistory and one parliamentary (though both of a highly exceptional nature), namely those of Lady Byron[40] and Queen Caroline;[41] extensive records of both cases survive. The records of the Consistory Court itself also survive, and allow a picture to be formed of the nature of the court's business and, in particular, of its matrimonial business.[42] Lushington's reported judgments allow an assessment to be made of his attitudes to the points of matrimonial law that he had to decide, and these are supplemented by records of his participation, in and out of Parliament, in the process of law reform.

Probate of wills was, financially speaking, the most important part of the professional business of Doctors' Commons, but there are comparatively few judgments of Lushington's, because the Consistory Court had only a minor jurisdiction in probate matters. However, Lushington sat occasionally in the Prerogative Court, and he heard a substantial number of probate cases in the Privy Council. He also expressed views, in Parliament and elsewhere, on the reform of the law governing the execution of wills, and the jurisdiction of the courts. He strongly favoured the introduction of a formality for the execution of wills, and this was effected in 1837. The reform created

---

[40] Chapter 3, below.   [41] Chapter 4, below.   [42] Chapter 5, below.

some difficulties that probably had not been anticipated, as illustrated by some of Lushington's judicial decisions.[43]

By the time that Lushington came to preside in the Court of Arches, in 1858, the ecclesiastical courts had lost most of their secular jurisdiction. Church rates, however, remained, and constituted one-third of the court's business.[44] Cases of clergy discipline constituted the next largest group,[45] and included some cases of national import-ance.[46] Most of the remaining cases involved access to and use of church premises.[47]

Lushington held the office of judge of the High Court of Admiralty from 1838 to 1867.[48] Over opposition from the proctors,[49] he in-troduced a series of procedural reforms which greatly increased ef-ficiency and were said, by the Registrar, to have led to 'an entire change in the practice and procedure of the Court', and to have been 'attended with the best results'.[50] His contribution to all areas of substantive admiralty law was extensive.[51] In ship collision cases, he had to elaborate the principles underlying the measurement of money compensation, and his decisions form the basis of important parts of the modern law of damages for property loss.[52] No judge has better described the tension around which the law of damages is built between, on the one hand, the search for perfect compensation in the individual case, and, on the other hand, the need for rules that are predictable, consistent, and reasonably inexpensive in general appli-cation.[53] The examination of every aspect of admiralty law would scarcely be feasible in a work of this sort, even if it were desirable.

---

[43] Pp. 189–93, below.
[44] Seventeen of fifty-two cases. J. C. C. Houston, *Cases in the Arches, 1858–67*, compiled from the Assignation Book and Index to Cases in the Court of Arches, Lambeth Palace Library. See chapter 8, below.
[45] Thirteen cases.
[46] See chapter 10, below.
[47] Houston, *Cases in the Arches*.
[48] He was sworn on 18 Oct. 1838, Assignation Book, PRO HCA 7/25/176; notice of his resignation appears in *The Times*, 8 July 1867, 9a.
[49] *Law Times*, 25 Jan. 1873, 225.
[50] H. C. Rothery, *Memorandum on the Jurisdiction and Practice of the High Court of Admiralty of England*, PP 1867, lvii, 4.
[51] Holdsworth, *History of English Law*, xvi, 141–4.
[52] *The Amalia* (1864) 5 New Rep 164 (interest); *The Black Prince* (1862) Lush 568, *The Clarence* (1850) 3 W Rob 282 (loss of profits); *The Clyde* (1856) Swab 23, *The Ironmaster* (1859) Swab 441, *The Columbus* (1849) 3 W Rob 158 (value); *The Gazelle* (1844) 2 W Rob 279, *The Hebe* (1847) 2 W Rob 530 (cost of repair); *The Inflexible* (1857) Swab 200 (expenses).
[53] See *The Columbus* (1849) 3 W Rob 158, 162.

Attention is directed, therefore, to three topics, loosely intercon-
nected,[54] that illustrate Lushington's conception of his judicial role
and its relationship to political considerations. These are the cases on
civil salvage, the Crimean War prize cases, and a single case, at the end
of his career, on the law of booty.[55] Because of the connexions of
admiralty law with international law, Lushington was called upon, on
several occasions, to advise the Government on questions of foreign
policy.[56]

The ultimate court of appeal from the civilian courts was, until
1832, the High Court of Delegates, a court separately constituted for
each appeal.[57] Colonial appeals were heard by a committee of the
Privy Council.[58] Under the rather haphazard arrangements for constituting the High Court of Delegates,[59] Lushington himself had sat
as a delegate in several cases, the earliest in 1810 when he was a very
junior advocate.[60] He had argued cases before the Delegates, and
before the Appeals Committee of the Privy Council, including a
notorious case in which, on a special reference, he argued against the
abolition of *sati* in India,[61] a fact which suggests that the practice
did not arouse the same horror in Lushington's mind as among others
in the anti-slavery movement.[62] In 1833, following the report of a

[54] Prize law is sometimes called 'military salvage'. See K. C. McGuffie (ed.), *Kennedy's Civil Salvage*, 4th edn (London, 1958), 3.
[55] Chapter 6, below.
[56] Earl Grey to Lushington, 1 June 1833, and Lushington's reply, 2 June 1833, Earl
Grey Papers, University of Durham; Lord Granville to Lushington, 19 Feb. 1860,
Granville Papers, PRO 30/29/19/5/14; draft convention with France on suppression
of slave trade and comments, 29 May 1845, Aberdeen Papers, British Library, Add
MSS 43125, 319; Lushington to Aberdeen, 13 Mar. 1845, BL Add MSS 43244,
122. See chapter 6, below.
[57] G. I. O. Duncan, *The High Court of Delegates* (Cambridge, 1971).
[58] P. A. Howell, *The Judicial Committee of the Privy Council, 1833–1876* (Cambridge,
1979), 8–13.
[59] There was no permanent court; the judges were paid almost nothing; reasons were
not given; junior advocates were often appointed, because the senior civilians were
involved in the cases as counsel. Brougham described it as 'one of the worst
constituted courts which was ever appointed ... one of the greatest mockeries of
appeal ever conceived by man'. Law reform speech, 7 Feb. 1828, H. Brougham,
Speeches upon questions relating to public rights, duties and interests (Edinburgh,
1838), ii, 355. See also Dickens, *David Copperfield*, ch. 26.
[60] PRO DEL/6/54–7 (nineteen cases).
[61] *The Times*, 25 June 1832, 6a. Lushington based his argument on freedom of
religion, and Greville described it as 'able and ingenious', *The Greville Memoirs*, ed.
L. Strachey and R. Fulford (London, 1938), ii, 307–8 (12 July 1832).
[62] See C. Buxton (ed.), *Memoirs of Sir Thomas Fowell Buxton*, 3rd edn (London,
1849), 109.

commission on which Lushington sat,[63] the High Court of Delegates was abolished, and its jurisdiction transferred to the newly created Judicial Committee of the Privy Council, which also took over the functions of the Appeals Committee. Lushington was appointed to the Privy Council in 1838 where he sat for twenty-nine years. During that time, he held, simultaneously, three important judicial offices, the first in the ecclesiastical court (Consistory and, later, Arches), the second in the Admiralty Court, and the third in the Judicial Committee of the Privy Council. In 1851, he was offered a life peerage, which would have given him a fourth judicial office as a member of the House of Lords, the final court of appeal from the English courts of law and equity, but, as will be seen, Lushington declined that offer.

He resigned his judicial offices in 1867, after an illness, at the age of eighty-five,[64] but retained the ecclesiastical office of Master of the Faculties until his death in 1873, hearing disputed cases at his private house in his ninety-first year.[65] Lushington's retention of the Mastership of the Faculties caused inconvenience to his successor as Dean of the Arches, Phillimore, who went so far as to comment, in print, on the fact that there was practically no remuneration attached to the Deanship, and that he had been assured by the Archbishop that he would receive the Mastership (which had light duties and substantial remuneration) as soon as it fell vacant, implying that he expected the latter event considerably earlier than 1873.[66] Lushington's view of the matter may be deduced from a letter of 1858 from J. B. Sumner, then Archbishop of Canterbury, urgently requesting him to accept the Deanship, and expressly offering the Mastership as 'the equivalent' of the Chancellorship of the Diocese of London (which could not be held in conjunction with the Deanship).[67] Lushington probably considered that, had he declined Sumner's request in 1856, he could have retained the Chancellorship, with its remuneration, until his death, and that he was therefore justified in retaining the Mastership.

[63] Ecclesiastical Courts Commission, Special Report, PP 1831–2, xxiv, 1.

[64] Notices of his retirement appeared in *The Law Journal*, 12 July 1867, 322, and *The Law Times*, 13 July 1867, 156.

[65] R. Phillimore, *Ecclesiastical Law of the Church of England* (1873), 1245, referring to two decisions of 10 April 1872, *The Law Times*, 25 Jan. 1873, 226.

[66] R. Phillimore, *The Principal Judgments delivered in the Court of Arches, 1896 to 1875* (1876), iv–v (Preface).

[67] J. B. Sumner to Lushington, 21 June [1858], Lushington Family Papers. The letter is one of the few in the collection that relates to business, and may have been preserved by Lushington in case it should prove necessary to supply evidence on this point.

Doctors' Commons was, by its official title, a college,[68] and its
atmosphere was distinctly collegial. Consultation among judges was
common.[69] The line between judge and advocate was indistinct: all
the advocates could exercise judicial functions, as surrogates, and
Lushington's appointment as judge of the London Consistory Court
did not interfere with his practice as an advocate; the judge's title
(Doctor) was the same as the advocate's, and the design of the
courtroom also emphasized their equality of status.[70] Dickens, the
novelist, who was a shorthand reporter there, commented that the
judges and advocates changed roles 'like actors'.[71] The exclusion of
oral evidence from the civilian courts meant that the proceedings were
less adversarial, giving a trial more the appearance of a leisurely
discussion than of a battle, Dickens calling the proceedings a 'cosey,
dosey, old-fashioned, time forgotten, sleepy headed little family
party'.[72] There were, until the nineteenth century, no reports of
reasons for decisions, and this contributed to an unwillingness to be
too closely bound by precedent and rigorous logic.

Lushington's judicial philosophy was a product of this background.
His manner of thought preceded the 'scientific' school of jurisprudence, which flourished in the second half of the nineteenth century.[73] The traditions of Doctors' Commons, where law reports were
unknown in his own youth, did not lend themselves to a theory that
every point of law was objectively determinable. Nor did Lushington
lean towards such a view: his decisions in the Consistory Court, and in
the Admiralty Court[74] show his determination to retain a large
measure of flexibility, even at the cost of certainty and predictability,

68 See Squibb, *Doctors' Commons*, 37.
69 Evidence of this appears on pp. 239 and 265, below.
70 Squibb, *Doctors' Commons*, 72–3, and illustration, reproduced opposite, from
    Ackermann's *Microcosm of London* (1808); illustration in C. Knight (ed.), *London*
    (London, 1843), v, no. 101, 7, and descriptions in Dickens' *Sketches by Boz*, ch. 8,
    and *David Copperfield*, ch. 23.
71 Dickens, *David Copperfield*, ch. 23.
72 Ibid.
73 F. Pollock wrote that 'the really scientific treatment of principles begins with the
    decisions of the last fifty years'. Introduction to *Principles of Torts* (1886). Science
    came to ecclesiastical law a little later. R. J. Phillimore, in offering a new book on the
    subject wrote that 'the dictionary form adopted by Dr Burn [previous edition by
    Phillimore, 1842], however superficially convenient, appears to me fatal to any
    attempt to produce the law in the form of a system arranged according to the
    principles of science'. Preface to R. J. Phillimore, *Ecclesiastical Law of the Church of
    England* (1873).
74 Some of these decisions are discussed in chapters 5 and 6, below.

Aquatint view of the court room at Doctors' Commons, after Rowlandson.

and he expressed this determination at the end, no less than at the beginning, of his judicial career.[75] He generally gives the impression of a judge who has selected his own destination. The style of his judgments is confident, forceful, and persuasive, with frequent references to general considerations of justice.

On the other hand, flexibility did not exclude the notion of deference to law. The *Banda and Kirwee booty* case,[76] at the end of his judicial career, denotes the limits beyond which, as a judge, he thought he could not go, and in several highly controversial ecclesiastical decisions, he denied his power to depart from law that he found to be binding upon him. The discussion of these cases, below, will tend to show that Lushington's power was not so fettered as he suggested, and that his assurances that his own opinions had been suppressed cannot always be taken at face value. It would seem that he yielded, in these cases, to the temptation of clothing controversial decisions in the disguise of judicial powerlessness. Three points should, however, be made by way of qualifying this unflattering conclusion. The first is that all the evidence suggests that Lushington believed what he said about the proper limits of his judicial power: any deception was self-deception. He often gave signs of facing up to difficulties, when he perceived them, and said on one occasion that he held 'in great contempt a judgment apparently strong, but only made so to appear by concealing difficulties which ought to be encountered'.[77] Secondly, the tendency to disguise power is one that affects all decision makers, in every age, and at every level, and it would be surprising, even if it were possible, that it should be entirely avoided throughout a long judicial career. Thirdly, in assessing the ecclesiastical cases, we must remember that we see them in particularly sharp focus, because they involved disputes on points that were then supposed (but are no longer supposed in modern times) to have profound religious, social, and political significance. A comparison with judicial decisions on other questions is not entirely apt, unless we are similarly detached from the assumptions that underlie them; in short, other judges, in other times, may have used similar disguises, unperceived.

Almost all the distinctive features of Doctors' Commons appeared anomalous by the 1830s. The absence of law reports had produced

---

75 See chapter 6, below.   76 Discussed on pp. 230–7, below.
77 *Westerton* v. *Liddell, Report*, ed. A. F. Bayford (1856), 49 (London Consistory Court).

accusations that the advocates were preserving secret knowledge for their own advantage.[78] The reliance on oral evidence was attacked as an inferior method of proof.[79] There were many small local courts with practically no business, and, therefore, no experienced judges and practitioners.[80] Many of the offices were sinecures, the duties being exercised by deputies.[81] Even in London, business was so small that there were too few advocates to offer free competition and public choice.[82] The restricted jurisdiction of the courts in probate matters created constant problems of the relationship with the other superior courts, many relevant questions requiring determination in the courts of law and equity.[83] Several of the officers, judges, and practitioners in Doctors' Commons were related by family ties, attracting charges of nepotism and bias.[84] More substantively, the powers of the courts to punish defamation and brawling were thought to be, at best, quaint antiquities, and, at worst, offensive to individual liberty. Church rates were a substantial grievance. The ecclesiastical censures, of penance and excommunication, were plainly obsolete.[85] A sentiment that grew in force as English society grew more pluralistic was that it was offensive to religious freedom that Church of England courts, with episcopally appointed judges, should determine questions that affected the civil rights of all citizens.[86]

[78] *Decisions in the High Court of Admiralty during the time of Hay and Marriott . . . 1776–1779* (1801), Preface, i; W. S. Holdsworth, *Some Makers of English Law* (Cambridge, 1938), 226.

[79] See the questions addressed to Lushington by the Select Committee of the House of Lords on the Administration of Justice in the Privy Council, 1844 HL Sess Pap, xix, 323, esp. qq. 95–150.

[80] In addition to the provincial diocesan and archdiaconal courts, there were nearly 300 peculiars and manorial courts with local jurisdiction, Ecclesiastical Courts Commission, General Report, PP 1831–2, xxiv, 9, 21.

[81] Report of Ecclesiastical Courts Commission, appendix.

[82] Lushington's evidence to Select Committee on Admiralty Courts etc., PP 1833, vii, 379, 426, 427 (qq. 492, 501).

[83] Report of Ecclesiastical Courts Commission, 25, 31. See Lushington's evidence at 430 (q. 513).

[84] See *The Times*, 1 Feb. 1848, 4d ('an oyster bed where every oyster is called Jenner'), id. 7 Feb. 5e ('The court of the Jenners'). See A. H. Manchester, 'The Reform of the Ecclesiastical Courts', *American Journal of Legal History* 10 (1966), 51, 60–1. But Lushington defended the use of family patronage in 1828, Hansard, 2nd ser., xix, 1758, Mirror of Parliament 1828, 2591a (17 July). Dickens also commented on the family connexions in Doctors' Commons, *David Copperfield*, chs. 23, 26 ('family-party'; 'baker's proctor, and the judge, and the advocates on both sides, who were all nearly related'; 'family group').

[85] See pp. 171, 258, below, and Report of Ecclesiastical Courts Commission, 62.

[86] See Brougham's law reform speech, Hansard, 2nd ser., xviii, 153 (7 Feb. 1828).

There was force in these points, and they were pressed with the self-confidence of the reformers, and they prevailed. But this should not obscure the merits of some aspects of the civilian tradition. Flexibility may sometimes have advantages over a rigorous adherence to precedent and legal logic. A co-operative atmosphere may produce better results, in some kinds of cases, than an adversarial one. Oral evidence is not infallible, and pre-recorded evidence, despite its un-doubted deficiencies, may sometimes be more reliable; moreover, it saves court time, and saves witnesses from the embarrassment of public testimony, and from the necessity of assembling at a single time and place, and waiting during what may be a lengthy trial.[87]

Increasing opposition to the system of ecclesiastical courts demanded a political solution. An organization called the Society for the Abolition of Ecclesiastical Courts, in 1846, declared its object to be

> to emancipate the jurisprudence of our country, from the Ecclesiastical interference, which now renders it opposed to the Civil Liberty of British subjects, a source of oppression and hardship, and a national dishonour, because a moral wrong.[88]

Eventually, the solution was, by a series of separate statutes, to abolish or transfer away all the controversial areas of law, leaving the ecclesiastical courts in place, but with a jurisdiction practically con-fined to internal church matters. In retrospect, it has seemed inevi-table that the ecclesiastical jurisdiction should have been so curtailed, but in 1830 it was not obvious that this was to be the eventual solution. Lushington favoured reform on many of the matters just mentioned: the abolition of sinecures, and the consolidation of the ecclesiastical courts,[89] the opening of the bar in Doctors' Commons to all barris-ters,[90] the entire extinction of the court's criminal jurisdiction,[91] the

---

[87] These points were made by R. Phillimore, *Thoughts on the Law of Divorce in England* (1844), 40–1. The practice of the ecclesiastical courts was also defended by Sir J. Nicholl, in *Saph* v. *Anderson* (1822), 1 Add 195.

[88] See E. Muscott, *The History and Power of Ecclesiastical Courts* (London, 1846), 48.

[89] Report of Ecclesiastical Courts Commission.

[90] Select Committee on Admiralty Courts, 427, q. 501. However, in 1839, Lushington opposed an amendment to the Admiralty Court Act that would have opened practice in that court to all barristers; Hansard, 3rd ser., xlix, 351–2 (15 July 1839).

[91] Report of Ecclesiastical Courts Commission, 64.

abolition of church rates,[92] the use of oral evidence,[93] appointment and payment of judges by the Crown,[94] and reform of the substantive law so as to minimize litigation, particularly jurisdictional conflicts.[95] In 1839, in a debate provoked by the imprisonment of a Dissenter by an ecclesiastical court, after proceedings that Lushington thought irregular, he said:

The reform of these courts is necessary on three grounds; – first, for the sake of justice; secondly, for the sake of their own characters; and, thirdly, for an object which I have nearly and dearly at heart, namely, in order to remove that bitterness of spirit which tends, day after day, to desecrate, debase, and discourage true religion in this country. I can conceive nothing more injurious to the interests of the established church.[96]

This passage reflects the same hope that Lushington expressed in relation to all ecclesiastical privileges: that the Church of England would ultimately be strengthened by the removal of just causes of complaint against it.[97]

Brougham[98] had attacked the ecclesiastical courts in his well-known law reform speech of 1828,[99] and when the Whigs assumed office, in 1830, a commission was established to effect reform. Lushington was a member of the Ecclesiastical Courts Commission, and the principal draftsman of its report in 1832. The Report reflected the criticisms of the courts just listed. In an important respect, however, the reforms recommended by the Ecclesiastical Courts Commission may, in the light of later events, be called conservative, for the Commission proposed the retention by the ecclesiastical court, and in some respects, indeed, the extension, of probate and matrimonial jurisdiction. Lushington, though he favoured the abolition of the monopoly of advocates in Doctors' Commons, was influenced by a desire to preserve, in some part, the profession of civil law. The loss of

---

92 See chapter 8, below.
93 Select Committee of House of Lords on Privy Council, HL Sess. Pap., 1844, xix, 323, q. 116, but adding a qualified defence of the practice of the ecclesiastical courts at qq. 202, and 213.
94 Select Committee on Admiralty Courts, 435 (q. 546).
95 Report of Ecclesiastical Courts Commission, 31.
96 Mirror of Parliament 1839, 2080a (25 April).
97 See the discussion of church rates, in chapter 8, below.
98 Henry Peter Brougham, first Baron Brougham and Vaux (1778–1868), MP, 1810–12 and 1816–30; Attorney-General to Queen Caroline, 1820; Lord Chancellor, 1830–4; member of Judicial Committee of the Privy Council.
99 Hansard, 2nd ser., xviii, 153 (7 Feb. 1828).

testamentary business, said by Sir John Nicholl[100] to be 'about nine tenths of the whole business in Doctors' Commons'[101] would be fatal. Lushington said, on this point

that it would be the ruin of the profession; the advocates are not many in number, and perhaps any consideration of their interests might not be deemed of so great importance to the public in this point of view; but with respect to the proctors practising in Doctors' Commons, the clerks and other dependents upon them, I consider it would be an infliction of a great hardship, not to say injustice, if such an alteration was effected, which must inevitably involve them in ruin, unless the public interest imperatively demanded it.[102]

The same concern is manifested in a private letter to Brougham (then Lord Chancellor) at about the same date:

Whatever be done there are two bodies of persons whose interests ought to be considered – the officers & clerks of the Prerogative Registry; the proctors & their clerks. The former consist of above 30 persons with their families – the latter of more than 130 proctors and clerks amounting to several hundreds, so that at least a thousand persons owe their principal & in many cases sole maintenance to this branch of the profession.[103]

This argument, standing alone, appears weak, for almost every reform has an adverse effect on some who have a vested interest in the unreformed system. A report published in 1833 did, in fact, recommend the abolition of the testamentary jurisdiction of the ecclesiastical courts, the effect of which was compared with 'a shell thrown into Doctors' Commons'.[104]

The Ecclesiastical Courts Commission published two separate reports. The first recommended the abolition of the High Court of Delegates, and the transfer of its jurisdiction to the Privy Council.[105] The principal objections to the High Court of Delegates were that it had no permanence as a court, being constituted anew for each case, that it included usually only the most junior civilians, and that it gave

[100] John Nicholl (1759–1838), civilian, Dean of the Arches and judge of the Canterbury Prerogative Court, 1809–34; Admiralty Court judge, 1833–8, MP, 1802–21 and 1822–32.
[101] Report of Select Committee on Admiralty Courts, 394, q. 50.
[102] Report of Select Committee on Admiralty Courts, 425, q. 492.
[103] Lushington to Brougham n.d. but with letter endorsed, in Brougham's hand, June 1833, Brougham Papers, University College, London, 4159.
[104] Fourth Report of Real Property Commission, PP 1833, xxii, 1; *Law Magazine* 11 (1834), 447–8.
[105] Special Report of Ecclesiastical Courts Commission, PP 1831–2, xxiv, 1.

no reasons for its decisions.[106] This was relatively uncontroversial, and the recommendation was promptly implemented.[107] The second report, called the General Report, recommended the consolidation of the ecclesiastical courts into a single court,[108] the judges to be appointed and paid by the Crown, various substantive amendments to the law of wills, transfer of church rates to secular tribunals, the transfer of clergy discipline cases to the personal jurisdiction of bishops, the introduction of oral evidence and jury trials, and the abolition of all the criminal jurisdiction, and defamation. The net effect would have been to preserve a modernized ecclesiastical jurisdiction, in a single court with little more than matrimonial and an enlarged testamentary jurisdiction.[109] Admission as an advocate was to be opened to anyone holding the degrees of Master of Arts, or Bachelor of Laws (the doctorate being no longer a requisite). But Doctors' Commons (though no longer to be the preserve of doctors) and the separate profession of civilians, were to be maintained. There can be detected, in this part of the Commission's report, a defensive note, reference being made to the national interest in maintaining expertise in international law, in case of war:

[The] connexion between the Ecclesiastical and Admiralty Jurisdictions has long subsisted, and probably owes its origin to the similarity of the form of proceedings in both courts, and of the course of study necessary to qualify the Practitioners for the proper discharge of the duties entrusted to them. The study of the Ecclesiastical Law requires an accurate acquaintance with the principals of the *Civil Law*, upon which the Law of the Admiralty is founded; and the Civilian is led to the investigation of those principles of general jurisprudence by which the intercourse of Nations is governed, and the rights and obligations of belligerents and neutrals in time of war are defined. In this point of view, the maintenance of these two branches of the Profession, in connexion with each other, has been always considered an object of importance; and as the Ecclesiastical business is that alone upon which, in time of peace, the Practitioners must depend, it is humbly submitted that the

---

106 See Special Report of Ecclesiastical Courts Commission, Brougham, law reform speech, Hansard, 2nd ser., xviii, 153–4.

107 3 & 4 Wm IV c. 41. See Howell, *Judicial Committee of the Privy Council*, 25–31.

108 The Commission suggested, without positively recommending, the abolition of the York Provincial Court, Report, 73. The Commission was said by the Select Committee on the Admiralty Court, 382 'to incline to that opinion'. Lushington himself, in the paper referred to below at note 119, argued strongly in favour of abolition of the York Court.

109 PP 1831–2, xxiv, 9. A few minor matters were to be left to the court, including pews, dilapidations, and sequestrations.

alterations proposed to be made in the Practice and Constitution of those Courts should be considered with reference to this object; so that the general character of their proceedings may be preserved, whilst their efficiency, for the purposes for which they are designed, may be improved and increased by the amendments which it may be deemed expedient to apply to them.[110]

Lushington made the same point in his evidence in 1833 to the Select Committee of the House of Commons on Admiralty Courts, of which he was also a member.[111] As a contemporary legal journal commented, the preservation of a monopoly of testamentary business to the proctors in Doctors' Commons seems a circuitous way of securing expertise in international law.[112]

The Commission's Minute Book survives,[113] an examination of which shows that Lushington was the moving force behind the production of the Report. He drafted the questions to be addressed to the ecclesiastical judges,[114] and he prepared background papers on no fewer than twenty separate subjects.[115] Lushington was asked to communicate, on the Commission's behalf, with the two common-law judges who, though members of the Commission, were infrequent attenders.[116] Lushington is referred to as the draftsman of several parts of the report.[117]

The Minutes record that 'Dr Lushington also laid before the meeting a paper containing his own individual opinions respecting some of the matters which had been agreed upon and throwing out for the consideration of the Board suggestions as to their probable effect'.[118] One of the very few documents to be found among the Lushington family papers that is not a private letter, is what is probably the draft

---

[110] Report of Ecclesiastical Courts Commission, 65.
[111] Report of Select Committee on Admiralty Courts, PP 1833, vii, 425, q. 492. See also his comments in Hansard, 3rd ser., xlix, 352 (15 July 1839).
[112] *Law Magazine* 11 (1834), 454.
[113] In the custody of the Church Commissioners.
[114] Minute Book, 22 April 1830.
[115] Pews and church seats, sequestrations, jurisdiction as to legacies and intestates' effects, tithes, defamation and parish registers, process for enforcing decrees and orders, general registry for wills, compensation, archdeacons, advowsons, dilapidations, *duplex querela*, Easter offerings, fees of clergy, parish clerks, simony, publication of notices in churches, common form probate practice, donatives. Minute Book, 27 May 1831; 4 Aug. 1831.
[116] Minute Book, 28 Jan. 1832. Evidence of Lushington to Select Committee on Admiralty Courts, 433, q. 539.
[117] Minute Book, 19 July 1831, 26 July 1831, 2 Feb. 1832.
[118] Minute Book, 17 Aug. 1831.

version of this paper.[119] It reveals that Lushington, not unnaturally, agonized about making recommendations likely to destroy his own profession. The document commences:

> It is my wish to offer to the consideration of the Board, certain opinions which I have formed after long & patient deliberation as to the existing state of the profession to which I belong & to which I am under so great obligation.[120]

He then described the existing state of the advocates' profession, which was bleak:

> I apprehend that at this period with perhaps only one solitary exception there is not an advocate whose expenditure is defrayed by his emoluments arising from his professional practice in Doctors' Commons; that with the exception of the profits arising from the office of King's Advocate the whole gains of the profession amount to scarcely more than one half of the income derived by a single eminent Counsel at other bars; that the inevitable consequence of this state of things is that the profession must decline, not only in public estimation, but in real talent and acquirements for I must think that there is no present inducement & little future prospect to bring men of ability & industry to the civil law bar . . . I think it injurious to the public that this state of things should continue.[121]

He went on to consider the effect on the profession of change:

> Looking at all contingencies I am free to confess that if the maintenance of the profession in its present condition were the great object sought to be attained, the best chance is to avoid all alteration whatever, but I must also add that in my judgment alterations will be made whatever may be the determination of this Board.[122]

He then deals with the alterations that he considers essential in the public interest: the consolidation of the courts, the introduction

---

119 The paper is in Lushington's hand, undated and untitled, but internal references appear to be conclusive. In addition to those in the passages quoted may be added a reference (f. 22) to 'the other business which will remain when the other resolutions of the Board are carried into effect viz as to Brawling Defamation & other matters'. An interesting question is whether the survival of this document, almost alone of Lushington's business papers, was accidental. Possibly Lushington chose to preserve it in order to establish what his position had been in 1831 on the future of the profession, a question that, no doubt, arose on the dissolution of Doctors' Commons in 1858.
120 Lushington Family Papers. Draft Paper, f. 1.
121 Draft Paper, ff. 2–3.   122 Draft Paper, f. 4.

of oral evidence, the requirement of formal execution of wills, and
the enlargement of jurisdiction to enable all questions concerning a
disputed will to be determined in one court. He estimates that the
business of the new court will occupy the time of one judge only, and
draws a conclusion about the future of the profession:

> With respect to the Bar it is my opinion that there will not be sufficient
> business to maintain it in efficiency & respectability; to ensure the respect &
> confidence of the public there must be at least a certain number of advocates in
> practice out of which suitors may select their counsel. To ensure this there is
> not enough business at present & it will be diminished.[123]

The proctors, he thought, would survive, with the increased common
form business, but his own branch of the profession was doomed.
Though evidently torn, he had no doubt that the public interest
should prevail:

> Notwithstanding the effects upon the Bar in Doctors' Commons not long able
> as I believe even without a change to sustain itself & which for many reasons I
> sincerely regret I must add, that the abolition of all the Courts save one, the
> introduction of parol evidence, & the subjecting wills of personal estate to the
> same formalities as devises of real property appear to me advantages to the
> public of the greatest value, calculated to render justice more speedy and less
> expensive & to destroy a large portion of litigation, the very profitability of
> which will be removed, the subject matter no longer existing.[124]

He expressed similar sentiments in a private letter to Brougham:

> when the Ecclesiastical Report comes to be carried into execution, a still
> further diminution of the Ecclesiastical business must take place. This I hold
> to be a great public benefit for it will be a diminution of litigation not arising
> from expence delay or difficulty discouraging suitors, but by the removal of
> the causes of litigation & the introduction of certain & fixed rules instead of
> leaving many matters in the discretion of the judge . . . [U]nless there be two
> judges it is obvious that there will not be a sufficient inducement to keep up a
> competent bar; this perhaps is a more questionable reason [for appointing two
> judges]. My own opinion is & long has been that the profession must fall; it is
> vain I think to expect that talent will now come in on the bare hope of war.[125]

Brougham had evidently suggested that, if there were two civilian

[123] Draft Paper, f. 24.
[124] Draft Paper, ff. 24–5.
[125] Lushington to Brougham, 5 Oct. 1833. Brougham Papers 4160. Prize cases in
wartime were lucrative.

judges, Lushington might himself go to the Admiralty Court,[126] but Lushington adhered to his opinion of the sufficiency of a single judge:

I have to thank you for your kind consideration of me with respect to the Admiralty Court. Unfortunately my own evidence will be found to militate in some degree against two judges, but this was unavoidable without departing from the truth.[127]

Lushington's role in the Ecclesiastical Courts Commission was known to his contemporaries. In introducing a government bill based on the Commission's Report, during the brief Tory administration of 1835, the Attorney General[128] said, paying tribute to a political opponent:

A more learned and valuable document than that Report, which I now hold in my hand, I have rarely met with, to the composition of which the Honourable and Learned Member for the Tower Hamlets [Lushington], I believe, has considerably contributed.[129]

He went on to mention that Lushington had approved the present bill.

Despite its bilateral party support, the bill failed to pass, as did several subsequent attempts,[130] until, ultimately, in 1857, the matrimonial and probate jurisdictions of the ecclesiastical courts were extinguished. Reform of the ecclesiastical courts was, by this time, linked with reform of the substantive law of divorce. Lushington was a member of the Commission on divorce law, and a signatory of the report that recommended the transfer of the matrimonial jurisdiction to a new tribunal. Again, however, in the light of actual events, there may be detected a conservative element in this recommendation, in that it preserved a link between ecclesiastical and matrimonial law, for

126 At this point Sir J. Nicholl was judge of the Admiralty, Prerogative, and Arches Courts, but he told the Select Committee on Admiralty Courts that he would not be prepared to do this permanently, *Report*, 383; Jenner succeeded him as judge of the Prerogative and Arches Courts in 1834.
127 Lushington to Brougham, 5 Oct. 1833, Brougham Papers, 4160.
128 Sir Frederick Pollock, first baronet (1783–1870), Attorney-General, 1834–5 and 1841–4; Lord Chief Baron of the Exchequer Court, 1844–66.
129 Mirror of Parliament 1835, 309a, 12 March. The next day, in the House of Lords, Brougham described the report as 'drawn up chiefly by ... Dr Lushington', Hansard, 3rd ser., xxvi, 931 (13 Mar.).
130 See W. L. Mathieson, *English Church Reform 1815–40* (London, 1923), 158–61; Manchester, 'The Reform of the Ecclesiastical Courts', 71–4. Lushington's account of the attempts to enact the Commission's recommendations appears in Mirror of Parliament 1839, 2079a (25 April), when he still expected that an Ecclesiastical Courts Bill would be introduced by the (Whig) government.

the proposed tribunal was to include an ecclesiastical court judge.[131] Lushington was a member also of the Ecclesiastical Revenue Commission, which laid the foundations for the reform of church finances, and a member of the Ecclesiastical Commission, the Church Building Commission, and other ecclesiastical commissions of enquiry.[132]

It will be recalled that Lushington sat briefly in the House of Commons between 1806 and 1808. Though out of Parliament after 1808, he gained a favourable reputation in Whig political circles and, having, in 1820, first refused an opportunity to re-enter Parliament, he then accepted the nomination for Ilchester.[133] He sat, between 1820 and 1832, for Ilchester, Tregony, and (briefly) for Winchelsea, with a short absence in 1830–1 on account of an unsuccessful contest at Reading in the general election of 1830.[134] After the Reform Act, he sat for the newly created and very populous[135] London borough of Tower Hamlets until his retirement from Parliament in 1841.[136]

He was a consistent supporter of the Whigs, and described himself, at the close of his parliamentary career, as 'still a party man and strongly attached to those principles which he had hitherto professed'.[137] However, he voted independently, opposing the party on the crucial question of sugar duties in 1841.[138] Nor did he hesitate to

[131] First Report of Divorce Commission, PP 1852–3, xl, 249, 274.

[132] Ecclesiastical Revenue Commission, *Reports*, PP 1834, xxiii, 5; PP 1835, xxii, 15; Ecclesiastical Commission, appointed 3 & 4 Vic. c. 113, s. 78. Lushington rarely attended meetings: see report of Select Committee on the Ecclesiastical Commission, PP 1847, ix, 1, 244, app. H. no. 2; PP 1856, xi, 1, 39 (evidence of J. J. Chalk, q. 414); PP 1862, viii, 305 (appendix); PP 1863, vi, 199; Church Building Commission (*ex officio* as Consistory Court judge) from 1828, PP 1825, xv, 91, 101, but his name does not appear in the annual reports after 1845. See G. F. A. Best, *Temporal Pillars: Queen Anne's Bounty, the Ecclesiastical Commissions and the Church of England* (Cambridge, 1964), O. J. Brose, *Church and Parliament: the reshaping of the Church of England* (Stanford, 1959), M. H. Port, *Six Hundred New Churches: a study of the Church Building Commission, 1818–1856* . . . (1961); Commission to inquire into the state of the several dioceses of Canterbury . . . etc, PP 1857–8, xxiv, 123.

[133] The patron was Lord Darlington (later Lord Cleveland) from whom there are two letters in the Lushington Family Papers. Brougham wrote, in 1830, that Lord Cleveland left Lushington free to follow his own political inclinations, see H. P. Brougham, *Life and Times of Henry, Lord Brougham* (London, 1871), iii, 28. The borough of Ilchester was one of those disfranchised by the Reform Act of 1832.

[134] Lushington to Brougham, 12 Aug. 1830, Brougham Papers, University College, London, 24, 645. See p. 54, below.

[135] Population 359,864; average English constituency 27,794, C. R. Dod, *Electoral Facts, 1832–1853* (London, 1853).

[136] C. R. Dod, *Parliamentary Companion* (1833, and years following).

[137] Hansard, 3rd. ser., lviii, 1014 (2 June 1841).

[138] See pp. 79–81, below.

Stipple engraving of Lushington, aged 42, by W. Holl after A. Wivell.

praise political opponents when he thought that they were right, speaking in glowing terms, for example, of Peel's[139] support, in 1829, of Catholic emancipation.[140] In 1820 he was a strident critic of the government, closely associated with Queen Caroline, who became, for a time, a focus of radical opposition.[141] Later, his views moderated. Party affiliations were rather fluid during his time in Parliament. C. R. Dod, the editor of *The Parliamentary Companion*, describes Lushington in the 1830s as a 'reformer', thereby placing him between the categories of 'Whig', and 'radical reformer'.[142] Though Lushington has occasionally been called a radical,[143] Dod's classification seems apt, at any rate in respect of the 1830s. Lushington supported most of the liberal reforms of his era, and was best known for his anti-slavery views, but, as will be seen, on the important questions of parliamentary reform, he supported only about one-half of the principal radical demands. He spoke comparatively rarely on foreign policy, except as it affected the slave trade; he said to his constituents, in 1832, that he 'was of opinion that peace was our best policy, and that we should meddle as little as possible with foreign politics.'[144] Nevertheless, he thought that there were occasions when 'the honour and policy of the country' might require war.[145] He described the independence of the South American countries as an 'emancipation from tyranny and despotism.'[146] He thought that the people of Poland were justified in an insurrection against Russia in 1832 'both by the law of God, and the law of nations ... would to God they had been successful'.[147]

Lushington's debating style, in and out of Parliament, was forceful, as is evidenced by the records of his speeches, and by the comments of

---

[139] Sir Robert Peel, second baronet (1788–1850), Prime Minister 1834–5 and 1841–6.

[140] Mirror of Parliament 1829, 149–50 (16 Feb.). Lushington's praise of Peel was picked out for special notice by Disraeli, *Whigs and Whiggism*, ed. Hutcheson (London, 1913), 33.

[141] See chapter 4, below.

[142] Dod, *Parliamentary Companion* (1833), 136; (1835), 139; (1837), 136; (1838), 137; (1840), 178.

[143] By Professor Gash, in a passing reference: N. Gash, *Sir Robert Peel* 2nd edn (1986), 102–3; by W. S. Holdsworth, *History of English Law*, xiv, 140, and by D. Eltis, 'Dr Stephen Lushington and the Campaign to Abolish Slavery in the British Empire', *Journal of Caribbean History*, 1 (1970), 41, 45; W. R. Cornish and G. de N. Clark, *Law and Society in England, 1750–1950* (London, 1989), 642. O. Chadwick, *Victorian Church*, 1, 260, calls him 'a Whig with radical affections'.

[144] *The Times*, 29 Oct. 1832, 3d.

[145] Hansard, 2nd ser., xxii, 153 (5 Feb. 1830).

[146] Hansard, 2nd ser., ii, 378 (11 July 1820).

[147] Hansard, 3rd ser., xiii, 657 (18 April 1832).

himself[148] and others.[149] In a pre-election speech in 1834, he was reported to have compared the Duke of Wellington[150] and Sir Robert Peel to swindlers and prostitutes. Peel, perhaps remembering Lushington's tribute to him over Catholic emancipation, accepted his explanation that the newspaper report was distorted, and that Lushington had not intended 'to make any personal allusion disrespectful to' him.[151] Lushington was widely attacked,[152] however, and Buxton,[153] who considered the speech 'rash',[154] went so far as to ask to withdraw his name from Lushington's election committee.[155] Peel no doubt had this incident in mind when he argued – ultimately successfully – in 1839, for the exclusion from Parliament of the Admiralty Court judge, on the ground that a judge should not appear to be a 'political partisan'.[156]

Some common themes run through Lushington's approach to the diverse matters on which he supported reform. Considerations of humanity, justice, religion, and national pride were strong reasons enough for reform, but what made the case conclusive was that reform was compatible also with – even actually demanded by – considerations of self-interest. Thus, removal of the privileges of the Church of England would not (as conservatives said) weaken the established church, but would strengthen it; abolition of slavery would bring, not ruin, but prosperity to the West Indies; a more lenient criminal law would tend towards the suppression of crime; political reform would strengthen the government. Another striking feature of Lushington's approach to reform – or perhaps rather a consequence of those just mentioned – is his sense of certainty, both in his objects and in his

---

148 He often recognized that he had 'used very strong expressions', Mirror of Parliament 1828, 2588a (17 July), or spoken with 'warmth'.
149 S. Walpole, comment quoted at p. 151, below; [J. Grant], *Random Recollections of the House of Commons* (London, 1836), 256–7.
150 Arthur Wellesley, first Duke of Wellington (1769–1852), victor at Waterloo, 1815, Prime Minister 1828–30, Foreign Secretary, 1834–5.
151 See *Morning Chronicle*, 12 Dec. 1834, 2f–3a; British Library, Add Mss 40405, 92–7, 150; *Annual Register*, 1834 (Chronicle), 177–8.
152 See Buxton to Lushington, 19 Dec 1834, Buxton Papers, 13, 268 ('this burst of Tory indignation against you and your speech'). Col. Sibthorpe, Hansard, 3rd ser., xxvi, 199–200 (24 Feb. 1835) (language 'neither becoming nor decent').
153 Sir Thomas Fowell Buxton, first baronet (1786–1845), MP, 1818–37, successor to Wilberforce as leader of the anti-slavery movement.
154 Buxton to Sir Robert Hanbury, n.d. but about 20 Dec 1834, Buxton Papers, 13, 271 (copy).
155 Buxton Papers, 13, 268–70, 271–2, 273–6.
156 Hansard, 3rd ser., xlix, 1115 (1 Aug. 1839).

means. 'This is an age of improvement,' he asserted confidently, 'and I, for one, will never consent to stand still on the ground that ancient usages interfere.'[157]

The period between 1820 and 1841, during which Dr Lushington was a Member of Parliament, was one of considerable activity in the reform of the criminal law. Lushington was among the active reformers.[158] His view of punishment was a utilitarian one. He said that he saw 'no reason for any punishment, but the prevention of offences and the reformation of offenders'.[159] 'If we execute a man,' he said, 'it is not for his guilt, but because his punishment shall act as an example to, and deter others from committing similar crimes.'[160] He considered that certainty of punishment was a far more effective deterrent than severity,[161] that punishments ought to be set at their minimum effective level,[162] and that education and religion were the best long term preventives.[163] Lushington, unlike some of the other reformers in 1821,[164] foresaw that these objectives would necessitate an 'active, vigilant, and preventive police', in addition to 'well regulated prisons'.[165] He certainly allowed that property should be protected by the law, and he introduced a bill to extend the criminal law to the destruction of wills,[166] not formerly punishable at all.[167] But 'although the acquisition and just security of property were advantageous to the community as well as to the possessor, there were limits

---

[157] Mirror of Parliament 1833, 1456a (25 April).

[158] In addition to the activities mentioned below, Lushington was a member of the select committee on the law relating to prisons, 77 HC Journal, 81 (5 Mar. 1822), a select committee on consolidating and amending the criminal law, 79 HC Journal, 168 (16 Mar. 1824), and a select committee on the causes and increases in the number of criminal commitments and convictions, 82 HC Journal, 483 (23 May 1827).

[159] Mirror of Parliament 1840, 1545, Hansard, 3rd ser., lii, 931 (5 Mar.).

[160] Mirror of Parliament 1837, 1528b (19 May).

[161] Hansard, 3rd ser., xxxiii, 1205 (31 May 1836), Mirror of Parliament 1840, 1547a (5 Mar.).

[162] Hansard, 2nd ser., xvi, 1136 (12 Mar. 1827), referring to discipline in the army.

[163] Mirror of Parliament 1840, 1547a (5 Mar.).

[164] See L. Radzinowicz, *A History of English Criminal Law* (London, 1957), iii, 357–74; N. Gash, *Mr Secretary Peel* (London, 1961), 310.

[165] Hansard, 2nd ser., v, 959 (23 May 1821).

[166] Hansard, 2nd ser., viii, 704 (25 Mar. 1823).

[167] Hansard, 2nd ser., v, 957 (23 May 1821), *Substance of the Speeches of S. Lushington ... and J. Sydney Taylor ... on the Resolution Relative to the Punishment of Death* (London, 1831), 25.

beyond which neither the acquisition nor the possession ought to be protected'.[168] The infliction of death transgressed the limit.

The attention of the reformers focussed, naturally, on capital punishment. By 1820, a very large number of offences had been made punishable by death, and though, as Stephen[169] pointed out, the number of offences capitally punishable is not a reliable indicator of the severity of the law,[170] the law was undoubtedly very severe. But it was mitigated in practice by the exercise of the royal prerogative of mercy.[171] In 1819, for example, of 1,254 persons sentenced to death, 97 were executed.[172] Between 1821 and 1831, an average of 1,236 persons were convicted in each year, of whom 61 were executed.[173] During the following decade, capital punishment was removed from a long series of offences,[174] and the average annual number of convictions and executions declined dramatically. During Lushington's last five years in Parliament (1836–41), there were, on average, nine executions in each year.[175]

Lushington had been an active opponent of capital punishment from at least as early as 1813.[176] He was a member of the Committee of the principal abolition society,[177] and spoke on the subject inside and outside Parliament. He said, at a public meeting, that capital punishment was 'a direct violation of humanity, and repugnant to the law of God'.[178] In Parliament he declined to enter into 'theological argument',[179] but he said that capital punishment was irremediable, in

---

[168] Hansard, 2nd ser., xvii, 898–9 (17 May 1827) on a bill to prohibit the setting of spring guns.

[169] Sir James Fitzjames Stephen (1829–94), legal historian and codifier; judge of the High Court, 1879–91.

[170] J. F. Stephen, *History of the Criminal Law of England* (London, 1883), i, 470. The Black Act, of 1722 (9 Geo. 1, c. 27), could be construed to create fifty-four capital offences, ibid., 471.

[171] See J. M. Beattie, *Crime and the Courts in England, 1660–1800* (Princeton, 1986), 430–49.

[172] Select Committee on Criminal Laws etc., PP 1819, viii, 1, 127 (appendix I).

[173] Return, showing capital convictions by five-year periods, PP 1847, xlvii, 289.

[174] Stephen, *History of the Criminal Law*, 474–5.

[175] Return showing capital convictions . . ., PP 1847, xlvii (767 convictions; forty-four executions).

[176] W. Tallack, *Howard Letters and Memories* (London, 1905), 151.

[177] The Society for the Diffusion of Information on the Subject of Capital Punishments. See Radzinowicz, *History of English Criminal Law*, i, 350.

[178] *Substance of the Speeches of S. Lushington . . . on the Punishment of Death*, 24.

[179] Mirror of Parliament 1840, 1545b; Hansard, 3rd ser., lii, 929 (5 Mar.).

case of error,[180] and he pointed out that errors had occurred.[181] An account survives of Lushington's unsuccessful efforts to secure the reprieve of a man, convicted of a robbery to which another had subsequently confessed.[182]

Lushington's principal arguments were pragmatic, and motivated, he said, not by sympathy for those executed, but by 'the interests and feelings of the population at large'.[183] Though he conceded that capital punishment might have a deterrent effect in some cases,[184] he considered that any advantage to the community on this account was greatly outweighed by other considerations. He allowed that capital punishment might be justifiable in case of necessity,[185] but denied the necessity.[186] He thought that capital punishment – then carried out in public – had a demoralizing and brutalizing effect on those who witnessed it,[187] maintaining 'that every execution does harm; that it defiles the purity of the well-disposed and innocent portion of the community, while it renders the impure still more depraved and demoralized'.[188] 'It is a matter of history,' he said, 'that the punishment of death has never proved effective for the prevention of crime.'[189]

An argument that he included in almost every speech on the subject

---

[180] Hansard, 2nd ser., vi, 959 (23 May 1821), *Substance of the Speeches . . . on the . . . Punishment of Death*, 22.

[181] Hansard, 2nd ser., vi, 959; Hansard, 3rd ser., lii, 930–1; Mirror of Parliament 1840, 1546 (5 Mar.), Mirror of Parliament 1840, 4588 (15 July).

[182] Lushington Family Papers. The case is that of William Knight, aged seventeen. The account describes the efforts on Knight's behalf, of William Crawford, Peter Bedford, T. F. Buxton, Dr Lushington, and Samuel Hoare. It is apparently written by Peter Bedford (writing appears similar to that in Bedford's Journal, Friends' House Library, and it is accompanied by a letter signed P.B.). A brief account of the trial and conviction appears in *The Times*, 30 Oct. 1818, 3c. Lushington referred to the case in his evidence to the Select Committee on Criminal Laws, 117.

[183] Hansard, 3rd ser., lv, 1084.

[184] Hansard, 2nd ser., v, 957 (23 May 1821); Hansard, 3rd ser., xi, 953; Mirror of Parliament 1832, 1471a (27 Mar.); Second Report of Commissioners on Criminal Law, PP 1836, xxxvi, 183, 238 (Lushington's evidence).

[185] Mirror of Parliament 1832, 2058; Hansard, 3rd ser., lii, 930; Mirror of Parliament 1840, 1546 (5 Mar.); Second Report of Criminal Law Commissioners, PP 1836, xxxvi, 238.

[186] Mirror of Parliament 1840, 1546; Hansard, 3rd ser., lii, 931.

[187] Hansard, 3rd ser., xxxviii, 920 (19 May 1837); Hansard, 3rd ser., lii, 932; Mirror of Parliament 1840, 1547a (5 Mar.). But he did not favour private executions, Second Report of Criminal Law Commissioners, PP 1836, xxxvi, 242.

[188] Mirror of Parliament 1840, 1547a (5 Mar.).

[189] Mirror of Parliament 1832, 1471; Hansard, 3rd ser., xi, 954 (27 Mar.).

was that capital punishment induced a reluctance to prosecute.[190] He himself had declined to prosecute a servant who had stolen money from him 'for no other reason but that I could not induce myself to run the risk of taking away the life of a man'.[191] The Tory newspaper *John Bull* records that, in 1825, Lushington's pocket having been picked, and the offender arrested, Lushington, on finding that the offender was not regularly known to the police, 'begged that he might be discharged; and, calling him aside into the private room, made him a present'.[192] Lushington stressed, also, the reluctance of witnesses to give evidence,[193] of judges to encourage convictions,[194] of juries to convict,[195] and of the executive to carry the law into effect.[196] He objected to the random implementation of severe punishment,[197] considering that certain punishment, duly proportioned to the crime, was the most effective deterrent,[198] and he thought that tangible proof of progress could be derived from the reduction in the occurrence of forgery since the abolition of the death penalty,[199] and from the rates of prosecution and conviction for highway robbery,[200] and for rape,[201] before and after abolition of capital punishment for those offences. The law was more humane; crime was reduced; very many lives had been saved; 'was not this carrying a good principle into effect with benefit and advantage to all mankind?'[202]

---

190 Hansard, 2nd ser., vi, 958–9 (27 May 1821); ibid., 1113 (6 June 1821); Mirror of Parliament 1832, 2058 (17 May); Hansard, 3rd ser., lii, 931 (5 Mar. 1840); *Substance of the Speeches . . . on the . . . Punishment of Death*, 24, Second Report of Criminal Law Commissioners, PP 1836, xxxvi, 236.

191 Evidence to Select Committee, note 172 above, 116. See also Hansard, 3rd ser., xi, 954, Mirror of Parliament 1832, 1471a (27 Mar.).

192 *John Bull*, 5 (1825), 381. Of course, this account does not establish that Lushington would not have been equally lenient if the punishment were transportation, or imprisonment.

193 Hansard, 3rd ser., lii, 930 (5 May 1840).

194 Ibid.

195 Hansard, 3rd ser., xi, 953 (27 Mar. 1832); Mirror of Parliament 1840, 4588a (15 July); *Substance of the Speeches . . . on the . . . Punishment of Death*, 23.

196 Hansard, 3rd ser., xi, 953; Mirror of Parliament 1832, 1471a (27 Mar.).

197 Mirror of Parliament, 1835, 1408 (17 June).

198 Hansard, 3rd ser., xi, 953; Second Report of Criminal Law Commissioners, PP 1836, xxxvi, 236, 241.

199 Mirror of Parliament 1840, 1546b (5 Mar.).

200 Mirror of Parliament 1840, 5030; Hansard, 3rd ser., lv, 1085 (29 July).

201 Mirror of Parliament 1840, 1530; Hansard, 3rd ser., lv, 1084 (Lushington said that capital punishment had been abolished for rape 'de facto' in 1838. It was not abolished formally until 1841, by 4 & 5 Vic. c. 38).

202 Ibid. Hansard, 1085.

There was little support in Parliament for abolition of capital punishment for murder, but Lushington made it clear that his arguments extended to this case also,[203] though recognizing that, here, public opinion was in favour of retention.[204]

Lushington was, from 1816, a member of the committee of the Prison Discipline Society,[205] and, in later life, a patron of the Howard Association, though not an active participant in its affairs.[206] During his parliamentary career he spoke, on several occasions, on the subject of prison conditions. He objected to arbitrary powers over prisoners,[207] to lack of clothing for them,[208] to the mixing of the sexes,[209] and of prisoners of different categories,[210] and to conditions that allowed riots and assaults.[211] He drew attention to horrifying details: 'eighty or ninety prisoners actually crowded into one room; the sleeping space allotted to each was less than sixteen inches'; the turnkey reported that, when he opened the door in the morning, 'such is the dreadful stench, I am almost suffocated by it'.[212]

Lushington opposed the use of corporal punishment, both as a means of military discipline, and as a civil sentence. He thought that public whippings were disgusting, and that private whipping was open to the objection that its severity would be arbitrary.[213] He pointed out that past mitigation of corporal punishment had not had the disastrous effect on army discipline that its defenders had predicted.[214] He was denounced for his attitude to this subject by

---

[203] Hansard, 3rd ser., xxxviii, 920 (19 May 1837); Mirror of Parliament 1840, 1546 (5 Mar.).

[204] Mirror of Parliament 1837, 1528b (19 May), and also in cases of treason, and robbery and attempted murder with actual violence, Second Report of Criminal Law Commissioners, PP 1836, xxxvi, 237.

[205] Buxton, *Memoirs*, 54; Tallack, *Howard Letters and Memories*, 4. Two letters from Lushington to F. P. Douglas, MP, on this subject, are in the Bodleian Library, Oxford, MS Eng Lett C. 563, ff. 31–4.

[206] G. Rose, *The Struggle for Penal Reform* (London, 1961), 17.

[207] Hansard, 2nd ser., i, 703 (31 May 1820); ibid, vi, 893–4 (4 Mar. 1822).

[208] Hansard, 2nd ser., v, 161 (11 April 1821); Mirror of Parliament 1828, 411a (28 Feb.).

[209] Ibid.

[210] Hansard, 2nd ser., vi, 1325 (27 Mar. 1822; young and innocent with felons), Mirror of Parliament 1828, 411b; Hansard, 2nd ser., xviii, 808 (28 Feb.; condemned and reprieved).

[211] Mirror of Parliament 1828, 411a; Hansard, 2nd ser., xviii, 807 (28 Feb.).

[212] Ibid.

[213] Hansard, 2nd ser., viii, 1441 (30 April 1823).

[214] Hansard, 2nd ser., xvi, 1135 (12 Mar. 1827).

Palmerston[215] as having 'wasted a vast deal of very respectable and constitutional indignation, which he might better have reserved for some occasion on which it would be more necessary or useful'.[216]

Lushington opposed the activities of some of the private prosecution societies. He thought that a society called the Constitutional Association, which instituted prosecutions for seditious, blasphemous, and criminal libel, was usurping the proper functions of the government[217] and curtailing 'the liberty of the press, under the specious pretence of repressing disloyalty'.[218] He roundly denounced another such society, called the Society for the Suppression of Vice, which sought to suppress, among other vices, obscene libels and sabbath breaking, as 'worse than useless',[219] and as 'a set of cowardly pusillanimous hypocrites',[220] thereby incurring the censure of Wilberforce,[221] who was one of its principal members.[222]

Lushington favoured an investigation into the 'Peterloo' disturbance, twelve years after the event, not for the purpose of punishment, but 'to teach a great moral lesson to persons in possession of political power'.[223] He particularly objected to the use of government informers,[224] 'a system of espionage, under which the freedom of the people might be annihilated',[225] for 'they too generally stimulated men to commit the actions they denounced'.[226]

He had occasion to comment on the conduct of several particular trials, including the trial of the missionary, John Smith, in Demerara,[227] the trial of slaves in Jamaica in 1825,[228] and the trial by

215 Henry John Temple, first Viscount Palmerston (1784–1865); MP from 1807, Foreign Secretary, 1830–4, 1835–41, and 1846–51; Prime Minister, 1855–8, and 1859–65.
216 Hansard, 2nd ser., xvi, 1136.
217 Hansard, 2nd ser., v, 1114 (6 June 1821); ibid., vi, 1313 (27 Mar. 1822).
218 Hansard, 2nd ser., v, 1114, 1118 (6 June 1821); ibid., vi, 1310, 1313 (27 Mar. 1822).
219 Hansard, 2nd ser., v, 1117 (6 June 1821).
220 Hansard, 2nd ser., v, 1491 (3 July 1821).
221 William Wilberforce (1759–1833); MP, 1780–1825, leader of the anti-slavery movement, and of the evangelical 'Clapham Sect'.
222 Hansard, 2nd ser., v, 1492; E. P. Thompson, *The Making of the English Working Class* (London, 1980), 60–1, 90, 442–3.
223 Mirror of Parliament 1832, 1225a (15 Mar.).
224 Ibid.
225 Hansard, 2nd ser., viii, 676 (24 Mar. 1823).
226 Hansard, 3rd ser., xi, 269 (15 Mar. 1832). On the use of government spies, see E. P. Thompson, *The Making of the English Working Class* (1980), 532–9, 715–26.
227 See pp. 66–8, below.
228 See Hansard, 2nd ser., xiv, 1044 (1 Mar. 1826).

court-martial of an army captain in New South Wales.[229] In his speeches on these trials, Lushington emphasized the need for fairness to the accused in such matters as securing an unbiased tribunal,[230] specifying the charges in sufficient detail,[231] using the most reliable evidence available,[232] avoiding hearsay[233] and unsworn evidence,[234] using due caution in accepting evidence of accomplices[235] and of witnesses who had been influenced,[236] and giving opportunity for a full defence.[237]

English criminal procedure did not, until 1836,[238] permit a person accused of felony to be represented by counsel. Counsel were permitted to cross-examine witnesses, but not to address the jury. Lushington spoke in 1824, and again on the 1836 Bill, in favour of allowing counsel in such cases. He denied that the judge could be (as was said in support of the existing system) a counsel for the prisoner.[239] In answer to those who said that the prosecutor was not allowed to play on the emotions of the jury, Lushington stressed the 'manifest injustice' of permitting counsel for the Crown to present an intricate circumstantial case against the accused, all the more effective because it was unemotional, and then expecting the accused to answer it unaided: 'not one prisoner in five thousand could be competent to such an undertaking'.[240] He maintained that the system led, not only to the conviction of the innocent, but also to the opposite danger, the acquittal of the guilty 'from the compassion of the jury'.[241] It was anomalous to allow a right to counsel in cases of misdemeanour, but to deny it in the more serious case of a felony.[242] He pointed out that in France, the Code Napoléon not only permitted counsel to an accused,

[229] Captain Robison. See Hansard, 3rd ser., xvi, 1142 (27 Mar. 1833); ibid., xix, 592 (11 July 1833).
[230] Hansard, 2nd ser., vi, 1310–11 (27 Mar. 1822); ibid., xi, 1228–9 (11 June 1824).
[231] Hansard, 2nd ser., xi, 1223–4 (11 June 1824); Hansard, 3rd ser., xvi, 1144 (27 Mar. 1833).
[232] Hansard, 2rd ser., xvi, 1144 (27 Mar. 1833).
[233] Hansard, 2nd ser., xi, 1229 (11 June 1824); ibid., xiv, 1046 (1 Mar. 1826).
[234] Hansard, 2nd ser., xiv, 1046 (1 Mar. 1826).
[235] Hansard, 2nd ser., xi, 1212 (11 June 1824).
[236] Hansard, 2nd ser., xiv, 1048 (1 Mar. 1826); Hansard, 3rd ser., xix, 593, 594 (11 July 1833).
[237] Hansard, 3rd ser., xvi, 1144 (27 Mar. 1833).
[238] Prisoners' Counsel Act, 6 & 7 William IV c. 114.
[239] Hansard, 2nd ser., xi, 210 (6 April 1824).
[240] Ibid.   [241] Ibid., 210–11.   [242] Ibid., 211–12.

but allowed him the last word.[243] To the objection that the presence of counsel would take the time of the court, he pointed out that the same time might be consumed in a civil action – 'in a trumpery action at *nisi prius*', where 'mere property' was at stake.[244] He suggested, moreover, that the existing system wasted time, by requiring counsel to address the jury under the guise of cross-examining witnesses,[245] adding that the law 'was a disgrace to the country'.[246]

The desire of some of the reformers, it has been suggested, was not so much to secure the greater efficiency of the criminal justice system, as to present a more pleasing image of justice.[247] Such an assessment would be true, in respect of Lushington, only in part. He was, indeed, concerned that the laws should be 'assimilated to the feelings of the people',[248] and that 'a conviction should receive the approbation of the public':[249] 'now that general civilization has advanced', there was a 'general feeling against ... severity of punishment'.[250] The acceptability of reform was 'proof of the increased intelligence and civilization of the nation'.[251] But the recorded expressions of Lushington's views suggest that, in his mind, the efficiency, the justice, and the popularity of reform were hardly to be dissociated: it was desirable that crime should be prevented, and that this object should be effected by measures that were just, humane, and efficient; the popularity of such measures confirmed their merits, and, at the same time, operated as an independent reason in their support.

There were, in Lushington's mind, as in the minds of most of his contemporaries, indissoluble links among education, religion, morals, and the welfare of the community: education, 'under the providence of God', was 'the surest safeguard against temptation to evil'.[252] In speaking of the prevention of crime, he said that the aim should be

---

[243] Ibid., 212.
[244] Second Report of Criminal Law Commissioners, PP 1836, xxxvi, 240 (Lushington's evidence).
[245] Hansard, 3rd ser., xxviii, 870; Mirror of Parliament 1835, 1408b (17 June).
[246] Hansard, 3rd ser., xxxi, 499 (17 Feb. 1836).
[247] R. McGowen, 'The Image of Justice and Reform of the Criminal Law in Early Nineteenth-Century England', *Buffalo Law Review* 32 (1983), 89, 96.
[248] Hansard, 2nd ser., v, 959 (23 May 1821).
[249] Hansard, 2nd ser., xii, 971 (10 Mar. 1825).
[250] Mirror of Parliament 1832, 1471b (27 Mar.). See also Mirror of Parliament 1837, 1528b (19 May).
[251] Hansard, 3rd ser., xxii, 157 (13 Mar. 1834, on hanging murderers in chains).
[252] Mirror of Parliament 1837–8, 4778 (18 June).

to improve the general moral condition of the people at large, to educate them, to impress upon their minds the great doctrines of the Christian religion, the great moral obligations they had to perform, and the great future consequences of departing from those great principles which the Author of that religion inculcated.[253]

At the age of eighty, Lushington was called upon, in his judicial capacity, to decide whether a clergyman of the Church of England might disavow a belief in the eternal punishment of the wicked.[254] The reference to 'future consequences' in his speech of 1840, indicates that there were, in his mind, social as well as theological consequences to belief in Hell, a common opinion at the time.[255]

Like many of the reformers, Lushington confidently expected, and sought to assist, the spread of enlightenment, morality, and progress through public education. He expressly associated himself with Brougham's often quoted saying, 'the schoolmaster is abroad', which Lushington described as 'more powerful than thirty sentences'.[256] The Society for the Diffusion of Useful Knowledge,[257] principally promoted by Brougham,[258] flourished between the years 1826 and 1846. Lushington was a founding committee member of the Society,[259] and was still a committee member when the operations of the Society were discontinued.[260] The society, the object of which was to

[253] Hansard, 3rd ser., lii, 932 (5 Mar. 1840).
[254] See pp. 330–1, below.
[255] See R. Brent, *Liberal Anglican Politics* (Oxford, 1987), 122; Best, *Temporal Pillars*, 50; G. Rowell, *Hell and the Victorians: A Study of the Nineteenth-Century Theological Controversies Concerning Eternal Punishment and Eternal Life* (Oxford, 1974).
[256] Hansard, 2nd ser., xxii, 882 (23 Feb. 1830).
[257] See H. Smith, *The Society for the Diffusion of Useful Knowledge, 1826–1846* (London, and Halifax, Nova Scotia, 1974); S. Bennett, 'Revolutions in Thought: Serial Publication and the Mass Market for Reading', in *The Victorian Periodical Press: Samplings and Soundings*, ed. J. Shattock, and M. Wolff (Leicester and Toronto, 1982); J. Percival, *The Society for the Diffusion of Useful Knowledge, 1826–1848; Handlist of Correspondence and Papers* (London, 1978); C. New, *Life of Henry Brougham to 1830* (Oxford, 1961), 347–57; R. Stewart, *Henry Brougham, 1778–1868: His Public Career* (London, 1986), 187–93; R. K. Webb, *The British Working-Class Reader, 1790–1868* (London, 1955), 66–73.
[258] See *Address* of the Committee of the Society for the Diffusion of Useful Knowledge (London, 1846), 3.
[259] See the appendix to the Society's first publication (by Brougham; see New, *Life of Henry Brougham*, 351), *Discourse of the Objects, Advantages, and Pleasures of Science* (London, 1827).
[260] *Address* of the Committee of the Society for the Diffusion of Useful Knowledge (London, 1846), preface. Nine other names are to be found in both lists.

distribute educational literature to a wide market, 'testified', it has been said, 'to a sudden desire for popularizing knowledge'.[261] Partly because of a name that was quaint, even in its own time, it was the object of considerable satire and ridicule,[262] and it eventually failed financially on account of an over-ambitious attempt to produce a universal biographical dictionary. But it did succeed, to a considerable extent, in creating a mass market for literature.[263]

The SDUK claimed to avoid questions of controversial politics,[264] but 'the Society took an appearance of political colour from the fact that almost all its original supporters were of one party in politics,[265] and the Society's commitment to a link among education, progress, and political reform was made evident in its address on suspending operations in 1846:

A spirit was awakened of which they [the Committee] have been the instruments – a spirit which led to the successive foundation of University College, King's College, and the University of London, and which had previously established the Mechanics' Institutes; which overthrew the laws excluding Roman Catholic and Protestant Dissenters from the public services; which reformed the representation in spite of the utmost efforts of wealth and power; which broke the chain of slavery throughout the British Empire, and is still at work in forwarding the best interests of the whole human race.[266]

The foundation of London University, referred to here, was another enterprise in which Lushington was engaged. He was one of the initial proprietors and shareholders,[267] on whose behalf he

---

[261] L. Stephen, article on Harriet Martineau, *DNB*.
[262] See Bennett, 'Revolutions in Thought', 226, 247, n. 1, cartoon; M. D. George, *Catalogue of Political and Personal Satires* ... (1952), 17267, reproduced in Stewart, *Henry Brougham*, facing p. 87 ('patent penny knowledge mill'); T. L. Peacock, *Crotchet Castle* (1831), Universal Library edn, 8 ('Steam intellect society'); Thompson, *The Making of the English Working Class*, 801n. (Societies for the Diffusion of 'Really' Useful Knowledge).
[263] Bennett, 'Revolutions in Thought', 237, supports the *Penny Magazine*'s claim to be the first mass-market periodical published in Great Britain. Webb, *The British Working-Class Reader*, 72, considers that the SDUK failed to reach working classes but that its experiments in quantity publishing were striking and encouraging.
[264] *Address*, 4.
[265] Ibid., and see New, *Life of Brougham*, 350 ('nearly all ... liberal Whigs').
[266] *Address*, 7–8.
[267] *Statement* by the Council of the University of London explanatory of the Nature and Objects of the Institution (London, 1827), appendix.

delivered a public address at the laying of the foundation stone.[268] He became, in 1828, a member of the Education Committee,[269] and he took the chair at a Special General Meeting of the Proprietors in 1828.[270] He was a member of the Council in 1828.[271] He attended the initial lectures (which were in medicine), on which he reported to Brougham 'that we have the most ample cause to be satisfied with our Professors'.[272] He went on to urge the speedy institution of lectures in the classics,[273] of which he said, in a later letter to Brougham, 'we want Pupils. Our present number for the Greek & Latin Classes does not exceed 20'.[274] Lushington was a governor of Guy's Hospital for over 50 years, and a promoter of medical education.[275]

In his speech at the laying of the foundation stone of London University, Lushington explained the principal objects of the new university as making available the advantages of education to those excluded from the ancient universities by lack of wealth and by religious persuasion:

Have we not all with one common consent of all parties and denominations agreed to educate the whole population of the country? Are we to stop short in this splendid career? Will any one argue for limiting the degree of cultivation which the human intellect shall receive, or establishing a monopoly to be enjoyed only by the few, whose wealth renders expense undeserving of consideration, and who are of one denomination of the Christian Church only?[276]

He added that wider education would add, not only to individual comfort and happiness, but to 'the welfare of the whole community'.[277] 'Promotion of education,' he said at a public meeting

---

268 Ibid., 52–4 (30 April 1827); H. H. Bellot, *University College, London, 1826–1926* (London, 1929), 36.
269 Bellot, *University College*, 52.
270 Bellot, *University College*, 75; *The Times*, 1 Oct. 1828, 3 d–e.
271 *Second Statement* by the Council of the University of London explanatory of the Plan of Instruction (London, 1828).
272 Lushington to Brougham, 6 Oct. 1828, Brougham Papers, University College, London, 5630. See also H. Brougham, *Life and Times of Lord Brougham*, ii, 498–9.
273 Ibid.
274 Lushington to Brougham, n.d., Brougham Papers, 6292. (The letter, which is incomplete, contains an instruction that it should be burned.)
275 *Guy's Hospital Gazette*, 1873, 99, reprinted in *The Times*, 27 Jan. 1873, 6b.
276 *Statement* by Council, appendix 4, 54. Similar sentiments are expressed in Hansard, 3rd ser., xxvii, 285 (26 Mar. 1835), together with the advantages of parental supervision at a non-resident university.
277 Ibid.

in 1838, 'was absolutely necessary for the welfare of the population.'[278]

Though there was widespread agreement on the link between education and religion, there was, by this date, no universal consensus as to what form religious instruction should take. The Society for the Diffusion of Useful Knowledge excluded from its objects any attempt at religious instruction, which, like politics, was apt to create 'angry discussion'.[279] But omission was itself controversial, and the Society was attacked more for irreligion than for its politics.[280] Lushington, though himself a firm adherent of the established church, was politically active in removing the disabilities of dissenters;[281] the foundation of London University was, as indicated in the speech quoted above, a part of this movement. The university was initially established without religious affiliation, but was soon reorganized, with the addition of a religious element by the foundation of King's College.[282]

Of elementary education, Lushington said: 'it is the duty of the state to confer the benefit, and . . . it is the right of the subject to have it'.[283] He supported the establishment of a national educational system, with 'separate and adequate religious instruction' for 'Churchmen, Catholics and Dissenters',[284] but the plan was abandoned in the face of opposition by Church and Dissent.[285] On the laying of a foundation stone for a day school in London in 1849, a hymn was sung that had been composed for the occasion by Lushington. This composition, though unlikely to earn for Lushington a high place in the ranks of hymnographers, is illustrative of the link, in his mind, between religion and education. One verse (of the full six) is sufficient for this purpose:

---

[278] *Globe*, 12 Dec. 1838 (meeting of inhabitants of Bethnall-green and Haggerstone for the purpose of promoting education in those districts). From Buxton Papers, Rhodes House Library, Oxford, 17, 289.

[279] *Address*, 4.

[280] Ibid., 5.

[281] See chapter 8, below (church rates) and pp. 57–9, below.

[282] Incorporated in 1829, and opened in 1831.

[283] Mirror of Parliament 1839, 3128 (19 June).

[284] Ibid.

[285] Lushington was denounced by Gladstone as indifferent between one religion and another, Hansard, 3rd ser., xlviii, 631. See E. Halevy, *History of the English People in the Nineteenth Century*, 2nd edn (London, 1949), iii, 224; Education Commission, 1861, evidence of Sir John Shuttleworth, PP 1861, xxi, pt vi, 300–1 (q. 2310). See G. I. T. Machin, *Politics and the Churches in Great Britain 1832–1868* (Oxford, 1977), 65–6.

> Grant thy blessing, God of truth,
> To instruct the rising youth;
> Fix their hope on Christ alone, –
> Christ, the sure foundation stone.[286]

Lushington, like other liberal reformers of his time, had to grapple with some intractable problems on questions of social welfare. He desired, as an objective, 'that the poor should support themselves by their own industry', but he disagreed with the means proposed to achieve this object by one of the forerunners of modern socialism, Robert Owen.[287] Lushington described Owen's communitarian proposals as 'visionary' and 'impracticable': the people 'were to be fed at certain hours like horses, and to be exercised at stated times'. Illustrating again the central role, in his mind, of religion, Lushington agreed that it was 'very desirable' to improve the morality of the people, 'but he was not prepared to do so by the exclusion of all religion'.[288]

Lushington enjoyed no immunity from the blind spots in the liberal enlightenment. The Poor Law Amendment Act, of 1834, which abolished monetary relief, and deliberately created conditions in workhouses that were inferior to those of the poorest paid outside, was enacted with liberal intentions, but with illiberal consequences.[289] It is likely that Lushington supported this Act.[290] He had said, in 1821, that 'his settled conviction was that the increase of poor-rates was an increase of misery',[291] and he had some correspondence on the subject with Lord Althorp,[292] the principal proponent of the 1834 Act.[293]

But he could not, probably, be described as one of the 'ideologues of laissez faire'.[294] During the debate, in 1841, on the prolongation of the

---

[286] S. Lushington, *The Foundation Stone: a hymn* (privately printed, Newcastle, 1850) British Library.

[287] Robert Owen (1771–1858), philanthropist, and founder of communitarian societies in Great Britain and the United States.

[288] Hansard, 2nd ser., v, 1323–4 (26 June 1821).

[289] Halevy, *History of the English People in the Nineteenth Century*, iii, *The Triumph of Reform* (1950), 119–29; Thompson, *The Making of the English Working Class*, 295.

[290] His vote is not recorded, but the Act passed by a large majority (187–50, third reading) Hansard, 3rd ser., xxiv, 1061 (1 July 1834), being opposed by an alliance of ultra-radicals and ultra-Tories. Halevy, *History of the English People*, iii, 341–2; G. D. H. Cole, *The Life of William Cobbett* (London, 1927), 415.

[291] Hansard, 2nd ser., v, 1482 (2 July 1821).

[292] John Charles Spencer, third Earl Spencer, Viscount Althorp (1782–1845); MP, 1804–34, leader of Whig party in House of Commons, 1830–4.

[293] Althorp to Lushington, 27 June 1834, Lushington Family Papers (on the question of compulsory unification of London parishes).

[294] The phrase is Thompson's, *Making of the English Working Class*, 333.

Poor Law, Lushington manifested some sympathy for those on the receiving end. He opposed a clause that would have compelled deserted wives to go into the workhouse as a condition of receiving relief for their children,[295] and he welcomed evidence of attempts 'to afford greater comfort to the unfortunate inmates of workhouses'.[296] Letters to his daughters show that, later in his life, he gave them, in his absence, 'command of his purse' for the relief of poor persons living in Ockham, the Surrey village where Lushington had his country house.[297]

In 1818, Lushington made two speeches to a committee of the House of Lords in favour of the protection of chimney-sweepers' boys.[298] He painted a vivid picture of the cruelty to which the boys were subjected, describing the practice of employing them as 'an enormity disgraceful to a civilized people'.[299] In 1825, and again in 1833, he supported restrictions on the hours of work for children in factories, calling the former system 'revolting to humanity, and to every principle of British justice'.[300] In 1836, when it was proposed, on free trade principles, to ease the restrictions by extending (to twelve hours) the permitted work day for children over twelve years old,[301] Lushington was opposed. He said, though he was a strenuous and uniform supporter of the principles of free trade, 'free trade . . . can only exist when both parties between whom it is carried on are equally capable of judging for themselves what is their own interest, and protecting that interest when they have formed their judgment'.[302] Like many of the liberals of his time, he was unable to see the need for state intervention to ameliorate the general condition of the

---

295 Hansard, 3rd ser., lvii, 785 (1 April 1841).
296 Mirror of Parliament 1841, 1146b (1 April).
297 Lushington to Alice Lushington, 3 Dec. 1856: 'You have now sole charge of Ockham. Should the weather continue severe remember you have the command of my purse & God has blessed me with great prosperity & I ought not to be niggardly'. Lushington to Fanny Lushington, 13 Jan. 1867: 'If this frost should last I fear for our poor people. What think you of asking Mr Onslow *in our absence in urgent* cases to give relief at my expense.' Lushington Family Papers.
298 *Speech of Dr Lushington in support of the Bill for the better regulation of chimney sweepers and their apprentices and for preventing the employment of boys in climbing chimneys . . . 13 March . . .* (London, 1818); *The Reply of Dr Lushington in support etc . . . 20th April . . .* (London, 1818).
299 *Reply*, 27.
300 Hansard, 2nd ser., xiii, 648 (17 May 1825); Hansard, 3rd ser., xvii, 103 (3 April 1833). See M. W. Thomas, *The Early Factory Legislation* (Leigh-on-Sea, 1948), 27–8, 63–4; Thompson, *The Making of the English Working Class*, 366–84.
301 See Halevy, *History of the English People*, iii, 284; Thompson, *Making of the English Working Class*, 366–84; Thomas, *Early Factory Legislation*, 89–93.
302 Mirror of Parliament 1836, 1392a (9 May).

working poor, accepting that, for adults, 'the fullest liberty should be allowed to them to bargain as they best may for the sale of their own labour'. But for children 'the rules of political economy are inapplicable': children in factories demanded protection as much as the chimney-sweepers' boys.[303]

Lushington supported street improvements in London as contributing to 'happiness, comfort, health, and morality'.[304] Even when improvements required a tax that he would otherwise have opposed, he considered them 'essential to the diminution of crime – of human suffering – and necessary to raise the lower orders to that state which every man of common humanity would wish to see'.[305]

Undoubtedly the most important political event, during Lushington's time as a Member of Parliament, was the Parliamentary Reform Act of 1832. This abolished fifty-six 'nomination' boroughs,[306] created new seats in populous areas, and substantially enlarged the electorate.[307] Lushington supported the Act, saying that 'the English nation will never be contented so long as the House of Commons is not constituted by their virtual representatives', and describing the Act as 'a measure on which depends the safety of the country, and perhaps the stability of the throne'.[308] The system of nomination boroughs, of which he had extensive personal experience,[309] he described as 'the mockery of representation'.[310]

As has been mentioned, Lushington was seen, in the political context of the mid-1830s, as a moderate reformer. The three principal demands of the radicals, in the 1830s, were universal [adult male] suffrage, the secret ballot, and annual Parliaments.[311] Lushington

303 Ibid.   304 Hansard, 3rd ser., xlix, 726 (24 July 1839).
305 Hansard, 3rd ser., lv, 1111 (30 July 1840).
306 Also known as close, rotten or pocket boroughs. The list appears in Hansard, 3rd ser., xiii, appendix, Sch. A, and includes the borough (Ilchester) for which Lushington sat.
307 See Halevy, *History of the English People*, iii, 28 (increase in UK from under 500,000, to 813,000), but see p. 49n (increase not much exceeding 800,000); E. L. Woodward, *The Age of Reform* (Oxford, 1938) 88 (increase in England from 435,000 to 652,000).
308 Mirror of Parliament 1831, 1629b (21 April). See also Hansard, 2nd ser., xxii, 881 (23 Feb. 1830; representation for Manchester, Birmingham, and Leeds).
309 See above pp. 3, 22.
310 Mirror of Parliament 1831, 577a (14 July).
311 Cole, *The Life of William Cobbett*, 372; Halevy, *History of the English People*, iii, 295 ('People's Charter', 1836). These items were on the radical agenda from an early date: Thompson, *The Making of the English Working Class*, 691. Lord Grey specifically declared his opposition to these three items in November 1831, ibid., 892.

supported just about one half of this agenda. He said, in 1833, that 'he knew that something final was called for, but he could not say that such a term was applicable to any measure – not even to the Reform Bill'.[312] He was not a democrat, in the modern sense of the word: he did not support universal suffrage,[313] and he had voted, albeit reluctantly, to restrict the franchise of the Irish electorate in 1829, in exchange for Catholic emancipation.[314] On the other hand, he was a wholehearted supporter of the secret ballot (a reform not introduced until 1872), maintaining that it was the only sure preventive of bribery and intimidation,[315] citing his own experience of 'intimidation of the most revolting character . . . exercised among the voters of the lower orders'.[316] He also supported a reduction in the length of Parliaments from the seven-year period then in force, in order to encourage a 'more honest and faithful, a more diligent and assiduous' discharge of the duties of members. He went only part way towards the radical position, however, thinking that 'three years is the most fit and proper period for which the duration of Parliaments should be fixed'.[317] The length of Parliaments was reduced to five years, only in the present century.[318]

Lushington favoured the requirement that a Member of Parliament, on accepting government office, should resign, and stand for re-election,[319] but he did not see any reason why a Member appointed to be a judge should not, having been duly re-elected, continue to sit in Parliament. In 1838, Lushington was offered the judgeship of the Admiralty Court, and wrote to Lord John Russell,[320] asking, among other things, 'whether the Office is to be tenable with Parliament – as

---

[312] Hansard, 3rd ser., xv, 430 (8 Feb. 1833).

[313] Halevy, *History of the English People*, 28n, estimates that 1 in 30 of the population of the UK had the vote in 1832. C. R. Dod, *Electoral Facts, 1832–1853*, gives the figures, for the UK, as 1 in 37 (counties), and 1 in 18 (boroughs).

[314] See Hansard, 3rd ser., xxii, 34 (11 Mar. 1834); see Halevy, *The History of the English People*, ii, 223, 272.

[315] *The Times*, 29 Oct. 1832, 3d (speech to constituents); Hansard, 3rd ser., xv, 430 (8 Feb. 1833); Mirror of Parliament, 1833, 1455 (25 April); Hansard, 3rd ser., xxxvii, 45 (7 Mar. 1837).

[316] Mirror of Parliament 1833 (25 April).

[317] *The Times*, 29 Oct. 1832, 3d (speech to constituents), Mirror of Parliament 1833, 3264a (23 July).

[318] Parliament Act, 1911, 1 & 2 Geo. V. c. 13.

[319] Hansard, 3rd ser., xxiii, 391 (1 May 1834).

[320] John Russell, first Earl Russell (1792–1878); MP, 1813–60, Home Secretary, 1835–9, Colonial Secretary, 1839–41; Prime Minister, 1846–52, and 1865–6.

at present'.[321] Lushington accepted the appointment to the court,[322] and he resigned his parliamentary seat and was re-elected.[323] This indicates that Russell's response to the question about Parliament was in the affirmative, and when the point arose in the House of Commons, both Russell,[324] and Lushington himself spoke against the introduction of a disqualification, as did Melbourne (the Prime Minister),[325] in the House of Lords.[326]

Lushington here showed himself disinclined to accept the principle of separation between law and politics, or, at least, disinclined to accept what has been taken for granted in modern times as a necessary implication of the principle, namely, the exclusion of judges from political activity. His argument was that 'all disqualifications of Members of Parliament ought to be avoided', as a fetter on the freedom of the electorate, except where acceptance of an office would necessarily exclude performance of parliamentary duties.[327] This position was supported by the consideration that several other persons, besides the Admiralty Court Judge, who exercised judicial functions were eligible to sit in the House of Commons.[328] The arguments on the other side, cogently marshalled by Peel, and supported by Brougham in the House of Lords, were, in essence, that a judge who was an active political partisan, in Parliament, and on the hustings, could not preserve the appearance of calm deliberation and unbiased decision-making required of a judge.[329] The Admiralty Court Bill was defeated in the House of Lords in 1839, after Brougham's opposition, and, when the Bill was re-introduced into the House of Commons in the following year, an amendment to exclude the

---

321 Lushington to Russell, 4 Oct. 1838, Lushington Family Papers. The letter is endorsed (presumably by Russell, or a secretary), indicating that it was sent and received.

322 He was sworn on 18 Oct. 1838: PRO, HCA/7/25, 176.

323 Dod, *Electoral Facts*, s.v. Tower Hamlets (Feb. 1839); the election was unopposed.

324 Hansard, 3rd ser., xlix, 1113 (1 Aug. 1839); ibid., liii, 1074 (13 April 1840).

325 William Lamb, second Viscount Melbourne (1779–1848); Home Secretary, 1830–4; Prime Minister, 1834, and 1835–41.

326 Hansard, 3rd ser., xlv, 259 (12 Feb. 1839); ibid., l, 243–4 (13 Aug. 1839).

327 Hansard, 3rd ser., xlix, 1119 (1 Aug. 1839).

328 See Hansard, 3rd ser., xlix, 1121 (1 Aug. 1839).

329 Hansard, 3rd ser., xlix, 1114–6 (1 Aug. 1839). Brougham spoke forcefully to similar effect in the House of Lords: Hansard, 3rd ser., xlv, 258–9 (12 Feb. 1839); ibid., l, 240–1, 245–6 (13 Aug. 1839), and wrote to Lushington on 24 Dec. 1847, 'I turned you out of the H. of Comms', Lushington Family Papers. see p. 46, below.

judge from Parliament, though first defeated,[330] was later carried, Russell declaring that, though personally still opposed to exclusion, he would not, 'perceiving that the sense of the House was against him', press for a division.[331] The voting on this question certainly must have been, as has been said,[332] influenced by party political considerations. But the eventual abandonment by the government of its original intention, after two unsuccessful attempts to effect it, suggests that Lushington's view of the compatibility of judicial and political activity was, by this date, in the minority.[333] The exclusion had prospective effects only, but there was a dissolution within a year of the passage of the Bill,[334] and so, at that date (June 1841), Lushington's parliamentary career came to an end.

Ten years later, Lushington was offered an opportunity to re-enter Parliament, as a life peer. The House of Lords, as a judicial supreme court, fell very far short of the standards of the mid-nineteenth century. The evidence given before a select committee of the House in 1856, reveals astonishing deficiencies.[335] There was no system of appointment of judicially qualified peers; appeals were heard by the Lord Chancellor and any former Lord Chancellors who cared to attend. Peers were unpaid, and there was no obligation to attend the hearing of appeals. Cases could be heard only when the House was in session. There was no system of ensuring that any particular number of law peers attended, so that, in many cases, two law peers divided equally, and other cases were heard by one law peer alone.[336] Appeals were not infrequently heard by judges who had themselves

330 Hansard, 3rd ser., liii, 1078 (13 April 1840). Lushington is not recorded as speaking or voting.
331 Hansard, 3rd ser., liv, 1410 (22 June 1840). Brougham, expressing himself as satisfied, supported the Bill in the House of Lords: Hansard, 3rd ser., lv, 73 (25 June 1840).
332 G. Stephen, *Anti-Slavery Recollections* (London, 1854), 67; *The Times*, 21 Jan. 1873, 9f.
333 George Stephen's suggestion (*Anti-Slavery Recollections*, 67), that Lushington was excluded from Parliament because of his anti-slavery views, seems improbable in light of the wide variety of political opinion in favour of exclusion. J. Hume, a radical (Dod, 1835) who had moved the exclusion in 1839, and seconded it in 1840, said that he did so on principle and with regret, as it would exclude 'his hon. Friend the Member from Tower Hamlets', Hansard, 3rd ser., liv, 1410.
334 Royal Assent: 7 Aug. 1840, Hansard, 3rd ser., lv, 1378; dissolution: 23 June 1841, Hansard, 3rd ser., lviii, 1598.
335 HL Sess. Pap. 1856, xxiv, 1.
336 See Report of Select Committee of the House of Lords on Appellate Jurisdiction, PP 1872, vii, 193, 313 (evidence of Sir J. G. S. Lefevre).

participated in the case at an earlier stage.[337] The quorum (of three peers) was made up by lay peers, who sat chatting and writing letters, with the natural consequence that an uninformed observer would think, as a witness said to the Committee, that 'they are not attending to their duty'.[338] The atmosphere of the hearing was not judicial: the law peers sat in various places, at a distance from counsel; they came and went during the course of argument, and, even when present, allowed their attention to be distracted by lay peers. In 1855 Bethell,[339] the Solicitor-General, went so far as to say, in the House of Commons, that the House of Lords was 'inferior to the lowest tribunal in what ought to be the accompaniments of a court of justice'.[340] Another source of criticism was that Scottish appeals were often decided by peers who had no knowledge of Scots law.

Lushington himself, in a letter to Lord Granville[341] in 1856, summed up the objections as he saw them:

> First it is complained that only two judges sit & therefore if they disagree there can be no decision – 2d that there are no judges save Brougham familiar with Scotch law (about half the appeals are Scotch) – 3d that some Lords give judgments who do not hear the causes *through*.[342]

It was still not finally settled that appeals were to be decided by the law peers alone. In a notorious appeal in 1844 from the conviction for sedition of the Irish radical Member of Parliament, Daniel O'Connell,[343] where political feeling ran high, lay peers desired to vote, but were persuaded by the government to refrain.[344] Although it turned

---

[337] See evidence of Malins to House of Lords Select Committee, 1856, HL Sess Pap xxiv, 1, at 66. An example is the church rate case (*Gosling* v. *Veley* (1853) 4 HLC 679) where Lord Truro gave the judgment of the House of Lords, having dissented in the Exchequer Chamber. See pp. 266–7, below.

[338] Ibid. at p. 11.

[339] Richard Bethell, first Baron Westbury (1800–73); MP, 1851–61, Solicitor-General, 1852–6; Attorney-General, 1856–8; Lord Chancellor, 1861–5.

[340] Hansard, 3rd ser., cxxxix, 2120 (11 Aug. 1855).

[341] Granville George Leveson-Gower, second Earl Granville (1815–91); MP, 1836–46; Foreign Secretary, 1851–2, 1870–4, and 1880–5; Liberal leader in the House of Lords from 1855.

[342] Lushington to Granville, 25 Feb. 1856, Granville Papers, PRO 30/29/23/6 f.146.

[343] Daniel O'Connell (1775–1847); Irish Nationalist; first Roman Catholic to sit in the Commons after 1829; imprisoned for seditious conspiracy, 1843, but released on writ of error by House of Lords, 1844.

[344] See R. B. Stevens, *Law and Politics: The House of Lords as a Judicial Body, 1800–1976* (Chapel Hill, N. Carolina, 1978), 32–3. O'Connell was, on many issues, in political alliance with Lushington.

out that this was the last time that the monopoly of the legally qualified peers was seriously challenged, this could not have been clear in 1850. Lay peers were regularly used for purposes of a quorum. It was commonly asserted, even in 1856, that voting by lay peers was proper, and indeed desirable in some cases.[345] As late as 1883 a lay peer attempted to vote, but the vote was ignored.[346] The notion that the House of Lords could reverse a judicial decision on overtly political grounds ran entirely counter to the separation of law from politics that was, by the mid-nineteenth century, gaining ascendancy as an essential aspect of the rule of law.

Reform of the judicial proceedings in the House of Lords was, by this time, therefore, an urgent necessity. But the shape of the reform was not obvious, because the political power of the House of Lords was an exceedingly sensitive issue. One possibility was to create peers specifically on the ground of their legal attainments and judicial competence. But there were difficulties. A hereditary peerage was generally conceded to be unsuitable in a case where the peer had insufficient wealth to sustain it,[347] particularly where there was likely to be a surviving heir (Dr Lushington had five sons). Life peerages might appear to offer a solution, but life peerages had not been used for hundreds of years, and, in the climate of the mid-nineteenth century, an assertion of a power in the government of the day to create life peers had political implications. A power, in a government responsible to the House of Commons, to create unlimited numbers of life peers threatened the independence of the House of Lords, and the hereditary principle as an integral part of a mixed constitution. Eventually, the solution lay in a statutory provision for a limited number of law lords appointed as life peers: a prerogative power to create life peers did not prove acceptable until a century later, when the political role of the House of Lords was quite different.

---

[345] See letter of Croker to Lord Lyndhurst, 21 Feb. 1856, B. Pool (ed.), *The Croker Papers, 1808–1857*, 265; Stevens, *Law and Politics*, 42, mentioning that Lord St Leonards held the view that lay peers could vote in some cases.

[346] See Stevens, *Law and Politics*, 34; R. E. Megarry, 'Lay Peers in Appeals to the House of Lords', *Law Quarterly Review* 65 (1949), 22.

[347] See Queen Victoria's letter, below. Also Lord Granville: 'Now, if these individuals [life peers] possessed fortune enough to sustain the dignity of an hereditary peerage – and without such a fortune any man would be a fool to wish for it . . .' Hansard, 3rd ser., cxl, 293 (7 Feb. 1856).

The possibility of an offer to Lushington was canvassed in 1847. Brougham, who had opposed the Admiralty Court Bill because he favoured the exclusion of the judge from the House of Commons, now wrote to him:

> You will naturally say I turned you out of the H. of Comms. from a fanatical regard as you might call it for judicial purity. Be it so. I have a still more fanatical hatred of the Slave Trade, and no man could object to your being in the House of Lords. Melbourne told me t'other day that John Russell gave as the reason for not offering you a Peerage that 'then Brougham would have a stout supporter on Slavery & Sugar' or some such thing – a saying which does my friend Johnny little credit, either as to sense or anything else, for assuredly *he* – J.R. – would have had a stout supporter on all other matters. I mentioned that this was just a case where Life Peerages would have been of great use – because I did not know how far having sons you might wish to curtail such a burthen on them.[348]

In 1851, Lord John Russell did offer a life peerage to Lushington. The Queen personally approved the offer, writing:

> With regard to the creation of Dr Lushington as a peer without remainder, the Queen has again thoroughly considered the question, and is of opinion that the establishment of the principle of creation for life, in cases where public advantage may be derived from the grant of a peerage, but where there may be no fortune to support the dignity in the family, is most desirable. The mode in which the Public will take the introduction of it will however chiefly depend upon the merits of the first case brought forward. Dr Lushington appears to the Queen to be so unobjectionable in this respect that she cannot but approve the experiment being tried with him.
>
> It would be well however that it should be done quietly – that it should not be talked about beforehand or get into the papers, which so frequently happens in creations of this kind and generally does harm.[349]

Lushington, however, declined the experiment, though, according to Greville, the clerk to the Privy Council, the offer was 'pressed upon him':[350]

> I am disposed to believe that a just discharge of my present judicial duties in the Privy Council[351] and the Court of Admiralty, the latter recently so much

---

[348] Brougham to Lushington, 24 Dec. 1847, Lushington Family Papers.
[349] The Queen to Lord John Russell, 25 Jan. 1851, PRO 30/22/9A/232.
[350] *The Greville Memoirs*, vii, 199 (15 Feb. 1856).
[351] In 1849 Dr Lushington sat on thirty days in the Privy Council; in 1850, twenty-four days; in 1851, thirty days, Howell, *Judicial Committee of the Privy Council*, appendix.

increased,[352] would leave me very little time or power to render any useful service in the decision of causes in the House of Lords – It is true that at one time I was conversant with Scotch Law, but 12 years have since elapsed, and I truly doubt whether at my age[353] I could by any exertion consistent with my other duties recover my knowledge of that Law so as to be really serviceable.

I have thus without reserve stated my opinion, because I infer from your observations, that the main reason for the proposition made by you was the prospect of some service in appeal causes.

I am not insensible to the high value of the honor you are disposed to advise her Majesty to confer upon me, but I feel that I should be placed in a very peculiar situation, if I were the first & only person at present of the legal profession promoted to a peerage for life – I doubt not that to create peers for Life may be a right measure, but whether it will be so received by the legal profession I am not so certain – tho' it may be a weakness I must admit that it would be painful to me to be subjected to censure by that profession.

Weighing all these considerations carefully, I beg leave most respectfully to decline the honor, which notwithstanding all difficulties I would not do, if I had more confidence in my own power of being useful.

I trust I may not be deemed ungrateful for the favor shewn me nor thought unwilling at any time to devote myself to her Majesty's service.[354]

It is evident, from this letter, that the offer was not so attractive as might at first sight be supposed. No remuneration was attached to the proposed peerage, and no relief contemplated from Lushington's duties in the Admiralty Court and the Privy Council.[355] Further, Lushington rightly foresaw that the appointment would not be welcomed by the existing law peers, who would probably regard the appointment as an implied reflection on their ability to deal with

---

[352] *Return of the Proceedings in the High Court of Admiralty from 1841 to 1866*, PP 1867, lvii, 21, p. 9 shows a steady increase in the number of days on which the court sat from 1847 to 1850 (1847: thirty-eight days; 1848: forty-one days; 1849: forty-six days; 1850: fifty-eight days). The number of days diminished in 1851 and 1852 (forty-seven and forty-four days) but rose again in the period of the Crimean War (1853: sixty-seven days; 1854: sixty-six days; 1855: eighty-one days). See also F. L. Wiswall, *The Development of Admiralty Jurisdiction and Practice since 1800* (Cambridge, 1970), 58–9, mentioning enlarged jurisdiction under the Act of 1840, and increased numbers of collisions in the steamship era, and also, at 96, Lushington's high reputation as a judge.

[353] Sixty-nine.

[354] 6 Feb. 1851, PRO 30/22/9/51–56.

[355] He says nothing of his duties in the London Consistory Court, which would account for about eighteen days a year (four sessions in each term, with some extra days). See Assignation Book, Greater London Record Office.

appeals, without offering any permanent improvement to the system. More generally, the legal profession would tend to sympathize with the fear that life peerages were a threat to the independence of the House of Lords, and to the political balance of the constitution. Nor was the suggestion that lawyers were unfit to be hereditary peers flattering to the profession.[356] The appointment would be widely opposed, not only on the ground of objection to Lushington's political links with the government,[357] but also in fear of the precedent that his appointment would create.[358] Acceptance of Russell's offer would have put Lushington at the centre of a political controversy, and into an environment in which he would have faced active hostility from his legal and non-legal fellow peers alike.

In 1856 Lord Granville referred in the House of Lords to this offer, in terms that plainly identified its recipient:

In order to show that this is not the first occasion on which the creation of life peers has been contemplated, I have permission to state that, in 1851, under the Administration of Lord J. Russell, an offer of a life peerage was made to a most distinguished judge, who would in every respect have been an ornament to this House. The offer was, however, refused, the learned Judge assigning as his reasons that his time was already fully employed in the discharge of his judicial functions; that he would be unable to devote much attention to appeals in this House; that he had been unable to keep up his knowledge of Scotch law; and that – and this he told me was the decisive reason – although he thought the exercise of the prerogative quite fitting as he now considers it legal, constitutional and expedient, he knew the step would be very unpopular among his learned brethren; and that, to use his own words, he had the weakness to shrink from being alone the first man to set the example.[359]

After Bethell's criticisms of the House of Lords in 1855, the government felt bound to act. In January 1856, the offer to Lushington was repeated, and again declined.[360] Then a life peerage was offered to

356 Lord Lyndhurst said: 'It is said sometimes . . . that these creations [life peerages] are to be confined to members of the legal profession. What, I would ask your lordships, has the profession of law done to merit this indignity?' Hansard, 3rd ser., cxl, 277 (7 Feb. 1856).
357 Russell had attempted, unsuccessfully, to secure Lushington's continued membership of the House of Commons, after his appointment (by the Melbourne government) to the Admiralty Court in 1838; see pp. 42–3, above.
358 This is made clear by O. Anderson, 'The Wensleydale Peerage Case and the position of the House of Lords in the mid-nineteenth century', *English Historical Review* 82 (1967): 486, at 487 and throughout.
359 Hansard, 3rd ser., cxl, 282 (7 Feb. 1856).
360 Anderson, 'Wensleydale Peerage Case', 490n.

Parke,[361] a baron of the Exchequer Court, and accepted. This precipitated a crisis.[362] The appointment was opposed by many peers, including all four of the law peers (excluding Cranworth,[363] the Chancellor).[364] The question was referred to the Committee of the House of Lords for privileges, and Parke's claim to sit and vote in the House was rejected. He was made a hereditary peer, and the main question was shelved for almost twenty years. The fear was that Parke's appointment was really meant, not to ameliorate the appellate functions of the House of Lords, but to set a precedent for an unlimited prerogative power to create life peers, which would be used for political reasons. This fear was reinforced by the fact that Parke could perfectly well have been appointed a hereditary peer, if the intention were really just to secure the benefit of his legal abilities, since he was wealthy, aged seventy-four, and had no son.[365]

Lushington was thus proved correct in his prediction that the appointment of the first life peer would not be smooth. Parke's own opinion, as reported by Greville, was that 'if he had had an idea of all the bother it had made, he never would have had anything to do with it'.[366] Lushington was, however, active in his support of the view that the appointment was perfectly legal. Greville referred to Lushington as 'the highest authority in favour of it'.[367] Lushington wrote to Lord Granville[368] on the eve of the debate, describing research conducted by his son on the question, mentioning his fruitless search for a pamphlet[369] (all copies were in the hands of law lords), and enclosing

[361] James Parke, Baron Wensleydale (1782–1868); junior counsel in support of bill again Queen Caroline, 1820; judge of court of King's Bench, 1828–34; member of Judicial Committee of Privy Council from 1833; judge of the Exchequer Court, 1834–56.
[362] See Greville, *Memoirs*, viii, 21 'menaced great embarrassment, if not danger'; Anderson, 'The Wensleydale Peerage Case'; T. E. May, *Constitutional History of England since the Accession of George III* (London, 1861), i, 246–9.
[363] Robert Monsey Rolfe, Baron Cranworth (1790–1868); judge of the Exchequer Court, 1839–50; Lord Chancellor, 1852–8, and 1865–6; married, in 1845, Laura Carr, Lushington's sister-in-law.
[364] 'All the lawyers but the Chancellor are dead against the Life Peerage', Greville, viii, 15. All spoke against it: Hansard, 3rd ser., cxl, 263, 1153 (Lyndhurst), 296 (St Leonards), 327 (Campbell), 376, 1193 (Brougham) (7 and 22 Feb. 1856).
[365] See Anderson, 'The Wensleydale Peerage Case', 491.
[366] Greville, *Memoirs*, viii, 52.
[367] Ibid., 15.
[368] Lord Granville was the government leader in the House of Lords.
[369] Sir H. Nicolas, *A Letter on the propriety and legality of creating Peers for life*, 3rd edn (1834), referred to by Lord Granville, Hansard, 3rd ser., cxl, 295 (7 Feb. 1856). The pamphlet favoured the power to create life peerages.

his son's copies of extracts from three other sources,[370] and concluding that 'I do not think the power of the Crown can be seriously disputed'.[371] Lord Granville spoke in the House of Lords the next day, evidently making use of Lushington's letter, and referring to the research.[372]

As has been shown, Lushington's view of the question was not a popular one in legal or conservative circles, and it did not prevail in the House of Lords. It is evident from his letter to Granville that Lushington went to considerable time and trouble (not to mention his son's) to lend support to the government position, even though he had no personal interest in the outcome. His political views, though less radical than in 1820,[373] were still disinclined to make any large accommodation to the interests of the hereditary peerage.

Lushington's career crossed, at many points, that of his brilliant contemporary, Brougham. The contacts between them, including considerable correspondence by letter,[374] cover a period of over forty years. Both were advisers to Lady Byron in 1816.[375] Both were counsel to Queen Caroline in 1820. Both were active in the cause of anti-slavery. They were joint founders of the Society for the Diffusion of Useful Knowledge, and of London University. They were in close contact over the reform of the ecclesiastical courts in the 1830s. They worked together, for many years, as fellow members of the Judicial Committee of the Privy Council. Brougham first suggested Lushington's appointment to the Admiralty Court. Brougham was instrumental in excluding Lushington from the House of Commons, but sought a place for him later in the House of Lords. They were alike in their political opinions, but dissimilar in many other ways. Brougham's defence of Queen Caroline is spectacular; Lushington's is solid. Brougham's role diminished after the trial; Lushington stayed to

---

370 Blackstone's *Commentaries*, referred to by Lord Granville, Hansard, 3rd ser., cxl, 287–8 (7 Feb. 1856); *Coke upon Littleton* referred to by Lord Granville, Hansard, 3rd ser., cxl, 286–7 (7 Feb. 1856); W. Cruise, *A Treatise on the Origin and Nature of Dignities etc.*, 2nd edn (1823), referred to by Lord Granville, Hansard, 3rd ser., cxl, 288 (7 Feb. 1856).
371 Lushington to Granville, 6 Feb. 1856, Granville Papers, PRO 30/29/23/6 ff. 95–9.
372 Hansard, 3rd ser., cxl, 294 (7 Feb. 1856). See also Fitzmaurice, *Life of Granville*, i, 157–8.
373 See chapter 4, below.
374 Brougham Papers, University College, London (forty-eight letters from Lushington), Lushington Family Papers (four letters from Brougham).
375 See chapter 3, below.

manage the funeral.[376] Brougham made brilliant parliamentary speeches against slavery;[377] Lushington put in many hours behind the scenes preparing cautious advice for the anti-slavery movement.[378] Brougham attacked the system of ecclesiastical courts in his famous law reform speech;[379] it was Lushington who did the background work for the Ecclesiastical Courts Commission that was supposed to implement reform. As a judge, Brougham is chiefly known for the speed at which he disposed of his cases; Lushington has left behind hundreds of carefully considered judgments. Brougham rose, for a short time, to great political height, and is known to every historian of the period; Lushington is hardly known, except to specialists, but it would be wrong to conclude, on that ground, that his long-term influence on the legal and political institutions of his time was the less substantial.

There is another very well-known figure with whom Lushington was closely associated, and with whom extensive correspondence survives. This is T. F. Buxton, Wilberforce's successor as the leader of the anti-slavery movement. Lushington and Buxton were alike in their 'indefatigable perseverence'[380] in opposition to slavery, as will appear from the fuller discussion of the subject below. But anti-slavery was, to Buxton, 'the one single object of his heart'.[381] Buxton called himself, in a letter to Lushington, a 'fanatic', and Lushington used the same word (of Buxton) in his reply.[382] Lushington, on the other hand, though he once described the abolition of slavery as the principal object of his life,[383] carried on, throughout the anti-slavery campaign, a busy professional practice, besides being a Member of Parliament, holding (after 1838) three judicial offices, and directing energy, in and out of Parliament, to many other reform causes. Buxton wrote to him, 'you can do 3 or 4 things at a time – I but one. You like Parliament – I hated it. It refreshes you – it slays me with fatigue.'[384] Buxton saw Lushington as possessing political discretion,

[376] See chapter 4, below.
[377] Brougham, *Speeches*, ii, 1–283.
[378] See chapter 2, below.
[379] Hansard, 2nd ser., xviii, 151–4 (7 Feb. 1828); Brougham, *Speeches*, ii, 319, 352–6.
[380] Stephen, *Anti-Slavery Recollections*, 67 (of Lushington).
[381] Stephen, *Anti-Slavery Recollections*, 234.
[382] Buxton to Lushington, 8 May 1839, Buxton Papers, 18, 93; Lushington to Buxton 9 May [1839], ibid., 92n.
[383] See p. 91, below.
[384] Buxton to Lushington, 10 May 1839, Buxton Papers, 18, 94 (copy).

in contrast to Buxton's own dogged determination.[385] Buxton and Lushington were both churchmen, but of rather different theological outlook. Buxton was driven by an evangelical fervour that was never, despite the close association between the two, manifested in Lushington's letters. Buxton's notebooks include a prayer for Lushington on the death of his wife.[386] Lushington's letter to Buxton during her last illness has only the conventional 'God's will be done'.[387] Buxton regretted that Lushington did not share his religious outlook, writing to an evangelical friend 'what would I give that the truth were disclosed to him [Lushington] with the same force'.[388] In a similar vein, Buxton's daughter, writing of Lushington, said 'How I did long for him, to open his eyes and see the blessings he might have! He does so *deserve* to be truly religious!'[389] She considered his opinions 'radical and almost irreligious'.[390]

Lushington, though he may not have been 'religious' by evangelical standards, was very closely involved with a wide variety of religious issues. Religion, in nineteenth-century England, was intimately linked with law and politics, and nowhere were the links manifested more plainly than in Lushington's career. The Church of England, in the middle third of the nineteenth century, was embroiled in external and internal controversies. All of them had political implications, and several led to notorious disputes, which engaged Lushington also in his judicial capacity.[391]

The external controversies had to do with the status of those who dissented from the Church. Though the Dissenters were, by the 1830s, eligible for almost all public offices, they still had several grievances against the Church of England, all of which sprang from the ancient assumption, long obsolete by this date, that membership in the Church of England comprised the whole population.

Dr Lushington's early attitude to Dissent, and to evangelical enthusiasm in general, was unfriendly, and even jocular. He spoke disparagingly of 'that class of religious enthusiasts, called

[385] Buxton to Bishop of Calcutta, 20 Feb. 1840, Buxton Papers, Rhodes House, Oxford, 19, 164.

[386] 16 Sept. 1838, Buxton Papers 4, 387–8 (a year after her death, if the diary entry is correctly dated).

[387] Lushington to Buxton, 31 July 1837, Buxton Papers 16, 57 aj.

[388] T. F. Buxton to J. Jeremie, 20 Mar. 1837, Buxton Papers 15, 240.

[389] Priscilla Buxton to Sarah Buxton, 23 Aug. 1833, Buxton Papers, 12, 61 g–h.

[390] Priscilla Johnston (née Buxton) to Sarah Buxton and Anna Gurney, 9 April 1835, Buxton Papers, 13, 442.

[391] See chapters 8, 9, and 10, below.

Methodists',[392] and of 'canters and methodists'.[393] In a speech in 1824, supporting the building of new churches, he permitted himself to indulge in humour at the expense of an evangelical organization called the Home Missionary Society:

To the operation of that society he felt reluctant that the field should be left open. And what the nature of those operations were, the House might gather from a pamphlet which he held in his hand, and which purported to be the Society's third report. Some agent of the Society, who had been pursuing his labours through the county of Worcester, described it in terms: 'I shall here attempt a description of the very deplorable state in which I have found the people of this dark county. It puts me at my wit's end when I think of the depravity of its thoughtless inhabitants. I shall only touch upon the manner in which they profane the Holy Sabbath'. Here the learned doctor said, he feared the House would be lost in horror when they should hear of the enormities which were committed by the people of this 'dark' county. 'They play against each other at foot-ball, and at hurling in a field adjoining to the church. Some of them play at fives, some at ball, some with sticks upon the green, some go to the river with lines and nets, and the youth of both sexes' (Oh, monstrous!) 'assemble together, and spend the evening in social mirth'. The zealous agent recommended that a march should be immediately commenced, and that, invested in gospel armour, they should go from house to house (and this was literally done) to collect subscriptions, the object of which was to spread the progress of dissent through the benighted county of Worcestershire.[394]

This was probably an injudicious indulgence: it attracted adverse comment in the next speech, and Lushington rose again to beg 'most distinctly to disclaim every species of hostility to the Dissenters'.[395]

Lushington's subsequent references to Dissenters, recorded in Hansard, are all extremely courteous. He spoke of the 'number and respectability of those who conscientiously dissented from the doctrines of the Church'.[396] He presented the petition in 1834 for the redress of the Dissenters' grievances, and spoke frequently of the justice of their grievances and demands.[397] His more respectful

[392] Hansard, 2nd ser., iv, 611 (13 Feb. 1821). The term 'methodist' was not necessarily confined to Dissenters. See E. Jay, *Religion of the Heart* (Oxford, 1979), 21, mentioning usages in 1809 of the word to include evangelical churchmen.
[393] Hansard, 2nd ser., vi, 959 (6 March 1822).
[394] Hansard, 2nd ser., xi, 347–8 (9 April 1824).
[395] Ibid., 357.
[396] Hansard, 3rd ser., xxxvii, 380 (14 March 1837).
[397] See Hansard, 3rd ser., xxii, 3 (11 March 1834); ibid., 401 (18 March 1834); ibid., xxviii, 80 (25 May 1835); ibid., xxxvii, 378 (13 March 1837); ibid., xlvii, 538 (25 April 1839); ibid., lviii, 796 (25 May 1841).

attitude was probably due, in part, to his close association with Dissenters in the anti-slavery movement.[398] It may well have been due, also, to the growing number and wealth of the Dissenters, and to Lushington's increasing political dependence on their support. In a letter to Brougham, explaining his loss of an election in 1830, he said:

The contest has been most desperate the Church and a large portion of the party called Semi-Evangelicals having united against me. The old Dissenters stood firm by my side.[399]

Ten years later he said, in Parliament, with reference to his post-Reform Act constituency of Tower Hamlets, that:

He had great confidence in the body of the Dissenters. He had the honour of representing a greater number of Dissenters probably, and more respectable than were contained within any constituency in the kingdom.[400]

The internal ecclesiastical controversies arose from divisions of theological thought within the Church of England. In the early years of the century the Church of England, and most of the Protestant dissenting churches, were profoundly influenced by what was called the Evangelical Movement, emphasizing personal conversion, individual salvation, fervent prayer, scripture reading, strict Sunday observance, and missionary endeavour. From 1833, partly in reaction to the evangelical movement, a revival occurred, associated with what is called the Oxford Movement, of Catholic doctrine and practice within the Church of England. The Protestant reformation of the sixteenth century had taken a comparatively conservative form in England, and had left considerable Catholic doctrine and practice in place, or not expressly forbidden. The ecclesiastical formularies, and independent historical sources, were now combed – with a fair degree of success, to the delight of some, the embarrassment of others, and the astonishment of many – for the purpose of supporting a high view

---

[398] See chapter 2, below.
[399] Lushington to Brougham, 12 Aug. 1830, Brougham Papers 24, 645. The constituency was Reading. The expression 'semi-evangelical' was used by Lushington as though it might be unfamiliar to Brougham; perhaps it was meant to include Wesleyans and others. A 'hard fight' for Lushington was predicted by Macaulay, T. Pinney (ed.) *Letters of T. B. Macaulay* (Cambridge, 1974), i, 278 (letter dated 16 July 1830).
[400] Hansard, 3rd ser., lii, 133 (11 Feb. 1840). See also Hansard, 3rd ser. xxviii, 80 (25 May 1835) to similar effect.

of the episcopacy, of the sacraments, and of the Church as the proper means of salvation for its individual members. The effect of the Oxford Movement (whose followers were also called Puseyites, Tractarians, Anglo-Catholics, and, later, Ritualists) was to remind the Church of England of its Catholic heritage, and to revive practices, some of which were ancient and long discontinued, and others of which were frankly copied from the nineteenth-century Roman Catholic church. A third influence, which flourished in the intellectual climate of the nineteenth century, was the application to theological subjects of scientific, rationalistic, and liberal thought. The adherents of these three schools were commonly described as the low-church, high-church, and broad-church parties. Though the divisions were imprecise, and the names of them, in some respects, misleading,[401] the usage was established by the middle of the century.[402] The legal disputes had important consequences: the high-church cases determined whether there would be a place, within the Church of England, for a Catholic tradition;[403] the broad-church cases whether there would be room for an academic tradition.[404]

Lushington's own religious ideas had been formed in the previous century, and were little affected by any of the principal schools of nineteenth-century religious thought. Though sympathetic with the evangelicals and closely allied politically with the dissenters, he was not himself an evangelical, as has been shown by his relation with Buxton. He was not a strict Sabbatarian.[405] He denounced the activities of some of the evangelical societies.[406] In a letter to his sister-in-law, shortly after his wife's death, he wrote, with reference to a letter of consolation from 'Mr Marsh,[407] the celebrated evangelical preacher', that 'I cannot view all things in their light' and that 'humanly speaking I cannot but think, that a greater evil, a more

---

[401] 'Low church' is too negative to be a synonym for 'evangelical'. 'High-churchman' was formerly used with a different sense, like, and often with 'High Tory', to denote one strongly in favour of the privileges and status of the Church.

[402] W. J. Conybeare, *Edinburgh Review* (1853), 273.

[403] See chapter 9, below.

[404] See chapter 10, below.

[405] See his comments on the Home Missionary Society, above, and Hansard, 2nd ser., xi, 1224 (11 June 1824).

[406] See comments on Home Missionary Society, and on Society for the Suppression of Vice, above.

[407] William Marsh (1775–1864), evangelical divine.

entire destruction of this world's happiness, could not have occurred'.[408]

On the other hand he had no sympathy whatever with the high-church party, and there is ample evidence in the cases discussed below of his hostility to Catholic doctrine and practice within the Church of England.[409] He was not, however, puritanical in matters of church ceremony. He wrote, of a visit to Canterbury Cathedral, 'fortunately too there was an anthem. The service was in my judgment beautifully performed'.[410] He approved of 'simplicity ... grandeur and beauty ... and pure and severe dignity', but not of what he considered alien importations of 'gorgeous pageantry'.[411]

It is debatable to what extent the broad church can properly be called a third ecclesiastical party,[412] but it is clear from his hostility to the high-church party that Lushington did not share the tolerance for diversity of theological views that is generally associated with the broad church. His condemnation in 1862 of a book of theologically liberal essays[413] also indicates a lack of sympathy with the broad-church party.

Lushington was, in short, a churchman 'of the old school',[414] more or less untouched by the ferment of nineteenth-century theological debate, as conservative in theology as he was radical in politics. He was a strong supporter of the link between church and state, tending, like many of the Whigs, towards erastianism, that is, the subordination of church to state.[415] He was a staunch supporter[416] of the parish church at Ockham, which stands in the grounds of the principal house – Ockham Park – which Lushington occupied, filling the

---

[408] Lushington to Frances Carr (sister-in-law), 4 Oct. [1837], Lushington Family Papers.
[409] See chapter 9, below.
[410] Lushington to Frances Carr, 2 Oct. 1837, Lushington Family Papers.
[411] A. F. Bayford (ed.), *The Judgment of the Right Hon. Stephen Lushington ... in Westerton v. Liddell* (London, 1855), 60.
[412] See I. Ellis, *Seven against Christ: a study of 'Essays and Reviews'* (Leiden, 1980), 2–3; Chadwick, *Victorian Church*, i, 544–5.
[413] See chapter 10, below.
[414] Trollope used the phrase in 1857, in *Barchester Towers*, ch. 32, where Slope says of the old dean that he was 'of the old school, of course, as any clergyman over 70 years of age must necessarily be'. Lushington was seventy-five when these words were published.
[415] See Machin, *Politics and the Churches*, 28–31, 182.
[416] Lushington presented communion plate to the church, *Surrey Archaeological Society Collections* (1859), x, 359–60.

role of village squire,[417] and using the principal pew in the church,[418] for the last twenty-six years of his life.

As a Member of Parliament, Lushington spoke frequently on the question of the civil disabilities of the religious minorities. In 1820, there was a high degree of religious toleration, in the sense that religious minorities were not actively persecuted.[419] But there was far from full equality, in the sense of 'admission without distinction to all civil privileges'.[420] The legal position of religious minorities at this date was complex, depending on distinctions among the religious groups, and among various kinds of civil privileges, and on the effect of a long list of ancient and recent statutes, orders, declarations, practices, and forms of oaths and declarations.[421]

Lushington, throughout his parliamentary career, spoke and voted in favour of the granting of full civil rights to Protestant dissenters, to Catholics, and to Jews. An important step in this direction was the repeal, in 1828, of the parts of the Corporation[422] and Test[423] Acts that required holders of public office to receive the sacrament of the Lord's supper according to the rites of the Church of England.[424] These provisions were widely regarded as obsolete,[425] and as an abuse of the sacrament.[426] Lushington voted in favour of their repeal.[427] In

[417] 'The squire is Dr Lushington, the freshest and heartiest as well as the kindest of old gentlemen. His family has been all that we could desire for friendliness and for parish activity.' F. Maurice, *The Life of Frederick Denison Maurice*, ii, 354. On the marriage of his son, Vernon, in 1865, the poor of the village received gifts of food and clothing, *Surrey Advertiser*, 4 March 1865, 3d.

[418] This fact is noted on a small plaque marking the site of the pew. The church underwent a Gothic restoration two years after Lushington's death, in which the old pews were removed; it may be deduced from Lushington's attitude to church furnishings, discussed in chapter 9, below, that he would not have welcomed this restoration.

[419] See U. Henriques, *Religious Toleration in England 1787–1833* (Toronto, 1961); C. Roth, *A History of the Jews in England* 3rd edn (Oxford, 1964), 248.

[420] The phrase is from Paley, *Moral and Political Philosophy* (1785), quoted in Henriques, *Religious Toleration*, 70.

[421] See Henriques, *Religious Toleration*, 83–4 (on the Test and Corporation Acts in practice), and 137–8 (on Catholic disabilities in practice).

[422] 13 Car. II st. 2, c.1 (1661).

[423] 25 Car. II c.2 (1672).

[424] 9 Geo. IV c. 17. The statutes were repealed in full by the Promissory Oaths Act, 1871 (Corporation Act), and the Statute Laws Revision Act, 1863 (Test Act).

[425] Since 1727, Parliament had passed an almost annual series of Acts of Indemnity to excuse violators. See Henriques, *Religious Toleration*, 15, and speech of Russell, Hansard, 2nd ser., xviii, 686–7 (26 Feb. 1828).

[426] See Hansard, 2nd ser., xviii, 687 (Russell), 709 (Wilbraham), and 1482–3 (17 April 1828: both archbishops).

[427] Hansard, 2nd ser., xviii, 782 (26 Feb. 1828).

1834, he presented a petition on behalf of the Dissenters, listing their complaints as 'of the state of the law as regards the solemnization of their marriages – of the want of a proper registry of births and deaths – of their exclusion from the benefits of the Universities – and . . . of being compelled to pay church-rates.'[428]

Marriages were required, by Lord Hardwicke's Marriage Act of 1753,[429] (with exceptions only for Jews and Quakers) to be performed according to the rites of the Church of England. Lushington described the relief sought by the Dissenters as 'a concession which should, in justice, be received',[430] and as a 'just and well-deserved measure of relief'.[431] He described the right of marriage as a 'natural right',[432] not to be restricted by the legislature except insofar as necessary to prevent clandestine marriages.[433] He pointed out that the requirement of solemnization by clergy was comparatively recent in the history of ecclesiastical law.[434] He thought it was unjust to Dissenters, and harmful to the Church, to 'compel parties to submit to ceremonies which were revolting to their religious principles and feelings'.[435] He went so far as to suggest the introduction of a compulsory civil form of marriage, leaving it to the parties to choose such subsequent religious rites as they should desire,[436] recognizing, however, that he could not press this suggestion 'without violating the conscientious feelings of a very large proportion of those who were attached to the Established Church'.[437] That proposal never did become part of English law, but the Marriage Act of 1836[438] permitted marriages to take place in dissenting chapels, or in a registry office.

The problem of registration, like all the other grievances, had at its root the presumption that membership of the Church of England was co-terminous with the English population. Reliance had to be placed,

---

428 Mirror of Parliament 1834, 629b, Hansard, 3rd ser., xxii, 3 differs slightly (11 Mar. 1834). The question of church rates is discussed in chapter 8, below.
429 26 Geo. II, c. 33.
430 Hansard, 2nd ser., xii, 1238 (25 Mar. 1825).
431 Hansard, 3rd ser., xxi, 783 (25 Feb. 1834).
432 Hansard, 2nd ser., xii, 1239 (25 Mar. 1825).
433 Hansard, 3rd ser., 492 (13 June 1836); Hansard, 3rd ser., xxxiv, 1022 (28 June 1836).
434 Ibid., 1239–40, Hansard, 3rd ser., xxi, 782 (25 Feb. 1834), Hansard, 3rd ser., xxvi, 1094–5 (17 Mar. 1835).
435 Ibid., 1241, and Hansard, 3rd ser., xxi, 782 (25 Feb. 1834).
436 Ibid., 1242; Hansard, 3rd ser., xxi, 781 (25 Feb. 1834); Hansard, 3rd ser., xxvi, 1094 (17 Mar. 1835).
437 Hansard, 3rd ser., xxi, 781 (25 Feb. 1834).
438 6 & 7 Wm IV c. 85, s. 18.

where it was necessary to prove a birth or death, on the parish records, but these were records of baptisms and burials performed in the parish church, not of births and deaths as such. Lushington supported the Births and Deaths Registration Act of 1836,[439] not only for the relief of the just grievance of Dissenters, but for the benefit to the general population of an accurate national register.[440]

Lushington spoke in favour of admission of the Dissenters to the ancient universities, which he described as 'great national institutions' and which he thought would be strengthened by the change.[441] Lushington deprecated as a 'solemn mockery',[442] (as much for the Church of England as for the Dissenters) the practice at Oxford of requiring seventeen-year-old boys to subscribe to the Articles of Religion at matriculation. Of Cambridge, where the practice was to admit Dissenters to study, but require subscription before awarding a degree, Lushington was equally critical, on the ground that it added insult to injustice to withhold a degree from one who refused subscription on conscientious grounds.[443] He made the further point that the practice at Cambridge showed that there was no insuperable difficulty in admitting Dissenters to either university. He thought that the true interests of religion were best consulted by following the path of conciliation, thereby promoting good-will, and 'the general well-being of the whole realm'.[444] Admission of Dissenters to Oxford and Cambridge did not occur until 1856,[445] and religious tests were not entirely abolished until 1871.[446]

In supporting the Roman Catholic Relief Act, of 1829,[447] Lushington discounted the fear that the Catholics were a threat to the civil order, praising them for their patience in the face of injustice and discrimination.[448] He deprecated the 'No Popery' riots of former times (having himself been attacked by an anti-Catholic mob in 1807), and welcomed the decline of hostility as a triumph 'of knowledge and reason over strong feeling and prejudice'.[449] One of the prejudices still

---

[439] 6 & 7 Wm IV c. 86.
[440] Hansard, 3rd ser., xxxiv, 141 (6 June 1836).
[441] Mirror of Parliament 1834, 1103 (17 April).
[442] Mirror of Parliament 1834, 1104.
[443] Ibid.
[444] Ibid., 1104b.
[445] O. Chadwick, *Victorian Church* 3rd edn (1971), i, 480.
[446] Universities Tests Act, 34 & 35 Vic. c. 26, College Charter Act 34 & 35 Vic. c. 63.
[447] Introduced by Peel. See Gash, *Mr Secretary Peel*, 545–98.
[448] Mirror of Parliament 1829, 149b (16 Feb.).
[449] Hansard, 2nd ser., xx, 909 (9 Mar. 1829).

powerful was that Catholics were untrustworthy, because they believed that 'no faith is to be kept with heretics'. Lushington said that Lord Coke had laid down that no faith should be kept with infidels, but Protestants were not on this account mistrusted: 'in the progress of time, we have all – both Protestants and Catholics – become wiser'.[450] The Act of 1829 removed most of the Catholic disabilities, but required a special form of oath for Catholic Members of Parliament, to the effect that they would not subvert the established church.[451] In 1834, Lushington supported the abolition of this requirement, partly because of its ambiguity,[452] and partly because he saw no need, in a reformed House of Commons, for oaths of any kind:

I know not why a member of the Church of England, or a Dissenter, should have his lips closed, and be prevented from stating anything which, in his opinion, might be beneficial to the interests of the kingdom. I ask why we should seem to shut up the windows of truth?[453]

The form of oath was not altered until 1866.[454]

Catholic relief was intimately connected with the government of Ireland. Lushington, though no friend of the Roman Catholic religion, which he described as 'superstition',[455] was even less friendly to enforcement by law of the Protestant establishment, which he said was 'opposed to every sense of justice and of sound policy among men',[456] the main cause of the evils of that country,[457] and 'neither sanctioned by the authority of the Scriptures on which the Protestant religion rests, nor consonant with the immutable principles of justice and truth'.[458] He warned that failure to give relief would be 'tantamount to a declaration of perpetual civil war against a large majority of the population of Ireland'.[459]

[450] Mirror of Parliament 1829, 873–4 (27 Mar.).
[451] Chadwick, *Victorian Church*, i, 21.
[452] See Hansard, 3rd ser., xv, 426 (8 Feb. 1833); ibid., xvi, 1353 (1 April 1833); Mirror of Parliament 1834, 641b (11 Mar.).
[453] Mirror of Parliament 1834, 641b (11 Mar.), referred to, with approval, by J. S. Mill (Notes on the newspapers, 12 Mar. 1834), J. M. Robson (ed.), *Collected Works of J. S. Mill* (Toronto, 1982), vi, 187.
[454] Chadwick, *Victorian Church*, i, 24.
[455] Mirror of Parliament, 1829, 744 (20 Mar.).
[456] Mirror of Parliament 1834, 3091a (29 July).
[457] Mirror of Parliament 1835, 669b (1 April).
[458] Ibid., 670a.   [459] Ibid., 670b.

Lushington was active in the cause of removing Jewish disabilities. He gave advice in 1829,[460] and 1830[461] to Jewish organizations, spoke on the subject in the House of Commons in 1830 and 1833, and presented a petition in 1833.[462] Three Bills were passed by the Commons during the 1830s, but defeated by the Lords, full equality not being attained until 1858.[463] Lushington pointed out some anomalous features of Jewish disabilities,[464] and asserted that 'with perfect safety . . . we can grant to the Jewish community their just rights'.[465] He spoke scathingly of those who sought to preserve the existing law:

Nothing has struck me with greater astonishment than that those who profess such peculiar attachment to the Christian faith should, as it appears to me, violate its most fundamental doctrine by upholding intolerance, and endeavouring to fix, for ever, upon an unoffending, moral, honest, and intelligent people all those deprivations and exclusions against which if they suffered one-twentieth part of them in their own proper persons, they would cry out as the greatest injustice which the malignity of bigotry could inflict.[466]

Lushington considered it an injustice to exclude anyone from Parliament on religious grounds,[467] and called on the House no longer to 'impose civil disabilities on the poor foundation of an epithet of religious abuse'.[468]

Lushington frequently avowed his own loyalty to the Church of England, and specifically dissociated himself from those Dissenters who favoured its disestablishment.[469] But he had two answers to those who accused him of weakening the Church. The first was that the claims of the religious minorities were founded on justice:[470] no one had a right to decide for others in matters of religion, or to say, however much he might be convinced of the truth, that what appeared to him to be true must necessarily appear to others to be true.[471] The

[460] T. D. Endelman, *The Jews of Georgian England* (Philadelphia, 1979), 283.
[461] U. Henriques, *Religious Toleration*, 186.
[462] On behalf of R. Grant, Hansard, 3rd ser., xv, 599 (12 Feb 1833).
[463] C. Roth, *History of the Jews*, 250–66.
[464] Mirror of Parliament 1830, 1246a (5 April) (a Jew might hold an advowson, i.e., a right to present a clergyman to a living, and might participate in the election of a clergyman).
[465] Mirror of Parliament 1830, 1247a (5 April).
[466] Mirror of Parliament 1833, 1931b (22 May).
[467] Ibid., 1932a.
[468] Ibid.
[469] Hansard, 3rd ser., xxii, 2–3.
[470] Hansard, 2nd ser., xx, 369 (16 Feb. 1829); Hansard, 3rd ser., xviii, 57 (22 May 1833).
[471] Hansard, 3rd ser., xlviii, 573 (19 June 1839).

second answer was that the Church of England was 'too well fixed in the affections of the people' to be weakened by loss of its privileges:[472] on the contrary, it would be strengthened, in that it would become the freely selected choice of an increasingly enlightened population.[473] So, in this matter, as in the other causes that Lushington supported, progress, justice, religion, and utility were united into a combination that made the reformers irresistible in their time. On his retirement from the House of Commons, he stated his own vision of progressive reform as the 'maintenance and promotion of the cause of civil and religious liberty all over the world' and 'extending free institutions in this country and in foreign nations', saying that this was 'the surest road to secure the peace, the prosperity and the happiness of mankind'.[474]

The topic of religious freedom encapsulates the tension that dominated Lushington's approach to reform. Politically, he was firmly on the side of the reformers in asserting the primacy of individual rights where they conflicted with the privileges of the Church. But he was, at the same time, very closely attached, personally and professionally, to the Church of England, and was a supporter, in principle, of the establishment. The political ideas that he favoured led directly to the loss of most of the Church's privileges, and made inevitable the demise of Lushington's own profession. The tension was resolved by his belief – based on the confidence that enlightened individuals would choose rightly – that Church, nation, and establishment would ultimately be strengthened by reform.

---

[472] Hansard, 2nd ser., xxiii, 1327 (5 April 1830); Mirror of Parliament 1833, 1932a (22 May). However, he thought that it should be made easy for the people to follow these affections, favouring construction of new churches to prevent their 'taking shelter in dissenting chapels', Hansard, 2nd ser., xi, 347 (9 April 1824).

[473] Mirror of Parliament 1829, 744a (20 Mar.).

[474] Hansard, 3rd ser., lviii, 1014 (2 June 1841).

2

ANTI-SLAVERY

Lushington's involvement in the anti-slavery movement requires separate attention: it was by far the most important of his spheres of activity outside his professional career; it occupied an enormous amount of his time and energy, and he exerted a significant influence on what was the most important political, social, and moral issue during his time in Parliament.

The anti-slavery campaign was directed first at the abolition of the slave trade, which was achieved in 1807, and only later at the prohibition of slavery itself,[1] which was not achieved until 1833. The slave trade was the easier target: the horrible methods used in seizing and shipping slaves[2] from Africa were seen, by the nineteenth century, to be indefensible, and the abolition of the trade did not seem to involve an actual legislative confiscation of property. A statute abolishing the slave trade was enacted in 1807.[3] Lushington spoke in Parliament in favour of this Act, despite, as he pointed out, a family interest in the other direction, his sister-in-law having inherited a plantation in Jamaica:[4]

---

[1] See J. Walvin, *England, Slaves and Freedom 1776–1838* (Basingstoke, 1986), 107, 124.

[2] See W. L. Mathieson, *Great Britain and the Slave Trade, 1839–1865* (London, 1929), 40–1.

[3] 5 Geo. IV, c. 113.

[4] He explained this in a letter to T. Clarkson, 26 Aug. 1828, British Library, Add Mss 41266, 272. His sister-in-law, Fanny, (wife of his elder brother, who had just, in 1807, succeeded to the baronetcy: Burke's *Peerage and Baronetage*, 105th edn, 1970, 1677) inherited Jamaica estates from her family. The will was litigated: *Lushington* v. *Sewell* (1827) 1 Sim. 435, (1830) 1 Russ & M 169. Lushington's brother later described himself as a 'Jamaica Planter', Sir H. Lushington to Lushington, n.d., marked '1832' in another hand, Lushington Family Papers. Dame Fanny Lushington (Lady Lushington's formal title) claimed compensation for 241 slaves: Report of slavery compensation claims, PP 1837–8, xlviii, 633.

One of the nearest connections I have in the world, has a great interest in this
important question; yet whatever may be the concern which those I most love
may have in it, when I read in the preamble of the bill that the Slave Trade is
inconsistent with justice, humanity, and sound policy; admitting that to be a
correct statement of the fact, I can have no option whether to preserve or
abandon the trade; for, Sir, I have never been accustomed to balance the
social duties of justice and humanity against the commercial estimates of
exports and imports... Whatever may be the conduct of Portugal, or of any
other country which may have facilities for the prosecution of this trade, let us
not continue a species of commerce, inconsistent with every principle of
justice and humanity.[5]

In 1830, he referred to 'the general disgrace of the odious traffic in
slaves'.[6]

The abolition of the slave trade in 1807 did not prevent the transfer
of slaves between British colonies, a practice which continued until
1824. Lushington, who returned to the House of Commons in 1820
after an absence of twelve years, was chiefly responsible for an amendment that prohibited the intercolonial trade.[7] The *Anti-slavery Reporter* said, of this amendment:

Indeed before the passing of Dr Lushington's consolidated Abolition Act of
1825, whole bodies of slaves had, in some cases, been forcibly taken from their
houses, in colonies, where from the unfitness of the soil for sugar, they had
enjoyed comparative relief from the severity of forced labour; and had been
transported to the colonies of Demerara and Trinidad, where, from various
causes but especially from the increased exertion of labour in the cultivation of
sugar, they perished in great numbers. One of the objects of Dr Lushington's
Act was wholly to suppress this intercolonial slave trade, perhaps the most
cruel of any.[8]

Buxton wrote in 1835 that Lushington was 'hardly known as the
author of the measure which stopped the inter-colonial slave-trade,

---

[5] *Substance of the debates on the bill for abolishing the Slave Trade ... passed into law
on the 25th March 1807* (London, 1808), 77–80. Hansard, viii, 962–3 (23 Feb. 1807)
gives only a summary.
[6] Hansard, 2nd ser., xxv, 406 (15 June 1830).
[7] 5 Geo. IV c. 113, ss 13, 14. Cf. 47 Geo. III c. 36, s. 1.
[8] *Anti-Slavery Reporter* 3 (1829), 403. See also *Report of the Committee of the Society
for the Mitigation and Gradual Abolition of Slavery, etc., read at the General Meeting
of the Society* ... (1824), Rhodes House Library, and also, G. Stephen, *Anti-Slavery
Recollections* (1854), 66.

which, had it been permitted to continue, would have . . . thrown no slight impediment in the way of emancipation'.[9]

For many years after the British abolition of slavery, in 1833, the slave trade was carried on under the flags of other nations,[10] and Lushington was active in the campaign to suppress it, using his professional knowledge of admiralty and international law. Britain entered into treaties with foreign powers, giving the Royal Navy power to search, and to seize, ships found to be carrying slaves, or fitted out for the slave trade. In 1842, Lushington, then judge of the Admiralty Court, was appointed to preside over a committee to draw up a code of instructions for British naval officers engaged in suppressing the trade.[11] Since these instructions had to take into account the varying treaties between Great Britain and each foreign state, it was a complex task, and the committee's report fills a whole volume of the Parliamentary Papers.[12] The instructions give detailed guidance in a wide variety of circumstances, with reference to the treaties with each foreign country; they are said to have been 'acted on without serious friction for the next fourteen years'.[13]

In 1845, Lushington sat with a representative of the French government on a commission to investigate the right of mutual search in the suppression of the slave trade, under a treaty of 1831 between the two countries.[14] Following the Commission's work, a new treaty was signed,[15] by which France undertook to maintain a squadron of her own cruisers to co-operate with the British. This arrangement was not, however, perceived subsequently by the British to have worked well.[16] Lushington also influenced the drafting of a number of the

---

9 Buxton to Scoble, 19 Dec. 1835, Minute Book of Anti-slavery Society, 23 Dec. 1835, Anti-slavery Papers, Rhodes House Library, Oxford, BE S 20 E2/4. See also, Buxton to G. Stephen, 19 Dec. 1835, Buxton Papers, Rhodes House Library, Oxford, 14, 223, at f. 237.

10 See Mathieson, *Great Britain and the Slave Trade*.

11 Lord Aberdeen to Lushington, 10 Nov. 1842, and Lushington's reply, 11 Nov., Aberdeen Papers, British Library, Add Mss 43240.

12 PP 1844, 1 (vol. 50). See W. L. Mathieson, *Great Britain and the Slave Trade* (1929), 71.

13 Mathieson, *Great Britain and the Slave Trade*, 72.

14 For the treaty, see PP 1844, 1 (vol. 50), 28–31. Correspondence relating to the Commission is in PRO/FO 84/615 ff. 35–114, and 616 ff. 91–276, and in the Aberdeen Papers Add Mss 43244, ff. 263, 272, 294, 301, 302. The proceedings were published: PP 1847, lxvii, 1.

15 Lushington was invited to sign it: PRO/FO 84/615, f. 110.

16 Mathieson, *Great Britain and the Slave Trade*, 72–3, 148–9.

treaties against slave trading,[17] and actively promoted, in and out of Parliament, the suppression of the slave trade.[18]

In 1823, a slave uprising occurred in Demerara. The Reverend John Smith, a Dissenting (Independent) missionary, was accused of having fomented the rebellion and of having concealed advance knowledge of it. He was tried by court martial, and sentenced to death; he was reprieved by the British government, but before the news of the reprieve reached Demerara, he died in jail.[19] His case was taken up by the anti-slavery movement as a demonstration of the evil consequences of slavery, and Smith became a symbolic martyr.[20]

Lushington spoke forcefully and at length[21] in the House of Commons, condemning the manner in which Smith had been treated. He said that it was his purpose to show that

not only all the forms of law were overlooked or disregarded, but that the most sacred principles of justice, fundamental rules indispensable to fair inquiry, without adhering to which guilt can never be satisfactorily established, were, on this memorable occasion, in almost every stage of the proceeding, shamelessly abandoned and culpably violated.[22]

Lushington examined the evidence against Smith on the charge of concealment, which was the evidence of slaves who had themselves participated in the rebellion. He pointed out, first, that the colonists generally rejected slave evidence, even in trivial matters affecting property. Secondly, the evidence was the uncorroborated evidence of accomplices (always to be treated with caution in criminal procedure) and given in hope of escape themselves from sentence of death or

worse than death, the torture of a thousand lashes – a sentence which this humane tribunal passed on several of the unfortunate beings, who were

---

17 See R. Anstey, 'The Pattern of British Abolitionism' in C. Bolt (ed.), *Anti-Slavery, Religion and Reform* (Folkestone, 1980), 34.
18 Hansard, 3rd ser., xlii, 1141 (10 May 1838), id. l, 128 (8 Aug. 1839); *Report on the Manuscripts of Earl Bathurst* (London, 1923), 607, 608, 610; *The Holland House Diaries*, ed. A. D. Kriegel (1977), 407; J. K. Laughton, *Memoirs of the Life and Correspondence of Henry Reeve* (1898), 108.
19 See E. A. Wallbridge, *Martyr of Demerara* (London, 1848), D. Chamberlin, *Smith of Demerara* (London, 1924), W. C. Northcott, *Slavery's Martyr* (1976), F. J. Klingberg, *The Anti-Slavery Movement in England: A Study of English Humanitarianism* (Newhaven, 1926), 219–22.
20 See Walvin, *England, Slaves and Freedom*, 140–1.
21 The report of the speech occupies over thirty columns in Hansard's report, an unusually large allowance for a private member.
22 Hansard, 2nd ser., xi, 1207 (11 June 1824).

placed at their bar, and which to the everlasting disgrace of the British name, was, in some instances, actually carried into execution.[23]

He then dwelt on the improbabilities of the prosecution case. The witnesses who testified to what Smith had said contradicted themselves and each other, and the only evidence of help to the prosecution attributed to Smith illiterate expressions that it was incredible he should have used.

On the charge of encouraging the revolt, Lushington complained of the unspecific nature of the accusation:

Sir, I never before heard of any tribunal especially of any tribunal acting under English law, putting a man on his trial for all his actions and all his words during a period of six years continuance, and that too without specifying time place and circumstances – merely one sweeping accusation, that by his general conduct, during a residence of six years, he had greatly contributed to the creation of dissatisfaction and discontent among the negroes. Where, Sir, is the man who would dare to trust his life to the issue of such an investigation? Where, Sir, is the individual so bold as to challenge such an inquiry? Where, Sir, is the tribunal so unjust as to pronounce sentence upon any individual so accused?[24]

Lushington made scathing comments on the conduct of the court martial, which he accused of having knowingly and wilfully given a false verdict. He adduced procedural rulings of the tribunal that exhibited bias against Smith, and he objected to the admission of hearsay evidence 'two or three deep'.[25] He ended by commenting on the animosity still evident in Demerara to a clergyman of the established church who had defended Smith's conduct, and calling on the House to mark an act 'alike repugnant to British justice and British feeling'.[26] Brougham called it a speech 'of the very highest merit'.[27] The motion, however, was lost.[28]

In the course of his speech, Lushington referred to a plantation called 'Success', adjoining the plantation on which Smith had lived, and had mistakenly identified it with another plantation, also called 'Success', where Smith had asserted that the slaves were overworked. This error drew a protest from the owner of the former property, who was John Gladstone, a member of Parliament, and the father of the

[23] Ibid., 1212.   [24] Ibid., 1223–4.   [25] Ibid. at 1229.   [26] Ibid., 1237.
[27] H. Brougham, *Speeches, Upon Questions Relating to Public Rights, Duties and Interests* (Edinburgh, 1838), ii, 104n.
[28] By a vote of 193–146, Hansard, 2nd ser., xi, 1313.

future Prime Minister, demanding an apology, and protesting[29] that he had always treated his slaves with consideration and kindness, and had supplied ample medical services. Lushington's reply was correct but cool:

Sir, I beg to acknowledge the receipt of your letter with its inclosure, which I return & I have great pleasure in perceiving that you have manifested so correct a desire to cooperate with the Government in ameliorating the condition of the Slaves. There is no doubt that the passage from Mr Smith's letter read by me on Friday does not apply to your plantation Success but to another Plantation of the same name, & I was from want of local knowledge clearly mistaken in apprehending that the writer referred to a plantation lying contiguous to Resouvenir. It was a mistake however which any man however cautious might naturally have made & in which I neither had nor could have the slightest wish to persevere. I instantly put into your hands the passage which had misled me & had you expressed any wish I would that night have corrected the error. I shall certainly in my place tomorrow explain the error; an explanation to which you are in justice intitled & which I have never shewn the least disposition to with-hold & which I must observe should have been asked in terms less peremptory.[30]

Despite the occurrence of an error in this case, the letter shows that Lushington was careful with his facts. In a letter many years later to the Secretary of the Anti-slavery Society, he said, of a document that had been sent to him:

There are many facts & statements therein of the truth of which I cannot possibly judge; & with respect to these I can only say that I have ever considered it essential to our cause not only to state the truth, but always to be ready with the proof.[31]

The West Indian colonies contained a substantial number of free persons who were black, or of mixed race, known at the time as free coloured people. Lushington did much for the amelioration of their condition. In 1823 two such persons, L. C. Lecesne, and J. Escoffery, were summarily expelled from Jamaica, where they had lived since childhood, having incurred the displeasure of the local government by

---

[29] He called the error 'so injurious to me, and so painful to my feelings', J. Gladstone to Lushington, 12 June 1824 (copy), Glynne-Gladstone Papers, Clwyd Record Office, Hawarden, 334.

[30] Lushington to J. Gladstone, dated Sunday night [13 June 1824], Glynne-Gladstone Papers, 334.

[31] Lushington to Scoble, 13 Jan. 1840, Anti-slavery papers, BE S18 C19/65, 66.

presenting a petition for the redress of their grievances. Lushington presented a petition on their behalf to the House of Commons, strongly objecting to discrimination on the basis of colour:

> He was at a loss to conceive what excuse could be offered for so gross a violation of the rights of British subjects. It could not, he was sure, be said, in an English House of Commons, that because men were a shade darker than those who were born in our own climate, they were therefore to be deprived of the privileges which the constitution of Great Britain extended equally to her most exalted and her meanest subjects.[32]

Lushington objected vigorously to a number of discriminatory laws 'depriving the numerous and loyal free coloured population of Jamaica, of rights which ought to be equally enjoyed by every free man'.[33] He said that 'In England, thank God! no such odious distinctions have obtained,' adding, perhaps over-optimistically, 'English justice would never endure them'.[34]

Both Lecesne and Escoffery were slave owners, and it might perhaps be supposed that this fact would diminish Lushington's enthusiasm for their case. But he adverted to the fact in their favour in order to establish their respectability, and so the greater injustice of their deportation.[35] He concluded a long speech, with many detailed facts, by appealing not only to principles of justice but also to the importance to Jamaica of retaining the loyalty of its free black population.[36]

The *Anti-slavery Reporter* recorded that Lushington's speech 'produced a deep impression upon the House', and extracted an assurance from the government of an investigation, with a view to compensation, if justified.[37] Reparation was eventually effected, and in 1830 Lecesne paid handsome tribute to Lushington:

> It is inexpedient, for obvious reasons, to point public attention to individuals in this island [Jamaica] who have been our friends and benefactors, during our protracted sufferings; but there is one in England, whose name must not, cannot, be suppressed. It is to Dr Lushington we are indebted, under heaven, for all we now enjoy – our return to our homes – our indemnity for our losses – and, above all, our restoration to the credit and good fame we formerly

---

[32] Hansard, 2nd ser., xi, 798 (21 May 1824).
[33] Hansard, 2nd ser., xiii, 1174 (16 June 1825).
[34] Ibid., 1177.   [35] Ibid., 1178.   [36] Ibid., 1192.
[37] *Anti-slavery Reporter* 1 (1825), 28. The *Anti-slavery Reporter*, in a four-page account, does not mention the fact that Lecesne and Escoffery were slave-owners.

enjoyed – are derived from his beneficence – from his energetic advocacy of our case – his firm and reiterated appeals in our behalf to the House of Commons – and his unwearied exertions in unravelling the tangled web of accusation in which we were involved. His reward for this can only be obtained from God.[38]

Lushington subsequently directed his energy to a more general amelioration of the condition of the free black population of the West Indian colonies, presenting a petition, in 1827, from 'the freeholders of the mixed race, and others, from inhabitants of the island of Jamaica, for admission to the full protection of the law and the privileges of British subjects; and also a similar petition . . . on behalf of the free people of colour in the colony of Honduras'.[39] He described the state of the free black people as 'little short of slavery'.[40] He pointed out the size and wealth of the mixed race population, and its increasing importance.[41] He enumerated their disabilities (exclusion from public office, from jury service, from the franchise and from the benefits of public education), comparing their position with that of the Jews in Jamaica:

He meant no offence to the Jews: he was far from entertaining the unjust, absurd, and mischievous, prejudices which existed against them. He could not, however, refrain from regretting that the House of Assembly should have extended to them those privileges which they had refused to the free men of colour, who were Christians; and who, even in point of complexion, could scarcely be distinguished from the whites themselves.[42]

He enlarged upon the anomalies and injustices of colour discrimination:

The children of slaves might be slaves by virtue of the law of property, but the children of brown persons were deprived of their privileges, for no other reason, but because their complexion happened not to be white.[43]

[38] *Anti-slavery Reporter* 4 (1831), 157–8, quoting *Jamaica Watchman* of 4 Dec. 1830. Lushington's actions on behalf of Lecesne and Escoffery were noted, with approval, by Wilberforce in his diary: R. I. and S. Wilberforce, *Life of Wilberforce* (London, 1838), 273.

[39] Hansard, 2nd ser., xvii, 1249 (12 June 1827). This speech was vigorously attacked by a Mr Barret, a member of the Jamaica House of Assembly, in a publication entitled *Reply to the Speech of Dr Lushington in the House of Commons on the 12 June, 1827, on the condition of the free coloured people of Jamaica* (1827), Rhodes House Library.

[40] Ibid., 1242.   [41] Ibid., 1243.   [42] Ibid., 1246.   [43] Ibid., 1248.

In 1829, an Order in Council repealed the disabilities of the free
black people of Trinidad,[44] who gave credit to Lushington, presenting him with an ornate silver tray,[45] inscribed:

To Stephen Lushington LL.D. M.P.
&c &c &c
The eloquent & intrepid advocate of the just rights
of the human race
This tribute of Gratitude
for his eminent & successful services is
presented
by the free inhabitants of African Descent of the
Island of Trinidad
16 July 1832

The political campaign for the abolition of slavery gathered force in
the early 1830s, with an organized campaign to demand pledges from
parliamentary candidates.[46] Success was obtained in 1833. In 1831, a
debate on slavery took place, in the House of Commons, on a motion
by Buxton. Lushington, in his speech, argued that the abolition of
slavery was by then universally accepted as desirable in principle. 'No
one now is hardy enough to defend slavery in the abstract', he said,
'but I remember a time when the case was very different ... Now,
however, the question is admitted on all hands to be merely one of
time.'[47] His speech linked expediency with morality: he denied any
danger of opposition from the free black people (themselves owners of
70,000 slaves), and suggested that prosperity for the colonies would
only be attained by the abolition of slavery:

I conceive it to be utterly impossible to continue the horrible system of negro
slavery much longer. In my conscience I should as soon hold highway robbery
a sacred profession, as believe that the trading in our fellow-men can much
longer be tolerated. Sooner or later the vengeance of Providence will overtake
those who support such a system.[48]

[44] Dated 13 March, 1829, *Anti-slavery Reporter* 3 (1829), 16; Klingberg, *Anti-Slavery Movement*, 243.
[45] Formerly in the possession of Dr Lushington's great-great-grandson, and now in the National Museum, Trinidad.
[46] See text at pp. 97–8, below.
[47] Mirror of Parliament 1831 (9th Parliament), 1467 [Hansard, 3rd ser., iii, 1455, 15 April 1831].
[48] Ibid., 1468.

He did not advocate instant emancipation, but he advocated an immediate commitment to the most rapid emancipation consistent with the prevention of bloodshed:

I do not mean to say that they should be set free tomorrow, but that efficient means should be adopted and be adopted immediately, for the purpose of bringing about, and that very speedily, the extinction of slavery.[49]

He opposed further committees of inquiry, seeing them as a delaying tactic, saying that 'I conceive that the House will stultify itself, if it again enter on inquiry, and express doubt and hesitation as to what it ought to do'.[50] Lushington mentioned, in his conclusion to this speech, that emancipation could not much longer be refused 'with safety', and in a speech in the following year, he said:

If I wanted a recipe to raise a rebellion and desolate these islands in blood, I should say, that to drive the negro to despair was the best. Leave them to believe that the legislatures of the islands alone are to emancipate them, that the Legislature of Great Britain will not interfere, and the consequences must be dreadful.[51]

He almost hinted at a threat, when he said:

I will not utter a syllable that can be construed into an attempt to excite the slaves to rebellion, but I should consider myself a coward if I did not boldly state that I have yet to learn that it is to be considered a moral offence in a British House of Commons for any man to endeavour to break the chains by which he is unjustly bound.[52]

Although he opposed committees to enquire into the merits of emancipation, he thought that a committee was necessary to propose the details of actually effecting it. In this he showed himself more cautious than some others in the anti-slavery movement. Writing to Brougham in 1832, he said:

The Anti Slavery Committee in London, the Committees thro' the country & the whole body of the Evangelicals & Dissenters look to Emancipation & nothing short of it. On several occasions during the last 3 weeks I have stood almost alone, when advocating any other course of proceeding ... When I suggested that Buxton should move a Committee in the Commons I was left with a single supporter. Viewing the consequences of these proceedings with great alarm I have used my utmost personal influence with Buxton to induce

---

[49] Ibid.   [50] Ibid.
[51] *Mirror of Parliament* 1832, 2262a (24 May); the version in Hansard, 3rd ser., xiii, 80, differs slightly.
[52] *Mirror of Parliament* 1832, 2861.

him to adopt a wiser course. He will now I believe consent to move for a Committee in the Commons nearly in the same terms as Lord Harewood adding these words 'to consider the safest mode of effecting speedy emancipation'. This last is a sine qua non with him & in truth without it he & his supporters would at once separate.[53]

Buxton's motion for a committee of inquiry was carried, with a government amendment,[54] and Lushington was a member of it. The committee assembled a considerable volume of evidence against slavery, but reported inconclusively, as it had been unable to complete its work before the passage of the Reform Act, and the subsequent dissolution of Parliament.[55]

In 1833 the government introduced, in the reformed Parliament, its own plan for the abolition of slavery. Before the committee stage Lushington persuaded the government to adopt a reversal of a judicial decision of Lord Stowell[56] (in which Lushington had argued unsuccessfully as counsel) that a slave who became free on visiting England, reverted to a condition of slavery on returning to a colony. Lushington said:

I propose by this resolution, that any slave who may have been brought over here with the consent of his or her possessor, shall be entitled to his or her liberty, to the same extent as any British subject, whether in England or elsewhere, in the event of such party returning to the West Indies. I am content to admit, however, that I am the more urged to propose this instruction from a decision given some years since by the Noble and Learned Lord Stowell, in the case of a female slave who had been born in the West Indies, – was brought over to this country and educated here, – and who having returned again to the West Indies, was again made a slave. The decision of Lord Stowell was, that if under any circumstances a slave, or the

---

53 Lushington to Brougham, unsigned, n.d. but internal evidence indicates between 17 April 1832 (Lord Harewood introduces petition in House of Lords: Hansard, 3rd ser., xii, 596) and 24 May 1832 (Buxton introduces motion in House of Commons: Hansard, 3rd ser., xiii, 38); Brougham Papers, University College, London, 10, 376. Lushington's fear was that a motion for instant emancipation, without transition or compensation, would fail, forcing the government into alliance with the slave-owning interests (ibid., at folio 3). The actual wording of Buxton's motion was 'that a select committee be appointed to consider and report upon the means which it may be expedient to adopt for the purpose of effecting the extinction of slavery throughout the British Dominions, at the earliest period compatible with the safety of all classes in the colonies'.
54 Lushington voted against the amendment which added a reference to the resolutions of 1823, and thereby, by implication, to the interests of the planters, Hansard, 3rd ser., xiii, 97 (24 May 1832). See Klingberg, *Anti-Slavery Movement*, 199.
55 PP 1831–2, xx, 1.
56 *The Slave, Grace* (1827), 2 Hagg 94.

offspring of a slave, after even enjoying the rights of freedom in Great Britain, should return to the colonies, he or she would be liable to be cast back into slavery. I am compelled therefore to admit, on the authority of my Lord Stowell, that such is the present iniquitous state of the law; and though I am compelled to submit to Lord Stowell's high legal authority, I cannot forbear from expressing my abomination of law so unjust. I admit, I say, the doctrine, coming as it does from so distinguished an authority; but I take the liberty of asserting that as I reprobate the injustice of such a principle of law, so I do not, for my own part, agree to the doctrine laid down.[57]

The government accepted the motion to instruct the committee accordingly.[58]

The government plan included two concessions to the planters, one, a period of semi-slavery, called apprenticeship, whereby, for a period of years, all slaves except young children were to be required to give three-quarters of their working time to their former owners; the second, money compensation to be paid to the slave owners.[59] These proposals created a division in the anti-slavery movement: some favoured unconditional emancipation, while others were prepared to compromise. Lushington voted in favour of Buxton's motion to re-serve half of the compensation money until the expiry of the appren-ticeship period.[60] On the issue of compensation itself he supported the eventual government policy of paying £20,000,000 to the slave owners:

To the present Government I pay the tribute of my gratitude for the risk I know they have run, for the hazard at which they have placed their popularity in this country, by proposing to take from the pocket of a distressed people 20,000,000*l* for the accomplishment of negro emancipation.[61]

But he could not bring himself to support apprenticeship in principle:

I should be glad to hear upon what ground it is that my noble friend defends, as a matter of justice, the principle that the slaves themselves shall now pay their masters seven years' labour of their lives, before they are made com-pletely free.[62]

Nevertheless, he supported the Bill, with the period of apprenticeship

57 Mirror of Parliament 1833, 3324a (25 July).
58 Hansard, 3rd ser., xix, 1237 (25 July 1833).
59 See Mathieson, *British Slavery and its Abolition 1823–1839* (London, 1926), H. Temperley, *British Antislavery, 1833–1870* (London, 1972), 17.
60 Mirror of Parliament 1833, Division Lists, cv (11 June).
61 Mirror of Parliament 1833, 3343b (25 July).
62 Ibid., 3342.

Anti-slavery 75

reduced to seven years from the twelve years originally proposed, as a
political necessity:

I may be asked, 'if your objections are so strong, why do you sanction any
period of apprenticeship at all?' My answer is direct and straight; because I
cannot help it. The principle of apprenticeship has been confirmed by the
House, and it now only remains for those who are opposed to it, to endeavour
to make the period as short as possible.[63]

He went on to express the hope that the apprenticeship system would
prove impracticable.[64] He spoke in favour of its abolition in 1838[65]
and, in fact, it was abandoned in that year.[66] Lushington's influence
on the debate of 1833 is attested by Lord Althorp, who said to
Lushington that he and Buxton 'had wielded a power too great for any
individuals in this House. I hope we shall never see such another
instance.'[67]

Although willing to accept the best arrangement attainable in a
political forum, Lushington's own opinion of compensation and apprenticeship is illustrated by a letter to Buxton about events in Mauritius[68] in 1835:

How do you feel after very nearly sacrificing your life for the blacks of the
Mauritius? 2,000,000 compensation for Felons, 5 years apprenticeship without the power of leaving the estate & 21 years for the children![69]

Buxton was involved in a bitter dispute on the question of compen-
sation in Mauritius with George Stephen, who wrote a letter to *The
Times*,[70] and an article in the *Christian Observer*,[71] accusing the
Anti-slavery Society of supporting slave-owners' interests. Buxton

[63] Ibid., 3344a. See also Hansard, 2nd ser., xv, 1328; Hansard, 3rd ser., xix, 1060.
[64] In a letter to Brougham (5 Oct. 1833) he predicted that 'apprenticeship will in great
part die a natural death', Brougham Papers, University College, London, 4160.
[65] Hansard, 3rd ser., xlii, 208 (30 Mar. 1838); ibid., xliii, 427 (28 May).
[66] Temperley, *British Antislavery*, 41.
[67] C. Buxton (ed.), *Memoirs of Sir Thomas Fowell Buxton* (London, 1849), 281–2
(account of Miss Buxton, based on report to her by Lushington). T. B. Macaulay
then secretary to the Board of Control, was anxious to retain the support of Buxton
and Lushington for the government: T. Pinney (ed.), *Letters of T. B. Macaulay*
(Cambridge, 1974), ii, 239 (Letter to Z. Macaulay of May 1833).
[68] See W. L. Mathieson, *British Slave Emancipation, 1839–1849* (London, 1932),
225.
[69] Buxton Papers 14, 207d. But it should be noted that the objection in Mauritius was
not just to compensation to slave owners, but to illegal slave traders (hence 'felons' in
a precise sense).
[70] *The Times*, 28 Nov. 1835, 2f (signed G.S.). See also letter (signed G.S.) in *The
Times*, 14 Jan. 1836, 6a.
[71] 30 Nov. 1835.

defended himself, and the correspondence was entered into the Minute Book of the Society.[72] Lushington used his influence with Buxton to restore peace:

I have read thro' the whole correspondence relating to the differences between you & [G. Stephen]. J. Forster dined with me yesterday & has most maturely discussed and considered the whole. We are both decidedly of opinion that the only wise & prudent course was to expunge. I cannot state in writing all my reasons but my own judgment was fully satisfied. I feel perhaps most strongly the mischief which must ensue to the cause from publicity.[73]

The Minute Book of the Anti-slavery Society shows that a resolution was passed to expunge the record of the dispute, and the relevant pages are crossed by diagonal lines.[74]

On questions of self-government, Lushington's political instincts favoured representative government. On the other hand he realized that colonial self-government often meant government by the whites at the expense of the slaves. Speaking of the Cape of Good Hope, he said, in 1830:

I admit that the Government should be for the benefit of the many, and not the few; but I do not think that that end would be obtained by a representative form of government at the Cape. If I could believe that it would have the effect of producing better regulations with respect to slaves – that it would improve the condition of the Hottentot population – I could readily consent to it, but until I see some disposition evinced by our colonies which have representative governments to improve the condition of the slaves – until I see among them a disposition of the strong to protect the weak – I shall object to any extension of a system, particularly where slave population exists, which I have reason to believe would not produce these effects.[75]

In 1839, a Bill was introduced by Melbourne's government to suspend the constitution of Jamaica on the ground of Jamaican obstruction of British anti-slavery measures. Lushington spoke in favour of the Bill. Though a constitution 200 years old was not lightly to be abrogated, he thought that Parliament had a duty to protect the blacks from the local colonial government:

Sir, the black population look with alarm and fear upon the House of Assembly – they consider them not their natural protectors; but they look to this country – to the Parliament of Great Britain – for the protection they

72 See Temperley, *British Antislavery*, 33–4.
73 Lushington to Buxton, 16 Jan. 1836, Buxton Papers 14, 335d.
74 Anti-slavery papers BE S20 E2/4 121.
75 Mirror of Parliament 1830, 1920 (24 May).

require, and which they believe will not be honestly extended to them by their own Legislature.[76]

Three days later, Lushington wrote to Buxton in urgent terms:

What is to be done in the present exigency as to *our friends* & the Bill for suspending the House of Assembly in Jamaica. This is really a most important question & I wish to call your most serious attention to it.

I do not know whether you now read the parliamentary papers, but the point is this. The House of Assembly has refused to act. Labouchere has brought in a Bill to suspend for five years the Assembly. This Bill will be most promptly opposed. If defeated two consequences may arise. 1. To overthrow the Government. 2. Most seriously to affect the success of emancipation in Jamaica. They cannot go on with the present laws. That is impossible & the Assembly will pass no good laws as matters now are. If emancipation fails in Jamaica . . . it will operate most prejudicially against the cause of freedom later in the U.S., the French, Dutch, &c, Colonies. The Anti-slavery body ought to support the Government on this question & strongly too. You especially must do so for your Committee postponed all legislative measures till the Hour of Freedom & now it is come without preparation. The existence of some unjust laws & the want of good laws are causes of the greatest evils & if not checked I fear it will become most difficult to restore a habit of industry much broken. Josiah Forster abroad & you absent I feel left alone. Pray write to me & say what you think can be done. Believe me the exigency is most urgent as well as important.[77]

Buxton offered to come to London and summon a public meeting,[78] but Lushington declined, saying 'We cannot effectively move without the Sturgites. I shall see Joseph Sturge[79] & prepare the ground.'[80]

On 6 May, he spoke again in the House of Commons, supporting the Bill, even at a risk to the government. He wrote to Buxton that the government, if it fell, would fall having taken a principled stand.[81] The next day he wrote to Buxton, giving an account of the vote (the Bill passed by a majority of five), saying that so narrow a majority 'will

[76] Mirror of Parliament 1839, 1648a (9 April).
[77] Lushington to Buxton, 12 April 1839, Buxton Papers 18, 48a–d.
[78] Buxton to Lushington (copy), 13 April 1839, Buxton papers 18, 50.
[79] Joseph Sturge (1793–1859), founder of the 'agency committee', representing the radical and activist section of the anti-slavery movement. See Mathieson, *British Slavery and its Abolition*, 205–6, Temperley, *British Antislavery*, 12–14, R. Brent, *Liberal Anglican Politics: whiggery, religion and reform, 1830–1841* (Oxford, 1987), 291–2.
[80] Lushington to Buxton, 15 April, Buxton Papers 18, 50a. A meeting was called by Lushington and Buxton on 26 April, Minutes, Anti-slavery Society, Anti-slavery Papers, BE S20 E2/15.
[81] Mirror of Parliament 1839, 2366a (9 May).

render the proceeding with the Bill impossible & most probably will lead to a Resignation of Ministers'. He asked 'What is to be done as to Jamaica? There will now be no law at all for 6 months to come. Ought then the old Anti-slavery Party or can we do anything? Are we impotent?' adding that 'the Government with too much justice complain of being driven forward & then deserted, but neither you nor I are to blame'. He continued:

I have scarcely slept during the night & I am too much bewildered to have any clear opinion. I feel however that happen what may we have still most ample reason to rejoice even in the present state of Jamaica but the Planters will suffer severely & the diminished prosperity of Jamaica will be a sad discouragement to general emancipation. The Negroes have in two instances . . . bought land & are proceeding to divide into small allotments. The rate of labour will rise enormously. If the Tories come in we shall have no good laws, no good Governors, no special magistrates. These are useless lamentations. Do you think anything can be done.[82]

The government did resign, as Lushington had predicted, and he wrote to Buxton:

The resignation took place yesterday. Ld Melbourne, whom I myself heard, declared that he resigned because power had been refused to him to carry into full effect the emancipation Act, protect the negroes & keep faith with Parliament. He spoke with great spirit & energy. I entirely approve of the resignation. It was impossible to govern Jamaica, when the power required by the Bill was refused. Is it not singular that at last a Whig Administration, in substance the same which carried the Abolition Act should be shipwrecked by the consequences of that very measure. Now ought not the Anti Slavery Party, whom I am as anxious as you to keep clear of politics, to express their regret that the Resignation has taken place *on these grounds*? I can take no part in it because I am so closely politically allied with Ld Melbourne & Ld John, neither should I wish it to be at all of a political nature for I have ever been most anxious to prevent it as far as circumstances would allow. Yet I think it well worth consideration. 1st on the ground of justice because the Anti Slavery Party most properly pressed the Government to secure equal laws in Jamaica, & 2d for the sake of the future, that there may be a solemn declaration that our Society will not be content with less than full justice to the negroes. I fear as Macaulay would fear were he alive, laws specious in form, useless in execution. I fear for I know it is required by certain West Indians the removal of the Specials & the substitution of some 3 or 4 Barristers to go circuits. Sir L. Smith will be forthwith removed – a Tory high church Lord his successor. I feel the utmost confidence that the negroes of Jamaica will do

82 Lushington to Buxton, 7 May 1839, Buxton Papers 18, 92a–c.

well and be happy, but I fear Jamaica will not prosper . . . Ponder on these
things & remember that it was your committee of 1836 that prevented laws
being then made & consequently brought about the necessity for immediate
legislation. I think that the Government & I ought in candour to say so, would
never had this question not come in this way have been compelled to resign,
but I am right glad that the Resignation has been placed on the great principle
tho' I lament deeply lament the consequences in Jamaica. The Queen is
greatly distressed by the event. I know not if any one has yet been sent for, but
if I know any news in time for Post you shall hear.[83]

The next news was that Peel was forming an administration,[84] and
then that 'Ld Melbourne is Minister again. Peel quarrelled with the
Queen as to the Household.'[85] The Jamaica Bill was eventually passed
in a less drastic form.[86]

Another issue on which liberal and anti-slavery principles came into
conflict, and, again, an issue that caused the fall of a government, was
free trade. The anti-slavery party was divided on this issue. Lushington favoured the retention of duties on foreign grown sugar because it
came from Cuba and Brazil, where slavery was still in use, and he
thought that removal of the duties would benefit slave owners, retard
emancipation, and increase the slave trade.

He spoke and voted against the Whig government on this issue in
1840, describing the proposed reduction of duties as 'a measure which
cannot but lead to the perpetuation of slavery, and, at the same time,
aggravate the misery of the slave trade'.[87] Gladstone wrote that Lushington had been influential in this debate, saying that he had 'laid
down a principle upon which the duties were to be maintained:
namely in order to give our own Colonies and India a fair opportunity
of trying their productive powers with . . . an exclusive possession of
the home market'.[88] In the following year, Lushington said:

I have ever been the friend of free trade . . . but I have always voted against
every measure that tended to increase the slave trade or give to it fresh vigour

[83] Lushington to Buxton, 8 May 1839, Buxton Papers 18, 92e–1.
[84] Buxton to Lushington, 9 May, Buxton Papers 18, 92p.
[85] Lushington to Buxton, 11 May, 1839, Buxton Papers 18, 94a. The reference is to the
'bedchamber' crisis; see *The Greville Memoirs*, ed. L. Strachey and R. Fulford
(London, 1938), iv, 162–7 (10 May 1839), N. Gash, *Sir Robert Peel: the life of Sir
Robert Peel after 1830* 2nd edn (1986), 220–7.
[86] See Mathieson, *British Slave Emancipation*, 26–30.
[87] Mirror of Parliament 1840, 4025b (25 June). Hansard, 3rd ser., lv, 95 omits 'trade',
probably erroneously.
[88] W. E. Gladstone to R. Gladstone, 30 June 1840, Glynne-Gladstone Papers 568,
139.

... I believe that if this question were put to the working classes of this country, – whether they would take sugar, if cheapened in the manner suggested (that sugar being the product of slave labour, and producing fresh calamities by the importation of new slaves) – I believe that the great majority, even of those who suffer by the want of that article, would be content to reject it.[89]

It may, or may not, be matter for regret that the sophistication of political polls at the time did not permit this proposition to be put to the test. The political division caused unusual alliances. Buxton's daughter wrote: 'to see Dr Lushington & Gladstone on one side & Mr Evans[90] against them seems a strange disjointing of one's notions.'[91] The government fell on a subsequent vote of no confidence.[92]

The debate in the anti-slavery party, however, continued. Two years later, at the Anti-slavery Convention of 1843, Lushington gave forceful explanation of his opinion:

I will not buy [cheap sugar] at the expense of African blood . . . I will bear the charge of being an advocate of monopoly, if by so doing I can put a stop to the horrors of the slave-trade, and a spell over desolating the coast of Africa.[93]

Lushington wrote to Scoble, the Secretary of the Anti-slavery Society, in 1844, arguing that the Society had no business, in view of its objects, in taking a stand against the sugar duties:

I think that our bond being the suppression of the slave trade, it is not competent to any one on purely free trade principles to ask the Society in his capacity of member to support the importation of Slave Trade sugar without proving that the Trade would not be thereby increased[94] – out of the Society all are free to do as they please.

89 Mirror of Parliament 1841, 1549, 1551b (7 May). Hansard, 3rd ser., lviii, 80–1, 88, differs slightly. Lord John Russell refers to the speech in a letter to Queen Victoria, A. C. Benson (ed.), *Letters of Queen Victoria* (London, 1907), i, 277 (16 May 1841).
90 William Evans (1788–1856), MP, 1818–26, 1830–4, 1836–53; consistent supporter of Buxton on anti-slavery.
91 Mrs Johnston to Miss Gurney, 14 May 1841 (copy), Buxton Papers 20, 250. For reference to William Evans' support of the government in this debate see Temperley, *British Antislavery*, 150.
92 See Temperley, *British Antislavery*, 151. Lushington voted for the government on the confidence motion. See N. Gash, *Reaction and Reconstruction in English Politics, 1832–52* (Oxford, 1965), 185 and appendix B.
93 J. F. Johnson, *Proceedings of the General Anti-slavery Convention 1843* (1843), 157.
94 Lushington's meaning is that the only arguments that should be heard by the Society from its members were those tending towards suppression of the slave trade.

To tell me that the people will get sugar cheaper would not weigh with me *as a member*, tho' I am ready to admit the fact. Such an argument is not hujus loci unless to it be added, that the Slave Trade would not be increased.[95]

The Anti-slavery Society was strongly influenced by pacifism on account of its Quaker membership.[96] In the same letter as that just quoted, Lushington said that 'as a *member* of the Anti-slavery Society' he had agreed not to advocate the use of force, though privately his opinion was in favour of its use and 'when acting not in unison with the Society' he did advocate it. Brougham also made reference to the Quakers in this context, considering that they had so far forgotten their traditional opposition to the slave trade as to 'become free trade fanatics'.[97]

Lushington was very active in the anti-slavery societies. He was a director of the African Institution, the oldest of the nineteenth-century anti-slavery bodies.[98] He was a vice-president of the Anti-slavery Society[99] founded in 1823, and present at the committee that planned its first general meeting in 1824, at which he moved one of the official motions and spoke.[100] He spoke at general meetings in 1825, 1830, 1831, and 1832,[101] and at the two general anti-slavery conventions in 1840 (where he is shown in a painting of the scene standing on the platform next to Buxton[102]), and 1843.[103] He was a vice-president of the Society from 1825,[104] and played a leading role in establishing

[95] Lushington to Scoble, 21 May 1844, Anti-slavery Papers, BE C19/77, 80. For the context of this debate, see Temperley, *British Anti-slavery*, 159–60.
[96] C. Bolt, *The Anti-slavery Movement and Reconstruction: a study of Anglo-American Cooperation, 1833–1877* (London, 1969), 22.
[97] Brougham to Lushington, 24 Dec. 1847, Lushington Family Papers.
[98] *19th Report of Directors of the African Institution* (London, 1825), Anti-slavery Society Office, London. Lushington is listed as a subscriber (donation: 10 gns; annual subscription: 3 gns) in the *16th Report* (1822).
[99] The Society was originally called by the rather cautious name of The Society for the Mitigation and Gradual Abolition of Slavery throughout the British Dominions. See *Report of Committee etc.* (1824), printed for the Society, Rhodes House Library.
[100] Anti-slavery Papers BE S20 E2/1 117 (25 June 1824). He was a member of the committee to prepare the report for publication, id., ff. 124–5.
[101] *Anti-slavery Reporter*, i, 6 (30 April 1825); i, 79 (31 Dec. 1825); iii, 263 (15 May 1830); iv, 263 (23 April 1831); v, 154 (12 May 1832). The speech of 1831 is separately published: *Speech of Dr Lushington, delivered at a General Meeting of the Society for the abolition of Slavery throughout the British Dominions etc.* (1831).
[102] Painting by R. B. Haydon, National Portrait Gallery 599, and key list.
[103] *Proceedings of the General Anti-slavery Convention ... held in ... 1840* (London, 1841), 377–80, 535–7, 539–40; Johnson, *Proceedings of 1843 Convention*, 155–8, 210–12, 320–1.
[104] Anti-slavery Papers, Minute Books, BE S20 E2/1 to E2/6.

The Anti-slavery Convention of 1840, by B. R. Haydon.
(Lushington is second from the left in the second row from the top).

the British and Foreign Anti-slavery Society (in effect, the successor society) in 1839,[105] from which he resigned in 1845, shortly after Buxton's death. The Minute Book includes a tribute to him at that time, second in warmth only to that adopted for Buxton.[106] Meetings of the Society were, several times, held at Lushington's house,[107] and, on occasion, he took the chair at meetings.[108] He was appointed to several subcommittees, or asked to advise on particular issues[109], and was formally asked to act on behalf of the Society in Parliament, where he raised several other issues besides those already mentioned.[110] He was a trustee of the Mico Charity, which promoted black education and welfare.[111]

It is evident from the Buxton Papers, as well as from the records of the Society, that Lushington was exceedingly diligent in the anti-slavery cause, though he derived no professional advantage from it – rather the contrary in Buxton's opinion[112] – and he had no independent income. Buxton's daughter wrote of Lushington:

He is working most marvellously 15 & 16 hours a day *often* Mrs L told us & *yet* he has undertaken Jeremie's Case. Of a man who *acts* in this way – what can be said? For that *mountain* of filthy papers in bad French & clothed in Jeremie's obscurity was enough to try the benevolence of most men. He

[105] Anti-slavery Papers BE S20 E2/6, 12, 14, 18, 20. See Temperley, *British Anti-slavery*, 62–5.
[106] BE S20 E2/7, 668 (4 April 1845).
[107] Anti-slavery Papers BE S20 E2/5, 78, 95. Buxton Papers 17, 106; 18, 181.
[108] Anti-slavery Papers, BE S20 E2/3, 129 (4 April 1832). He accepted an invitation to take the chair at a public meeting (BE S18 C19/82a, 23 April 1847), and declined another such invitation in view of his 'situation as Judge of the Admiralty Court', on 12 Nov. 1850 (BE S18 C19/85). He was invited again to chair a meeting in 1851 (BE S20 E2/8, 512, 517; reply not recorded).
[109] Anti-slavery Papers BE S20 E2/1, 124; E2/6 320, 430, 435; E2/7, 79–82, 222.
[110] Anti-slavery Papers BE S20 E2/6, 35, 45–6, 53. The other issues were the mistreatment of missionaries in the West Indies, Hansard, 2nd ser., xiii, 1343 (23 June 1825), ibid., xvi, 1166 (13 Mar. 1827); the trial of slaves in Jamaica, Hansard, 2nd ser., xiv, 1044–52 (1 Mar. 1826); the administration of the law in Mauritius, Hansard, 3rd ser., xxxi, 420 (15 Feb. 1836). See Temperley, *British Antislavery*, 128; the importation of slaves from Texas into the United States, Hansard, 3rd ser., xxxiv, 1107 (30 June 1836); the condition of Hill Coolies in India, Hansard, 3rd ser., liv, 937–41 (4 June 1840); and duties on East India rum, Hansard, 3rd ser., lvi, 612 (12 Feb. 1841).
[111] PP 1837–8, xlviii, 312, and many references in Buxton Papers. In a letter to Brougham (end. March 1836) he recounts 'some progress in the administration of the Mico fund', Brougham Papers, 8142.
[112] Buxton to Jeremie, 20 Mar. 1837, Buxton Papers 15, 238. G. Stephen expressed the same opinion, *Anti-Slavery Recollections*, 69.

has done it however, condensed the thing & says the Case is an *excellent* one.[113]

Many letters, to and from Buxton, attest to extraordinary commitment of time and energy to the cause.[114] A letter written shortly after his wife's death, in 1837, though proposing a reduction in his anti-slavery activities, actually paints a vivid picture of his dedication:

[After three pages on anti-slavery business] My situation is now totally changed, new duties have fallen upon me to which I am wholly unaccustomed not to say unfit, & I have less energy than formerly. Under these circumstances it is matter for serious consideration whether I should not contract as far as possible my sphere of action feeling convinced that even then there will be very much inadequately done. With regard to my children it is obvious that both my life and time have now acquired an importance such as they had not before – indeed from the ages of the youngest it is almost a matter of certainty that some must be left orphans before they attain majority: this consideration weighs with me & induces me to think that all ought to be dedicated to them.[115]

There are many indications in the papers of the reliance that Buxton and others placed on Lushington's judgment. Buxton wrote to Macaulay, in 1832, that he was 'waiting for Lushington's plan'.[116] In 1838, he wrote to Stephen, 'such are my impressions; but before I can give any further opinion, I must, at least, have permission to consult Lushington'.[117] On another occasion, he wrote, 'Lushington, I find, leaves town on the 14th & I think it so important that we should have a general meeting before he goes that I have written to Stokes to summon one'.[118] In a family letter, he said, 'Is it not famous that the

---

113 Priscilla Johnston to Sarah Buxton, 19 April 1835 (copy), Buxton Papers 13, 442. Jeremie was appointed Procureur and Advocate-General of Mauritius, but rejected by the white population there. Lushington defended his conduct in the House of Commons, Hansard, 3rd ser., xxi, 420 (15 Feb. 1836). See S. B. De Burgh-Edwardes, *History of Mauritius* (London, 1921), 65, 70; Mathieson, *British Slave Emancipation*, 218–23. Other letters of Lushington on Mauritius are in the Brougham Papers, 8142, 8146, 8149.

114 See, for example, Lushington to Buxton, 31 July 1835, Buxton Papers 14, 81a; Lushington to Buxton, 31 July 1837, Buxton Papers 16, 57ah–al; Lushington to Buxton (copy), 23 Dec. 1837, Buxton Papers 17, 4; Buxton to Miss Jeremie (copy), 29 Oct. 1838, Buxton Papers 17, 225; Buxton to J. J. Gurney (copy), 7 Dec. 1838, Buxton Papers 17, 277.

115 Lushington to Buxton, 6 Nov. 1837, Buxton Papers 16, 159q–r.

116 Buxton to Macaulay, Dec. 1832, Buxton, *Memoirs*, 252.

117 Buxton to Stephen (copy), 12 Mar. 1838, Buxton Papers 17, 81.

118 Buxton to Trotter (copy), 30 Sept. 1840, Buxton Papers 19, 421.

Dr will undertake it [the East Indian question[119]]. It saves my life –
for if he had not, I must have gone into Parlt which would soon have
finished me up.'[120] Macaulay wrote to Buxton, 'Lushington is master
of the subject & has the ear of the House.'[121]

Buxton's letters to Lushington himself show the same. For instance, he wrote, in 1839, 'I know also that I have leaned much upon
you, but the case of Africa is almost such as to justify distressing her
few real & capable friends',[122] and in the same year, 'What you say out
of Shakespeare about doing things in right season & considering is
well but you may die & nobody could do it with a tenth part of the
advantage that you could'.[123] Buxton considered Lushington more
cautious than himself:

> Lushington thought it inexpedient to bring on the question of Indian Slavery;
> this discretion is hardly in consonance with my disposition. I am more
> inclined for working in season or out of season with the tide or against it but on
> the other hand Lushington is most true and faithful to the cause, knows far
> better than I do the temper of the present House of Commons, & is swayed by
> no other motive than a desire to act for the best.[124]

On the same matter (East Indian slavery) he wrote to Lushington:

> You are the only man capable of doing it justice & at the same time of
> exercising that degree of prudence which this case particularly requires.[125]

Buxton was a hard taskmaster – Lushington called him a fanatic[126] –
but he recognized some limits to Lushington's capacity:

> Lushington would be exactly the man for Liverpool. His presence there
> would ensure success; but I really know not how to ask him. We trouble him
> enough upon matters even more important than the Liverpool meeting. He
> wants rest as much as any man, & yet he is of so free and ardent a nature that he
> will kill himself, rather than not do any thing he can. I could wish the matter
> were thrown before him for consideration, but I do not like putting it in the

---

119 Slavery continued in India into the 1840s, Temperley, *British Anti-slavery*, ch. 5.
   Lushington acted, but Parliament was dissolved without substantial progress,
   ibid., 103–4.
120 Buxton to Anna Gurney and Sarah Buxton, 24 May 1838, Buxton Papers 17, 159d.
121 Macaulay to Buxton, 23 June 1837, Buxton Papers 15, 329.
122 Buxton to Lushington (copy), 27 Aug. 1839, Buxton Papers 18, 357.
123 Buxton to Lushington (copy), 17 Nov. 1839, Buxton Papers 18, 440.
124 Buxton to Bishop of Calcutta, 20 Feb. 1840, Buxton Papers 19, 164.
125 Buxton to Lushington (copy), 16 April 1841, Buxton Papers 20, 226.
126 Lushington to Buxton, 9 May 1839, Buxton Papers 18, 92n.

shape of a request; & still less do I like that I should be the person so to put it.[127]

On occasions when they did not see eye to eye, Buxton was distressed. His daughter said that 'difference of opinion with him [Dr Lushington] is worse than anything to my father'.[128] Buxton wrote to Lushington that 'I suspect, when I see my views differ from yours that I must be under the influence of some great error'.[129] On another matter, he wrote:

I am most sincerely sorry that you & I do not see this one thing in exactly the same light, but tho' we differ, pro hac vice, there shall be no separation between us, so do not expect it. Why, Man, have you not borne for the last 20 years more than half my burden, & have you ever failed to render me every assistance which could be furnished by your better judgment, your great experience, and your unquestionable industry, and am I to let you go so easily at last?[130]

Of Lushington's part in the movement, George Stephen wrote:

Dr Lushington is one of those able and energetic friends of the cause who has never had full justice done to him by the scanty labours and ill-informed pens of our abolition historians ... his personal sacrifices have been large and generous, and ungracefully rewarded ... Dr Lushington knows exactly when and where to stop; most men are at a loss where to begin; and a certain ardour of temperament, which even age has scarcely suppressed, renders this prudential facility of self-arrest a quality as valuable as it is rare; it combined with his other excellences to give him much weight with his Anti-slavery colleagues, among whom he has from the first held most conspicuous rank.[131]

Buxton's son, Charles, in his account of his father's life, stressed his close association with Lushington, saying that 'every idea, and every plan, was originated and arranged between them'.[132] In 1866, Charles Buxton erected a monument to commemorate the emancipation of the slaves, and in memory of his father. Lushington's is one of the five names, in addition to Buxton's, inscribed there.[133]

127 Buxton to J. Washington (copy), 5 Oct. 1840, Buxton Papers 19, 430–1.
128 Buxton, *Memoirs*, 243 (letter of May 1832).
129 Buxton to Lushington, 1 Jan. 1840, Buxton Papers 19, 61.
130 Buxton to Lushington (copy), 3 Jan. 1843, Buxton Papers 20A, 330.
131 Stephen, *Anti-Slavery Recollections*, 66–8.
132 Buxton, *Memoirs*, 132–3. In the index to Buxton's papers, Lushington's name appears more frequently than any other, except immediate family: P. M. Pugh, *Calendar of the Papers of Sir Thomas Fowell Buxton* (London, 1980), 321.
133 The monument now stands in the gardens between the Houses of Parliament and Lambeth Bridge. The other names are Wilberforce, Clarkson, Macaulay, and Brougham.

Lushington was intimately involved in the last project of Buxton's life, an unsuccessful attempt to establish a settlement on the west coast of Africa. It was intended that land would be settled and farmed, and eventually that the slave trade would be destroyed by the introduction of free commerce and prosperity among the Africans, and with this prosperity, by an association of ideas common at the time, civilization and Protestant Christianity.[134] In 1839, the inaugural meeting of the society was held at Lushington's house in Great George Street, which must have been crowded, as the minutes indicate the presence of fifty-nine persons.[135] Lushington gave a guarantee of debts,[136] subscribed twenty guineas, and was one of three deputy chairmen.[137]

The full name of the society was the Society for the Extinction of the Slave Trade and for the Civilization of Africa. Christianization was seen by Buxton as an essential part of the enterprise, and a printed flier describing the Society includes this:

Sir Fowell Buxton emphatically declares, that next to Christianity (the great and only effectual cure) the deliverance of Africa is to be sought in 'calling out her own resources'.[138]

Buxton's letters contain expressions (showing that the path of progress does not always run in a straight line) such as 'the conversion of a barbarous people to civilization and Christianity'.[139] Buxton relied on Lushington to draw up instructions for the commander of the expedition and a model treaty

which shall be as close as possible to perfection. No doubt it is a laborious task, it requires not only the examination of existing treaties & a knowledge of African character, but a deep insight into human nature, so look to it, I pray you, with your whole mind & let it be as just towards the African as was the Treaty of William Penn towards the Indians.[140]

134 See Reports of Select Committee [on] ... Native Inhabitants of Countries where British Settlements are made ... to promote the spread of Civilization among them, and to lead them to the peaceful and voluntary reception of the Christian religion, PP 1836, vii, 1; id. 1837, vii, 1, esp. at 76. Buxton and Lushington's younger brother, Charles, were members. Buxton's view of Catholic missionary work in Africa was that Catholic converts were little removed from paganism: see Buxton to Lushington (copy), 25 Jan. 1840, Buxton Papers 19, 99–101.
135 Buxton Papers 30, 341 (23 July 1839).
136 See Buxton Papers 19, 19 (B. to L. (copy), 18 Dec. 1839).
137 Buxton Papers 30, 346.
138 Buxton Papers 30, 345.
139 Buxton to Lushington (copy), 6 April 1842, Buxton Papers 20A, 67.
140 Buxton to Lushington, 18 Dec. 1839, Buxton Papers 19, 19–20.

This manifests the not uncommon assumption that a standard form can be supplied for every kind of contract. Lushington declined the invitation:

Now as to your former letter respecting the Treaties &c I am really at a loss to do what you desire. You say that Stephen said *I* was exceedingly anxious on the subject of the Instructions & Treaties. I never opened my lips on the subject. You indeed were more anxious & called for a *pattern* treaty. To this I felt & now feel that there is great difficulty, because I know not how by possibility any one Treaty could be made applicable to circumstances which must vary. I have again considered the subject but I really am at a loss to know what to do . . . The Instructions are in my judgment much more important & more practicable.[141]

Lushington attended a meeting on behalf of the Society, having been summoned '*vi et armis*', but adjudged it a failure, commenting on the absence of the Quakers.[142]

Lushington negotiated with Lord Normanby[143] and drafted resolutions for the Society. A draft in his hand shows that attention was given to the risk of sickness:

That assuming the practicability & sufficient salubrity of settlements in Africa, the adoption of such measure would be expedient as one means of abolishing the Slave Trade & also be calculated to produce other beneficial results.

2. That Mr Buxton be requested to collect & lay before the Ministry information as to the salubrity of the districts most likely to be chosen for settlements and also as to any progress hitherto made by any nation in the cultivation of African produce.[144]

The risk, though foreseen, was not prevented, and the expedition ended in disaster with forty-one deaths from fever.[145] Lushington wrote a letter of consolation:

I very well know how deeply you will feel the afflicting news from Africa & I would most willingly have abstained from adverting to the subject, did I conceive that so doing would have spared you a single pang.[146]

141 Lushington to Buxton, 29 Oct. 1840, Buxton Papers 19, 455m–o.
142 Lushington to Buxton, 29 Oct. 1840, Buxton Papers 19, 455j.
143 Buxton Papers 30, 279; 32, 169.
144 Buxton Papers 30, 309–10.
145 See Temperley, *British Antislavery*, 60; Mathieson, *Great Britain and the Slave Trade*, 51–7.
146 Lushington to Buxton, 19 Jan. 1842, Buxton Papers 20, 437e.

He went on to blame himself for precipitate action, and to absolve Buxton from any blame, expressing a hope that 'you will not allow the recent intelligence to make any painful impression upon your mind'.[147] Lushington was right in anticipating that Buxton would be distressed by the failure of the expedition, and it appears that he was unsuccessful in his attempts to offer consolation, for Professor Temperley writes that 'the deaths . . . preyed on his mind'.[148]

In 1853 an American slave, John Anderson, in the course of escaping from Missouri, killed a man who was entitled by American law to arrest him. Anderson reached Canada, and, in 1860, the United States made a formal demand for his extradition. The treaty then in force allowed for extradition where the conduct of the fugitive constituted a crime both in Canada and in the United States. This raised a point of acute legal difficulty because, while murder was a crime in both countries, using reasonable force to escape from slavery was not a crime by Canadian law. The question was whether killing to resist an arrest that was lawful by American law constituted murder by Canadian law.

It happened that Lushington had foreseen this precise problem seventeen years earlier, when the treaty was drafted, and had suggested an express exception for fugitive slaves:

Still I am bound to say, that there is a point connected with the case of a fugitive slave, for which not even the foresight of the Government at home, or of the executive abroad could adequately provide. I refer not to the common charge of stealing a horse or stealing clothing – because, were an individual to be surrendered on such grounds, it would be an abuse of authority, and not its exercise – but to instances which might be brought forward of a party committing murder to effect his escape. That case would puzzle any Government whatever . . . Before the article be adopted there should be an exception of fugitive slaves in so many words.[149]

The legality of a proposed extradition could be challenged, at that time, like the legality of any detention or imprisonment, by application for a writ of habeas corpus. Anderson applied for such a writ to the Canadian court of Queen's Bench, but the application was rejected.[150] The decision caused a great stir, both in Canada and in

---

[147] Ibid., 437l.
[148] Temperley, *British Antislavery*, 61.
[149] *Proceedings* of 1843 Convention, 321.
[150] *Re Anderson* (1861) 20 UCQB 124. Sir J. B. Robinson CJ, in giving the judgment of the majority, pointed out that it was open to the executive to refuse to surrender Anderson, despite the court's decision.

England.[151] Lushington, then seventy-nine years of age, took an active interest in the case, and may well have exercised a significant influence on the events. On 4 January 1861, a letter from him was read at a meeting of the Anti-slavery Society[152] urging the Society to approach the Duke of Newcastle (the Colonial Secretary), and the committee resolved to do so 'in accordance with the suggestion of Dr Lushington'.[153] Five days later, Newcastle sent a letter to the Government of Canada, with instructions, in strong terms, not to surrender Anderson without further directions from London, even if his pending appeal against the decision of the Canadian Court of Queen's Bench should be dismissed.[154] The arrival of this letter in Canada[155] may be considered to have assured Anderson's safety. Meanwhile, on 14 January, the Anti-slavery Society held a special meeting, which Lushington attended as a visitor.[156] The next day a successful application was made 'with Dr Lushington's energetic encouragement'[157] to the English court of Queen's Bench for a writ of habeas corpus.[158] This expansive assertion of English jurisdiction surprised many, and the power was removed by statute in the following year.[159] The arrival of the English writ in Canada, on 1 February, caused Anderson's advisers to apply to the Canadian Court of Common Pleas, which ordered his release on a technicality.[160]

It will be seen that, between the ages of forty-two and sixty-three, anti-slavery must have occupied almost all Lushington's time outside his professional career. But this statement is inadequate, because it suggests that anti-slavery was a secondary concern, and because it fails to depict the enormous energy that Lushington devoted to the

---

[151] Many letters and petitions were addressed to the Colonial Secretary: PRO/CO 42/629 (index), 631. There were questions and debate in Parliament; see Hansard, 3rd ser., clxi, 218, 339, 821, clxii, 252.

[152] Minute Book, Anti-slavery Papers, BE S20 E2/9, 125.

[153] Ibid., 126.

[154] PRO/CO 43/152/447, 449 (Duke of Newcastle to Officer administering the Government of Canada, 9 Jan. 1861), PP 1861, lxiv, 296.

[155] It was acknowledged by Lt.-Gen. Williams, for the Government of Canada, on 26 Jan., PRO/CO 42/626/60, PP 1861, lxiv, 300.

[156] Minute Book, Anti-slavery Papers BE S20 E2/9, 133 (14 Jan. 1861).

[157] *Anti-slavery Reporter*, 1 April 1873 (obituary).

[158] (1861) 3 El & El 487, 3 LT 622, 30 LJQB 129. See *Law Magazine* 11 (1861), 42, and *Upper Canada Law Journal* 7 (1861), 53, 36 LT 162, 176, 210. See P. Brode, *The Odyssey of John Anderson* (Toronto, 1989).

[159] 25 & 26 Vic. c.20.

[160] *Re Anderson* (1861) 11 UCCP 9 (interim writ, 1 Feb., final decision 16 Feb.). See note, 20 UCQB 193, and Brode, *Odyssey*, 90, 97.

cause.[161] In 1831, he called it 'the principal object of my life'.[162] He received no tangible reward for these services. He opposed the pecuniary interests of his own relatives.[163] He alienated himself from those in power of both political parties. He attacked the actions of the Church of England, to which he was personally and professionally attached. It is of interest to ask what combination of religious, political, social, and legal views led him into a path so little to be expected of a nineteenth-century ecclesiastical lawyer.

His speeches were forceful in style, as many of the extracts already quoted illustrate. To the charge of enthusiasm he replied that moderation in respect of slavery was no virtue:

[I will] advocate this truth . . . regardless of the outcry that I am a wild enthusiast . . . I hold him to be an enthusiast who, ignorant of the subject matter – without taking pains to investigate, imagines that he has come to the just conclusion; and, regardless of the ordinary process of arriving at the truth, professes himself at once the advocate of a cause without being able to explain the reasons of his opinion. But I hold, if a man has learned what the truth is by patient and deliberate inquiry, if he does know the system in all the atrocities of its villainy – to speak mildly, to utter sentiments (as they call them) of moderation on the subject, is to betray the truth – is to suppose that a man of feeling, honour and honesty, can behold these things, and yet talk of them as if they did not violate the laws of God and man, and outrage the feelings of every right-minded individual who justly appreciates them.[164]

He was, on occasion, sarcastic:

I well remember the time when we were entertained with representations of the peace, the happiness, the tranquillity, the enjoyments of a state of slavery. I remember the time when we were told, that the negroes were well fed and comfortably clothed at the expense of the master – and comfortably maintained in old age and sheltered in sickness; having no other return to make for all these numberless favours, than easy labour for his benefit. We were taught to believe that there was nothing but merriment and joy in the West Indies;

---

[161] Buxton wrote 'You can do three or four things at a time – I but one', Buxton Papers 18, 94.

[162] General Meeting of Anti-slavery Society, 9 May 1831, *Anti-slavery Reporter*, 5 (1831), 265.

[163] See above pp. 63–4. Hansard, 3rd ser., xiii, 80.

[164] 'Speech of Dr Lushington delivered at a General Meeting of the Society for the Abolition of Slavery throughout the British Dominions, April 23, 1831', *Anti-slavery Reporter* 4 (1831), 263, 267. Also separately printed.

that the negroes danced in their chains, and praised the master under whose
domination they lived.[165]

Nor did he treat his political opponents gently:

I declare that there is no more bitter enemy to the abolition of slavery than he
who pronounces pompous eulogiums on the blessings and advantages of
liberty; but when measures are brought forward tending to abolish slavery,
turns round upon their promoter, and charges him with endeavouring to
induce the House to do that which must be productive of evil.[166]

Sometimes he aroused an emotional response. The report of a speech
in 1832 records that 'Dr Lushington's statement of this case was given
in language so forcible and affecting that many of the audience shed
tears, and the ladies wept, many of them audibly'.[167] The shorthand
reporter, whose social status and sex are not disclosed, must have been
among those affected, for the report continues 'this part of his speech
has been so imperfectly reported that we adopt the following narrative
of the facts from the Official Despatch . . .'[168]

On the question of racial equality Lushington expressed very firm
views. With respect to the free coloured people of Jamaica, he said:

It is not in the nature of things that a large body, increasing in wealth and
intelligence, should for ever submit in silence to restrictions so unjust and
degrading founded upon no other principle, resting on no other basis, than
the darkness of the colour with which the God of nature has distinguished
their skin.[169]

With reference to the emancipated blacks, he said:

I am willing briefly to bear my testimony, as far as I have had an opportunity
of forming an opinion by experience, that the coloured races as well as the
pure black, possess, by the blessing of Providence, the same talents and the
same capability of cultivating them as have been given to those of a different
complexion . . . I wish that . . . all who cherish an absurd feeling of superior-
ity, arising from the colour of their skin, may become ashamed of themselves;
and that the old adage of 2,000 years' date may be felt to be a true one, 'Virtue
constitutes the soul of man'.[170]

[165] Ibid., 263–4.
[166] *Mirror of Parliament* 1832, 2262b (24 May). The reference is to Lord Sandon (later
  Earl of Harrowby), the Member for Liverpool. Peel described one of Lushington's
  speeches as 'full of vituperation': Hansard, 3rd ser., 1458 (15 April 1831).
[167] *Anti-slavery Reporter* 5 (1832), 156–7.
[168] Ibid., 157.
[169] Hansard, 2nd ser., xiii, 1174.
[170] Speech at 1843 Convention, Johnson, *Proceedings . . . 1843*, 210, 212.

He recognized that, even after emancipation, continued vigilance was needed to protect the blacks from white oppression.[171]

From an early date, Lushington was committed to total abolition of slavery. In 1824, when the newly founded anti-slavery society ventured only to call itself the Society for the Mitigation and Gradual Abolition of Slavery throughout the British Dominions,[172] Lushington said, at its first general meeting:

I am desirous to declare my firm opinion that it is the *abolition* of slavery we must seek, and that all attempts to ameliorate the conditions of the slaves, unless the ultimate result be the entire abolition of the state itself, will prove vain and perplexing ... The truth is, Sir, that when God made men, he made them not to be slaves ... I mean not to say that the immediate emancipation of the Negroes would be a blessing to them, or that it is possible under existing circumstances; but I do mean to say that we should never lose sight of these principles; that we should never suffer ourselves to consider a state of slavery as permanently to be endured, or to be endured longer than the well being of the Slave himself may render necessary; and that we should never omit any means or any opportunity of accelerating its ultimate extinction.[173]

In the House of Commons he said, in the same year, that 'emancipation, complete emancipation, was the only system to which we could look, as that which would put an end to their sufferings'.[174] In 1831, he declared, 'I profess myself the advocate for the speedy and entire emancipation of every slave'.[175]

Lushington's speeches include many appeals to religion:

If there was any truth in philosophy; if they were to place confidence in the sacred Word of God himself – it was impossible to believe that such a system could continue to exist. It was never given by God to man to hold his fellow-man in Slavery.[176]

Slavery was incompatible with Christianity, as slave owners had recognized,[177] asking, 'can you ... use the words "dear brother" or

[171] Speech at 1840 Convention, *Proceedings ... 1840*, 535–6.
[172] See note 8, above, Temperley, *British Antislavery*, 271.
[173] Speech at 1824 General Meeting, 89, 91.
[174] Hansard, 2nd ser., x, 1178. D. Eltis, 'Dr Stephen Lushington and the Campaign to Abolish Slavery in the British Empire', *Journal of Caribbean History* 1 (1970), 41, 45, describes him as a 'radical' in the anti-slavery movement.
[175] General Meeting of Anti-slavery Society, 1831, 263.
[176] *Anti-slavery Reporter* 1 (1825), 80. See also speeches to Anti-slavery Society in 1831, 263, 266; 1832, 162, and to Anti-slavery Convention 1840, 374, 535.
[177] See Walvin, *England, Slaves and Freedom*, 38, 52, 78.

"sister" to those you hold in bondage?' and drawing the conclusion that Christianity should not be taught. Lushington agreed with the premise, but drew the opposite conclusion:

Most true were the words they uttered ... Make the slaves Christians – and (harder task yet!) make the owners of them Christians, and slavery must speedily cease.[178]

References to religious truth do not usually stand alone, but are closely linked to secular expressions of humanitarian values: 'happiness, justice, charity, and a regard for the Word of God';[179] 'mercy, humanity, religion and truth'.[180] He spoke of 'justice and humanity'[181] and 'the eternal purposes of truth and justice'[182] or 'the laws of God and the inalienable rights of man'.[183]

Another theme that frequently appears, in combination with references to religion, is that of national duty and national shame. He expected a successful candidate for election to say 'my soul sinks under that sin, and with the blessing of God, every effort shall be made by me to remove the load from my country and my conscience'.[184] He spoke of 'a time when the household fire of liberty was burning in every British bosom',[185] and of an oppressive colonial law as 'a law enacted within one year from the present hour by Christian men, boasting to be Englishmen, and followers of Christ'.[186] He often asserted that the people of England were opposed to slavery, and would make sacrifices for its abolition:

When I sat on the other side of the House, with but few friends to support me, actuated only by the spirit of truth, and when sometimes my courage failed me, I found the feelings of the people of this country rising to my support, encouraging every effort, and stimulating me to fresh exertions and fresh hopes ... I have such faith in their principles and good feeling, that I believe

[178] Speech (1831), 264. The inconsistency of Christianity with slavery is also asserted in Hansard, 2nd ser., xiii, 1344 (23 June 1825).
[179] Speech (1831), 263.
[180] Ibid., 265.
[181] *Substance of the Debates on the ... slave trade* (1807), 80.
[182] Speech, General Meeting of Anti-slavery Society, *Anti-slavery Reporter* 1 (1825), 80.
[183] Speech (1843), 156. 'Inalienable right' occurs also in the speech of 1832, *Anti-slavery Reporter* 5 (1832), 162.
[184] Speech (1830), 264.
[185] Speech (1832), 154.
[186] Speech (1832), 156.

they would prefer their dinner of herbs to the stalled ox that is offered to them by this measure [reduction of sugar duties].[187]

Lushington, unlike most of the leaders of the anti-slavery movement, was neither an evangelical,[188] nor a Dissenter. As a churchman, he did not altogether welcome the occupation of the missionary field by Dissent. Nevertheless, he did not hesitate to praise the work of the Dissenting missionaries in the West Indies:

To them was the praise of the legislature and the country due. He cared not whether they were Methodists, or Baptists, or Anabaptists, or Presbyterians, or by which of the numerous names distinguishing the religious sects of the country they were called. It was enough for him that they were Christians, and that they had nobly and fearlessly discharged their duty towards their fellow creatures.[189]

He contrasted, in very unfavourable terms, the actions of the Church of England:

The Church of England, he must say, had for a century and a half been grossly negligent in giving instruction to the slave population of our colonies. Whatever was done in that way (and much had been done for the dissemination of Christianity amongst the slaves) was done, not by the Church of England, but by the Moravians, Baptists, and Wesleyans. He was aware that he laid himself open to misrepresentation in this matter, but this was a time at which the truth ought not to be concealed.[190]

He reserved special praise for the Wesleyans:

To the Wesleyan Methodists is due all the amelioration which has yet been effected in the condition of the slaves, all the progress which has been made in their education, and all the success in their conversion.[191]

He praised the Baptist missionaries, also, calling them 'excellent and pious men'.[192]

In 1826, an attack took place in Jamaica on the Methodist chapel

187 Hansard, 3rd ser., lviii, 88 (7 May 1841). Mirror of Parliament 1841, 1551b differs slightly.
188 For the attitude of the evangelicals to slavery, see F. K. Brown, *Fathers of the Victorians: the Age of Wilberforce* (Cambridge, 1961), 373–83.
189 Hansard, 2nd ser., x, 1174 (16 Mar. 1824).
190 Speech (1832), 161. On the ambivalence of the Church of England, see Walvin, *England, Slaves and Freedom*, 131.
191 Mirror of Parliament 1831, 1468b (15 April). The same sentiments appear in Hansard, 2nd ser., xvi, 1167–8 (13 March 1827). See Walvin, *England, Slaves and Freedom*, 103–4.
192 Mirror of Parliament 1839, 2366a (6 May) See also Buxton Papers 18, 92p.

and on the house of the minister. The attack was said to have been encouraged by a sermon preached in the parish church by G. W. Bridges, chaplain to the Bishop of Jamaica, and a supporter of slavery.[193] Lushington was scathing in his references to Bridges:

the Reverend Mr Bridge – no Wesleyan Methodist, thank God for that! but a clergyman of the Church of England, forgetful of the feelings of a man and disregarding the character of his cloth – ordered his female slave to be flogged for overroasting a turkey.[194]

Lushington did not neglect what he maintained would be the practical advantages of abolition: it would free the colonists from the fear of insurrection, and it would enhance their prosperity by fostering free commerce:

I believe, as far as relates to the property of the white inhabitants, their interest will be most materially improved. Instead of living, as now, in perpetual fear and agitation; instead of exacting an unwilling and precarious labour under the influence of the lash, they would then have a body of labourers, who, if paid but a very small proportion in the way of hire, would discharge a double duty with satisfaction to themselves and benefit to their proprietors.[195]

Free labour was, at the same time, financially profitable and compatible with the workings of Divine Providence:

There must be some motive to actuate man. You now actuate him by the fear of the lash, and, alas! by the infliction of it. Make him a freeman, and reward him for his labour, and you hold out to him the very motive which God has designed to actuate mankind – the hope of benefiting himself and improving his condition.[196]

According to all the principles which God has given to govern man, the free spirit of the individual working for his own benefit will infinitely surpass the greatest exertion which the slave can make.[197]

Referring to his relatives' interest in slavery, he said that 'for their sakes he hoped that the emancipation of the negroes would be

---

[193] Lushington spoke on the case: Hansard, 2nd ser., xvi, 1166 (13 Mar. 1827), and was himself attacked for his speech in *John Bull* 7 (1827), 278.

[194] Mirror of Parliament 1831, 1468a (15 April).

[195] Speech, above note 101 (1831), 264. In 1840 he thought that abolition had reduced crime in Jamaica: Speech, above note 103 (1840), 378.

[196] Ibid.

[197] Speech, Johnson, *Proceedings* (1843), 156. See also the reference to free labour, Hansard, 2nd ser., x, 1172 (16 Mar. 1824).

undertaken by the legislature of this country and steadily pursued'.[198] He spoke of the 'happiness and prosperity' in which the West Indies could not share 'so long as slavery continued'.[199] He verged, at times, on the visionary, looking forward to 'the vindication of the rights of humanity, the promotion of commerce, and the establishment of eternal liberty over the whole earth'.[200]

Lushington, for all his idealism, was a practical political campaigner. In a phrase that well illustrates the relation, in his mind, of religion and politics, he wrote to Buxton that 'Providence works not by miracles in these matters but by human action'.[201] He welcomed an advance, even though it might be less than he desired. 'Let us have the good by little and little' he said, in another context.[202] Thus he supported the payment of compensation to slave owners, and he was willing (after unsuccessful opposition) to accept a short period of apprenticeship. He supported the rights of Lecesne and Escoffery, even though they were slave-owners. He praised a clergyman who had supported Smith in Demerara, though he was a planter ('a prejudice which he has overcome').[203]

He advocated practical political action:

When a candidate seeks the favour of an elector, ask him not whether he be the friend of the Duke, or my Lord Grey, of Sir Robert Peel. Let no such question be proposed by a friend to Negro emancipation; but let him ask this question: 'In your heart do you detest abhor and abjure Slavery?' Let his next question be – 'Will you vote for the extinction and abolition of the system?' Mark him well – no general professions of abhorrence of slavery, no low bows and smiling countenances will do: – what Englishman is there who can refrain from expressing his detestation of slavery? But ask him whether he will lend his cordial assistance and co-operation to its immediate extinction? Should he urge – (for I am pretty well versed in the ingenious shifts with which candidates evade these questions) – should he urge this objection – 'Consider the danger to the whites' . . . inquire what his reasons are for apprehending danger . . . But should he go a step further, and say, 'I am an advocate for

[198] Hansard, 3rd ser., xiii, 80 (24 May 1832).
[199] Hansard, 3rd ser., xiv, 1115 (3 Aug. 1832).
[200] Hansard, 3rd ser., xviii, 491 (7 June 1833).
[201] Lushington to Buxton, 9 May 1839, Buxton papers 18, 92n.
[202] Mirror of Parliament 1836, 2544b (25 July). See also Hansard, 2nd ser., xvii, 898 (17 May 1827).
[203] Speech, *Report of Committee of Society* (1824), 92. Lushington moved a vote of appreciation to this man (Austin) in the General Meeting of the Anti-slavery Society, Anti-slavery Papers BE S20 E2/1, 25 June 1824.

amelioration, with a due regard to existing interests', if once these words escape his lips, *vote against him*.[204]

He said in 1840:

Throughout the whole of our enterprise . . . the great object of my life has been to look difficulties in the face . . . I have always looked to see what were the obstructions in the way, and how they could best be overcome, and the desired result obtained.[205]

He added:

We should be careful in all our proceedings, strong yet prudent; energetic but still cautious; and never imagine that we are the whole world . . . Let us therefore go on in our course, increasing in activity and energy, but tempered with caution and prudence, yet thinking nothing done, until all be obtained.[206]

Lushington was a lawyer, and his views were reflected in his opinions of law, which 'ought to be made for the administration of impartial justice between man and man', 'for the protection of the peace', and 'for the preservation of the great bonds of human society', not 'to strengthen the strength of the strong, and to weaken the weakness of the weak'.[207]

Lushington was also an advocate (albeit unpaid, in this cause) and it may naturally be supposed that, to some extent, he adapted his arguments to suit his audiences: religious references are more frequent in his speeches to anti-slavery bodies than to the House of Commons. There are no arguments, however, that do not appear in both forums. His private correspondence with Buxton and Brougham confirms, what could hardly be doubted, that he was personally committed to the arguments he used.[208]

204 Speech (1831), 265. The tactics were effective: see Klingberg, *Anti-Slavery Movement*, 255, R. Anstey, 'Pattern of British Abolitionism', 27.

205 Speech, at 1840 Convention, *Proceedings* (1840), 379.

206 Ibid., 380.

207 Ibid., 377. See also 536.

208 E. Williams, *Capitalism and Slavery* (1944, rep. 1964), 191, suggests that Lushington's motive was to destroy the West Indian sugar monopoly, not in the interest of the slaves, but in that of sugar refiners in his constituency. But the evidence taken as a whole, particularly Lushington's later position on sugar duties, does not appear to suggest that this was a substantial motive. (This is the only reference to Lushington, whose name does not appear in the index to the 1964 edn.) Immediately following the passage cited by Williams, Lushington said 'They [his constituents] acknowledged the title of the West Indian colonies to supply the home market', Hansard, 3rd ser., xix, 1177 (24 July 1833). Williams may well, however, be right about the motives of Lushington's constituents in supporting him.

There has been some debate among historians as to whether the abolition of slavery was primarily caused by moral and religious principle, or by economic self-interest.[209] It will be seen that, in Lushington's mind, religious, moral, humanitarian, legal, nationalistic, and economic considerations all pointed in the same direction, and, indeed, were hardly to be separated from each other.[210]

There is, perhaps, a tendency to discount religious motives that are not manifested in fervent expression or pious conduct. It is true that Lushington's actions do not appear to be motivated by religious considerations, standing alone. But religious truth was not the less real to him because it was also reflected in moral, legal, and social terms; on the contrary, Divine Providence worked not by miracles but by human action, and not only through individual piety, but also through the actions of human communities. Hence, Lushington's simultaneous attachment to reform, and to the established Church of England.

[209] Williams, *Capitalism and Slavery*. R. T. Anstey, '"Capitalism and Slavery": a critique', *Economic History Review* 21 (1968), 307; Temperley, *British Anti-slavery*, 273–6.

[210] Greville comments on the mixture of humanitarian and economic motives among the abolitionists, *Memoirs*, ii, 346–7 (26 Jan. 1833). Walvin, *England, Slaves and Freedom*, also comments, at 154, on the unison of morality, religion, and economics, and on the national disgrace of slavery.

3

LADY BYRON'S SEPARATION

Lord Byron was, in 1815, a very well-known literary figure. His poetry was enormously popular. His contempt for social conventions had an ambivalent effect on his reputation: to some, he was a welcome scourge of cant and hypocrisy; to others, a dangerous threat to moral standards. His marriage, in 1815, to a young heiress aroused widespread interest, and his separation from her a year later, shortly after the birth of a daughter, was the talk of the country. As the reasons for the separation were shrouded in mystery, ample scope was given to scandalous rumour, which charged Byron with almost every kind of offence, before and during his marriage, including murder, incest, homosexual and heterosexual sodomy, adultery, and brutality.

Dr Lushington was Lady Byron's legal adviser. The facts of the separation, in outline, were these. After a year of marriage, Lady Byron left Lord Byron's London house, in January 1816, at his request, with her infant daughter for what was supposed to be a temporary stay with her parents in Leicestershire. Lady Byron, shortly after her departure, wrote two affectionate letters to Lord Byron, but within a week her mother, Lady Noel, had travelled to London, been referred to Lushington, and had consulted him about a separation. In February Lady Byron herself came to London at her own insistence to consult Lushington personally. Lady Byron's father, Sir Ralph Noel, had, meanwhile, written formally to Lord Byron, proposing a separation. Byron resisted this proposal initially, and wrote several letters to Lady Byron, pleading for a reconciliation, but she was adamant, and in April Lord Byron signed the separation papers and left England.

Much has been written about the separation,[1] but little attention

[1] See bibliography in L. A. Marchand, *Byron: a Biography* (New York, 1957). Since, have appeared G. W. Knight, *Lord Byron's Marriage: the evidence of the asterisks* (London, 1957), G. W. Knight, *Byron and Shakespeare* (London, 1966), P. Gunn,

has been paid to the legal aspects of the dispute. Although the case never went to court, and so never produced an official legal record, the unofficial documentary evidence is extensive, and affords a unique view of the conduct of a matrimonial dispute in the early nineteenth century. Much of Lushington's advice to Lady Byron was given by correspondence. His letters to her, and hers to him, are, for the most part, preserved, though Lushington's own records of the case were said, by his grand-daughter, to have been destroyed by him before his death.[2] Lady Byron's letters to others, commenting on the progress of the case, are preserved, and many are published. Lord Byron's letters, too, recently published in a definitive edition,[3] show his point of view throughout the negotiations. Hobhouse, Lord Byron's closest friend, kept a diary which has survived.[4]

Lushington, when he was first consulted by Lady Byron, was thirty-four years of age, and had been an advocate in Doctors' Commons for seven years. He was still one of the junior members of what was a very small profession.[5] Lushington's name was, however, apparently familiar to Hobhouse, who wrote in his diary that 'the family have retained Lushington & make no doubt of success'.[6] His reputation at the time may be judged from a letter of Lady Byron's mother, who called him 'the most rising man in the Spiritual Court and the Man most looked up to'.[7]

My Dearest Augusta: a Biography of the Honourable Augusta Leigh, Lord Byron's Half-Sister (London, 1968), M. Elwin, *Lord Byron's Wife* (London, 1962), M. Elwin, *Lord Byron's Family* (London, 1975), D. L. Moore, *The Late Lord Byron: Posthumous Dramas* (London, 1961), D. L. Moore, *Lord Byron: Acounts Rendered* (London, 1974), D. L. Moore, *Ada, Countess of Lovelace: Byron's Legitimate Daughter* (London, 1977), E. H. P. Longford, *Byron* (London, 1976), L. A. Marchand, *Byron: a Portrait* (London, 1971), T. A. J. Burnett, *The Rise and Fall of a Regency Dandy: the Life and Times of Scrope Berdmore Davies* (Oxford, 1981).

2 Marchand, *Byron: a Biography*, 582n (letter of Miss Susan Lushington to Professor Marchand).

3 L. A. Marchand, *Byron's Letters and Journals: the complete and unexpurgated text of all the letters available*, 12 vols (London, 1973–82).

4 The portion covering the period of the separation is in the New York Public Library (Berg Collection). Other portions are in the British Library. References without manuscript number are to the manuscript in New York. Where portions have been published, this is noted.

5 Five advocates only had been admitted after Lushington, and, of these, only one made a career in the profession. See G. D. Squibb, *Doctors' Commons* (Oxford, 1977), 198–9.

6 Hobhouse *Diary*, 12 Feb. 1816.

7 Lady Noel to Lady Byron, 26 Jan. 1830, Lovelace-Byron Papers, Bodleian Library, Oxford, 36/15, Elwin, *Lord Byron's Wife*, 379.

Divorce, in the modern sense of dissolution of marriage, did not exist as an ordinary legal remedy in 1816. Dissolution of marriage could be obtained by Act of Parliament, but Parliamentary divorces were rare, and, more to the point, virtually unobtainable by women.[8] The proceedings contemplated by Lady Byron in the ecclesiastical court would, if successful, have led to a divorce *a mensa et thoro*, having the effect of a judicial separation; she would have been entitled to live apart from Lord Byron, and he would have been required to support her. If her suit had failed, she could have been required to return to Lord Byron's home.

Lord Byron, if he had wished to do so, could have forced the matter into court himself by instituting a suit for restitution of conjugal rights, which would (if successful) have led to an order requiring Lady Byron to return to him. A letter to his solicitor shows that, as late as 4 March, he was contemplating this course of action:

> Before *we cite* – it will be better to ascertain whether *they really* mean to go into court – because – if they do not – or *she* does not – this measure on our part may be a pretext for them to urge & induce her to go on – by saying that we have set the example – and that it is mere self defence & so forth.[9]

It was a defence to a restitution suit that there were grounds for divorce. So, as a matter of theoretical legal principle it made no difference which party commenced the suit: if Lady Byron could establish grounds for divorce, the same grounds would constitute a defence to a restitution suit commenced by Lord Byron; on the other hand, if she had no grounds for divorce, she had no defence to a restitution suit.[10] There were, however, practical advantages to occupying the position of defendant. Hobhouse reported in his diary that Lord Byron was advised that he should not cite, but that he had a good defendant's case.[11] The reason was that a greater particularity in

---

8   S. Wolfram, 'Divorce in England 1700–1857', *Oxford Journal of Legal Studies* 5 (1985), 155, says that there had been only one case, in 1801. Shelford, *Practical Treatise on the Law of Marriage and Divorce* (London, 1841), 364n, mentions another, in 1704. See also pp. 173–4, below.

9   Lord Byron to J. Hanson, 4 Mar. 1816, L. A. Marchand, *Byron's Letters*, vol. 5, *So Late into the Night*, 42.

10 This point was discussed by the Court of Appeal in *Russell* v. *Russell* [1895] P 315, 330–1, where it was concluded, citing decisions of Lord Stowell (Sir William Scott) and of Dr Lushington himself, that it was settled in the ecclesiastical courts that only a danger to personal safety would constitute a defence to a restitution suit.

11 Hobhouse *Diary*, 5 March 1816. L. A. Marchand, *Byron: A Biography*, 584, Burnett, *Regency Dandy*, 108. See p. 119, below.

allegations was required of a promoter of a suit, than of a respondent, possibly a crucial point where there were suspicious circumstances suggesting adultery, but no precise proof.[12]

The main question turned on the grounds for divorce, which were adultery and cruelty.[13] Only conduct occurring after the marriage constituted a ground for divorce; pre-marital sins, it was supposed, had been forgiven. The law on these questions was not always clear. The leading work on ecclesiastical law consisted of an alphabetical list of topics, with a series of quotations and summaries of decisions, loosely arranged by topic, but with no analysis, or attempt by the author of the book to reconcile or explain the extracts.[14] Adultery had a plain meaning, though proof was often difficult. Cruelty was more flexible and uncertain. The courts at the time took a narrow view. Sir William Scott,[15] then the judge of the London Consistory Court before whom Lady Byron's case would have come, had said, in a case often quoted[16] (later by Lushington himself, when a judge[17]) that it was in the public interest to confine the grounds of divorce very narrowly, for the stability of marriage would be threatened if a spouse could lawfully abandon a marriage for slight causes. 'The general happiness of the married life is secured by its indissolubility . . . Necessity is a powerful master in teaching the duties which it imposes . . . the happiness of some individuals must be sacrificed to the greater and more general good.' Cruelty was such conduct as made it unsafe for the wife to remain in the matrimonial home, and the test was usually stated to be a reasonable apprehension of bodily hurt. Scott had said that 'It is the duty . . . of the Courts to keep the rule extremely strict.'[18] In principle, insulting language or conduct was insuf-

---

[12] In *Moore* v. *Moore* (1840) 3 Moo PC 84, Dr Lushington himself, giving the judgment of the Privy Council, held that acts of adultery might be alleged in a responsive allegation to a restitution suit, without the particularity required in a libel to support a divorce suit. See p. 187, below.

[13] R. Burn, *Ecclesiastical Law* 7th edn (London, 1809). A. Waddilove, *Digest of Cases decided in the Ecclesiastical Courts* (London, 1849), includes unnatural practices under the heading of cruelty. L. Shelford, *Marriage and Divorce*, 364, includes unnatural practices as a separate ground, but deals with it only in a footnote.

[14] Burn, *Ecclesiastical Law*.

[15] William Scott, Baron Stowell (1745–1836); judge of the London Consistory Court, 1788–1821, and of the High Court of Admiralty, 1798–1828. Created a peer in 1821.

[16] *Evans* v. *Evans* (1790), 1 Hagg Con 35.

[17] See, for example, *Neeld* v. *Neeld* (1831), 4 Hagg Ecc 263, and chapter 5, below.

[18] *Evans* v. *Evans* (1790), 1 Hagg Con 37.

ficient,[19] though insulting language and conduct might be admissible as proof that the wife's fear of bodily harm was reasonably grounded, or to defeat a defence of condonation.[20]

Condonation was an important feature of the law. Even if a wife established adultery, or cruelty, or both, she would lose the right to a divorce if she had forgiven, or condoned the offence. Voluntarily remaining in her husband's house, and treating him with apparent affection, after knowledge of the offence, though not conclusive, were weighty evidence of condonation.[21] Lady Byron's affectionate letters, for this reason, constituted a serious weakness in her case.

In considering the relative positions of spouses in a matrimonial dispute, account must be taken of property law, though this was outside the province of the ecclesiastical courts. At that time married women were severely restricted in their rights to own property. The husband obtained a freehold interest in the wife's real property for the parties' joint lives, and all personal property of a married woman, with some minor exceptions, vested in her husband.[22] These disabilities could, however, be evaded by the device of trust, whereby property could be vested in one person (the trustee) for the use of another. This device was commonly used in cases of separation in order to secure the use of a part of the matrimonial property to the wife, and such an arrangement was made in favour of Lady Byron when the articles of

[19] 'Mere austerity of temper, petulance of manners, rudeness of language, a want of civil attention and accommodation, even occasional sallies of passion, if they do not threaten bodily harm, do not amount to legal cruelty.' Per Sir W. Scott, in *Evans* v. *Evans*, note 16 above. In *Harris* v. *Harris* (1813), 2 Phill Ecc 111, the same judge said: 'It is not the habit of the court to interfere in ordinary domestic quarrels; there must be something which makes cohabitation unsafe; for there may be much unhappiness from unkind treatment and from violent and abusive language, but the Court will not interfere – it must leave the parties to the correction of their own judgment; they must bear, as well as they can, the consequences of their own choice. Words of menace are different.'
[20] *D'Aguilar* v. *D'Aguilar* (1794), 1 Hagg Ecc 773.
[21] See *Bateman* v. *Ross* (1813), 1 Dow 235 (HL), *D'Aguilar* v. *D'Aguilar* (1794), 1 Hagg Ecc 773.
[22] See R. S. D. Roper, *Treatise of the Law of Property arising from the Relation between Husband and Wife* (new edn by Jacob, London, 1841), 3, 169. Eversley, *The Law of Domestic Relations* (London, 1885), 307, writes: 'Marriage at common law operated as an absolute conveyance of the wife's personal property to the husband, and to give him an interest in her realty for his and her joint lives.' This position was not changed until the Married Women's Property Acts of 1870 and 1882; see L. Holcomb, *Wives and Property: Reform of the Married Women's Property Law in Nineteenth-Century England* (Toronto, 1983).

separation were eventually signed by Lord Byron in April, 1816, with Lushington signing as trustee.[23]

Another area of law, also outside the field of the ecclesiastical courts, but very relevant to the dispute between Lord and Lady Byron, is child custody. Here the basic principle was that the father was entitled to custody, and his right could be enforced in the common law courts by a writ of habeas corpus, a procedure for testing the legality of any detention of a person, even against the mother.[24] However, the Court of Chancery had jurisdiction to interfere with the father's rights, where the child was in physical, or – what was more to the point in the Byron case – moral danger.[25] Further, the father's power to obtain a writ of habeas corpus in the common law court could be defeated if the child was already a ward of the Court of Chancery, in which case the question would come exclusively before the latter court, which was more amenable to challenges to paternal power. A book published in 1841 explained this point as follows:

It seems that when a parent applies to a common law court for a writ of habeas corpus to recover his children, who have been taken from him, the court will

---

[23] Lovelace-Byron Papers, 151/14. See Lushington to Lord Holland, 3 Mar. 1816, R. E. Prothero, *Letters and Journals of Lord Byron* (London, 1899), iii, 319. The validity of deeds of separation is discussed at length in Roper, *Husband and Wife*, ii, 267–324. See also the discussion in Eversley, *Law of Domestic Relations*, 466–8, from which it appears that, by 1816, separation deeds were enforceable both at law and in equity, at least in respect of property. Roper expresses a doubt whether the Court of Chancery would actually restrain, by prohibition or injunction, a husband's suit for restitution of conjugal rights. The ecclesiastical courts did not recognize a separation agreement as a defence: *Mortimer* v. *Mortimer*, 2 Hagg Con 310, 318. No question seems to have arisen of Lord Byron's breaking the agreement by instituting such a suit. Probably he would have considered it dishonourable to go back on his word.

[24] See *DeManneville* v. *DeManneville* (1804), 10 Ves 52. The law was modified in 1839 by The Custody of Infants Act, 2 & 3 Vic. c. 54. See J. Perkin, *Women and Marriage in Nineteenth-century England* (London, 1988) 27, 107–8.

[25] A year after the Byron separation, the Chancellor deprived the poet, Shelley, of custody of his child on the ground that he held atheistical and immoral views: *Shelley* v. *Westbrooke* (1817), Jac 266. The parallel with Byron's situation is remarkable, and was not lost on Byron himself, who wrote to his publisher: 'You will recollect that if the publication [Don Juan] is pronounced against on the grounds you mention as *indecent and blasphemous*, I lose all right in my daughter's *guardianship* and *education* – in short all paternal authority – and every thing concerning her – except the pleasure I may have had in begetting her. It was so decided in Shelley's case – because he had written Queen Mab &c &c.' (4 Dec. 1819, L. A. Marchand, *Byron's Letters*, vol. 6, *The Flesh is Frail*, 252), and he made a similar point in a letter to Hobhouse on 22 June 1820 (L. A. Marchand, *Byron's Letters*, vol. 7, *Between Two Worlds*, 121).

not grant the writ if the lord chancellor has previously interfered in the matter.[26]

Some understanding of the rules of evidence and procedure in use in the ecclesiastical courts is necessary, as references to evidential and procedural points recur throughout the period of the negotiation. A matrimonial suit was commenced by a citation, i.e. an order requiring the opposite party to appear. The party initiating the proceedings (the 'promoter') would then submit a document called a libel, which contained a very detailed statement of the grounds for the relief sought. The ecclesiastical courts did not receive oral evidence. All disputed facts had to be proved by the written depositions of witnesses. Nor were the parties, or their representatives, present during the examination of witnesses. The examination was conducted in private by a person (a proctor not otherwise concerned in the case) acting as an officer of the court, examining solely on the allegations in the libel.[27] The statement of alleged facts in the libel was, therefore, crucial, and the procedure for examination of witnesses made it essential that every fact, in minute detail, should be specified in the libel.[28] There was no question of starting the proceedings with a general claim, and then waiting for the trial to reveal the details of the case. It is known, from a statement of Lushington's in 1870 that will be discussed more fully below, that a libel was actually prepared.

[26] Shelford, *Marriage and Divorce*, 677–8, citing *Wellesley* v. *Wellesley*, 1 Dow & Clark 152 at 161, 2 Bligh NS 124. In that case (2 Bligh NS 142) Lord Manners said: 'on a writ of habeas corpus being applied for by the father, to have the children restored to him, in the Court of King's Bench, that Court enquires whether they are wards of the Court of Chancery, and whether there are any proceedings in that Court respecting them. If the Court of King's Bench finds there are such proceedings, it declines to grant the writ.'

[27] Waddilove, *Digest*, 171.

[28] H. Coote, *Practice of the Ecclesiastical Courts* (London, 1847), 320–35 gives a sample libel for divorce for adultery, and, at 350–7, a libel for cruelty. An extract will indicate the tone of the documents: 'And the party proponent doth expressly allege and propound, that from such time until dinner-time on the same day, which was six o'clock, the said Arthur Vincent and Maria Theresa Grant were for the most part alone together, either in the said front drawing-room, or in a room called the back drawing-room adjoining thereto, and communicating therewith by folding doors; into which back drawing-room a sofa, which usually stood in the front drawing-room, was removed by her, the said Maria Theresa Grant's orders, at between one and two o'clock on that day by the servant, for whom she rang the bell at that time, and whom she then also ordered to bring up luncheon. And the party proponent doth further expressly allege that the said Arthur Vincent and the said Maria Theresa Grant, whilst so alone together on that day, had the carnal use and knowledge of each others bodies, and thereby committed the foul crime of adultery.'

Proceedings were not commenced, and the libel was never served, but the negotiations depended largely on Lady Byron's threat to commence proceedings and to produce the libel. This was a weapon that could only be used once. Byron demanded often to know the precise grounds of Lady Byron's complaint, but Lushington would not reveal his hand, and, ultimately, Lord Byron was not willing to face the risk of a show-down.

Two aspects of the law of evidence were significant. One was the civil-law rule that the evidence of one witness alone was insufficient to establish disputed facts. The ancient rule had been that two witnesses were required, but by 1816 it was sufficient if there were independent evidence of any sort to corroborate the testimony of a single witness.[29] Even more important was the rule, then in force in the common law courts also, that parties could not give evidence.[30] After her interview with Dr Lushington in February, Lady Byron wrote to her mother:

The misfortune of my case is that so little has passed before witnesses – and the wife's deposition *unsupported* is of no avail.[31]

Other references to this feature of the law indicate that it was of crucial importance in the case.[32]

It will be appreciated from this brief survey of the law, that Lady Byron's legal position was, on the face of it, very weak. But the case shows that, with adequate financial backing, and good advice, success could be had. Lady Byron had two primary, and two subsidiary objectives. She wanted a permanent separation that would effectively bind Lord Byron, and she wanted custody of her child. The subsidiary objectives were to achieve these things without the publicity attendant upon proceedings in open court that would have compelled

[29] Waddilove, *Digest*, 172.
[30] Ibid., 364.
[31] Lady Byron to her mother, 23 Feb. 1816, Lovelace-Byron Papers, 30/24, Elwin, *Lord Byron's Wife*, 417. Even if corroborated, the wife's deposition could not be evidence, since parties could not be witnesses.
[32] In a letter of 12 Feb. 1830 to Mrs Lushington, she wrote: 'I think that the most plausible argument against the supposition of any *serious* causes for the separation will be that if Lord B were conscious of such he would never have given so decided a testimony in my favor. But the truth is that he always relied upon the invalidity of a wife's testimony against her husband, unsupported by any witness – & frequently mentioned that circumstance to me. Mrs Leigh also endeavored to impress it upon my mind in one of her letters at the time of the separation, as follows: "without witnesses your depositions will go for nothing – the same with regard to those who have only learned circumstances from you". Is not this a curious proof of the *plot*? But I did not see through it then.' Lovelace-Byron Papers, 91/36. See also Dr Lushington's statement to H. A. Bathurst, quoted below, p. 114.

her to reveal some matters that she wanted to keep secret, and to salvage some part of the matrimonial property for her own separate use. Despite the weaknesses of a wife's legal position at the time, she attained all these objectives.

The initial consultation with Lushington was by Lady Noel, Lady Byron's mother, who recorded favourable impressions, describing Lushington as '*gentlemanlike*, clear headed and clever'.[33] Lord Byron was advised by a solicitor, J. Hanson, and, although Lord Byron retained three advocates in Doctors' Commons,[34] Lushington dealt directly with Hanson. This was, it seems, unusual. Lady Noel wrote:

Lushington has *most kindly condescended* to be the professional Person on our side. I say *condescended*, because it is quite out of *Etiquette* for him to meet a *Solicitor*, and I told him that I believed Hanson would probably be fixed on by Lord B.[35]

Lady Noel had also arranged, through a family friend, Serjeant Heywood, a direct introduction to Lushington, 'without the intervention of a *proctor* which in the *Civil Court* answers to a *Solicitor* in the other Courts'.[36]

Lady Noel brought, for Lushington's use, Lady Byron's written statement of her grievances. It happens that this document is preserved, with Lushington's annotations made, probably, during the interview with Lady Noel.[37] With it are Lushington's own notes, consisting of eleven numbered points.[38] As evidence of what Lord Byron did, this document is triple hearsay, but it is first-hand, and almost unique, evidence of how a lawyer of the time began to put a matrimonial case into legal form, and for this reason, it is quoted in full. Lushington passes over general complaints about Lord Byron's character, and complaints of harsh words in private, and references to

[33] Lady Noel to Lady Byron, 25 Jan. 1816 (dated 24th), Lovelace-Byron Papers, 36/13, Elwin, *Lord Byron's Wife*, 375.

[34] Doctors Robinson, Adams, and Jenner. See Prothero, *Letters and Journals*, 308. All were senior to Dr Lushington, having been admitted in 1796, 1799, and 1803, respectively. See Squibb, *Doctors' Commons*, 196–7.

[35] Lady Noel to Lady Byron, 26 Jan. 1816, Lovelace-Byron Papers, 36/15, Elwin, *Lord Byron's Wife*, 379.

[36] Lady Noel to Lady Byron, 23 Jan. 1816, Lovelace-Byron Papers, 36/11, Elwin, *Lord Byron's Wife*, 373.

[37] Lovelace-Byron Papers 129/13–17 (dated 18 Jan. 1816). Parts of this statement are in Elwin, *Lord Byron's Wife*, 343–4, 345, 349–50.

[38] Lovelace-Byron Papers 129/24–7. Parts are in Elwin, *Lord Byron's Wife*, 328–9, 334, 344. Lushington added numerals to Lady Byron's statement, some of which correspond with the numbering of his notes.

Lady Byron's own feelings and motives; he picks out statements relevant to the two grounds of divorce (cruelty and adultery) and notes the presence of competent witnesses. The note is as follows:

1. and at that time stated to Mrs L[eigh] that he hoped that you & the child might die in the confinement. Lady B not present.
2. Lord B has declared his intention of making noise to disturb Lady B during her confinement (Mrs L) His conduct towards Lady B was so violent that strong apprehensions for her personal safety were entertained by Mrs L & Capt B. Fletcher his valet has declared that he was so much alarmed for Lady B's safety that he several times watched Lord B when he was preparing to go to bed until he was in bed, lest he should go up to Lady B & use personal violence. Lord B was in the habit of having pistols with him & Fletcher was afraid he might use them. Lady B being apprehensive of violence desired Mrs L to tell Fletcher to be upon the watch; Mrs L entertained the same apprehension & told Fletcher. Fletcher said he had before taken care to do so, & continued to watch afterwards. The day after Lady B's confinement Lord B came into the room, & being informed that Lady N[oel] was very ill expressed his joy at it. It is doubtful whether Mrs L overheard this or not.
3. Mrs L came to the house Nov 15 from that time can speak to great severity & harshness of treatment till the confinement frequently refusing to speak to her for a considerable length of time – & particularly also in April or May last when Mrs L was present, Lady B being very ill & great probability of miscarriage existing.
4. Lord B was in habit of getting intoxicated with Brandy. Fletcher & his wife both can prove the breaking etc – & his conduct was particularly outrageous to Lady B. Has confessed the breaking &c to Mr Le Mann
5. Lord B has admitted the fact to Lady B, to Mrs L, to Capt B & it is apprehended to Mr B. Lord B frequently visited Miss B [Susan Boyce, an actress] at her lodgings. This can be proved by Miss B's servants & Lord B's correspondence by letter between them. Mrs L & Fletcher. Lord B took her home frequently in his carriage from the theatre, & staid a considerable time with her at her lodgings. Coachman and Footman certainly – Miss B's servants – Lord B often took Miss B from the theatre after the play. Once Lord B found that Miss B had left a brooch in his carriage & the next morning sent his footman to search the carriage – he informed Mrs L of this fact & expressed great anxiety to have it found.[39]
Lord B has declared to Mrs L that Miss B had cost him considerable sums

[39] See letter of Susan Boyce to Lord Byron (16 Nov. 1815) informing him of the loss of a brooch in his carriage, so that he should be warned in case it were found and an explanation required, G. Paston and P. Quennell, *To Lord Byron* (London, 1939), 181, not the first instance of excessive caution in such matters proving counter-productive.

of money & also he ordered jewels of some value at Love & Shelly's Jeweller Bond St which jewels were carried to Miss B it is believed by Fletcher – Lord B has told this to Mrs L & to Lady B. Lord B used to permit Miss B to come to the private Box at the theatre (Boxkeepers). There must be witnesses to prove great intimacy. Mr Bac probably, and Mr R – & others also the Green Room. Miss B has made many demands for money upon Lord B & he has declared he has broken off intercourse with her on that account. Mrs L & also to Lady B. The connection has been acknowledged to Capt B.

6. Lord B has repeatedly threatened to commit suicide to Lady B & often to Mrs L but it is doubtful if he has done so when both were present.

7. When Lord B by letter desired Lady B to quit the house, this produces very great agitation in Lady B – (Mrs L can prove).

8. Conversation – blasphemous & indecent before Mrs L & Lady B. also Capt B

9. At Newmarket used repeatedly to send Lady B out of the room with very severe & violent language (Mrs L present)

10. Lord B has often stated to Lady B that he has been guilty of very atrocious crimes (perhaps in presence of Mrs L)

11. Nurse can speak to Lord B's violent deportment on the 3rd of Jan & to her locking the doors to guard against Lord B's coming in the night to do Lady B an injury.

Here we can see the list of witnesses, and the libel, taking shape in Lushington's mind; the instances of violent behaviour would tend to support an allegation of cruelty; the evidence relating to Susan Boyce, one of adultery. A libel was drafted, according to a statement of Lushington's over fifty years later, but destroyed when the separation was agreed.[40] Lushington advised that process should be served on Lord Byron if, but only if, he made preparation to leave England.[41]

Although rumour charged Byron with incest and homosexual sodomy,[42] neither of these, occurring before the marriage, would constitute grounds for divorce, and there is no proof, even today, that they occurred during the marriage. There is reason to take at face value a disavowal by Lady Byron of her reliance on these two charges.[43]

[40] J. C. Fox, *The Byron Mystery* (London, 1924), 58.

[41] Lushington to Lady Noel (copy), 26 Jan. 1816, Lovelace-Byron Papers, 375.

[42] The two charges were recorded by Hobhouse in his diary as 'incest and ———', Hobhouse *Diary*, 7 and 8 March. In the entry for 9 Feb. he recorded that 'C.L. [Caroline Lamb] accused B of ——— poor fellow – the plot thickens against him.' Marchand establishes that the blanks signified sodomy. *Byron: A Biography*, 587n.

[43] Fox, *The Byron Mystery*, 112. See Marchand, *Byron: A Biography*, 586–7, and Burnett, *Regency Dandy*, 105 and 108. As regards incest during the marriage, Lady

Adultery with Susan Boyce would, almost certainly, have been alleged. Lady Noel wrote, after her initial interview with Lushington:

Lushington observed today, that from Miss B's *character* which *he* well knew, your *health* was not safe if you continued with Lord B.[44]

The point about health might have had a legal significance, in that infecting a wife with venereal disease would be a danger to her health and would constitute cruelty – reasonable fear of infection would be an additional legal justification for Lady Byron's leaving her husband. On 26 January, Lushington wrote to Lady Noel that 'the admissions or rather declarations concerning Miss Boyce are very important'.[45]

The circumstances supporting the allegation of adultery were suspicious, but hardly conclusive, for Lord Byron had legitimate reason to meet Susan Boyce at the theatre and to accompany her to her home. It now appears that adultery had occurred, but it is far from clear that convincing evidence could have been assembled in 1816.[46]

The other branch of the case would have depended on an allegation of cruelty. The incidents listed in Lushington's note fall short of a convincing case: they might well have been considered by Sir William Scott as instances merely of the chances of married life: bad temper and bad manners, and harsh and insulting behaviour. Lady Byron would have had difficulty, even if all the facts alleged were proven, in establishing a reasonable apprehension of physical harm, especially in light of her amicable departure in January.

However, three weeks later, Lady Byron came to London in order to reveal some additional fact that could not be entrusted to writing, saying that 'there are things which I, and only I, could explain to you

Byron wrote to Mrs Villiers, on 17 July 1816, 'I have had an answer – all that it ought to be – or that I could desire. It *thoroughly* convinces me of her innocence in regard to all the period with which I was concerned. *Lady Byron and the Leighs* (London, 1887), 42; Elwin, *Lord Byron's Family*, 67.

[44] Lady Noel to Lady Byron, 25 Jan. 1816, Lovelace-Byron Papers, 36/14; Elwin, *Lord Byron's Wife*, 376.

[45] Lushington to Lady Noel (copy), 26 Jan. 1816, Lovelace-Byron Papers, 375.

[46] Marchand, *Byron: A Biography*, 548–50, Lord Byron to Kinnaird, 23 Aug. 1821, Marchand, *Byron's Letters*, vol. 8, *Born For Opposition*, 185. Paston and Quennell, *To Lord Byron*, ch. 9. Hobhouse, in his diary entry for 9 Feb., wrote: 'he told me that except with Miss B he had never been guilty of any infidelity towards her – & that she could not guess this': Hobhouse *Diary*. It is evident from Lady Noel's letter of 25 Jan. that Lady Byron had guessed; but proof was another matter. Fox, *The Byron Mystery*, 111, says that it was not expected by Byron that a charge of adultery would be made.

in conversation, that may be of great importance to the thorough understanding of the case'.[47]

It is certain that Lady Byron revealed an important fact at this interview in February. Its precise nature has been the subject of very much speculation, and still cannot be determined for certain. The fact that a significant revelation had been made to Lushington became generally known in 1830, following the publication, by Thomas Moore,[48] of a biography of Byron. In dealing with the separation, Moore suggested that Lady Byron had no very compelling reason for her conduct, and that she had sought to justify her position retrospectively.[49] Lady Byron perceived these comments as an attack on her parents, in that they seemed to lend support to a view Lord Byron had expressed, that Lady Byron had been improperly prevailed upon by her parents, without sufficient reason, to insist upon the separation. Lady Byron felt herself called upon to publish a defence, and she did so in the form of privately printed *Remarks on Mr Moore's Life of Lord Byron*, which Moore subsequently (with Lady Byron's reluctant concurrence)[50] published as an appendix to his book. Lady Byron included, in her *Remarks*, a letter from Lushington, written in 1830, in which he said that she had, at the interview in February 1816, revealed to him some facts 'utterly unknown, as I have no doubt, to' her parents, which had persuaded him that a reconciliation was impossible.[51] This publication caused enormous interest. 'And what think ye, sir, that a' this pollution could hae been that sae electrified Dr Lushington?' was the question asked in a contemporary journal,[52] and the same question has been asked by many others since. Some

---

[47] Lady Byron to Lushington, 17 Feb. 1816, Lovelace Byron Papers, 88/19, Elwin, *Lord Byron's Wife*, 412.

[48] Thomas Moore (1779–1852); Irish poet; Lord Byron's friend, literary executor, biographer, and editor.

[49] T. Moore, *Letters and Journals of Lord Byron, with notices of his life* (London, 1830), 1832 edn, iii, 212–13.

[50] She wrote to Lushington on 16 Mar. 1830: 'On further consideration I cannot reconcile myself to the idea of the union with Moore. There is another reason against it besides the objection which I mentioned viz. the *highly improper* character of the book even in the opinion of men of the world. Surely it would be a sort of degradation to me to accompany voluntarily a publication of an immoral character.' Lovelace-Byron Papers, 88/174. Lushington replied, 'It is my opinion that you should accede to Mr Moore's proposition' (same date): Lovelace-Byron Papers, 88/176. See D. L. Moore, *The Late Lord Byron*, 322.

[51] The original letter is in the Lovelace-Byron Papers 88/159.

[52] *Blackwood's Magazine*, May 1830, 828.

attention is given to it here because Lady Byron's theat to reveal her allegation had a crucial effect on the negotiations.

A number of points diminish the evidentiary value of Lushington's letter of 1830. First, it was written at Lady Byron's express request 'for the record'. It is inevitable, therefore, that it will have been influenced to some extent by Lady Byron's principal purpose, namely, to minimize her parents' role in the separation. Lushington will have been reminded by her of the aspects of the matter that conform to her present purpose. Secondly, Lushington expressly said that he was speaking only from memory. There is no reason to doubt that Lushington's memory was as good as most persons', and, of course, Lady Byron's was not a case to be readily forgotten, but still, fourteen years after the event, a letter written in these circumstances is not so reliable as a contemporary record. Lushington can hardly have been sure in 1830 to what extent he had thought a reconciliation feasible during a short period of time in 1816, the precise length of which he said that he could not remember. And, even in 1816, Lushington cannot have known, of his own knowledge, that what Lady Byron told him had been previously unknown to her parents. Making allowances, however, for all these points, Lushington's letter establishes that it stuck in his mind, fourteen years after the event, that Lady Byron had made a very significant disclosure to him in February 1816, and of something that her mother had not revealed to him at the initial interview.

The correspondence, preserved at Oxford, between Lady Byron and Lushington's wife, shows that revisions were made, in 1830, to Lushington's letter, at Lady Byron's instance. On 12 February 1830, she wrote to Mrs Lushington, an old friend of hers:

Suggest if you please to Dr L whether the last sentence of his letter, which is unnecessary for the point I wish to establish, does not convey too forcibly the truth I wish to suppress. If the letter were to end with the words 'reconciliation impossible' the purport of it, as far as I can see, would be perfectly answered. The concluding sentence is indeed *my* justification, but not that of my parents.[53]

From this, it would seem that Lushington must have agreed to an alteration. The second-last sentence concludes with the words 'reconciliation impossible', but the concluding sentence, as published,

---

[53] Lady Byron to Sarah Lushington, 12 Feb. 1830, Lovelace-Byron Papers, 91/41.

does not refer to any 'truth' that Lady Byron could plausibly wish to suppress.

Lushington also referred to the February interview in a conversation of 1870 with H. A. Bathurst, a trustee of Lady Byron's marriage settlement.[54] He is reported to have said that 'the real cause of Lady Byron's separation, when it was ascertained that there was no adequate ground in the opinion of the medical men for supposing him insane, was his brutally indecent conduct and language to her – and compelling her to listen when he returned from his profligate revels at a late hour, to the most disgusting descriptions of his adulteries and indecencies with loose women, toying with more than one at the same time naked'.[55] The complaint of insulting language is confirmed by Lady Byron's contemporary accounts.[56]

Lushington's views of marriage were conservative, as is revealed by his later judgments in matrimonial cases. He would certainly have considered conduct of the sort described to be a very gross dereliction of the deference and respect due by a husband to his wife. But it is doubtful whether any words, however insulting, would constitute a legal ground for a divorce, unless they threatened physical harm.[57] Nor could events that had occurred in private be proved. The evidentiary aspect of the matter remained in Lushington's mind in 1870:

Dr L, speaking with much feeling and emotion, described Lord B's conduct as most foul and gross, but of this there could hardly have been any evidence; and I gathered that Lady B would have been most reluctant or positively unwilling to charge him with such offences if legal proceedings became necessary – she would naturally shrink from doing so . . . On my suggesting it, Dr L confirmed my belief that it would have been very difficult to get any legal evidence of Lord B's incest or conduct to Lady B. She could not have given evidence, and, in case of hostile proceedings and the graver charges failing for want of proof, the father would have had control over the infant daughter.[58]

The indication is that Lushington thought his client's case morally strong, but legally weak.

The terms of Lushington's letters to Lady Byron confirm a sense of strong moral sympathy. After a meeting between Lady Byron and

54 Lovelace-Byron Papers, 152/18.
55 Lovelace-Byron Papers, 374 (copy), in Fox, *The Byron Mystery*, 57 (last thirty-nine words omitted).
56 Lovelace-Byron Papers 131/89, Elwin, *Lord Byron's Wife*, 331.
57 See note 19, above.
58 Fox, *The Byron Mystery*, 57–8.

Lady Caroline Lamb,[59] who accused Lord Byron of incest and of homosexual offences, Lushington wrote, congratulating his client on her 'escape from all proximity to, or intercourse with, such contamination'.[60] After the separation was concluded, he wrote:

I shall consider it my duty without detailing the particulars of the past, to establish as far as I can to the world a complete justification of your conduct, & to prove that your resolution of finally separating was a measure dictated by imperious necessity.[61]

Perhaps in pursuance of the promise just recorded, he discussed the matter with Sir William Scott, the judge of the Consistory Court, before whom the case would have come, a discussion that illustrates the intimate atmosphere of Doctors' Commons:

Sir W Scott introduced the matter to me, when there was no other person present. I read him your explanatory letter & also entered more into detail with him than I should have thought myself justified in doing towards any other person, & I am quite sure that I entirely satisfied his mind as to the merits of the respective parties. He put one or two questions as to the nature of the charges, which showed he was not so much unacquainted with what had passed as he would have had me suppose. The questions I evaded as well as I could, for it would not have been right to have given a direct affirmation or negation. P.S. I am almost ashamed of my caution, but pray do not mention Sir W Scott's name.[62]

This shows a strong personal feeling, on Lushington's part, of the merits of Lady Byron's case, and an anxiety to ensure Scott's good opinion, both of Lady Byron, and perhaps also of his own conduct.

Other letters from Lushington to Lady Byron after the separation agreement was concluded, include advice, in very strong terms, that she should continue her policy of silence in respect of the precise details of her complaints. In response to Byron's publication of the poem 'Fare thee well', accusing her of heartless and callous conduct, she proposed to make a public statement, apparently intending to reveal the terms of a declaration that she had prepared for Hobhouse, in which she disavowed reliance on the charges of incest and sodomy,

[59] Caroline Ponsonby (1785–1828); married, in 1805, William Lamb, later second Viscount Melbourne, and Prime Minister; had amorous affair with Lord Byron, 1812–13.
[60] Lushington to Lady Byron, 27 Mar. 1816, Lovelace-Byron Papers, 88/94. Moore, *The Late Lord Byron*, 244n.
[61] Lushington to Lady Byron, 25 April 1816, Lovelace-Byron Papers, 88/110. Moore, *The Late Lord Byron*, 164.
[62] Lushington to Lady Byron, 20 April 1816, Lovelace-Byron Papers, 88/112.

and to make a different allegation.[63] Lushington firmly advised against this course of action, on two grounds. The first was that such a use of the declaration would look like devious conduct:

Until that declaration be given to Mr Hobhouse (which I think should not be done until he asks for it), the contents should not be made known by you, & if afterwards used, it should be with great caution. The impression that you gave a declaration which did *not* clear up Lord B's character & that you afterwards used it *against him* (for tho' circulated for your own protection only, such must be its operation to protect you,) ought I think to be avoided for perhaps such conduct might be distorted into a species of double dealing. Honestly I would rather you were deemed a Pharisee for the next three months (at least six weeks longer than is possible) than that there should be a shadow of ground for impeaching the candour of your conduct.[64]

The second ground of Lushington's advice was that revelation of her charge would be likely to do her more harm than good:

It is infinitely better to be deemed by some 'righteous over much' than for any to believe you could have endured without disgust and horror scenes even remotely connected with these iniquities which are so widely circulated, believed in their full extent by some, to a certain degree by a very large proportion. An indifference to right & wrong is a much more serious imputation than even an affected abhorrence of venial errors. – You must be satisfied if by a very few the less important deviation from the right line should for *a very short time* be imputed to you.[65]

In 1820 Lord Byron offered Lady Byron the opportunity of seeing his memoirs, which were said to contain a detailed account of the marriage. In drafting her reply (addressed to Augusta Leigh), she consulted Lushington and Colonel Doyle. In this case Doyle was the more cautious. Lushington's initial draft included the following passage, the portions in angle brackets being marked for proposed deletion by Doyle:

Indeed if his statement alone went forth I should lament it on account of Ada [Lord and Lady Byron's daughter], to whom such an event must be inevitably injurious; an effect which Lord B seems to have overlooked – but this would not & indeed could not be the termination. It would become a duty imperative

[63] See pp. 128–9, below. The letter itself is missing. See Elwin, *Lord Byron's Wife*, 529.
[64] Lushington to Lady Byron, 13 April 1816, Lovelace-Byron Papers, 88/105.
[65] Ibid. Parts of this letter are quoted in Elwin, *Lord Byron's Wife*, 464, and Moore, *The Late Lord Byron*, 164.

upon me for Ada's sake ⟨(for to her welfare the purity of her mother's character must always be important)⟩ to make a full & unreserved disclosure to the world of all those circumstances which would at one establish my own justification ⟨& involve Lord B & others in infamy⟩.[66]

Lushington's first inclination, therefore, had been to use what looks like rather a heavy-handed threat to restrain publication, and to make what seems to have been an incautious reference to a perceived attack on Lady Byron's 'purity'. In the end, a short letter was sent, declining the opportunity of inspection, and saying that Lady Byron would lament some of the consequences of publication. The memoirs were eventually burned, after Lord Byron's death, with the participation of Lady Byron's advisers.

From these events, it may be deduced that the revelation of the precise details of Lord Byron's conduct would not have been in Lady Byron's interest, any more than in Lord Byron's.[67] Publication would, it seems, have laid her open to the charge that she had 'endured without disgust & horror scenes' that suggested 'an indifference to right & wrong', and would have affected the 'purity' of her character. In a letter to Mrs Leigh during the separation negotiations, Lady Byron had explained her demand for the separation by saying: 'Now, independent of any advice whatever, I deem it my duty to God to act as I am acting.'[68] This again suggests that some conduct had occurred on account of which she would have had reason to feel ashamed if she had allowed it to continue.

To these considerations must be added the evidence of the reaction to the negotiations of Lord Byron and his friends and advisers. Lushington's tactics were to conceal the details of Lady Byron's case in order to put maximum pressure upon Lord Byron to agree to a separation out of court. There is no doubt that the tactic was effective, and that it was greatly assisted by the notoriety of Lord Byron, and the love of the public for scandalous rumour. Lady Byron wrote to her mother that 'the silence of my friends has been very *dis*advantageous to Lord B in regard to opinion – since worse than the true causes are supposed'.[69] Byron himself wrote plaintively to his solicitor that 'it

---

66 Lovelace-Byron Papers, 375 (copy). See Elwin, *Lord Byron's Family*, 198.

67 'It would be a death-blow to me to be obliged to come forward publicly', Lady Byron to Lady Noel, 22 Jan. 1816, Marchand, *Byron: A Biography*, 570.

68 Prothero, *Letters and Journals*, iii, 310–11 (14 Feb. 1816). See *Don Juan* i, 27, Marchand, *Byron: A Biography*, 578–9.

69 Lady Byron to Lady Noel, 4 Mar. 1816, Lovelace-Byron Papers, 30/32, Elwin, *Lord Byron's Wife*, 424.

seems a little unfair, – that the parties should furnish all the world
with their charges – except the person against whom they are
directed'.[70]

To Lady Byron, he wrote 'I have requested to know with what I am
charged. It is refused. Is this mercy or justice?'[71] The effect on Mrs
Leigh was dramatic:

I have been for some days bordering on a state of distraction. I expect to hear
every hour of the *Citation* as it is called. I & all B's friends had hoped things
were in train to be settled amicably – or at least *quietly* arranged. [She then
indicates a desire that Lord B would accede to Lady Byron's terms as to the
Noel property] But what is most horrible dear Mr H[odgson] is this – that it is
intimated from Ly B's side – & I and others even think she has confided it to
Mr Wilmot – that there will come out what must *destroy him* FOR EVER in this
world – even what will deprive him of all right to his child, & so blast *his*
character that neither sister nor *Wife* who has lived under the same roof with
him can ever be considered as they *have* been again! What this mysterious
charge can be is beyond the utmost stretch of my imagination to guess. He
vows HE knows not.[72]

Pressure on Byron was intensified by the threat that Augusta Leigh,
and Byron's other friends, would know of this charge if the case went
to court. Hobhouse's diary reveals Lord Byron's anxiety to conceal the
full truth. At first, Hobhouse records, Byron denied all wrongdoing,
and said that 'he could make no sort of guess at the cause of this
measure'.[73] Then, after Hobhouse taxed him with rumours of 'very
great tyranny – menaces, furies, neglects',[74] 'I got him to own much of
what I had been told'.[75] Then, after Lady Byron's interview in
London with Dr Lushington, Wilmot (Byron's cousin, but acting for
Lady Byron), to whom Augusta thought the secret had been revealed,
urged Hobhouse in very strong terms to keep the matter out of court:

he took me into another room & there in great agitation told me that I knew
nothing of the case & that Byron was mad & that something horrid would be
proved against him – he conjured me therefore to advise B not to go into court

[70] Lord Byron to J. Hanson, 12 Feb. 1816, Marchand, *Byron's Letters*, vol. 5, *So Late
into the Night*, 26.
[71] Lord Byron to Lady Byron, 15 Feb. 1816, Marchand, *Byron's Letters*, vol. 5, *So
Late into the Night*, 27.
[72] Elwin, *Lord Byron's Wife*, 439.
[73] Hobhouse *Diary*, 5 Feb. See also further quotations in Burnett, *Regency Dandy*,
104.
[74] Hobhouse *Diary*, 12 Feb. 1816, quoted by Marchand, *Byron: A Biography*, 576, and
by Burnett, *Regency Dandy*, 104.
[75] Hobhouse *Diary*, 12 Feb. 1816, quoted in Burnett, *Regency Dandy*, 104.

and said 'if the matter should come out and you should find I have misrepresented it, I will give you leave to pull my nose'.[76]

Evidently, Hobhouse and Davies (another close friend) taxed Byron with this mysterious charge, urging him to reveal what it was since it appeared that it was soon to be made public in any event.

It appears that as court is inevitable B said to S.B.D. [Scrope Berdmore Davies] and me at last that he may have been *bereav'd of reason* during his paroxysm with his wife – it appears to me he has made some confession. I am still however in the dark utterly.[77]

From this it is clear that Byron admitted that he knew, or suspected, what the charge was. The fact that he would not reveal it to his closest friends (with whom he was not accustomed to be prudish) and that he ascribed it to loss of reason during a 'paroxysm', suggests something quite startling to the orthodox opinion of the time. Hobhouse recorded in his diary for the next day that 'he owns himself to have been deranged soon after marriage but whether this is an excuse or not for what is to come out is doubtful'.[78]

Hobhouse described the very unusual manner in which Lord Byron took legal advice from his civilian advisers:

Went with Byron to Doctors Commons met there with Hanson – Farquhar the proctor – Dr Jenner – Dr Adams – Sir I[79] Robinson. B stated his case first – he then retired and I stated all the bad points told me by Mrs Leigh & Capt Byron – on hearing them the three Doctors were unanimous not to cite, but said they thought Ld B had a good *defendant's* case. B then appeared happy at the decision.[80]

This entry is for 5 March, three days before Wilmot's warning mentioned above. Evidently the effect of asking Hobhouse to state the case against him was that Lord Byron's advisers gave their opinion in ignorance of the particular charge to which Wilmot referred, and Byron avoided the necessity of answering his lawyers' questions.

Putting together this evidence, with the evidence of Lady Byron's attitude, and Lushington's advice, it may be deduced that her

[76] Hobhouse *Diary*, 8 Mar., Elwin, *Lord Byron's Wife*, 430.
[77] Hobhouse *Diary*, 12 Mar., quoted by Burnett, *Regency Dandy*, 116, and, with minor variations from the Lovelace transcription, by Elwin, *Lord Byron's Wife*, 437.
[78] Hobhouse *Diary*, 13 Mar. 1816.
[79] Robinson's initial was C.
[80] Hobhouse *Diary*, 5 Mar. 1816.

allegation was of some highly unconventional behaviour, of a sexual nature, that had occurred in private.[81] From a strictly legal point of view it was probably insignificant: it did not constitute legal cruelty; it was condoned; and in any event, there was no legally admissible proof of it. But, as is not uncommon, legal negotiations were dominated by a non-legal issue. Both parties were anxious to keep the secret, but, in the end, Lord Byron was the more anxious. Lady Byron's negotiating power depended on her threat of disclosure, and her success was due to her ability to make that threat credible.

Nothing said here establishes that the conduct in question was the 'real cause' of the separation – a matter on which enough, perhaps, has already been written; but it does suggest that it was a substantial cause of the separation agreement.

Lady Byron was greatly concerned about the two affectionate letters that she had written to Lord Byron immediately after leaving London.' The second of these was as follows:

Dearest Duck, We got here quite well last night, and were ushered into the kitchen instead of the drawing room, by a mistake that might have been agreeable enough to hungry people. Of this and other incidents Dad wants to write you a jocose account, & both he and Mam long to have the family party completed. Such a W.C.! and such a *sitting* room or *sulking*-room all to yourself. If I were not always looking about for B, I should be a great deal better already for country air. *Miss* finds her provisions increased, & fattens thereon. It is a good thing she can't understand all the flattery bestowed upon her, 'little angel'. Love to the good goose,[82] and every body's love to you both from hence. Ever thy most loving Pippin . . . Pip——ip.[83]

She was aware that her case, morally and legally, was seriously weakened by the existence of this letter, since it tended to show that she perceived no very serious cause for complaint when she left. Her explanation was that the letter was sent in accordance with medical

[81] Marchand, *Byron: A Biography*, 586n, mentions a persistent rumour of an irregular sexual relationship between Lord and Lady Byron, and G. W. Knight, in *Lord Byron's Marriage*, argues, partly on literary evidence, for a particular irregularity (sodomy), a theory rejected by Marchand in *Byron: A Portrait*. The evidence available to me does not support so specific a conclusion. Against Knight's theory must be set the facts that Lady Byron did not at first perceive the conduct as making cohabitation impossible (in January she expected to resume sexual relations; see Prothero, *Letters and Journals*, 295, 296), and that she was ready to disavow a charge of 'unnatural crime'; see below, note 131. An irregularity of a different sort therefore seems more probable.
[82] i.e., Augusta Leigh.
[83] Lady Byron to Lord Byron, 16 Jan. 1816, Elwin, *Lord Byron's Wife*, 351.

advice and out of consideration for Lord Byron, on the assumption that he was insane.[84] But this was hardly consistent with the tone of the letter,[85] as she realized herself. 'I must have been mad to write so' she wrote to a friend a few days later.[86] She wrote to Lushington that she had written to her husband 'affectionately and cheerfully' not, at this point, telling him the precise terms of the letter ('I have not a copy'). She added:

Can this measure, dictated by humane & medical considerations, which I have already explained & can fully prove, impede the legal separation?[87]

Lushington's reply was this:

With respect to the letters you addressed to Lord B. after your departure from London, which contained kind & affectionate sentiments, it would certainly have been desirable that no such letters should have been written, because the production of such letters unexplained would naturally lead to an inference, that the mind which dictated kind expressions, could not be suffering from a succession of unmerited injuries. But I do not conceive that circumstance could deprive you of your right to legal redress – it could only produce an effect until the explanation was given & as you have the power of proving the motives which actuated the writing in such terms, that they did not arise from a light consideration, or oblivion of your past illtreatment but from a humane & laudable anxiety not to aggravate the personal maladies of Lord B., I trust, that if he should venture to ground his defence on such a basis, the explanation would not only overthrow it, but place your character as undoubtedly it deserves, in a still more favourable light.[88]

References to Lady Byron's good character appear more frequently than one might expect, and suggest that Lushington was not among Lord Byron's admirers. He described Lord Byron's suggestion that his financial embarrassments had caused the separation as 'repugnant to all my notions of truth, justice & liberal feeling'.[89] He himself felt

---

[84] Lady Byron said, in her *Remarks*, Moore, *Life of Byron*, vi, 277 (appendix), that the medical advice was to 'avoid all but light and soothing topics ... On the day of my departure, and again on my arrival at Kirkby, Jan 16th, I wrote to Lord Byron in a kind and cheerful tone, according to those medical directions.'

[85] Letters written to Mrs Leigh on the same day establish that her state of mind certainly was that she expected Lord Byron to join her at Kirkby, and to resume sexual relations. See note 81, above.

[86] Lady Byron to Mrs Clermont, 21 Jan. 1816, Moore, *The Late Lord Byron*, 310n.

[87] Lady Byron to Lushington, 8 Feb. 1816, Lovelace-Byron Papers, 88/12.

[88] Lushington to Lady Byron, 10 Feb. 1816, Lovelace-Byron Papers, 88/70. Elwin, *Lord Byron's Wife*, 405.

[89] Lushington to Lady Byron, 9 Feb. 1816, Lovelace-Byron Papers, 88/68. Elwin, *Lord Byron's Wife*, 405.

that he had gone beyond what was usual in a professional relationship, for he wrote:

> I have now only to add, that in the progress of this transaction I have unavoidably been led beyond the line of my professional duty. I have had occasion to advise in matters of prudence & feeling as well as with reference to legal proceedings. If in any observations I may have addressed to your Ladyship I have declared my sentiments too plainly or too strongly I hope you will attribute it to the real motive, a sincere wish of making myself as useful as my abilities permit.[90]

Ann Fletcher, Lady Byron's maid (and the wife of Lord Byron's valet) underwent a preliminary examination by Lord Byron's solicitor, and the questions asked of her (as recounted to Lushington by Lady Byron) give warning of the potential strength of Lord Byron's defence, and the likely significance of the letter that Lady Byron had written on 16 January:

> [She was asked] if she had seen Lord Byron use violence towards me? What was my state of spririts when I left London – on the road – and at Kirkby?[91]

On 25 April, when the separation documents had been finally signed, Lushington wrote to Lady Byron that 'the only act which requires explanation is the letter of the 16th'. It may be assumed that by this time he had seen the precise terms of the letter, and his words suggest that not all could be expected to be satisfied with Lady Byron's explanation, though he adds that the 'letter of which you have inclosed me a copy will be very beneficially used for that purpose'.[92] This must have been the letter written on 15 January to her friend Selina Doyle,[93] in which she indicated that she really did think that Lord Byron was insane, and that she was contemplating a permanent separation. Lushington later received a copy of the letter from Miss Doyle, and wrote to Lady Byron:

> The date renders it still more valuable authenticating it as entirely your own, before any 'cold caution'[94] of mine could have suggested it for other purposes.[95]

[90] Lushington to Lady Byron, 9 Feb. 1816, Lovelace-Byron Papers, 88/69.
[91] Lady Byron to Lushington, 29 Feb. 1816, Lovelace-Byron Papers 88/32. Prothero, *Letters and Journals*, 320–1, gives the full statement, from which it is clear that Lord Byron would have had a substantial defence.
[92] Lushington to Lady Byron, 25 April 1816, Lovelace-Byron Papers, 88/110.
[93] Lady Byron to Selina Doyle (copy), 15 Jan. 1816, Lovelace-Byron Papers 30/85, Elwin, *Lord Byron's Wife*, 351–2.
[94] The reference is to a letter from J. Perry, editor of the *Morning Chronicle*, to Sir R. Noel, 18 April 1816, Elwin, *Lord Byron's Wife*, 467: 'To this [the question why the

Nevertheless, the letter of 16 January has always been a principal weapon in the armoury of Lady Byron's critics, as, for instance, in Moore's biography in 1830.

Possibly Lady Byron needed no advice against writing any further such letters. However, Lushington told her expressly to be cautious, and explained the reason:

I have received a communication from Sir Ralph, that Lord B wrote to you himself on Saturday – I cannot refrain from writing this line to say that if that letter requires an answer & is not already answered, your ladyship must be particularly cautious in the reply . . . It is right that I should impress upon your mind that no reply should be sent which does not express a deep sense of the injuries you have received, or rather no reply from which it would be possible to infer that you do not feel deeply aggrieved.[96]

Those writing about Lord Byron have often sympathized, more or less explicitly, with his eloquent pleas to Lady Byron for a response to his letters. It may seem calculating and cold-hearted to make no response to his finely written letters. It is clear, however, that any sort of affectionate response would have been very damaging to her legal position. Lushington would hardly have been doing his duty if he had not warned her of the legal consequences.

Lady Byron feared that Lushington might himself be moved by the eloquence of Lord Byron's letters. In enclosing a letter she had received from Lord Byron[97] she wrote that 'Lord B particularly piques himself on a talent for equivocation which renders it impossible to discover the *real sense* of his words'.[98] Of a later letter[99] she wrote:

The enclosed copy of Lord B's letter will I think remove your surprise that I should have been greatly agitated by perusing it. It is the most forcible appeal to any tender recollection – and was perhaps written in that state of self delusion to which he has an extraordinary power of working up his

charges were not revealed] you answered that Lady Byron acted in this by the advice of Dr Lushington. What! A wife tears herself from the bosom of her husband and acts by the cold caution of a lawyer rather than by the dictates of her own heart!'
95 Lushington to Lady Byron, 1 May 1816, Lovelace-Byron Papers, 88/114.
96 Lushington to Lady Byron, 5 Feb. 1816, Lovelace-Byron Papers, 88/61.
97 The letter of 3 Feb. 1816, Marchand, *Byron's Letters*, vol. 5, *So Late into the Night*, 21.
98 Lady Byron to Dr Lushington, PS dated 5 Feb. to letter dated 4 Feb., Lovelace-Byron Papers, 88/6, Elwin, *Lord Byron's Wife*, 394.
99 Presumably that of 8 Feb., Marchand, *Byron's Letters*, vol. 5, *So Late into the Night*, 24.

imagination. In *this* letter I do not observe any *art* – but strong passion, principally, I conceive, *wounded pride* . . . I am too well acquainted with the sudden & dreadful transitions of his mind from Tenderness to Revenge, not to apprehend the *most fatal*, if I were in his power – though without supposing a *predetermination* The revolution takes place the moment its object is *in his power* – as I found within an hour after I was married.[100]

In addition to warning her about corresponding with her husband, Lushington advised her very strongly to refuse his requests for an interview. Lady Noel wrote to Lady Byron, after her interview with Lushington that Lushington '*insists* on Lord B not being allowed to remain *an instant* at Kirkby should he go there – and he says YOU must not see him on ANY ACCOUNT – and that your father should remain in the room *with you*.'[101] For similar reasons, Lushington sought to dissuade her from coming to London in February:

There is one objection which has made a very forcible impression upon us all; the risque of Lord B insisting upon a personal interview . . . We all think that no interview should take place upon any pretence, under any circumstances whether singly with Lord B. or in the presence of others.[102]

It may seem harsh that Lord Byron's pleas should be thus rejected, but it is essential to bear in mind the very precarious legal position of a wife in Lady Byron's circumstances: a personal interview was bound to be dangerous, legally (for it might supply grounds for alleging that Lady Byron did not feel compelled to leave him or had condoned his previous conduct), and physically (in view of Lord Byron's mood, and former violent behaviour).

On the matter of custody of the child, Dr Lushington was firm in advising Lady Byron to retain physical custody, saying to her that 'it is legally advisable and perfectly right that you should keep possession of the child'.[103] Lady Noel took precautions against an attempt to take the child by force, and wrote to her daughter, who was then in

---

[100] Lady Byron to Lushington, 11 Feb. 1816, Lovelace-Byron Papers, 88–114. Elwin, *Lord Byron's Wife*, 406.

[101] Lady Noel to Lady Byron, 24 Jan. 1816, Lovelace-Byron Papers, 36/13, Elwin, *Lord Byron's Wife*, 376. Upper case denotes multiple underlining.

[102] Lushington to Lady Byron, 18 Feb. 1816, Lovelace-Byron Papers, 88, Elwin, *Lord Byron's Wife*, 412.

[103] Lushington to Lady Byron, 8 Feb. 1816, Lovelace-Byron Papers, 88/66. Selina Doyle also reported an optimistic opinion: '[Dr] L. thinks under the existing circumstances that no judge would sentence you to give it up; though had you been the person to claim it, the same judge might not have thought it right to infringe the law by taking it from the father.' Selina Doyle to Lady Byron, 26 Jan. 1816, Fox, *The Byron Mystery*, 108.

London, that she had bought a pair of pistols.[104] A woman who had lived in the village recalled, years later, the local excitement that had been caused by the arrangements made for men to guard the child.[105] Lord Byron was hardly in a position, at the time, to provide a home for the child himself, but Lady Byron's fear was that he would arrange for his half-sister, Augusta Leigh, to look after the child.[106] Lady Byron's and Lushington's attitude to the charges against Augusta Leigh of incest must be understood in the light of a possible custody dispute.

Lushington's initial view of the custody question was, as reported by Lady Noel, favourable:

He is also of the opinion that you will not be interrupted in retaining the child – and is happy you have now possession of it. Ld B may move for a writ that the Child should be brought into court, but he does *not* think that in this case it would be granted, at all events the Lord Chief Justice of the King's Bench would *not decree*, without hearing the situations of the respective parties – which in this case would be highly advantageous to the Mother – as his habits of life & acknowledged *partial* derangement at least, would be proved even by *his* nearest Connections, also the extreme indecency of his language, before even Georgina – which obliges her mother to keep her out of the room.[107]

Lushington did not practise in the King's Bench, where writs of habeas corpus were issued, and was not an expert in the common law. It seems that his opinion may have been too optimistic. A less favourable opinion was later given by Brougham (the later Lord Chancellor):

Mr Brougham . . . considers that if Lord B were to apply for a habeas corpus to bring up the body of his child, and if upon the return to the writ the tender age of the child were set forth, the father could only obtain possession of it by offering to take back the mother – but if that offer were made, Mr B apprehends, that Lady B could not retain possession of the child from the father.[108]

On the other hand, again, Lady Byron received a favourable opinion from Sir Samuel Romilly,[109] a Chancery barrister:

104 Elwin, *Lord Byron's Family*, 21.
105 Moore, *Ada, Countess of Lovelace*, 7 (letter of 18 April 1859).
106 Lady Byron to Lushington, 9 Mar. 1816, Lovelace-Byron Papers, 88/43, Elwin, *Lord Byron's Family*, 21.
107 Elwin, *Lord Byron's Wife*, 376.
108 Elwin, *Lord Byron's Family*, 22–3.
109 Samuel Romilly (1757–1818); MP, 1806–18; criminal law reformer.

If the child were made a ward of the Court of Chancery I have no doubt that the Lord Chancellor would not suffer her to be removed from you. Neither at present, nor I think at any future time.[110]

Reliable legal advice, it will be seen, was not very readily available. Three courts were involved, and three separate branches of the legal profession. Only the Court of Chancery could actually remove the father's rights, and, as earlier explained,[111] there was support for the view that if the child were made a ward of the Court of Chancery, the common-law courts would not grant a writ of habeas corpus, but would defer to the jurisdiction of Chancery, where paternal rights were considered less sacred. At that time, a child could be made a ward in Chancery by vesting property in it and requiring the court to administer it. This procedure is described in the following letter from Mrs Clermont (Lady Byron's confidante[112]) to Lady Noel:

Dr Lushington advised that the Child should be made a Ward of Chancery & Lady B saw Sir S Romilly last night about it he is of the same opinion and this it seems can be done by giving it any little property Sir S said she had only to let her fathers Solicitor draw up the common deed for that purpose which he would know how to do Wharton comes tomorrow about it Dr Lushington named two hundred Pounds as being sufficient but Wharton they say will know how to do it but you must observe this transaction is desired to be kept a *profound secret* as it might have an ill effect if *he* knew it and is only a precaution to keep it out of the court of King's Bench which is more determined as to paternal right than Chancery.[113]

Lady Byron wrote to Lushington suggesting that Lord Byron should be asked to make a formal renunciation of paternal rights.[114] Lushington advised against putting this question on the bargaining table:

I doubt very much whether it would be advisable to bring forward this subject at all, until the articles are actually signed . . . The other reasons stated in your note are also exceedingly strong & render the object most desirable. But is it to be obtained? By what motive can Lord B's mind be influenced to the adoption

[110] Fox, *The Byron Mystery*, 147. He adds (149) that a bill was filed on 8 Mar. 1816, naming Ada as plaintiff, and Kinnaird and others and Lord Byron as defendants, and praying to have the trusts of Lady Byron's marriage settlement executed by the court.
[111] See pp. 105–6, above.
[112] Upon whom Lord Byron wrote a vicious satire, entitled *A Sketch*.
[113] Elwin, *Lord Byron's Family*, 21. In a letter to Lushington on 29 Feb. 1816, Lady Byron said that she had seen Sir Samuel Romilly about making Ada a ward of the court, Lovelace-Byron Papers, 88.
[114] Lady Byron to Lushington, 29 Mar. 1816, Lovelace-Byron Papers, 88/55.

of such a measure, to the concession of all power over you? By no motive, I apprehend, but fear, & how that can be brought to operate appears to me very difficult to form an opinion.[115]

He thought that Lord Byron was unlikely to agree to renounce his rights, and that, if Lady Byron remained in possession of the child, her position, while not quite so secure as it would be if protected by an express renunciation, would be reasonably secure.[116] The risk of insisting on a renunciation would be that the whole agreement would be jeopardized. Byron did not hear of the wardship proceedings until a year later.[117] He wrote a furious letter to his solicitor, instructing him to oppose the application.[118] He repeated his determination in letters to Augusta Leigh.[119] The elaborate legal precautions taken show the care and expense that was devoted to Lady Byron's case. Lord Byron's attitude a year later shows that the fears of Lady Byron's advisers were not wholly fanciful.

For some time after leaving London in January, Lady Byron kept up a friendly – indeed an intimate – correspondence with Augusta Leigh.[120] One of the most persistent theories about the cause of the separation has been that it was due to incest between Lord Byron and Mrs Leigh, and rumours to this effect were circulating in London in February.[121] It is now clear that incest had occurred at a period before Lord Byron's marriage'[122] though it has not been shown that it occurred during the marriage. Premarital incest, it will be recalled, would be no ground for divorce. It is also clear that the suspicion of incest was not Lady Byron's primary reason for desiring a separation.

115 Lushington to Lady Byron, 31 Mar. 1816, Lovelace-Byron Papers, 88/99. Elwin, *Lord Byron's Wife*, 458–9.

116 'In regard to the child, it appears to my advisers most advantageous that it should not be made a subject of discussion at present, or in any way suggested to him as such, because it is highly improbable that he would resign the power *in a formal manner*; and, by not making any particular provision for it, if he goes abroad, he will virtually, to a certain extent, acknowledge my guardianship. To let him know these reasons would be to defeat them.' Lady Byron to Mrs George Lamb, 1 April 1816, Prothero, *Letters and Journals*, 327.

117 Lord Byron to Lady Byron, 5 Mar. 1817, Marchand, *Byron's Letters*, vol. 5, *So Late into the Night*, 180.

118 Lord Byron to Lady Byron, 25 Mar. 1817, Marchand, *Byron's Letters*, vol. 5, *So Late into the Night*, 189.

119 Id., 190, 223–4. But in May, he wrote: 'I am aware they have made her a Chancery ward', Lord Byron to Augusta Leigh, 11 May 1817, Marchand, *Byron's Letters*, vol. 5, *So Late into the Night*, 224.

120 Prothero, *Letters and Journals*, 293–300.

121 See Elwin, *Lord Byron's Wife*, 426.

122 Marchand, *Byron: A Biography*, 583.

She wrote to her mother, of Augusta Leigh, on 24 January that 'she
has been the truest of friends to me and I hope you regard her, & *seem*
to regard her as such, for I very much fear that she may be supposed
the cause of the separation by many, & it would be a cruel injustice'.[123]
She saw Mrs Leigh on 5 March, and wrote to Lushington asking for
his approval of a plan whereby she would disavow the charge of incest
in return for a promise by Mrs Leigh not to accept custody of the
child, saying 'my situation in relation to Mrs Leigh becomes every day
more distressing, and cannot remain without change'.[124] But Lushington did not approve this idea:

I have just received your letter respecting Mrs Leigh, but cannot acquiesce in
your expedient at present ... I am fully aware of the very disagreeable
predicament in which you are placed ... but I do think that it would be
extremely improper to renew any intercourse with Mrs L. until the separation
is put past all doubt, & not even then until means have been taken to obviate
any injurious effects in the future. I have thought of a plan for that purpose
more safe than what we before discussed & will mention it tomorrow evening.
In the meantime I can only repeat my opinion that an interview with Mrs L
should be avoided & if you think that avowing that you do so under my advice
will save you any disagreeable solicitation, pray use my name to that effect. It
would not be right for any one to press you for reasons when you have so done,
but if further urged you may add that until the separation be finally concluded, I have advised you to have no intercourse *with any one* living under
Lord B's roof.[125]

The device that Lushington approved was that Lady Byron would
state that incest was not one of the grounds on which she was seeking a
divorce, but at the same time she would sign a declaration, carefully
dated and witnessed, in which she would record her suspicion of
incest, so that, in case of a custody dispute, she would not be pre-
cluded from proving that Lord Byron and Mrs Leigh were unfit
persons to have custody. This declaration was written in Dr Lushington's handwriting, including erasures and substitutions, presumably

---

[123] Lady Byron to Lady Noel, 24 Jan. 1816, Lovelace-Byron Papers 30/9. Also to
Lushington: 'Mrs L[eigh] seemed to think me quite mistaken & rather misguided –
said that there must be something more than she knew, or I would not object to
return. – I then revealed to her the *whole* tenor of Lord B's conduct, to which she
would say nothing but the old excuse of insanity.' Lady Byron to Lushington, n.d.,
Lovelace-Byron Papers, 88.
[124] Lady Byron to Lushington, 10 Mar. 1816, Lovelace-Byron Papers, 88/44. Elwin,
Lord Byron's Wife, 433–4.
[125] Lushington to Lady Byron, 10 Mar. 1816, Lovelace-Byron Papers, 88/86, Elwin,
Lord Byron's Wife, 434.

for the sake of confidentiality.[126] It explains that Lady Byron had
suspicions of incest that had at one time 'and might even still subsist',
but that as she had no proof, and thought it possible that the 'crime . . .
might never have been perpetrated since her marriage with Lord B',
she had not made the charge a part of her case. The document was
signed by Wilmot, Doyle, and Lushington, and concluded with an
expression of their opinion that 'the line now adopted by Lady B is
strictly right and honorable, as well as just towards Mrs L, and Lady B
ought not whatever may hereafter occur, be prejudiced thereby'.
Lady Byron wrote, in her own hand, 'the reasons above stated are the
genuine reasons which actuated my conduct'. This statement was
dated, and Lady Byron's signature initialled by Wilmot,[127] Doyle,
and Lushington. The device of drawing up this declaration shows that
Lady Byron and her advisers were by no means oblivious to the
damage that was done by rumour to Mrs Leigh's reputation, and that
they went to some lengths to repair her reputation, so far as they could
do so without damaging Lady Byron's legal position. A disavowal,
dated 9 March, was prepared for Hobhouse, signed and witnessed,[128]
and approved by him (though not delivered[129]) in which Lady Byron
'disavowed for herself and those most nearly connected with her
having spread any rumours injurious to Lord B's character',[130] adding
'And [she declares] that the two reports specifically mentioned by Mr
Wilmot do not form any part of the charges which, in the event of a
Separation by agreement not taking place, she should have been
compelled to make against Lord B'.[131]

126 Lovelace-Byron Papers, 129/76–9, Ralph, Earl of Lovelace, *Astarte: a fragment of truth concerning Lord Byron* (London, 1905), appendix.
127 Lord Byron's cousin, but an adviser of Lady Byron.
128 '[Wilmot] said to me should you consider such a document satisfactory if signed by Lady B and witnessed by me. I said I should – he then said it is signed by Lady B & witnessed by me – which he showed me to be the case.' Hobhouse *Diary*, 9 Mar.
129 'W read over the disavowal paper in my presence and then put it into his pocket to keep it until the affair should be concluded', Hobhouse *Diary*, 9 Mar., quoted in Burnett, *Regency Dandy*, 110–11. See also Dr Lushington's letter to Lady Byron of 13 April quoted at p. 116, above, and Fox, *The Byron Mystery*, 112, describing the original document in the Lovelace papers. The reason for non-delivery is given by Lord Byron in a letter to Wilmot, 11 Mar. 1816, Marchand, *Byron's Letters*, vol. 5, *So Late into the Night*, 48: he had promised not to use the disavowal in the event of a trial, and the case might still have gone to court.
130 Hobhouse *Diary*, 9 Mar., Lovelace-Byron Papers, 375 (copy). See Fox, *The Byron Mystery*, 112, for the terms of the original document.
131 Lovelace-Byron Papers 375 (copy), quoted in Fox, *The Byron Mystery*, 112. One of the charges specifically mentioned was incest: the other was sodomy. See notes 42 and 43, above. A paper, in Lady Byron's hand, undated, reads: 'A complete &

Lushington devoted considerable energy to the property questions. He told his client, very bluntly, that she could not expect too much. In response to a letter in which she had spoken of an 'equitable' division, Lushington replied:

I am afraid that is not the question at issue. The point is, how much it is prudent to sacrifice for certain peace & security – I will make up my mind on this as far as so difficult a consideration will allow.[132]

The marriage settlement was complicated, but the substance of the negotiation was based on the following figures. Lady Byron's fortune (that she had brought into the marriage) was £1,000 per annum. Her 'pin money' (i.e. money allotted to her for private use) was £300 per annum. Dr Lushington's proposal was this:

Lady Byron will be satisfied with L200 per an. in addition to her pin money, during the life of Lady Noel, and at her decease one half of the Noel property.[133]

The Noel property was property worth £6,500 per annum, that Lady Byron would inherit (and the income from which would therefore be Lord Byron's) on the death of Lady Noel. Lushington explained the net effect of his proposal, in submitting it for Lord Byron's perusal, in such a way as to make it sound attractive to him:

Under this arrangement Lord B will claim immediately a pecuniary profit of L500 per an. in consequence of his marriage with Lady B, and be relieved of all expense of maintaining her. At the death of Lady Noel he will be benefited to the amount of from L3,500 to L4,000 per an.[134]

The £500 is the difference between Lady Byron's fortune (£1,000) and the sum of the pin money and the £200 figure proposed. Lord Byron had initially proposed that Lady Byron should retain the full

unqualified disclaimer of the four following reports: 1. Unnatural crime; 2. Incest with Mrs L; 3. Personal violence of all & any sort of description; 4. Infidelities with any person in his house, or introduction of any person with whom he was suspected of infidelity.' Lovelace-Byron Papers, 129/69.

132 Lushington to Lady Byron, 28 Feb. 1816, Lovelace-Byron Papers, 88/78. She had written to him on 15 Feb. 'I have thought of Terms, as you desired, and should feel so very happy to be secured from molestation with the child, that I scarcely think of any other advantages ... I shall certainly resign my jointure altogether'. Fox, *The Byron Mystery*, 110. Jointure was property settled on a wife for her use after her husband's death, in lieu of dower. See Roper, *Husband and Wife*, i, 460ff.

133 Lushington to Lord Holland, 3 Mar. 1816, Prothero, *Letters and Journals*, 319. A memorandum of an agreement to this effect, signed by Hanson, on Lord Byron's behalf, dated 30 Mar. 1816, is in Lovelace-Byron Papers, 90/52.

134 Ibid.

£1,000 of her own fortune,[135] so Lushington was apparently giving something away in offering to be satisfied with £500. The offer was, no doubt, designed to tempt Lord Byron, whose need for ready cash was notorious, into accepting the principal terms of the separation, which were vital to Lady Byron, and in exchange for which she had to give up property that she might otherwise have claimed.[136] This is confirmed by Lady Byron's account, to her mother, of the same proposal, which shows that she considered that the proposal gave away a great deal, and also the reason for her assent to it, that is, her gloomy assessment of the legal position:

All offers of amicable arrangement have been refused – and perhaps when you know the terms, *you* may not be sorry. Half the Noel property was offered – and only L200 per ann. asked at present. It is a bad job – for I shall lose the cause – and can only obtain present security whilst the suit lasts.[137]

Lord Byron would not agree to give up half of the Noel property, but was willing to promise to make a fair provision to Lady Byron out of the property. Lady Byron was willing to agree to having this question determined by arbitration, provided Lord Byron bound himself immediately to such an arbitration, to take place at Lady Noel's death. But negotiations stuck on this point,[138] Lord Byron expressing simply a willingness to 'do what should be deemed fair & liberal by Lady B – in the event of the Noel property falling in'.[139]

[135] This is recited in the arbitration reference to Sir S. Shepherd, Lovelace-Byron Papers, 132/92, Prothero, *Letters and Journals*, 323.

[136] Lord Byron had written to Lady Byron that he would ultimately abide by her wishes, if she really desired a separation (letters of 3 and 5 Feb., Marchand, *Byron's Letters*, vol. 5, *So Late into the Night*, 21, 22), but he evidently did not feel bound by this later (see letters of 1 Mar. to Lady Byron 'I am prepared to meet your legal advisers and to try what force there is in the decrees of Venice' and 2 Mar. to Lord Holland 'I will now not only sign no separation – but agree to none – not even to verbal permission for Lady B's absence', id. 39), though Hobhouse thought that 'Lady B had a right to demand performance of this promise', *Diary*, 6 Mar. Dr Lushington, therefore, had good reason not to rely on the statements in the earlier letters, which, in any case, would not be legally binding.

[137] Lady Byron to Lady Noel, 4 Mar. 1816, Lovelace-Byron Papers, 30/32. Elwin, *Lord Byron's Wife*, 424. The last sentence refers to the requirement that a husband pay his wife's alimony and costs pending litigation.

[138] 'Hanson & Lushington had met on Sunday night & broke off at once on the article of the Kirkby property', Hobhouse *Diary*, 11 Mar.

[139] Lord Byron to Wilmot, Marchand, *Byron's Letters*, vol. 5, *So Late into the Night*, 48. Hobhouse thought that Lord Byron had assented to the settlement, and was in honour bound to accede to it. He records (*Diary*, 11 Mar.), that he received a stiff letter from Wilmot, and thought himeslf 'responsible either to persuade Lord B to comply or to give Mr W satisfaction if I could not persuade him'. A duel was,

This was probably considered too vague by Lady Byron's advisers, and an insufficient protection for her interests against Lord Byron's creditors, and the point was eventually submitted for arbitration to the Solicitor-General, Sir Samuel Shepherd, who decided it in favour of Lady Byron.[140] Use of arbitration to fix the terms of the settlement agreement, an unusual procedure, here offered an escape from the impasse (Lord Byron was willing to do what should be fair, but not to go back on his declared resolution about the Noel property).

The references to Lushington in Lord Byron's letters are, as one would expect, uncomplimentary,[141] though there is nothing comparable to the vituperation reserved for Sir Samuel Romilly,[142] who had acted for Lady Byron after overlooking an earlier retainer for Lord Byron. After Lady Noel's death, when a dispute over the Noel property was looming, Lord Byron wrote, in a letter to his solicitor:

You may show this letter to Mr Kinnaird or Dr Lushington: I will stand by what I say as to *Lushington's* and the Noel people's conduct [that he did not expect fair dealing from them], and give him satisfaction with the greatest pleasure, though I suspect that *his* weapons are only *libels in* and out of Doctors' Commons.[143]

Since Lord Byron was very proud of his ability with his pistols,[144] it is as well that this plan was not implemented, for it would have had the probable effect of cutting short Lushington's career by some fifty years.

Hobhouse, on the other hand, Byron's closest friend and adviser,

however, avoided. See Burnett, *Regency Dandy*, 113. A draft bill in Chancery was prepared to enforce the oral agreement: Lovelace-Byron Papers 151/5 (dated April 1816).

140 Lovelace-Byron Papers, 132/108, Prothero, *Letters and Journals*, 325. Hobhouse wrote: 'I never thought Sir S Sheppard's opinion could be otherwise', *Diary*, 28 Mar. 1816.

141 See Marchand, *Byron's Letters*, where references in the index (vol. 12) reveal that he was, at several times, vilified, usually as a specimen of a low profession generally.

142 See letters of 18 Nov. 1818 (to Lady Byron) and 24 Nov. 1818 (to Murray), Marchand, *Byron's Letters*, vol. 6, *The Flesh is Frail*, 80, 84.

143 Lord Byron to Hanson, 20 June 1822, Marchand, *Byron's Letters*, vol. 9, *In the Wind's Eye*, 177. An article in *Temple Bar* 1869, 364 [by John Fox] stated that Lushington accompanied Dr Baillie to visit Lord Byron to discover proofs of insanity, but Dr Lushington specifically denied this in the statement to Bathurst, and said that he had never met Lord Byron after the breach. Fox, *The Byron Mystery*, 58.

144 See Moore, *Life of Byron*, iii, 280: 'I can snuff out that candle with a pistol shot at twenty paces.' Also, Marchand, *Byron's Letters*, vol. 8, *Born for Opposition*, 31 (Journal, 21 Jan. 1821).

and the best man and a witness at the wedding, evidently held no grudge. Meeting Lushington in 1818 he wrote:

Dined with Burdett. Stephen Lushington there. This is Lady Byron's Dr Lushington, a nice fellow, I thought.[145]

Public opinion in 1816 seems to have been largely on the side of Lady Byron and her advisers,[146] but Lord Byron has had his supporters also.[147] It has been said, against Lushington, that, by his 'cold caution' he persuaded Lady Byron to disregard the dictates of her heart, and improperly loosened the sacred bonds of matrimony.[148] Lushington's later career shows that, on occasion, he was hot-tempered, and that his opinions in favour of the sanctity of marriage were stronger than most. It has also often been suggested by various writers, more or less explicitly, that Lushington was interested in his professional fees, rather than in attempting to save the marriage. But, as Lady Byron's legal adviser, his duty was to give effect, not to his own views about the desirability of saving the marriage, or even to his own views of his client's best interests, but, within the bounds of legal and professional propriety, to her objectives. Lady Byron herself, on

---

[145] Hobhouse *Diary*, 30 June 1818, British Library Add Mss 47235, f.29b, Lord Broughton, *Recollections of a Long Life*, ed. Lady Dorchester (London, 1909), ii, 100.

[146] See Moore, *Life of Byron*, iii, 215–16.

[147] See *Blackwood's Magazine*, July 1869, accusing Lady Byron of being a moral Brinvilliers, i.e., of poisoning Lord Byron's reputation by lending support to defamatory charges against him.

[148] See note 94, above (cold caution). In an anonymous poem, *Leon to Annabella*, purportedly by Lord Byron, the following reproach is addressed to Lady Byron, for taking advice from an ecclesiastical lawyer:

> How could'st thou go, *opinions* vile to beg,
> And hang thy conscience on a lawyer's peg? –
> Some lisping fool, with empty dictums big,
> Proud of his LL.D. and periwig.
> His mind was not the crucible to try
> The deep arcana of love's alchemy,
> Whose highest flight of genius seems to be
> To settle squabbles on a belfry key.
> Shall dolts like him a husband's rights define?
> Say wives may grant him this, must that decline,
> Arrest the tide with which our passions flow,
> And vainly cry no farther shalt thou go?

Quoted from Knight, *Lord Byron's Marriage*, 194.

her first interview with Lushington was 'very much satisfied',[149] and her sense of satisfaction apparently did not diminish, for she maintained connections with Lushington throughout her life, consulting him on a variety of subjects.[150] Lushington married, in 1821, a close friend of Lady Byron's, and for the last twenty-six years of his life he resided at Ockham Park, the family seat of the Earl of Lovelace, Lady Byron's son-in-law.

Another accusation made by Lushington's critics has been that he callously refused to reveal the details of his client's case, and took improper advantage of the pressure exerted upon Lord Byron by the effect of scandalous rumour. It is true that he gained an advantage from this pressure. There may have been an element of bluff in his strategy, for it is not at all clear that he would have succeeded in court. Lushington himself used a card-playing metaphor (not necessarily suggesting bluff[151]) when he said in 1870 that he had 'declined to show his cards and name anything, for obvious reasons'.[152] There is no impropriety in this, and an examination of the facts against the legal background shows that he acted throughout for his client, for whom he achieved a notable success, in a legal environment very hostile to her interests.

[149] Lady Byron to Lady Noel, 23 Feb. 1830, Lovelace-Byron Papers, 30/24, Elwin, *Lord Byron's Wife*, 417.

[150] He acted for her in 1843 in a delicate family matter, paying money on Lady Byron's behalf to redeem jewels that had been misappropriated and pawned by Ada: Lovelace-Byron Papers, 89, 173, 375; see D. L. Moore, *Ada, Countess of Lovelace*, 314, 328. He advised her in 1852 on an action threatened by a former servant of Medora Leigh: Lovelace-Byron Papers, 137/10, 33, 51, 84, 92, 100, 117, 119; 89/84; see C. Turney, *Byron's Daughter* (New York, 1972), 1975 edn, 235–6, Moore, *Ada, Countess of Lovelace*, 186–7. He also advised her, in 1853, in a case of threatened blackmail; see Moore, *Ada, Countess of Lovelace*, 341–4, W. Grieg to Lushington, 15 Jan. 1854, Lushington Family Papers. He was a trustee of the marriage settlement, and under Lady Byron's will: Lovelace-Byron Papers, 90, 152.

[151] In whist, a very popular game in 1870, success depends not only on a player's own holdings, but also on making an estimate of opponents' holdings, and on the order of the play of the cards.

[152] Bathurst statement, note 54 above.

4

THE DEFENCE OF QUEEN CAROLINE

In 1820 there occurred 'one of the greatest political sensations of all time.'[1] This was the introduction in the House of Lords of a Bill to deprive the Queen of England of her title, and to dissolve her marriage with the King. The Bill, called a Bill of Pains and Penalties, was legislative in form, but the proceedings were judicial in substance,[2] and are aptly called the Trial of Queen Caroline. Though far removed, in many ways, from an ordinary matrimonial dispute, the proceedings served to focus attention on the anomalies and injustices of the existing law of divorce.[3]

Six counsel were engaged on the Queen's behalf, all of whom, despite incurring the King's hostility, subsequently became judges.[4] The leading counsel was Brougham, later Lord Chancellor, but an

---

[1] The phrase is that of G. D. H. Cole, *The Life of William Cobbett* (1927), 247.

[2] Counsel controlled the presentation of the case on each side; witnesses were examined; the Lord Chancellor presided in a judicial manner. See *The Greville Memoirs*, ed. L. Strachey and R. Fulford (London, 1938), 108: 'The Chancellor is equally impartial, and as he decides personally all disputes on legal points which are referred to the House, his fairness has been conspicuous in having generally decided in favour of the Queen's counsel.' On the other hand, there were non-judicial features of the proceedings; the Lord Chancellor spoke and voted (in favour of the Bill), and the decision was by majority vote of a political body, and took into account political considerations. The House of Lords was called upon to perform functions that were partly judicial in ordinary divorce cases (of which there had been five in 1819, and one in 1820; see S. Wolfram, 'Divorce in England 1700–1857', *Oxford Journal of Legal Studies* 5 (1985), 155, 181), in trials of peers charged with crime, and in the rare cases of Bills of Attainder, and impeachment. It also heard appeals on points of law, but witnesses were not examined, and the lay peers generally did not attend. See A. S. Tuberville, *The House of Lords in the Age of Reform* (London, 1958), ch. 9, 'The House of Lords as a Court of Law'.

[3] J. Perkin, *Women and Marriage in Nineteenth-Century England* (London, 1989), 40, suggests that the case 'laid the groundwork' for reform of the divorce laws.

[4] Brougham, Denman, Lushington, Wilde, Tindal, Williams. S. Walpole, *History of England from the Conclusion of the Great War in 1815* (London, 1879), 583, wrote: 'Everything that the Court could do to retard the promotion of the advocates of the Queen was certain to be done. Yet the counsel for the Queen attained on the whole

important part was played by Lushington, who was the Queen's civilian adviser.[5]

Civilians, the Doctors of Civil Law, practised in the ecclesiastical courts, which had exclusive judicial jurisdiction over matrimonial disputes. The House of Lords in its legislative capacity was not bound by the rules of the ecclesiastical courts, but it was dealing with a matter that, had it arisen between private parties, would have come first before those courts. The proceedings in the House of Lords, though political as much as legal, were concerned with justice, if only because an appearance of injustice had political implications. The treatment that the Queen would have received in the ecclesiastical courts, had she been a private litigant, was, therefore, relevant to her case, and formed an important part of her argument.[6]

The marriage, in 1795, between Caroline of Brunswick, and the Prince of Wales (later George IV) had been a failure from the start. After a year the parties had separated, and Caroline had lived first in England and then in Italy, returning to England after the death of George III in 1820. It was her return to England, and her determination to claim recognition of her position as Queen, that precipitated the Bill. The case against her, which formed a long recital in the Bill, was that she had, after promoting a servant (Bergami) to unsuitably high position, committed adultery with him.[7] A succession of witnesses, many of them Italian former servants of hers, were called in an

higher positions, both in their profession and in the State, than those for the King . . . Rarely had any client been defended by counsel destined for such distinction.'

[5] The crowds outside the House of Lords shouted, as carriages arrived for the trial: 'Is it Brougham? Is it Denman? Is it Lushington?' R. Huish, *Memoirs of Her Late Majesty Caroline, Queen of Great Britain* (London, 1821), ii, 516. Several contemporary cartoons depict Lushington, along with Brougham and Denman, as the Queen's counsel, e.g. 'Stewards Court of the Manor of Torre Devon', 1820, BM, M. D. George, *Catalogue of Political and Personal Satires . . . in the British Museum* (London, 1952), 14013. Dr Lushington also appears in nos 13761 and 13768 (July 1820).

[6] Dr Phillimore was disparaging about the civilians appearing against Lushington: '[The King's] advisers are very unfortunate in the choice of their civilians: the King's Advocate [Sir Christopher Robinson] is clumsy and confused, and has no practice; Adams is injudicious and impracticable, and has no learning.' Phillimore to Duke of Buckingham, Duke of Buckingham & Chandos, *Memoirs of the Court of George IV 1820–30* (London, 1859), 66.

[7] Bergami had been her courier. The evidence occasioned much ribald humour: 'What newspaper does the Queen take? She takes in the Courier.' When reference was made to her visit to the Dey of Algiers, she was said to be 'as happy as the Dey is long'. Cartoons depicted scenes from the evidence, e.g. 'Steward's Court of the Manor of Torre Devon' (M. D. George, *Catalogue*, 14013) showing ten scenes, including one of Bergami dressing the Princess, and another of Bergami bathing her.

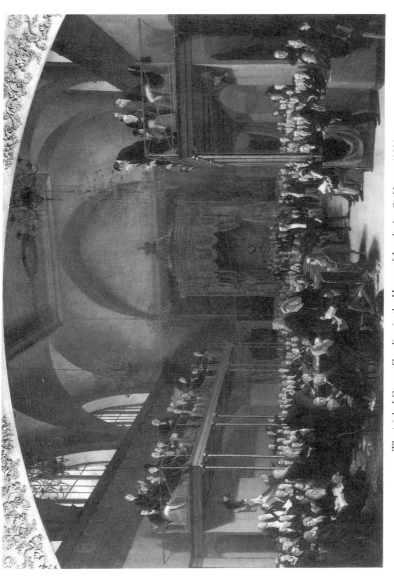

The trial of Queen Caroline in the House of Lords, by G. Hayter (1820). (Lushington is the central figure standing upright facing left).

attempt to prove the adultery. At the outset of the trial, the prevailing opinion was that the Queen had been guilty.[8] But several of the witnesses against her were discredited by Brougham's very effective cross-examinations. By the end of the case, the prevailing opinion probably was that, though the Queen might still in fact have been guilty, the evidence against her could not be said to be satisfactory.[9] Lushington's speech had two themes – to some extent inconsistent with each other: he set out to show that the evidence against the Queen was unpersuasive, and, at the same time, that, in any event, she would have had a successful defence in the ecclesiastical court.

He commenced his speech with what has been called 'a rather curious passage':[10] he drew attention to the Queen's age:

My lords; the first [circumstance] which I advert to, is the age of the party accused; and this I venture to say without fear of contradiction, that no precedent can be found in modern times, where a husband has sought to divorce himself from a wife, accusing her of adultery at the age of fifty.[11]

It obviously was not impossible for a fifty-year-old woman to be guilty of adultery. Lushington described it as an 'improbability'. This does not seem, at first sight, to be a particularly strong point, in view of the exceptional circumstances in which the Queen had lived, abroad, separated from her husband, and free from the restraints of English

---

[8] Lord Byron (who was in Italy and did not participate in the Trial) wrote to Hobhouse: 'Here (and we are in her late neighbourhood) there are no doubts about her and her blackguard Bergami.' 22 June 1820, L. A. Marchand, *Byron's Letters*, vol. 7, *Between Two Worlds* (London, 1977), 122. Byron also commented on the unreliability of Italian witnesses (ibid., 139), and welcomed the news of the abandonment of the Bill 'for it will prevent a revolution – though it may *hasten* a *reform*' (ibid., 237).

[9] Lord Grey, for example, said that he had changed his mind in the course of the trial; Hansard, 2nd ser., iii, 1574 (3 Nov. 1820). See G. M. Trevelyan, *Lord Grey of the Reform Bill* (London, 1920), 194–6.

[10] R. Fulford, *Trial of Queen Caroline* (New York, 1967), 214.

[11] Hansard, 2nd ser., iii, 1186 (26 Oct. 1820). Lushington later said that he thought that there were no cases even of a wife over forty-five (ibid., 1187). This was subsequently contradicted by the Solicitor-General (J. S. Copley, later Lord Lyndhurst) who referred to a case where the wife had been forty-six (*Report of the Proceedings in the House of Lords on the Bill of Pains and Penalties against the Queen* (Edinburgh, 1820), 228, but Dr Lushington's point had served its purpose, and may even have been strengthened by the production of a single instance only in contradiction. The Princess had been forty-eight in the summer of 1816 when the sea voyage took place during which adultery was alleged.

society. But the effect of making the point was to alter the focus of attention from the general to the particular. The most dangerous line of thinking, from the point of view of the defence, was that the Queen must, during the twenty-four years that she had lived apart from her husband, very likely have committed adultery at some time or other. This line of thinking was supported by what was known of the character of the Queen (recklessly indiscreet, at best), by the ill-treatment she had received from her husband, and by a general supposition of men of the world about human nature. Defence counsel in a criminal case faces the same kind of danger, when evidence of general bad character and of past similar acts is adduced. The effect of drawing attention to the Queen's age was to demand attention to the question of whether adequate proof had been adduced of the specific instance of adultery alleged, the only remaining credible allegation (as Lushington sought to show) at this stage of the trial being that adultery had occurred on a sea voyage in 1816.[12]

Lushington then turned to the aspect of the matter that lay within the area of his own expertise, that is, the weakness of the King's claim had it been prosecuted in the ecclesiastical courts. The ecclesiastical courts had jurisdiction to grant a divorce from board and bed (in effect, a judicial separation) for adultery, and such a divorce was normally an essential preliminary to a parliamentary dissolution of the marriage.[13] But it was a complete answer to a divorce suit that the petitioner had encouraged his wife's adultery (connivance), or that he had himself committed adultery (recrimination).[14] The King had disliked Caroline on sight, and had deserted her after a year of marriage. Desertion was not, by itself, a bar to a divorce,[15] but it might be relevant to a defence of connivance, and it was a fact calculated to elicit sympathy for the Queen:

12 This was the strongest point against the Queen, and was relied on heavily by Lord Liverpool, the Prime Minister, in his speech in support of the Bill (Hansard, 2nd ser., iii, 1574, 3 Nov. 1820), who also said (ibid., 1595) that Dr Lushington was 'the only advocate for her majesty who fairly grappled with the circumstance, and endeavoured to explain and justify it'. Lushington called it 'the last stay, the last cable of a falling cause' (ibid., 1219). Creevey wrote that this incident was the 'sole foundation of the Bill', H. Maxwell (ed.), *The Creevey Papers: a Selection from the Correspondence and Diaries of Thomas Creevey* (London, 1903, 3rd edn, 1905), 331.

13 See Wolfram, 'Divorce in England', 159.

14 See R. Burn, *Ecclesiastical Law*, 2nd edn (1767), ii, 433, A. Waddilove, *Digest of cases decided in The Court of Arches etc* (1849), 38–9, 41, L. Shelford, *A Practical Treatise on the Law of Marriage and Divorce etc* (1841), 440–4, 449–58.

15 See chapter 5, below.

My lords: there is one other circumstance – the husband of the lady accused has been twenty-four years separated from that wife – separated, my lords, by his own act, by his own choice, by his own free will – separated, my lords, not in consequence of even a breath of suspicion of any misconduct of that wife ... but in the wayward indulgence of his own fancy, breaking asunder the solemn bonds in which God had united them.[16]

Lushington took full advantge of the public sympathy for the Queen as a wronged woman.[17] He reminded his audience of the attitudes of the ecclesiastical court, where a wife had, in important respects, equal rights with her husband,[18] and where rank conferred no legal privileges:

My lords, then the King has no right to seek redress. Let no man dare to say, that though the King is relieved from various sanctions of the laws of men – let no one within these walls presume to say, that he is emancipated from the law of God.

Let no mind dare to say, that the assertion in this Bill is not founded in utter falsehood – 'Whereas her royal highness, further unmindful of her exalted rank and station, and of her duty to your majesty'[19] – what duty, my lords? what duty that is not reciprocal in the marriage life? Is there one law for woman and another for man? ... Is the plighted troth at the altar to bind the simple individual, and set free the king upon his throne? Is there one divine law for the common individual, and another for the sceptered monarch? ... But, my lords ... I say again, that unless your lordships are prepared to violate the law of God and man – unless that reverend bench which forms a part of those judges whom I now address, are prepared to forget and abandon the tenets of the gospel, it cannot – it dare not – pronounce for this divorce.[20]

Lushington reminded his audience of the King's misconduct:

My lords, what is the plighted troth, and how has it been kept and preserved? 'To love'! where shall I seek for the marks of it? 'To comfort!' where shall I look for one trace of it? ... 'To honour!' has that been observed?[21]

---

16 Hansard, 2nd ser., iii, 1187.
17 See Perkin, *Women and Marriage*, 36–7.
18 See chapter 5, below.
19 The phrase occurs twice in the long preamble to the Bill.
20 Hansard, 2nd ser., iii, 1187 and 1188–9, and *Trial of Queen Caroline* (1821), 'Speech of Dr Lushington', *Reports of Proceedings*, iii, 88. The reference to one law for woman and another for man does not appear in Hansard, but is in the other versions, and (in plural form) in J. Adolphus (ed.), *A Correct, Full, and Impartial Report of the Trial of Her Majesty Caroline, Queen Consort of Great Britain, before the House of Peers on the Bill of Pains and Penalties* (London, 1820), 396, and seems probably correct; the Hansard version is repetitive.
21 Hansard, 2nd ser., iii, 1187–8.

He offered an apology for his attack on the King, but in such a way as to reinforce, rather than to detract from, the point he was making:

My lords, it is to me inconceivably painful to dwell upon these subjects; because I know and feel that every discussion on these topics shakes the throne and weakens the monarchy. I know that when the private acts of kings are brought before the world, there are individuals without number to whom it is a pleasure and a delight to magnify their errors and to exaggerate their failings. My lords, that is not my will. It is the discharge of a solemn duty which has compelled me to advert to it. I have done it as speedily as I could; and I leave it with the greatest pleasure.[22]

That this was a rhetorical apology only appeared from his next words, which showed that he had by no means finished with the King's misconduct, for Lushington next turned to connivance, a topic which, he said, if mentioned in a case, 'at once rouses the attention of the judges':

My lords, what should I say of a husband insensible to his own honor – what should I say upon the offer of fifty thousand pounds a year on condition of living abroad, without a single restriction, without one single direction that the adulterous intercourse imputed should not be carried on in all its gross impurity? What should we say to an individual who came here and prayed for justice acting thus? who has said, 'go your ways,' not as my learned friend Mr Denman said last night, 'and sin no more',[23] but 'go and indulge your passion; revel in all the profligacy of degraded intercourse; and you shall be furnished with the means'.[24]

An attempt by the Queen to adduce evidence of the King's adultery would, probably, have alienated the peers. In any case, the King's adulterous affairs were notorious,[25] and it was probably decided that the greatest tactical advantage to the defence lay in reminding the peers of his adultery, and of its significance in the ecclesiastical court (which Lushington did by the device of announcing that he would say nothing about it), and claiming credit for the Queen for reticence:

---

[22] Hansard, 2nd ser., iii, 1188.   [23] See below, note 35.
[24] Hansard, 2nd ser., iii, 1188.
[25] See cartoons reproduced in I. McCalmon, 'Unrespectable Radicalism: Infidels and Pornography in early Nineteenth-Century London', *Past and Present* 104 (1984), 74–110, M. D. George, *Catalogue*, no. 13,847, 'An excursion to Brighton', published about September 1820.

My lords: I am happy to say that I am not under the necessity of introducing another topic to your lordships consideration – I am not under the necessity of saying one word upon recrimination. We have adduced no evidence – thanks to the wisdom of my learned friends who confidentially advise her majesty – thanks to her discretion and propriety – this House and the nation are saved the consequences of such a measure.[26]

Lushington then turned to the other strand of his argument, his attempt to show that the evidence against the Queen was insufficient. He started with a crucial question, namely, the cogency of the proof that should be required. Counsel for the Crown had laid stress on the fact that adultery could be established in the ecclesiastical courts without eye-witness proof of the actual deed, citing a decision of Sir William Scott, the principal matrimonial law judge, for that purpose.[27] Lushington pointed out that in the case cited there had been ample proof of adultery, and himself cited another decision of the same judge, for the proposition that strict proof was essential:

My lords, in the case . . . the proof was so strong that the counsel for the wife were upon the point of declining to argue it – that learned judge who, whatever be the station of the parties, never forgets the interests of justice, insisted upon that case being argued, and, my lords, it fell to me to argue it . . . When he gave sentence pronouncing that the husband had failed in proof of the adultery, he used these memorable words – 'I may have a moral conviction of her guilt; but I have no judicial proof.'[28]

Lushington had a difficult line to follow here: he wanted to bring it home to his audience, who were mostly non-lawyers, that they ought not to determine the fact of adultery without strict proof; moral conviction was not enough. On the other hand, he did not want it to appear that he was relying on a legal technicality, with which his audience would be very unsympathetic. In short, he had to perform the difficult task of bringing home to a non-legal audience the inherent merit of, that is the underlying reason for, the legal requirement of strict proof:

Again, I beseech your lordships, not for one instant to suppose that I am asking from your hands a verdict because there is a deficiency of legal proof

---

[26] Hansard, 2nd ser., iii, 1188–9.
[27] Sir William Scott, later Lord Stowell, was the judge of the Consistory Court for the Diocese of London. This was the court that dealt with most divorce cases, of which Lushington himself was judge from 1828 to 1858. See chapter 5, below.
[28] Hansard, 2nd ser., iii, 1190–1.

againt moral conviction. My lords, I ask for a verdict because I say that there is no proof in the present case which any man of honesty, of discretion, of judgment and of common diligence must not repudiate as utterly destitute of all credibility.[29]

The underlying reason for the requirement of strict proof in criminal cases (and adultery was treated as a crime by the ecclesiastical courts) is that the consequences of conviction to the individual accused are so heavy (and this was certainly true of proof of adultery against a wife at the time) that it is unfair to inflict them in the absence of a very high degree of certainty. If proof of opportunity were enough, Lushington suggested, no one would be safe.[30] He conceded that proof of opportunity, combined with proof of indecent familiarity and the seeking of opportunities in which a criminal intercourse might be enjoyed, would be sufficient, but he stressed that both elements (opportunity and inclination) must be strictly proved:

My lords; on whom, upon the present occasion, lies the burthen of proof? Those of your lordships who are even ever so little cognizant with proceedings in courts of law, know the duties which attach upon him who affirms any proposition. You know that the plaintiff in an action is bound to make out his demand. Much more, my lords, do you ever hold in sacred remembrance, that he who seeks to take away the life or character of an individual, is bound, by every principle of eternal justice, by every rule recognized by the law, to establish that guilt by full free unsuspected and unsuspicious testimony ... No individual yet alive in any country, in any mode of trial, I believe, since the dark ages, was ever put upon the task of first establishing his innocence – since the day when the folly and superstition of our ancestors led their miserable victim through ordeal fires and across burning ploughshares to take the risk of life and death – never since that day has any one yet been asked to prove his innocence in the first instance.[31]

This was a theme to which he often reverted in examining in detail the evidence against the Queen. All that Majoochi, the principal Crown witness, had been able to say was that there was 'rather a familiarity' between the Princess and Bergami, and Lushington said, of him, that 'This, the hand of their cause, can bear them out no further in their ground, than that there was "rather a familiarity"'.[32] He emphasized the difficulty, always faced by a person formally accused of crime, of having to explain incidents taken out of context from the distant past for the purpose of the prosecution case, and he attempted the difficult

---

[29] Ibid., 1191.   [30] Ibid.   [31] Ibid., 1192–3.   [32] Ibid., 1194.

task of inviting his hearers to imagine themselves in the prisoner's
dock:

> Your lordships must take it as a whole. You must not select this or that trifling
> occurrence, and say, at a lapse of six years, 'this cannot be explained, therefore
> I will affix upon it the stain of guilt.' Who, I ask your lordships, who in this
> House is so spotless, whose life so free, not only from guilt but even from the
> possibility of suspicion, that he would have the courage to say, 'Go back six
> years – every the most trifling iota of my conduct shall at the very first blush
> and glance prove its own incorruptible purity.' My lords, he who would dare
> to say that, has, I will venture to say, less honesty, less candor, or less
> knowledge, than falls to the general lot of human kind.[33]

Lushington's tone contrasts markedly with that of his fellow counsel. Brougham had ended his speech with a high-flown peroration that
stressed the political dangers of passing the Bill. Denman made a
rather extravagant comparison of the King to the Roman emperor,
Nero, and an obscene insult addressed to that emperor which he
thought necessary to obscure by quoting in Greek,[34] ended with the
reference, already mentioned, to the woman taken in adultery, and
Christ's reproach to her accusers: 'Go and sin no more'. This gave rise
to a jocular verse not helpful to the Queen's case.[35] Denman himself
bitterly regretted his conclusion.[36] Lushington's speech, probably by
arrangement among the counsel, adopted a wholly different line, by
exploiting the weaknesses in the evidence against the Queen. The
speech contains some strong language,[37] but the overall tone is one of
careful examination of the strength of evidence, and the concluding
words were 'I leave the honour of my client, not to your mercy, but to
your justice'.[38]

The defence of the Queen was successful, for the motion for
the third reading passed by only nine votes, which was judged by
the government to be an insufficient majority, and the Bill was

---

[33] Ibid., 1206.
[34] See Hansard, 2nd ser., iii, 1090 (24 Oct. 1820), (My mistress' [body] is cleaner than
your mouth).
[35]
> Most gracious Queen we thee implore
> To go away and sin no more;
> Or if that effort be too great,
> To go away at any rate.
>   (*DNB* sn Denman, and in many other accounts).
[36] J. Arnould, *Memoir of Thomas, first Lord Denman etc.* (London 1873), 172.
[37] Sarcastic treatment of witnesses' evidence, and expressions such as 'Gracious God!'
[38] Hansard, 2nd ser., iii, 1238.

abandoned.[39] The chief credit must go to Brougham,[40] who had overall charge of the defence, and whose cross-examination of Majoochi, the principal witness against the Queen, made the words '*non mi ricordo*' – I do not remember – a catchphrase for perjury. But Lushington's speech, which closed the Queen's defence, is entitled also to a large share of the credit, and has been praised by contemporary,[41] and later commentators.[42]

Even after reading the report of the speeches, it cannot be said with certainty what arguments finally prevailed. Perhaps few peers believed the Queen to be probably innocent,[43] but many must have thought that her guilt had not been satisfactorily established, and many more that in any case it was politically dangerous to send the Bill into the House of Commons. The points tended to reinforce each other. Lord Grey,[44] who was active throughout the trial in opposition to the Bill, and whose opinion was certainly influential,[45] emphasized the weaknesses in the government case, and its failure to discharge the burden of proof.[46] Other peers indicated that they were unwilling to

---

[39] Ibid., 1744 (10 Nov. 1820). It would have been formally possible to proceed, but the prospects for the Bill in the House of Commons were bleak. It has been said that the Bill passed only by the votes of the peers who held office as ministers, who could not be regarded as impartial: L. Melville, *An Injured Queen: Caroline of Brunswick* (1912), 501, R. Stewart, *Henry Brougham 1778–1868: His Public Career* (London, 1986), 157. E. L. Woodward, *The Age of Reform* (Oxford, 1938), 658, lists nine ministers who were peers, but the Earl of Harrowby abstained: *Report of Proceedings*, Appendix, Hansard, 2nd ser., iii, 1744–5.

[40] W. Holdsworth, *History of English Law*, xiii (London, 1952), 220.

[41] Sir F. Burdett, a radical member of the House of Commons, said: 'Denman was bald & confused & not eloquent – Lushington *excellent*.' M. W. Patterson, *Sir Francis Burdett and his Times* (London, 1931), ii, 519. Accommodation was provided for members of the lower house on the steps of the throne, and Sir Francis Burdett appears there in Hayter's painting (National Portrait Gallery, Reg. no. 999; Burdett is marked as no. 111 in the key).

[42] The speech was described as 'most masterly' in *Georgian Era* (1833), ii, 359, and has been preferred to those of Brougham and Denman by E. Parry, *Queen Caroline* (1930), 306, and called, 'from the legal side . . . perhaps the best' by Fulford, *Trial of Queen Caroline*, 214.

[43] See S. MacCoby, *English Radicalism, 1736–1832* (London, 1955), ii, 371.

[44] Charles Grey, second Earl Grey (1764–1845); prominent Whig peer; Prime Minister, 1830–4.

[45] The calls for his speech were so prevalent that other peers attempting to speak at the same time 'immediately yielded' to him, *Report of Proceedings*, 300. In the cartoon mentioned above (note 5; no. 14013) a verse of the text below the picture is devoted to Grey: 'And who in Grey do bow so civil? Oh dat be de great Bow Wow of de Kennel, A Whig & half & half a Radical. Doodle Johnny Calf.' See also Trevelyan, *Lord Grey of the Reform Bill* (1920), 194–6.

[46] Hansard, 2nd ser., iii, 1573–4 (3 Nov. 1820).

impose on the Queen a divorce that would not have been available in the case of a private individual.[47] The Queen herself undoubtedly approved of Lushington's speech, because she remained in close contact with him until her death, making him an executor, and a beneficiary, of her will.[48]

Lushington played a political, as well as a legal role. He corresponded with Lord Liverpool,[49] the Prime Minister, on questions concerning the Queen's income, and residence.[50] On 20 July, two months before the trial began, he signed a document concurring in the advice of the Queen's other counsel that she should defend the case in the House of Lords.[51] Dr Phillimore, a fellow civilian, wrote, in a not altogether friendly tone, in a letter dated 12 August:

> Lushington, I hear, now very much presides over the counsels of Her Majesty; in many respects he is well calculated to please her, for he is good-natured and obliging in his demeanour, rash in his advice, and a lover to excess of popular applause. He is everywhere with her now: airs with her, assists her in receiving addresses, etc.[52]

On several occasions Lushington spoke, in the Queen's interest, in the House of Commons. On 3 July 1820 he spoke in favour of a postponement of the coronation.[53] On 15 July he introduced a motion in support of the Queen's claim to a service of silver plate, that she said had been given to her by the Prince of Wales in 1808.[54] On 25 July

---

[47] Lord Falmouth, ibid., 1620 (4 Nov. 1820), and 453–4, Earl of Harrowby, ibid., 1714 (7 Nov.). Lord Falmouth said, at 1726, echoing Dr Lushington's argument, 'The King had private rights and duties to perform within his own family in particular, as well as the meanest of his subjects'. Lord de Clifford said that the separation probably occasioned the conduct they were now investigating, ibid., 1626 (6 Nov.).

[48] The other counsel were not beneficiaries. Creevey wrote that Brougham 'absolutely *hated*' the Queen, 'nor do I think that her love for her Attorney-General was very great'. Maxwell, *Creevey Papers*, 366.

[49] Robert Banks Jenkinson, second Earl of Liverpool (1770–1828); Prime Minister, 1812–27.

[50] Liverpool Papers, British Library, Add MSS 38565/227, 237, 244.

[51] A. Aspinall (ed.), *Letters, 1812–1830* by George IV (Cambridge, 1938), 355 (No. 833; 20 July 1820).

[52] Duke of Buckingham & Chandos, *Memoirs of the Court*, 66.

[53] Hansard, 2nd ser., ii, 158 (3 July 1820).

[54] Ibid., 477–8, 499–524. The motion was unsuccessful, as it transpired that the plate had not been given to the Queen outright, and Dr Lushington had to retreat. See *Annual Register*, 1820, 181 ('So complete was the overthrow of Dr Lushington that the very warmest partisans of her majesty in the House, were forced to allow, that he had no grounds for his motion', but adding that those who had misinformed Lushington of the facts were more to blame).

Lushington commented adversely on a libel against the Queen that had appeared in a provincial newspaper, not, however, supporting prosecution.[55]

One of the Queen's recurrent complaints was that her name had been excluded, by Order in Council, from the liturgy, that is, from the prayers in which it was customary to pray for the members of the royal family by name, it being ordered that the prayers should read simply 'our gracious king, George, and all the royal family'.[56] Even after the trial, much to her chagrin, the Order was not altered. Lushington introduced petitions in the House of Commons on this question, among others that concerned the Queen, in January and February of 1821.[57] Lushington's letters to Brougham, however, show that he had little hope of success. On 5 March he wrote 'She is very positive in her assertions that nothing shall induce her to leave England without having her name restored to the liturgy, but I doubt her patience and so I told her',[58] and on 8 March, 'She thinks there is a chance of obtaining the liturgy – I see none'.[59] On 24 March, he wrote:

The Q has received from Ld Liverpool a letter stating that the King sees no reason to depart from his determination made in Feb 1820 of excluding her from the liturgy – this was to be expected – I saw her this morning & she is extremely positive in her declarations that she will not leave England but I doubt her perseverance.[60]

It appears from this correspondence that Lushington had by this time replaced Brougham as the Queen's principal legal adviser. Lushington wrote, on 5 March, 'I will see her as often as I possibly can',[61] and it appears that Brougham was consulted only indirectly. Lushington wrote to him on 24 March:

I fully executed all your instructions as to thanks due which were most graciously received – Indeed I read your letter in substance to the Q herself

55 Hansard, 2nd ser., ii, 601 (25 July 1820).
56 The order, dated 12 Feb. 1820, is given in full in the appendix to *Report of Proceedings*. The order directed the omission of the words, in use during the reign of George IV, 'Their Royal Highnesses George Prince of Wales, the Princess of Wales, and . . .'.
57 Hansard, 2nd ser., iv, 78, 611 (25 July 1820).
58 Lushington to Brougham, 5 Mar. 1821, Brougham Papers, University College, London, 32,344.
59 Lushington to Brougham, 9 Mar. 1821, Brougham Papers, 10,147.
60 Lushington to Brougham, 24 Mar. 1821, Brougham Papers, 10,148 (endorsed 24 June by Brougham).
61 Lushington to Brougham, 5 Mar. 1821, Brougham Papers, 32,344.

... The Q intends holding a drawing Room Monday se'nnight – if you object let me know by return of post.[62]

After much vacillation, the Queen accepted a money allowance from the government, of which Lushington approved, though it inevitably weakened the Queen's popular support as a symbol of opposition to the government.[63] Lushington wrote to Brougham:

Indeed her mind was wholly occupied with the letter she had written to Ld Liverpool accepting the annuity, and of which letter she told me you should have a copy sent by tonight's post – So this is done, & I am right glad of it, for to this it must have come at last after a most disagreeable interval.[64]

In a later letter he said that 'The Q's acceptance of the money is an unpopular act but it could not be helped.'[65]

Lushington, like many others, friendly and hostile, who wrote of the Queen, derived some amusement from her imperfect command of English:

She has desired me to attend her on Sunday next to write a letter to Lord Liverpool asking for a sum of money for *a fit out* – This I must do & I think she has very just grounds for the demand tho' of course it will not be acceded to.[66]

On general tactics, Lushington was also evidently involved to some extent.[67] The Queen had threatened to attend a reception of the King's ('The Drawing Room'), in order to present a petition to him in person. Lushington wrote to Brougham agreeing 'in thinking the threat of going to the drawing Room worse than useless'.[68]

[62] Lushington to Brougham, 24 Mar. 1821, Brougham Papers, 10,148 (endorsed 24 June by Brougham).
[63] A. Wood, *Nineteenth-Century Britain* (London, 1967), 51.
[64] Lushington to Brougham, 5 Mar. 1821, Brougham Papers, 32,344. Reference to this question can be found in the Creevey Papers, Maxwell, *Creevey Papers*, 354, 357, and Melville, *Injured Queen*, 534–9, from which it appears that Brougham had advised the Queen to reject the allowance. Her letter refusing the allowance until her name should be restored to the liturgy is in Melville, *Injured Queen*, 535. See also MacCoby, *English Radicalism*, 373.
[65] Lushington to Brougham, 8 Mar. 1821, Brougham Papers, 10,147. See Woodward, *The Age of Reform*, 68: 'She was no longer a symbol of resistance to oppression; she had passed over to the side of the pensioners.'
[66] Lushington to Brougham, 8 Mar. 1821, Brougham Papers, 10,147.
[67] He had corresponded with Lord Liverpool in July and August 1820 on Caroline's financial affairs, and on the question of a house for her. Liverpool Papers, British Library, Add MSS 38565, ff. 227, 237, 242, 244.
[68] Lushington to Brougham, 24 Mar. 1821, Brougham Papers, 10,148 (endorsed 24 June). Correspondence between the Queen and Lord Liverpool relating to this threat is given by Melville, *Injured Queen*, 540–1. The government took the threat

Talk of revolution was widespread in 1819 and 1820, and some serious disturbances had occurred.[69] In August 1819 eleven people had been killed by troops, and hundreds wounded, at a public meeting in Manchester ('Peterloo'). In February 1820 a conspiracy to overthrow the government had been detected (the Cato Street conspiracy). The Queen became the focus of popular opposition to the King and the government. Crowds accompanied her into London on her return to England in June, and there were violent scenes in London that appeared to pose a serious threat to public order.[70] Lord Grey, who played a leading role in the trial, wrote that they would see, if they lived, 'A Jacobin revolution more bloody than that of France'.[71] There were large and noisy crowds in the streets during the trial,[72] and riotous celebrations after the Bill was withdrawn.[73] The Queen's case was identified to some extent with 'the cause of imperilled freedom'.[74] Erskine May wrote, in his *Constitutional History of England*, that 'many sagacious observers dreaded a civil war'.[75] A modern historian has written that the affair 'brought the ministry near to resignation or dismissal more than once during its course and even seemed at times to threaten revolution'.[76]

quite seriously and made detailed preparations for dealing with it; but the Queen contented herself with sending her petition to Lord Liverpool, Melville, *Injured Queen*, 541.

[69] E. Halevy, *History of the English People in the Nineteenth Century*, vol. 2, *The Liberal Awakening* (2nd edn, 1949), ii, 54–79. E. P. Thompson, *The Making of the English Working Class* (London, 1980 edn), 737, considers that 'revolution was possible' in 1819.

[70] Halevy, *History of the English People*, ii, 92–3, T. W. Laqueur, 'The Queen Caroline Affair: Politics as Art in the Reign of George IV', *Journal of Modern History* 54 (1982), 417.

[71] E. T. Lean, *The Napoleonists: a Study in Political Disaffection, 1760–1960* (London, 1970), 118.

[72] Creevey said that he saw 100,000 in Piccadilly; Maxwell, *Creevey Papers*, 334. See Halevy, *History of the English People*, ii, 98.

[73] Medallions were struck showing Minerva, holding a tablet inscribed Queen's Trial, dismissing Discord (description in offer from modern dealer).

[74] Halevy, *History of the English People*, ii, 101, J. Stevenson, 'The Queen Caroline Affair', in *London in the Age of Reform* (Oxford, 1973), 124. Cobbett, the leading radical of the time, wrote letters to the Queen, urging her to insist on her full rights (printed in Melville, *Injured Queen*, ii, 436 ff.). Cobbett drafted some of her letters, see Melville, *Injured Queen*, 528; J. M. and J. P. Cobbett (eds), *Selections from Cobbett's Political Works* (London, 1835).

[75] T. E. May, *Constitutional History of England since the Accession of George III* (1861), i, 110. Thompson, *Making of the English Working Class*, 832, considers that Cobbett 'nearly brought down' the Throne in the Queen Caroline agitation.

[76] J. Stevenson, 'Queen Caroline Affair', 117.

There is a flavour of revolution in some of Lushington's speeches in the House of Commons, manifesting sentiments rare in the most conservative branch of the legal profession, and on the lips of a future ecclesiastical court judge. On 3 July 1820, he said, in criticizing the expenditure of large sums of money on the coronation (which had not yet taken place):

If this measure were persisted in, he, for one . . . believed in his conscience that whatever excesses the people might commit they had been driven to them by ministers, by their arrogant and oppressive conduct, and their contempt of public feeling. Did the hon. gentlemen opposite suppose that the spirit of the country was to be fettered and manacled by those volunteers that were now raising, or that it was to be kept down by the barracks that were rising in every direction? This effect might indeed be produced for a short time – but only for a short time; for there was still spirit enough in the country to lay in the dust all the machinations of the hon. gentleman and his colleagues.[77]

When challenged to say whether he had declared that the extravagance of ministers was a just ground for expecting that the people would proceed to extremities and outrage, Lushington retreated a little, saying that 'What he had stated was, that the distress of the country was occasioned by the extravagance of ministers.'[78] On 24 January 1821, in presenting a petition in the Queen's interest, he said:

Would to God he could entertain any rational hope that the House would acquiesce in the prayer of the petition! But he could not expect that, so long as he saw the sentiments of the people opposed to the majority of their representatives. It would be well if they attended to the petitions of the people before the day came – and it might come much sooner than many persons imagined – when a reform would be hastily resorted to, instead of being the result of calm deliberation.[79]

On 13 February, in presenting other petitions relating to the Queen, he said:

That most unfortunate and illegal measure [excluding the Queen's name from the liturgy] had introduced nothing but confusion in divine service, and excited unbounded disgust throughout the country.[80]

And again:

The petitioners stated that the distress and discontent which prevailed throughout the country was to be mainly attributed to the ignorance,

[77] Hansard, 2nd ser., ii, 159–60 (3 July 1820).   [78] Ibid., 161.
[79] Hansard, 2nd ser., iv, 79 (24 Jan. 1821).   [80] Ibid., 612.

obstinacy, and inanity of ministers. He did, from the bottom of his heart, agree in that sentiment. To the conduct of the ministers, and to the defective state of the representation, did he attribute the national misfortunes.[81]

Lushington was regarded as one of the hotter heads on the reform side. Walpole wrote:

On the 4th of May, 1821, the reformers celebrated their cause by a great dinner at the London Tavern. Some of the most popular members of the Whig party in the House of Commons attended the dinner; and Lushington, who had been associated with Denman and Brougham in the defence of the Queen, distinguished himself among them all for the vigour, or rather the violence, of the language which he used at it.[82]

Yet the Queen was a most improbable figure as a revolutionary leader.[83] Her principal demand – that she should be prayed for in Church as Queen Consort – could hardly be less threatening to the establishment (church or monarchy). In the end, the affair seems to have acted as an extinguisher, and not an accelerant, of revolutionary fires. Her trial provided an opportunity for the expression of popular discontent with the King personally, and with the government, without endangering the monarchy itself. The outcome of the trial showed that government power could be constitutionally resisted. Lord John Russell said that 'the Queen's business' had 'done a great deal of good in renewing the old and natural alliance between the Whigs and the people and weakening the influence of the Radicals with the latter'.[84]

The Queen was determined to attend the coronation in July 1821, and consulted Lushington on how to attain her object. Lushington applied to the Prime Minister, Lord Liverpool, on the matter, but without effect.[85] In June, the Queen wrote to Lushington to ask him 'by what means and measures' she could 'obtain her perogatif and privilege to assist as Queen Consort equally as the reste of the royal

[81] Ibid., 613.
[82] Walpole, *History of England*, ii, 282. Walpole also mentions Lushington's reputation as a reformer in iii, 45.
[83] Laqueur says 'ludicrously ill suited for the role of radical heroine', 'Queen Caroline Affair', 418. See also G. Wallas, *The Life of Francis Place* (London, 1898), 151, Thompson, *Making of the English Working Class*, 778–9.
[84] Halevy, *History of the English People*, ii, 104. See Byron's comment, note 8 above. Laqueur suggests that a radical threat was rendered harmless by 'being transformed into melodrama, farce, and romance', 'Queen Caroline Affair', 418.
[85] Melville, *Injured Queen*, 542 (letter from Caroline to Liverpool referring to conversation between Liverpool and Lushington).

family to have a place allotted to her sole use'.[86] Her request was refused, but she resolved – most unwisely, as it turned out – to attempt to enter Westminster Abbey without a ticket. She was refused entry at several doors. If she had expected a popular rising in her favour, it was not forthcoming, and she drove away humiliated.[87]

Shortly afterwards she became ill, and she died on 8 August. Lushington was with her several times during her last days, and was present at her death.[88] He and his fellow executor stayed until between 2 and 3 o'clock the next morning to secure the Queen's possessions. Lushington was about to be married that very morning, 'so, having taken two hours rest, I went to Hampstead, was married, and immediately returned to town'[89] in time for an interview with Lord Liverpool at noon, who undertook that the government would pay the expenses of the funeral.[90]

---

[86] C. Hibbert, *George IV: Regent and King, 1811–1830* (London, 1973), 200. Evidently this was a lesser demand than that of actually sharing in the coronation ceremony.

[87] 'The refusal was peremptory at all the doors of the Abbey which she tried, and one was banged in her face', Brougham to Creevey (19 July 1821), Maxwell, *Creevey Papers*, 359. She received a mixed reception from the crowd. Brougham, in his letter to Creevey, says that she was cheered, but see Halevy, *History of the English People*, ii, 104 ('very few cheers and many hoots'). H. Twiss, *Public and Private Life of Lord Chancellor Eldon* (London, 1844), ii, 48, says: 'A few of the mob called Queen for ever! I am informed that, on the other hand, there was great hissing, cries of "shame, shame!" and a gentleman in the Hall told us that when her majesty got into her carriage again, she was weeping.'

[88] See account in Hansard, 2nd ser., vi, 957–8 (6 Nov. 1822). It was alleged that the Queen had revealed to Lushington, on her deathbed, that William Austin, a child whom she had brought up, and of whom she had been accused many years earlier of being the mother, was, in fact, her son. The *Morning Chronicle* doubted this, saying that, if so, Lushington would never have affixed the inscription to the coffin describing her as an injured queen. *John Bull*, a scurrilous Tory newspaper ('For God, the King, and the People'), which had hinted at this revelation, without actually asserting it, took the opportunity to attack Lushington: 'What! did Dr Lushington ever *believe* the Queen to have been injured or oppressed? Did Dr Lushington *think* the Queen innocent? . . . When we consider that . . . he saw her DIE – at 20 minutes after 10 o'clock at night, and that, in TEN HOURS and EIGHTEEN MINUTES from that time he led his blooming bride to the altar at Hampstead Church, we confess we are sceptical . . . Most of all we are surprised that they [Morning Chronicle] should stickle for Dr Lushington's delicacy or squeamishness.' *John Bull* 1 (1821), 302. See also attacks on Lushington in *John Bull* 2 (1821), 309, and *John Bull* 2 (1822), 660. In a letter to Brougham long afterwards, Lushington said that the Queen had 'on her death bed' expressly denied that William Austin was her son. Lushington to Brougham, 27 Sept. 1858, Brougham Papers, 10,268.

[89] Lushington to Brougham, 19 Aug. 1821, Maxwell, *Creevey Papers*, 364.

[90] Hansard, 2nd ser., vi, 950 (6 Mar. 1822).

The Queen had desired in a codicil to her will that 'three days after my death [my body] be carried to Brunswick for interment'.[91] Speedy removal of the body from England was desired also by the government, which, with good reason as events showed, was apprehensive of public disturbances. On the day of the funeral procession, Lushington was at Brandenburg House (which had been the Queen's residence) before six in the morning. Before the procession started, an altercation occurred between him and the undertaker,[92] Lushington objecting, not to the presence of troops, but to what he considered the undue haste in removing the body before adequate preparations had been made.[93] The government favoured a route for the procession that would avoid the City, in order not to give the opportunity to the City Corporation, which had consistently supported the Queen's interest,[94] to mount any kind of 'pageant'.[95] The crowd was determined that the procession should be made to go through the City, and it was successful in forcing this result by blocking (with carriages from which the wheels were removed) all other routes.[96] At Cumberland Gate, the troops opened fire on the crowd, and two persons were killed. A bullet passed through the panels of one of the carriages in the procession, but did not injure the occupants. The position of Lushington, and his wife, shut into their carriage, must have been most uncomfortable:

[91] Melville, *Injured Queen*, 602.
[92] See *The Times*, 15 Aug. 1821, Huish, *Memoirs of Caroline*, ii, 756, *Gentlemen's Magazine* 2 (1821), 177.
[93] Hansard, 2nd ser., vi, 954 (6 Mar. 1822), differing in several respects from the account in *The Times*. In a letter to Lord Liverpool dated 13 Aug., on behalf of both executors, Lushington protested 'against any removal until it can be ascertained that the due preparations are complete'. Liverpool Papers, Add Mss 38289/354.
[94] Alderman Wood was a radical opponent of the government, and one of the Queen's principal supporters. Lushington was awarded the freedom of the City in a box made of heart of oak of the value of one hundred guineas. The certificate is now in the possession of the Lushington family. The box appeared in a modern auction catalogue described as 'a fine George III freedom box, of oak with gold lining and finely pierced overlay decoration of scrolls surrounding the arms of the City of London, the edges chased with oak leaves and acorns, maker A. J. Strachan, 1820.'
[95] See Memorandum of Sir George Cockburn, Aspinall, *Letters of George IV*, 458, 460, explaining why he advised against taking the body by water from Hammersmith (Brandenburg House was on the river) 'If the city, as was suspected, wished to get up a pageantic display . . .'.
[96] See Memorandum as to the riotous proceedings on 14 August, Aspinall, *Letters of George IV*, 953.

I remained a passive spectator in my carriage while the shots were firing round me; I might almost say, a passive victim, for I was quite near enough to run the risk of suffering by that firing.[97]

At the first stoppage, Lushington was asked, as executor, to authorize a different route, but declined, adding that he 'thought the measure . . . proposed would be attended with deep responsibility'.[98] His own opinion, at least in retrospect, was that it would have been wise to permit the procession to go through the City:

And here I must take the liberty to deny that the wish for her majesty's remains to go through the city was the wish of the mob alone. I cannot yet be induced to believe that the whole corporation of London ought to be described as a mob . . . They [ministers] surely might have indulged the wishes of the people, without compromising either duty or principle; and it is with pain that I have heard words from a right hon. gentleman which may lead the House to believe that the route was marked out by one whom, by the forms of parliament, I am not permitted to mention . . . I cannot but think that, without offence to the Crown, they might have indulged the general wish of the people, and spared, by so doing, the bloodshed and confusion which ensued.[99]

In retrospect, no doubt Lushington was right. But at the time the route was planned, the government must have been in a difficult position, with the King's wishes to be taken into account, and the need to avoid, on the one hand, public disorder, and, on the other hand, undue 'pageantry' that might have led to graver disorders.

The procession did, after many delays, go through the City, and the Lord Mayor hastily left a meeting to admit the procession, and to accompany it to the eastern boundary.[100] The procession reached Romford at eight in the evening. 'All the persons attending upon her majesty's remains had, at that time, been thirteen hours in the mourning coaches, without an opportunity of leaving their seats.'[101] The undertakers then proposed that the procession should continue immediately to Colchester, but Lushington objected in the interest of the ladies and their female attendants.[102] The undertakers insisted, threatening to call in the military, and the procession continued, arriving at Chelmsford at four in the morning. Lushington, with extraordinary stamina, accompanied it ('personal fatigue was to me a

[97] Hansard, 2nd ser., vi, 955.   [98] Hansard, 2nd ser., vi, 954–5.
[99] Ibid., 955.   [100] Melville, *Injured Queen*, ii, 556.
[101] Hansard, 2nd ser., vi, 956.   [102] Ibid.

matter of no consideration'),[103] the ladies remaining to rest in Rom-ford. He still had the energy to write a vigorous letter of protest to Lord Liverpool, dated 'Chelmsford. A quarter before 5 a.m., Aug 15 1821'.[104] The undertakers gave a 'peremptory order' to be ready to start again at nine, but the horses were too tired, 'the convenience of the horses being attended to, however that of the human beings was neglected'.[105] They reached Colchester at four in the afternoon, and the undertakers proposed to go on again at eight. Lushington 'pro-duced a copy of a letter from Lord Liverpool . . . stating that the journey was not to be performed in two days, unless it would be done with convenience',[106] and this secured a delay until five the next morning.

The codicil to the Queen's will also desired that 'the inscription on my coffin be – Here lies Caroline of Brunswick, the injured Queen of England'.[107] This last instruction caused a serious controversy. Lord Liverpool, naturally, objected to the inscription, and said, according to Lushington's account, that 'it was impossible for the king's govern-ment to have such a plate fixed upon the coffin, because it would be pronouncing a censure upon them'.[108] Lushington interpreted this to mean that, though the government would take no active part in affixing the inscription, it would not object to the executors' doing so.[109] In this, he probably misinterpreted the Prime Minister. In a letter to the King dated 8 August, Lord Liverpool put the point more broadly:

With respect to the inscription which the Queen has directed to be put upon her coffin, it can obviously not be put upon it by authority or consent of Govt. nor while it is in the charge of any officers of Govt.[110]

103 Hansard, 2nd ser., vi, 956–7.
104 Liverpool Papers, Add MSS 38289, f. 376.
105 Hansard, 2nd ser., vi, 957.
106 Ibid., 957. The letter referred to is in the Liverpool Papers, Add MSS 38565, f. 421, Lord Liverpool to Lushington, 13 Aug. 1821: 'The procession may halt on the second night if necessary, so that it arrives in Harwich on Thursday in time to ensure embarkation on that day.'
107 Melville, *Injured Queen*, 602.
108 Hansard, 2nd ser., vi, 958.
109 Ibid.
110 Aspinall, *Letters of George IV*, 454. Castlereagh went even further: 'The king entirely concurs with you that the offensive inscription which the Queen has decided to be placed on her coffin, cannot be acquiesced in. It is impossible that either the British or Hanoverian Governments could be parties to such a measure, and as the interment must be conducted under their immediate orders, it is obvious that this direction of Her Majesty must be regarded as non avenue.' Ibid. It seems

At any rate, the executors ordered a coffin plate to be prepared, bearing the inscription:

Deposited / Caroline / of Brunswick / the injured / Queen / of England / Departed this life 7 Augt / in the year of our Lord / 1821 / aged fifty-three years.[111]

No attempt was made to attach the plate in London, but when the procession stopped at Colchester on the night of 15 August, the coffin was placed in the church, and Lushington took the opportunity to attach the plate. Objection was immediately raised by the undertakers, and a message was sent to Lord Liverpool, who instructed that the plate should be removed, and this was done, after the church had been cleared by soldiers.[112] Lushington was criticized for causing an unseemly altercation in a church. He defended himself at some length in the House of Commons in a debate on the conduct of the funeral, in March 1822. He stressed first that he had received express oral instructions from the Queen, solemnly repeated 'with her dying breath', that he had pointed out to her the difficulty that might occur, and that she had for this reason put her instructions in a codicil. Lushington described the scene at Colchester in this way:

No other opportunity occurred [to affix the plate] while the body remained in England, except that which was made use of at Colchester, and I do not hesitate to declare that it was after much painful consideration that I adopted the course which was finally carried into execution. On the one hand I did feel a reluctance to fixing the plate in the church; on the other hand it was the last opportunity likely to be afforded to me, of keeping the promise I had so solemnly made. Now, what is the course which under such circumstances, I ought in duty and in honour to have taken? For I do pray the House not to look at the matter with the cool calculation of after deliberation, but with reference to the feelings by which the parties at such a moment would be actuated. I took the alternative, which I believed to be the best; and if the thing were to occur again, and I had, as then, pledged my honour to my dying mistress, to fulfil her last intentions to the best of my power, so help me God! I would again pursue the same course. I know that I have been charged with having

probable that Lord Liverpool had intended to tell Lushington that the executors could do as they wished when the coffin had left England.

[111] Aspinall, *Letters of George IV*, 454, says that the plate cost £26 17s 3d, including six shillings for a man's time in taking it to Brandenburg House and fixing it. He says that the bill was paid, to P. Storr, on 14 Mar. 1822. This suggests that Lushington intended to have the plate affixed in Hammersmith, and he says so himself (Hansard, 2nd ser., vi, 958) and that there was no time.

[112] *The Times*, 17 Aug. 1821, 20 Aug. (correspondence and editorial note).

had no respect for the house of God – I know that canters and methodists, who, at the time, approved what I was doing, have since been base enough to tell other tales; but, if the House thinks that I have erred from the true path of my duty, I can only say that I have erred honestly, and with an intention to do the best. I took the opportunity when the church was nearly empty; the plate was fixed on in less than three minutes;[113] and it was not until after it actually was fixed on, that any representation was made to me upon the subject. As I was about to leave the church, a communication with regard to the plate was made to me by the illustrious Mr Thomas [the undertaker's representative]. I remonstrated against what was intended, and at last entreated that, before it was removed, an express might be sent to Lord Liverpool, that the orders of government might be taken; for I felt confident that his lordship would not order it to be taken off. Of the confusion which occurred afterwards I know nothing ... Nothing disgraceful or indecorous took place while I was present.[114]

This account invites some questions. Lushington must have known that there was at least an ambiguity in Lord Liverpool's instructions; they might possibly leave open the course that was followed, but Lushington could not have thought that his conduct had been expressly authorized. He must have known, too, that affixing the inscription would be provocative. He had told the Queen that it would be, and, by his own account, he went out of his way to affix the plate in an inconspicuous manner. Again, it is not clear, on his own account, that the Queen's instructions to him were specific in requiring the plate to be affixed before the coffin left England; more likely, her wish was that the plate should adorn the coffin in its final resting place,[115] and it might be said that Lushington's conduct made it less likely, not more likely, that her wish in this respect would be fulfilled.

In fact, the plate never did reach Brunswick. After its removal it could not be found, and it was thought to have been lost. In 1930, however, an account appeared in *The Times* to the effect that the plate had been stolen at Colchester by a servant of Lushington's, and returned to him many years later; it was then (1930) in the possession of Lushington's great-grandson, and a photograph of it appeared in

---

[113] Huish, *Memoirs of Caroline*, 806, and also J. Nightingale (ed. C. Hibbert), *Memoirs of the Public and Private Life of Queen Caroline* (London, 1820, rep. 1978), 343, say that it was screwed on 'after much altercation', but this seems unlikely, in view of the superior force at the command of the undertakers.

[114] Hansard, 2nd ser., vi, 958–9.

[115] The terms of the codicil, above, do not suggest that the plate was to be attached in England. She chose the wording 'Here lies . . .'. I do not know what significance can be attached to the substitution of the word 'Deposited'.

the newspaper.[116] Subsequent letters to the editor offered alternative versions of this story,[117] agreeing on the fact of theft by the servant. The plate is today still in the possession of the Lushington family, in very good condition, though slightly bent at one corner, where, presumably, it was prized off the coffin.

The next day (Thursday 16 August) the procession went on to Harwich,[118] the coffin being rushed on to the ship with what Lushington called 'needless and indecent haste'.[119] In Germany, Lushington had to deal with various further difficulties in connexion with the funeral arrangements,[120] and the Queen's body was finally placed in its vault in Brunswick on the night of 24 August. A box that had belonged to the Queen remained in his custody until 1858.[121]

Lushington was twice named in codicils to the Queen's will as beneficiary. She left him her coach, and, in a later codicil, a copy of a portrait of herself.[122] The estate, however, was insolvent,[123] and Lushington would have received no benefit from it. Evidently he did receive a necklace, probably as a gift from the Queen before her death, because his grand-daughter, who died in 1953, left, in her will, 'the pearl necklace with diamond clasp which belonged to Queen Caroline'.[124]

It is of interest to ask what motives induced Lushington to undertake a role in Queen Caroline's affairs so far beyond what might be expected of a legal adviser. An executor in his position, especially considering that the Queen died on his wedding day, might certainly

---

116 *The Times*, 15 Feb. 1930, 13f. and 16f. The whereabouts of the plate were earlier rumoured. See A. Greenwood, *Lives of the Hanoverian Queens of England* (London, 1911), 352n: 'It [the plate] is said still to be in the possession of Dr Lushington's descendants.'

117 Letter from Herbert Helme, *The Times*, 19 Feb. 1930, 15e (plate returned by servant's widow to Lushington's sister-in-law), letter from G. R. Y. Radcliffe, another of Lushington's great-grandsons, ibid., 22 Feb. 8e (plate returned to Lushington's son by servant's son).

118 *The Times*, 17 Aug. and Hansard, 2nd ser., vi, 959.

119 Ibid., 960. Huish, *Memoirs of Caroline*, 816, says that the mourners (including Lushington) arrived just in time to see the coffin slung onto the boat.

120 See Huish, *Memoirs of Caroline*, 828 (discussions about lying in state and time of burial), Nightingale, *Memoirs of the Public and Private Life of Queen Caroline*, 355–6.

121 It was then handed over to Cardinal Wiseman, acting under a power of attorney of an Italian donee: Wiseman to Lushington, 23 March 1858, two notes from solicitors, and a receipt, signed by Lushington, and counter-signed by Wiseman, Lushington Family Papers.

122 Melville, *Injured Queen*, 601.

123 Aspinall, *Letters of George IV*, 998, Liverpool Papers, Add MSS 38370, f. 34.

124 Will of Susan Lushington; probate granted 4 Jan. 1955 (Somerset House).

have been expected to take a less active personal part in the conduct of her funeral. In part, the explanation is, no doubt, that it was not in Lushington's character to leave a task unfinished. He always considered, as his motto, to 'think nothing done so long as anything remains to be done'.[125] But, in part, Lushington's actions, especially the affixing of the coffin plate, cannot be seen otherwise than as a political gesture of opposition to the government.

Lushington himself was conscious that he was seen to have played a political role, and, in his explanation to the House of Commons in 1822, he indicated that he felt some tension on this account:

Her majesty had been pleased to honour him with her confidence generally in the absence of the hon. members for Winchelsea and Nottingham (Messrs Brougham and Denman).[126] When the trial was over, he thought his vocation was at an end; but some months afterwards, when he had little time to spare, his professional exertions were again called for. He mentioned these circumstances, because he deprecated above all things the idea that he had become at any time her majesty's political adviser. That duty, he felt, was in much better hands.[127]

But even at the trial, which was the most legal kind of proceeding in the whole affair, politics played an important, and perhaps a dominant, part. Lushington's attitude to the trial altered after 1821.[128] His speech of March 1822, while critical of the funeral arrangements, was moderate in tone, and went out of its way to exonerate Lord Liverpool personally. In 1835, in response to a charge of disrespect to the then sovereign (William IV), he claimed that, at the Queen's trial, he had 'not spoken a syllable more' than duty required of him.[129] Nevertheless, the contemporary record shows that, in 1820 and early 1821, he was leaning towards an alignment with the more extreme manifestations of opposition to the government.

[125] Lushington to Fanny Carr (sister-in-law), 18 Oct. 1854, Lushington Family Papers. A similar phrase occurs in his speech at the Anti-slavery Convention, 1840, *Proceedings* (1841), 380. See p. 98, above.

[126] Lushington later described himself as 'the executor and the confidential adviser of the late Queen Caroline', to whom she 'confided all her secrets'. Mirror of Parliament 1835, 78b (25 Feb.).

[127] Hansard, 2nd ser., vi, 962.

[128] He was married in August 1821, but there is no independent evidence of the effect of his marriage upon his politics.

[129] Mirror of Parliament 1835, 78b (25 Feb.), Hansard, 3rd ser., xxvi, 270. See Hansard, ibid., 199–200 (Col. Sibthorpe, 24 Feb. 1835). Lushington said that he had received Lord Eldon's eulogium on not having exceeded the duty of an advocate. Contrast Eldon's reproof of Lord Brougham, Hansard, 2nd ser., iii, 1457–8 (2 Nov. 1820).

5

THE CONSISTORY COURT

THE BUSINESS OF THE COURT

In 1828, Dr Lushington became judge of the Consistory Court of the Diocese of London, by far the most important of the diocesan courts.[1] He held the office until 1858, the year in which matrimonial and probate cases were transferred to secular courts, and the profession of civil law came to an end. The business of the court during Lushington's time as judge, therefore, presents a picture of the closing years of Doctors' Commons.

The judgeship was not a full-time occupation, either in time or salary. The court sat on about twenty days each year,[2] but these, being scheduled in advance for the sessions of the court, were not necessarily full days.[3] The judge's annual remuneration was about £300.[4] Dr Lushington continued to practise as an advocate before the other civilian courts, until his appointment to the Judicial Committee of the Privy Council, in 1838.

The kinds of cases that made up the business of the court may be classified in various ways. Disputes between individuals were of three kinds: matrimonial suits, testamentary suits, and suits for

---

[1] He was sworn as the judge on 16 Feb. 1828, Assignation Book, Greater London Record Office, DL/C/132.

[2] Report of Ecclesiastical Court Commission, appendix B, PP 1831–2, xxiv, 400 (Answers of John Shephard, Deputy Registrar: nineteen days in 1827, twenty-one days in each of 1828 and 1829).

[3] A full judicial day was reckoned by Lushington at five hours, Report of Select Committee on Admiralty Courts, PP 1833, vii, 379, 430 (Minutes of Evidence, q. 513).

[4] Report on Emoluments of Ecclesiastical Courts, PP 1830, xix, 51, Report of Ecclesiastical Courts Commission 1831–2, xxiv, 9, 400 (Lushington's answers to committee questions. £160 in 1828; less than £280 in 1829; less than £330 in 1830).

defamation. Contrasted with these kinds of dispute were 'criminal' suits, which, though they could be instituted by anyone, were brought in the name of the judge against persons 'touching and concerning their soul's health, and the lawful correction and reformation of their manners and excesses'.[5] Criminal jurisdiction in secular matters was confined, by this date, to cases of incest and of brawling (i.e., unseemly conduct) in church. Another way of dividing the cases is between strictly ecclesiastical, and secular business.[6] What may be called the strictly ecclesiastical business included cases of church rates, faculties for alterations in church buildings, clergy discipline, disputes over rights to occupy pews, and church-wardens' accounts. The principal secular business was matrimonial and probate. By far the most numerous class of cases was matrimonial.[7]

The surviving records of the court in this period include the Assignation Books,[8] showing the dates of the court's sessions, and the names of the cases dealt with at each session, an index of cause papers,[9] and most of the cause papers themselves.[10] Table 1, below, is based on an examination of these records and shows the numbers of cases in each category instituted between the beginning of 1828 and the end of 1857.

The matrimonial causes in use at this period were divorce suits, restitution suits, and nullity suits. There were also a few cases of disputed alimony. Jactitation of marriage (falsely claiming to be married) is listed by Coote[11] as still current in 1847, but there were no cases in Lushington's time as judge, probably because the procedure had been discredited by its fraudulent use in a notorious case in

5 H. C. Coote, *The Practice of the Ecclesiastical Courts* (London, 1847), 151.
6 The Ecclesiastical Courts Commission used a threefold division: temporal, mixed, and spiritual. PP 1831–2, xxiv, 12–13. Defamation is treated as a spiritual and criminal suit 'of an anomalous character'. Church rates, seats, and faculties are treated as mixed.
7 See Report of Ecclesiastical Courts Commission, Appendix D, PP 1831–2, xxiv, 9, 471 (twenty-eight causes were instituted in 1827–9, of which twenty were matrimonial).
8 GLRO DL/C/132–141, 650.
9 GLRO DL/C/627.
10 Most of the matrimonial and testamentary cause papers are at the Greater London Record Office, DL/C/ AC 7377. Most of the other cause papers (except faculty papers) are at the Guildhall Library, MS 12185/2–7.
11 Coote, *Practice of the Ecclesiastical Courts*, 357 ('a suit of very unfrequent occurrence ... but at times a proceeding of great practical utility').

Table 1. *The business of the court, 1828–57*

Matrimonial	558
Testamentary	117
Defamation	37
Brawling	13
Incest	4
Church rates	30
Faculties	51
Clergy discipline	9
Miscellaneous	25[a]
Unidentified	9

[a] Includes sequestrations, churchwardens' accounts, perturbation of seat, vestry elections, burial fees.
Source: Cause Papers, and Index, Greater London Record Office.

1776.[12] Table 2 shows the numbers of cases in these categories, by five-year periods.

The total number of cases instituted gives a misleading picture of the actual business of the court, for many of the cases were abandoned

Table 2. *Matrimonial causes*

	Divorce	Restitution	Nullity	Alimony
1828–32	64	22	12	4
1833–7	61	10	7	4
1838–42	79	19	7	
1843–7	68	15	11	
1848–52	66	11	12	
1853–7[a]	57	6	4	
Totals	395	83	53	8

[a] Fifteen cases, apparently matrimonial cases, presumably pending at the date of the transfer of jurisdiction to the new Divorce and Matrimonial Causes Court, are listed in the Assignation Book, but not found among the cause papers, nor in the index, and not included in these figures. Four other cases, included in the figure of 558 in table 1, were not found among the cause papers, and are excluded from this table.
Source: Cause Papers, Greater London Record Office.

[12] *Duchess of Kingston's case* (1776) 20 St Tr 355 (the parties to a valid marriage colluded to allow a jactitation suit to succeed, so that the woman could obtain an annulment of her first marriage, and marry again; she did go through a second ceremony of marriage, for which she was convicted of bigamy).

without any dispute that required judicial attention. Writing to Brougham in 1833, Lushington said that 'as to Matrimonial Causes. There are not 6 in a year; no nor 4 in all the Country Jurisdictions.'[13] The records of the court show that, in 1832, twenty-two matrimonial causes were instituted, and, in 1833, nine,[14] but most of them probably did not require Lushington's attention. A table published in 1853, showing the causes of divorce determined in the six years 1845–50, gives a better picture of the judicial role. Fifty-four cases are listed, fifty-two resulting in sentences of divorce, and two in dismissals.[15] The total number of divorce and restitutuion suits instituted during these years was 103. This table also shows that an unopposed divorce might be obtained in two to three months. It should be noted that, even where a case was unopposed, the court required proof of grounds for divorce.[16] Some of the contested cases lasted much longer. *Dysart* v. *Dysart*, for example, lasted two and a half years, and has eighty-eight entries in the Assignation Books.[17] It is possible to determine from the Assignation Books the number of times each case

Table 3. *Divorce suits*

	Promoted by wife				Promoted by husband		
	Adultery	Cruelty	Both	Total	Adultery	Cruelty	Both
1828–32	16	9	15	40	24		
1833–7	15	10	8	33	28		
1838–42	18	5	5	28	50		1
1843–7	16	7	12	35	32	1	
1848–52	19	3	9	31	35		
1853–7[a]	18	8	10	36	21		
Totals	102	42	59	203	190	1	1

[a] See note to table 2.
Source: Cause Papers, Greater London Record Office.

13 Lushington to Brougham n.d. but endorsed by Brougham June 1833, Brougham Papers, University College, London, 4159.
14 Cause papers, GLRO.
15 Report of Divorce Commission, appendix, PP 1852–3, xl, 281.
16 The Deputy Registrar said six weeks to two months, but the table shows no case concluded in less than ten weeks. Lushington's own estimate was two to three months, Report of Select Committee of House of Lords on Privy Council, HL Sess Pap 1844, xix, 323, Evidence of Dr Lushington, q. 52.
17 GLRO DL/C/137, 138.

Table 4. *Sentences of divorce*

	In favour of wife		In favour of husband	
		percentage of cases instituted		percentage of cases instituted
1828–32	12	30	19	79
1833–7	9	27	21	75
1838–42	13	46	44	86
1843–7	21	60	25	76
1848–52	15	48	27	77
1853–7[a]	15	41	13	62
Totals	85	42	149	78

[a] See note to table 2.
Source: Cause Papers, Greater London Record Office.

was listed for hearing, but this only shows the time during which the case was pending, not whether it was vigorously prosecuted, nor whether it occupied judicial time: many of the entries in the Assignation Books show simply that the case was postponed from one session to the next.

A divorce suit in Doctors' Commons did not lead to the dissolution of the marriage, and did not permit either party to remarry. The sentence of the court was that the parties 'ought by law to be divorced and separated from bed, board, and mutual cohabitation ... until they shall be reconciled with each other'.[18] The grounds for divorce were adultery and cruelty. Table 3 shows the number of divorce suits promoted by wives and husbands, and the grounds alleged, divided by five-year periods. It will be seen that more suits were promoted by wives than by husbands, but more of the wives' suits were abandoned,[19] though whether with practical effects favourable to the promoters, or the reverse, cannot be determined from the cause papers. Table 4 shows the number of sentences of divorce granted in favour of wives, and husbands, divided by five-year periods.[20]

The papers relating to a disputed divorce case typically included the following documents: the citation (a summons in the name of the

[18] Coote, *Practice of the Ecclesiastical Courts*, 347.
[19] Very few cases were formally dismissed by judicial decree, see table published in 1853, Report of Divorce Commission, appendix (two of fifty-four cases).
[20] Figures include divorces granted to respondents in divorce and restitution suits.

bishop); proxies (formal appointments by each of the parties of their proctors); the libel (the promoter's plea); a responsive allegation (the respondent's plea); an answer to the allegation; depositions of the witnesses on the libel and on the allegation; interrogatories (a form of written cross-examination) to be administered to the witnesses on the libel and on the allegation; notes that the witnesses were duly sworn; an allegation of faculties (the wife's demand for alimony); answer to the allegation of faculties; an Act to lead a compulsory (i.e. a subpoena to compel attendance of a witness); the compulsory; the sentence of divorce; a bond (for £100) against remarriage; the wife's bill of expenses (taxed by the judge).[21] Since the court received no oral evidence, the depositions and interrogatories are, in a few cases, voluminous. On the other hand, few sets of papers are so complete as that just described. Many cases were unopposed,[22] and many were abandoned.[23].

The allegations of faculties, and the answers, do not occur often enough to support any reliable estimate of the overall wealth or social standing of litigants. The professions mentioned in the allegations[24] are those of wine broker,[25] perfumer and hairdresser,[26] barrister,[27] coal merchant,[28] upholsterer,[29] attorney and solicitor,[30] coach proprietor,[31] lieutenant in full pay,[32] lieutenant on half pay,[33] lieutenant-colonel in West India regiment,[34] paymaster of the Dragoons,[35] vict-

---

[21] These are the cause papers in *Cochran* v. *Cochran* (1831) GLRO DL/C AC 7377 53/1.

[22] See table in appendix to Report of Divorce Commission (eleven cases, of fifty-four, were opposed). In ten of the unopposed cases the respondent did not appear, and they were carried on *in poenam contumaciae* (on pain of contempt). See Ecclesiastical Court Commission Report PP 1831–2, xxiv, 16.

[23] Often the cause papers consist only of the citation, or of the citation and proxies.

[24] Nullity and restitution, as well as divorce cases, are included here. Allegations referring simply to property or income are omitted.

[25] *Bryan* v. *Bryan* (1828) GLRO DL/C AC 7377 62.

[26] *Page* v. *Page* (1829) GLRO DL/C AC 7377 53/1.

[27] *Turton* v. *Turton* (1830) GLRO DL/C AC 7377 53/2.

[28] *Tomlinson* v. *Tomlinson* (1831) GLRO DL/C AC 7377 62.

[29] *Phipps* v. *Phipps* (1830) GLRO DL/C AC 7377 19/2.

[30] *Story* v. *Story* (1831) GLRO DL/C AC 7377 46, *Owen* v. *Owen* (1831) GLRO DL/C AC 7377 53/1, *Archbult* v. *Archbult* (1835) GLRO DL/C AC 7377 40, *Rodgers* v. *Rodgers* (1839) GLRO DL/C AC 7377 45.

[31] *Waterlow* v. *Waterlow* (1831) GLRO DL/C AC 7377 46.

[32] *Sargeaunt* v. *Sargeaunt* (1835) GLRO DL/C AC 7377 17/1, 17/2.

[33] *Cood(e)* v. *Cood(e)* (1837) GLRO DL/C AC 7377 57/2.

[34] *Perry* v. *Perry* (1843) GLRO DL/C AC 7377 56/2.

[35] *Shearman* v. *Shearman* (1854) GLRO DL/C AC 7377 59/1.

ualler and wine and spirit merchant,[36] hop and clover-seed merchant,[37] silversmith,[38] general agent and metal broker,[39] sub-engineer of the London fire engine establishment,[40] cabinet-manufacturer,[41] partner in a brewery,[42] accountant,[43] clerk to Commissioners of Income Tax,[44] India-rubber waterproof manufacturer,[45] grocer and tea dealer,[46] surgeon and homeopathic physician,[47] standard-bearer in the Corps of Gentlemen at Arms,[48] merchant.[49] Two husbands are described as prisoners for debt.[50] The descriptions of the parties show that, in eighteen cases, titled persons were litigants,[51] and that ten cases involved clergymen. In his evidence to a committee of the House of Lords in 1844, Lushington said that, while many persons were deterred from litigation by the expense, the very poorest could proceed as paupers, and he estimated that there were always one or two such cases pending.[52] The cost of a divorce (to non-paupers) was at least £100, and sometimes much more,[53] but the descriptions in the cause papers show that litigation was not entirely confined to the wealthy.[54]

A suit for restitution of conjugal rights led to a decree requiring a husband to 'take his wife home and to treat her with conjugal

[36] *Broadbelt* v. *Broadbelt* (1833) GLRO DL/C AC 7377 63.
[37] *Collett* v. *Collett* (1837) GLRO DL/C AC 7377 57/1.
[38] *Walker* v. *Walker* (1834) GLRO DL/C AC 7377 64.
[39] *Anichini* v. *Anichini* (1839) GLRO DL/C AC 7377, 38, 40.
[40] *Hambleton* v. *Hambleton* (1838) GLRO DL/C AC 7377 57/1.
[41] *Dawson* v. *Dawson* (1847) GLRO DL/AC 7377 54/1.
[42] *Yea* v. *Yea* (1848) GLRO DL/C AC 7377 34/1.
[43] *Bunn* v. *Bunn* (1852) GLRO DL/C AC 7377 14/2.
[44] *Crace* v. *Crace* (1852) GLRO DL/C AC 7377 14/1.
[45] *Burke* v. *Burke* (1853) GLRO DL/C AC 7377 23.
[46] *Pringle* v. *Pringle* (1855) GLRO DL/C AC 7377 60/2.
[47] *Buckinghamshire* v. *Wilson* (1855) GLRO DL/C AC 7377 60/1.
[48] *Harmer* v. *Harmer* (1855) GLRO DL/C AC 7377 1/3.
[49] *Campbell* v. *Campbell* (1856) GLRO DL/C AC 7377 60/1.
[50] *Douglas* v. *Douglas* (1829) GLRO DL/C AC 7377 12, *Wynne, falsely called Morphew* v. *Morphew* (1831) GLRO DL/C AC 7377 63.
[51] Figure includes peers, daughters of peers, and baronets.
[52] Select Committee of House of Lords on Privy Council, HL Sess Pap 1844, xix, 323, Evidence of Dr Lushington, qq. 164–8. Paupers had to swear that they were not worth £5 after payment of debts, ibid., q. 168.
[53] Report of Divorce Commission, PP 1852–3, xl, 249, 279 (evidence of J. Shephard, Deputy-Registrar of the Consistory Court); R. Phillimore, *Thoughts on the Law of Divorce in England* (London, 1844), 42, estimated the (presumably, average) cost at £200.
[54] S. Anderson has shown that parliamentary divorces were not confined to the upper classes: 'Legislative Divorce: law for the aristocracy?', in *Law, Economy and Society, 1750–1914* (1984), 412.

Table 5. *Restitution suits*

	Promoted by wife	Promoted by husband
1828–32	16	6
1833–7	7	3
1838–42	14	5
1843–7	10	5
1848–52	7	4
1853–7[a]	4	2
Totals	58	25

[a] See note to table 2.
Source: Cause Papers, Greater London Record Office.

affection', or requiring a wife to 'return home and render to her husband conjugal rights'. These suits were not frequent in Dr Lushington's time, and declined during his tenure as a judge. They were, as will be seen from table 5, used more than twice as often by wives as by husbands. Grounds for divorce (that is, adultery and cruelty) constituted a defence to a restitution suit, and a divorce could be granted in favour of the respondent, without a separate suit.[55]

Table 6. *Nullity suits*

Grounds	Promoted by woman	Promoted by man	Annulments
Former marriage	8	15	12
Impotency and malformation	10	3	6
Nonage		5	3
Consanguinity and affinity[a]	1		1
Undue publication of banns	1	4	2
Insanity	2	1	3
Other[b]	2	1	
Totals	24	29	27

[a] Suits for incest (which also had the effect of annulment) are not included in this table. See table 2.
[b] Failure to comply with foreign law, absence of licence, fraud.
Source: Cause Papers, Greater London Record Office.

[55] Similarly, a respondent in a divorce suit, who recriminated, could obtain a divorce without instituting a separate suit.

Marriages could be annulled on several grounds. A decree annulling a marriage had the effect of setting it aside for all purposes, and therefore left both parties free to marry. As the effect was, also, to make illegitimate any children of the marriage, the courts naturally tended towards strictness. Table 6 shows the number of nullity cases in Dr Lushington's time as judge, the grounds on which nullity was sought, whether the suits were instituted by men or women, and the number of marriages annulled on each ground.

One of the interesting facts that emerges from these figures is that more matrimonial cases were instituted by women than by men (about 54 per cent). The theoretical recognition, by the ecclesiastical courts, of the separate legal personality of a married woman was noted, by Blackstone, as a marked exception to the common-law rule of unity of husband and wife.[56] But the ecclesiastical courts went a step beyond theory. Again, in marked contrast to the common-law rules on costs, a husband was bound to pay his wife's costs, and interim alimony, from day to day during litigation, whatever its ultimate outcome, the wife being described as 'a privileged suitor as to costs and alimony'.[57] These rules attracted some criticism[58] but were defended by Lushington[59] and others[60] as essential (because married women usually controlled no property) to making the courts accessible to those with just grievances against their husbands. The figures tabulated here show that women did in fact enjoy a considerable degree of access to the court, at least to the initial stages of the legal process.

The principal probate court was the Prerogative Court of the Province of Canterbury, but the diocesan courts had jurisdiction over small estates, which accounts for the 117 testamentary cases.

The court's jurisdiction over defamation was confined to cases not

---

[56] Blackstone's *Commentaries*, i, 444.

[57] L. Shelford, *A Practical Treatise on the Law of Marriage and Divorce* (London, 1841), 533. See *de Blaquiere* v. *de Blaquiere* (1830) 3 Hagg Ecc 322, 331, *Walker* v. *Walker* (1837) 1 Curt 560 (where, however, the husband was insolvent).

[58] Report of Select Committee of House of Lords on the Privy Council, qq. 86–7.

[59] Report of Select Committee of the House of Lords on the Privy Council, HL Sess Pap 1844, xix, evidence of Lushington, q. 84 ('as the truth cannot be known till it has been investigated, the husband must take the consequences of the investigation').

[60] Phillimore, *Thoughts on the Law of Divorce*, 45 ('That an abandoned woman may abuse such a right seems to be no reason why an innocent woman should be deprived of it').

actionable at law.[61] In every case the words complained of were spoken words imputing sexual misconduct (not actionable at law without proof of pecuniary loss[62]) and in all but one of the cases the promoter was a woman. The libel recited that all persons who utter words to the reproach, hurt, or diminution of the good name, fame, and reputation of any other person 'contrary to good manners and the bond of Christian charity' ought to be compelled to retract, and (to take a typical example) stated that the defendant

not having the fear of God before his eyes, did ... in an angry, reproachful, and invidious manner ... defame the said Ann Mills ... who was and is a person of good name, fame, and reputation, and character, and charged the said Ann Mills with having committed the foul crime of adultery, fornication, or incontinency, and speaking of and meaning and intending the said Ann Mills ... said, affirmed and published several times, or at least once, these or the like words, 'You, thou, or she are art, or is a whore' or words to that or the like effect, or of the same import and meaning.[63]

Where the case was proved, the order of the court was that the defendant should perform penance, which, at this date, involved a formal apology to the promoter:[64]

The said Benjamin Hall shall, on Sunday, the 17th day of July, 1831, immediately after Divine service and sermon are ended in the forenoon, come into the vestry room in the presence of the minister and churchwardens of the said parish, and likewise in the presence of Mary Ann King ... and five or six of her friends, if they be there, otherwise in their absence, and shall with an audible voice confess and say as follows: – Whereas I, Benjamin Hall, have uttered and spoken certain scandalous and opprobrious words of and against Mary Ann King ... to the great offence of Almighty God, the scandal of the Christian religion, and the injury and reproach of my neighbour's credit and reputation by calling her a whore; I therefore before God and you humbly confess and acknowledge such my offence, am heartily sorry for the same, and do ask her forgiveness, and promise hereafter never to offend her in like manner, God assisting me.[65]

---

[61] The papers relating to thirty-one of the thirty-seven defamation suits are at the Guildhall Library.
[62] Blackstone's *Commentaries*, iii, 128.
[63] Coote, *Practice of the Ecclesiastical Courts*, 266.
[64] No damages could be awarded by the ecclesiastical court. Public penance (in the presence of the congregation) could be ordered in case of a widely published slander: R. Burn, *Ecclesiastical Law* 2nd edn (London, 1767), ii, 121.
[65] Coote, *Practice of the Ecclesiastical Courts*, 272–3.

This jurisdiction was widely considered to be obsolete by the nineteenth century, and was thought particularly objectionable in that it did, sometimes, lead to imprisonment for failure to obey the citation, or to perform the penance, or to pay the costs.[66] In one of Lushington's cases, the defendant, having refused to perform the penance, petitioned for his release after spending twenty weeks in prison, saying that he did not know that he was liable to be imprisoned for speaking the truth.[67] The petition is marked in pencil, perhaps by the Registrar, 'Judge can do nothing – the penance must be performed'.[68] The Ecclesiastical Courts Commission, of which Lushington was a member, recommended abolition of this jurisdiction in 1833, and he said in Parliament:

I am rejoiced to find that one of the provisions of the Bill [based on the Commission's report] takes such offences as defamation out of the hands of the Ecclesiastical Courts. It was only in the month of May last, that I was myself compelled, in the discharge of my duty, to send an individual to gaol for defamation. I had no option, consistently with a due observance of my oath, but to act in the manner I have mentioned; although I know not by what law parties, so imprisoned, can be liberated.[69]

The Bill did not pass,[70] and the Commission's recommendation was not implemented until twenty years later.[71]

The ecclesiastical courts had jurisdiction to punish 'brawling and smiting in church'. This also was recommended for abolition by the Ecclesiastical Courts Commission, with a transfer of jurisdiction to the temporal courts.[72] The offence was not so uncommon as might be supposed, because 'brawling' included all use of angry words, and because 'church' included vestry rooms where meetings on controversial local questions were held. Dickens, in *Sketches by Boz*, presents a satirical account of a brawling case, in which the defendant was proved to have used the words 'you be blowed' for which he was excommunicated for two weeks.[73] One writer has identified the source as *Jarman* v. *Bagster*,[74] one of Lushington's decisions, of

66 See Report of Ecclesiastical Courts Commission, PP 1831–2, xxiv, 63 and appendix.
67 On the extent to which truth was a defence in the ecclesiastical courts, see R. H. Helmholz (ed.), *Select Cases on Defamation to 1600* (London, 1985), xxx–xxxii.
68 *Roberts* v. *Cornell* (1834) Guildhall Library MS 12185/3.
69 Mirror of Parliament, 1835, 309b (12 Mar.)
70 See W. L. Mathieson, *English Church Reform, 1815–1840* (London, 1923), 158.
71 Ecclesiastical Courts Act, 18 & 19 Vic. c.61.
72 Report of Ecclesiastical Courts Commission, 62.
73 'Scenes, no. 8, Doctors Commons'.
74 (1830) 3 Hagg 356.

which a note in Dickens' hand survives.[75] In that case the defendant had said 'you are a liar' and called the complainant 'a drunken church-warden'. Another of Lushington's cases, where, in respect of the words complained of, the reality is closer to the fiction, is *North and Little* v. *Dickson*,[76] in which the defendant said 'you are a wretch'. Probably Dickens drew his material from several sources.[77] In both cases the sentence was suspension from entering the church for two weeks.[78] The jurisdiction of the ecclesiastical courts over brawling was abolished in 1860.[79]

Four cases of incest were brought during Lushington's time as a judge, three in criminal and one in civil form.[80] These cases were commonly brought in order to annul a marriage, often of a man with his deceased wife's sister (incestuous by ecclesiastical law at that time). The order of the court, if the case were proven, was to declare the marriage void, require the parties to live apart, and order the defendant to perform penance. This took a more rigorous form than was usual for penance for defamation, for it was required to be performed in the church 'whilst the greater part of the congregation shall be then assembled to see and hear the same'.[81]

In a case in which such an order was made, the defendant applied for a remission of the penance, with a medical certificate to the effect that 'she would be exposed to dangerous risk if the penance be carried into effect'.[82] Lushington recognized the obsolete nature of penance:

Whatever may have been the reasons for the performance of penance in former days, certainly they do not apply with equal force to the present time. The facts stated in the certificate . . . render it the imperative duty of the Court not to enforce this part of its sentence, at least at the present time.[83]

He went on to remit the penance altogether, on the ground that the probable consequences of suspending it for an indefinite period

---

[75] W. J. Carlton, *Charles Dickens, Shorthand Writer* (1926), 58.
[76] (1828) 1 Hagg Ecc 730.
[77] Dickens set the scene in the Court of Arches, not the Consistory Court.
[78] Not, in fact, excommunication, which was reserved for cases of actual violence. See Report of Ecclesiastical Courts Commission, PP 1831–2, xxiv, 62.
[79] 23 & 24 Vic. c. 32. The papers at the Guildhall Library include a case dated 15 Dec. 1859. MS 12185/7.
[80] The distinction is explained by Dr Lushington in his evidence to the Select Committee of the House of Lords on the Privy Council, HL Sess Pap 1844, xix, 219.
[81] Form of schedule of penance in *Chick* v. *Ramsdale*, Guildhall MS 12185/4.
[82] 1 Curt 36.   [83] *Chick* v. *Ramsdale* (1835) 1 Curt 34, 37.

'would be almost as detrimental as the actual performance of it'.[84] The Ecclesiastical Courts Commission recommended the transfer of the power to punish incest to the temporal courts,[85] but this was not done until the present century.[86]

The more strictly ecclesiastical cases included church rates, which became a matter of high controversy during Lushington's time as judge. The most important test cases, known as the *Braintree* cases, were brought initially in the London Consistory Court, and are discussed in a later chapter.[87] Faculties for alterations in church buildings were usually matters of purely local interest, but church ornaments became a topic of national controversy in the 1850s, and Dr Lushington had to determine an important case on this matter, also discussed in a later chapter.[88] The clergy discipline cases (called 'correction of clerks') involved mainly cases of officiating without a licence. Five cases involved financial matters: sequestrations, and churchwardens' accounts. The court recognized rights to occupy pews, enforced by a suit known, rather quaintly, as perturbation of seat, and three cases were of this sort. One criminal case, arising out of a local dispute about church music, was for obstructing an organist.[89]

MATRIMONIAL LAW

The period immediately preceding the enactment of the Matrimonial Causes Act, 1857, is an important one in the history of family law, for this was the end of the ancient jurisdiction of the ecclesiastical courts over matrimonial causes, and the period immediately preceding the modern era. The Consistory Court of the Diocese of London, of which Lushington was judge from 1828 to 1858, was by far the most important matrimonial court, with about half of all the litigation in England.[90] He, therefore, in a sense, embodied the old order, and his opinions are of interest for this reason. But he was also a leading

---

[84] Ibid.

[85] Report of Ecclesiastical Courts Commission, PP 1831–2, xxiv, 64.

[86] 8 Ed. VII c. 45. The power of the ecclesiastical court was not expressly repealed by this Act, but all ecclesiastical power to punish the laity was said to be obsolete by Goddard LJ, in *Blunt* v. *Park Lane Hotel Ltd* [1942] 2 KB 253, 257.

[87] Below, chapter 8.

[88] Below, chapter 9.

[89] *Office of the judge promoted by Vivian* v. *Hibon & Williams* (1833), Guildhall Library MS 12185/3.

[90] PP 1844, xxxviii, 155 (87 out of 160 cases in 1840–3).

reformer, and a signatory of the report that eventually put an end to his own jurisdiction.[91]

Lushington's opinions on marriage and divorce are, therefore, known from extra-judicial as well as from judicial sources: he spoke on the question in Parliament; he gave evidence to a committee of the House of Lords in 1844, and he sat as a member of several Commissions, including that whose report in 1853, referred to above, led to the enactment of the Matrimonial Causes Act in 1857.

His opinion on the question of dissolution of marriage (then available only by Act of Parliament) was that there was some merit, from the point of view of morality, in a rule of indissolubility, though he recognized that 'in the present state of society' irregular unions were inevitable.[92] He considered the arguments quite closely balanced. But he also thought that, if dissolution of marriage were to be available at all, it ought not to be effected by Act of Parliament. His objections were the enormous expense of the parliamentary procedure, and the unsuitability of the legislative form for a process that had come to be perceived by this date as judicial. He used strong language to this effect in the House of Commons:

Would to God that the disgrace could be removed from this House, and that the law for the annulling of marriage were placed on some sound and solid foundation – that certain rules and principles were laid down, which should enable both high and low – and mark, also, – both male and female, – to obtain divorces upon just grounds; at little cost; and without the interposition of Parliament.[93]

These views were no doubt influential in leading him to join with the majority of the Commission in 1853 in recommending that a new judicial tribunal should be established, with power to dissolve marriages, a recommendation implemented in 1857, thereby putting an end to the jurisdiction of the ecclesiastical courts.

Lushington made reference, in the passage just quoted, to the disparate impact on the sexes of the existing system. He enlarged on this point, again with strong language:

[91] Report of Divorce Commission, PP 1852–3, xl, 249.
[92] Evidence to Select Committee of House of Lords on the Privy Council, HL Sess Pap 1844, xix, 323, q. 37, rep. PP 1852–3, xl, 287, q. 32. See also First Report of the Commissioners appointed to enquire into the state and operation of the law of marriage as relating to prohibited degrees of affinity etc., PP 1847–8, xxviii, 257 (Dr Lushington was a commissioner), where it is recognized that the prohibition on marriage to a deceased wife's sister could not be effective.
[93] Mirror of Parliament 1830, 1269a (6 April 1830).

It is a proof of the repulsive iniquity of the present system, that there stands upon the records of Parliament but a single solitary instance of a female having applied for a divorce bill. That instance occurred in 1801; and with that exception, even since the reformation, Parliament had never either the justice or the honesty to extend relief to any female.[94]

Two months later, he said:

A still greater objection [than inequality between rich and poor] perhaps is that whilst you allow the injured husband the power of resorting to Parliament freely for relief, you refuse to afford the same facilities to the unoffending and equally injured wife ... Ever since I have had an opportunity of considering this question, this anomaly has struck me. I never had an opportunity of reconciling the principle with justice or common sense by which we refuse that relief to the wife, which is granted to the husband. If there ought to be any distinction, or any greater favour should be shewn to one party than to another, I think it should be to the wife, as the weaker party.[95]

In the ecclesiastical courts at that time, the grounds of divorce (that is, divorce *a mensa et thoro*, later called judicial separation) were, in principle, the same for both sexes. Thus, cruelty could be alleged by a husband, though only one such case (unsuccessful) is reported in Lushington's time as a judge.[96] Conversely, adultery, standing alone, on the part of the husband or the wife was a sufficient ground of divorce. Ironically, it was the 1857 Act, following the recommendation of the 1853 report, that first introduced a formal inequality between the sexes in the grounds for divorce, by allowing divorce to a man on proof of adultery, but to a woman only on proof of adultery with aggravating circumstances.[97] Parliament, in practice, had given

94 Mirror of Parliament 1830, 1269b (6 April 1830). Another case occurred in the following year (1831); see S. Wolfram, 'Divorce in England 1700–1857', *Oxford Journal of Legal Studies* 5 (1985), 155, 174. S. Anderson, 'Legislative Divorce', 415, shows that two petitions from women were made in 1801–10, three in 1831–40, and two in 1841–50.

95 Mirror of Parliament 1830, 2088a (also Hansard, 2nd ser., xxiv, 1280–1) (3 June 1830).

96 *Furlonger* v. *Furlonger* (1847) 5 Not Cas 422. The court records reveal two other cases, in 1837, and 1840, in which husbands alleged cruelty and adultery; the sentences of divorce were for adultery only: *Anichini* v. *Anichini*, GLRO DL/C AC 7377, 38 and 40, *Cooper* v. *Cooper*, GLRO DL/C AC 7377, 66.

97 The Commission recommended 'that divorces a vinculo shall only be granted on the suit of the husband, and not (as a general rule) on the suit of the wife. That the wife, however, may also apply for a divorce a vinculo in cases of aggravated enormity, such as incest or bigamy', Report of Divorce Commission, 274.

divorces to women only where there were aggravating circumstances, and the terms of the 1857 Act resulted from the conservative nature of the reform, which aimed at continuing 'with as little change as possible',[98] in the new secular tribunal approximately the same powers and practices as formerly prevailed in the ecclesiastical courts and Parliament combined.[99]

Lushington did not hesitate to assert the common purposes of law, religion, morality, and social policy. He said (extra-judicially) that he considered matrimonial causes to belong to the temporal, rather than to the spiritual, side of the court's jurisdiction, but added, as a proviso, 'except insofar as the due Regulation of those Causes would tend to the Support of Morality or to the Suppression of Immorality'.[100] His theology did not embrace the notion of marriage as a sacrament, strictly speaking,[101] but he considered that it was by 'the settled law of all these courts, and impugned by no other ... an obligation co-existent with the lives of the parties,'[102] and that 'we must remember that the English ecclesiastical law is founded exclusively on the assumption that all the parties litigant are Christians'.[103] He referred to marriage as part of 'the evident design of Divine Providence',[104] and his judgments include other references to the divine purpose:

Under any other circumstances [than the need to protect the wife from injury] the Court cannot put asunder those whom God has joined ... Marriage is in this country considered of ... sacred and binding force.[105]

He spoke of adultery as able to 'sever the strongest ties by which God

98 Sir Francis Jeune (Lord St Helier), *Encyclopaedia Britannica* 11th edn, viii, 339, s.v. 'Divorce'. The new court also had the power (formerly exercised by the common law court) to award damages against an adulterer.
99 See O. R. McGregor, *Divorce in England: a Centenary Study* (London, 1957), 18 ('It altered the procedure for obtaining divorce, but introduced no new principles'). J. H. Baker, *An Introduction to English Legal History* 2nd edn (London, 1979), 408 ('the reform was modest'), L. Holcombe, *Wives and Property: Reform of the Married Women's Property Law in Nineteenth-Century England* (Toronto, 1983), 98–100.
100 Report of Select Committee of House of Lords on the Privy Council, q. 218.
101 See Report of Select Committee of the House of Lords on the Privy Council, qq. 223–7. On protestant attitudes to divorce, see R. Phillips, *Putting asunder: a History of Divorce in Western Society* (Cambridge, 1988), 77–94.
102 *Dysart* v. *Dysart* (1844) 3 Not Cas 324, 366.
103 *Cursetjee* v. *Perozeboye* (1856) 10 Moo PC 375, 415.
104 *D—e* v. *A—g* (1845) 1 Rob Ecc 279, 298.
105 *Neeld* v. *Neeld* (1831) 4 Hagg Ecc 263, 265–6.

and man can consecrate the marriage union'.[106] The formal decrees of the Court had a mediaeval flavour:

> In the Name of God, Amen. We, Stephen Lushington . . . having first called upon God, and having him alone before our eyes . . . do pronounce . . . that . . . the said Eleanor Cochrane . . . being altogether unmindful of her conjugal vow, and not having the fear of God before her eyes but being instigated and seduced by the Devil did . . . commit the crime of adultery.[107]

Lushington took it for granted – as few in his time would have doubted[108] – that a wife was bound, to a considerable extent, to submit to her husband's wishes. It was an age in which a marriage manual advised a bride to remember that 'your position as a woman . . . must be inferior to his [your husband's] as a man'.[109] Lushington said, reflecting similar assumptions:

> If a wife violates the rules and regulations of her husband (providing they are not absolutely absurd or irrational) he has a right to complain of it.[110]

He spoke of the 'just deference' due from a wife to her husband.[111] In a case of an unsuccessful allegation of cruelty by a wife, he said:

> If a wife can ensure her own safety by lawful obedience and by proper self-command, she has no right to come to this court. I know she has had a hard task to perform, but the path of duty is often beset with thorns. In one word [she] failed in the first great duty of submission.[112]

Corresponding to the wife's duty of submission was the husband's duty to control his wife's conduct. In refusing a divorce sought by a husband, he commented that he was 'bound to have exercised the control of a husband'.[113] In another husband's divorce suit, in which Dr Lushington granted the divorce with evident reluctance, he said

---

[106] *Davidson* v. *Davidson* (1856) Deane 132, 151. See also *Graves* v. *Graves* (1842) 3 Curt 235, 241 ('it would go to sap the foundations of all morality').

[107] Sometimes the 'foul' crime of adultery. The wording varied slightly from one decree to another. See Coote, *Practice of the Ecclesiastical Courts*, 345–7. The extract quoted is from the sentence of divorce in *Cochrane* v. *Cochrane* (1831) GLRO DL/C AC 7377 53/1.

[108] The wife's duty of submission was commonly derived from scripture ('Wives, submit yourselves unto your own husbands', Ephesians v, 22), and from the inclusion in the marriage service of a promise to 'obey'. See E. P. Thompson, *The Making of the English Working Class* (London, 1980), 453, quoting Paley (1809).

[109] S. Ellis, *The Wives of England: Their Relative Duties, Domestic Influence, and Social Obligations* (London, 1843), 17.

[110] *Wallscourt* v. *Wallscourt* (1847) 5 Not Cas 121, 133–4.

[111] *Davidson* v. *Davidson* (1856) Deane 132, 150–1.

[112] *Dysart* v. *Dysart* (1844) 3 Not Cas 324, 367, revd 5 Not Cas 194, 1 Rob Ecc 105.

[113] *Dillon* v. *Dillon* (1842) 1 Not Cas 415, 426.

that the husband was culpably inattentive to matters which ought to have excited

his vigilance, and induced him to take measures of protection . . . Of most culpable negligence I cannot acquit him, of the most supine inertness when his honour loudly called for the most active interposition, I must say he is guilty.[114]

As appeared in the discussion of Lady Byron's case, the prevailing legal view of cruelty, laid down by Lushington's most distinguished predecessor in the Consistory Court, Lord Stowell, was a very narrow one. It might be supposed that Lushington's evident sympathy with Lady Byron might have inclined him to take a more lenient view when he came to sit in Lord Stowell's chair, but Lushington followed very much along the lines of his predecessor, and for the same reasons. Thus, Lushington denied relief to women who complained of quarrelsome behaviour,[115] intoxication,[116] exposing a wife to a risk of venereal disease,[117] and disgusting and degrading language, unless there were a direct threat to bodily health.[118] Lushington recognized that these decisions led to harsh results to individuals (usually women, in the case of allegations of cruelty), but this consideration was overridden by the general interest, for married persons of both sexes, and for their children, in stability of marriage.[119] Lushington refused to allow himself 'to be led away, by an anxiety to relieve a hardship upon an individual, to do what might cause an infinitely greater injustice to the interests of the public at large'.[120] The happiness of individual litigants was not a legitimate consideration:

I say nothing of a probability of that peace and happiness which ought to belong to wedded life. Of such considerations I have no cognizance . . . I may, individually, regret the painful consequences to which my judgment may subject her; but this court is only a mouthpiece to declare the law, and is forbidden, for the wisest reasons, from interfering in matrimonial intercourse save for the protection of personal safety.[121]

114 *Phillips* v. *Phillips* (1844) 1 Rob Ecc 144, 154.
115 *Kenrick* v. *Kenrick* (1831) 4 Hagg Ecc 114, 129.
116 *Evans* v. *Evans* (1843) 1 Not Cas 470, 475–6.
117 *Ciocci* v. *Ciocci* (1853) 1 Sp 121, 132.
118 *Chesnutt* v. *Chesnutt* (1854) 1 Sp 196, 198.
119 *Evans* v. *Evans* (1790) 1 Hagg Con 35, Lord Stowell's famous decision to this effect is cited in *Neeld* v. *Neeld* above, and in the 1853 report of the Divorce Commission, PP 1852–3, xl, 249.
120 *Furlonger* v. *Furlonger* (1847) 5 Not Cas 422 (the husband was alleging cruelty).
121 *Dysart* v. *Dysart*, above, 369. The words 'only a mouthpiece' do not appear in Robertson's report.

A claim by a judge to quite so restricted a role must, however, invite scepticism, and some of Lushington's decisions on cruelty show that, when faced with a case where his sympathy for the wife was strongly engaged, he was not so fettered as the passage just quoted suggests. In *Saunders* v. *Saunders*[122] the wife sought a divorce for various insulting language and actions, including spitting in her face. Lushington described this as a 'gross outrage'[123] and he pronounced for the divorce, but it was only with considerable strain on the argument that he succeeded in demonstrating that it gave rise to a reasonable apprehension of bodily harm:

> Is it possible to imagine that when a husband has proved himself so utterly insensible to all those feelings which he ought to entertain towards his wife, so brutal, so unmanly, that he would, when his passion was excited, restrain himself within the bounds of the law, and that his wife would be safe under his control? Threats of personal ill usage have been deemed sufficient to justify a separation. I am of opinion that such an outrage as this is more than equivalent to any threat, for it proves a malignity of feeling which would require only an opportunity to shew itself in acts involving greater personal danger, but never surpassing it in cowardly baseness.[124]

It was argued, for the husband, that he was conscious that violence was prohibited, and had carefully confined his conduct to what was lawful, but so hostile was Lushington that he turned this point against him:

> Nor are such consequences less to be feared when it is proved, as it here is, that the husband supposed, though vainly so, that he was not within the cognizance of the law; for those who are resolved to go to the verge of the law are the most likely to overstep those bounds which their fear only, and not their sense of duty, prescribes to them.[125]

Adultery, on the part of a wife, was not to be excused by reason of cruelty,[126] or use of obscene language,[127] or want of supervision by

---

[122] (1847) 1 Rob Ecc 549, 5 Not Cas 408.
[123] 1 Rob Ecc 559.   [124] Ibid., 562–3.
[125] Ibid., 563. In *Russell* v. *Russell* [1897] AC 395 (HL), which was for many years the leading case on cruelty, *Saunders* v. *Saunders* was discussed by several of the law lords, and found difficult to reconcile with the narrow view of cruelty asserted elsewhere by Dr Lushington and others. Lord Herschell, at 451, deduced, from the strained reasoning, an affirmation of the narrow view, in that Dr Lushington felt compelled to force the facts into proof of personal danger.
[126] *Cocksedge* v. *Cocksedge* (1844) 1 Rob Ecc 90, *Scrivener* v. *Scrivener* (1835) ibid., 92–3.
[127] *Stone* v. *Stone* (1844) 1 Rob Ecc 99, 3 Not Cas 278.

the husband,[128] or by desertion.[129] Lushington manifested considerable sympathy in the case of the deserted wife. Nevertheless, he pronounced for the divorce, saying that she had no 'license'[130] to commit adultery, and adding:

I must administer the law as I find it, and not presume to say that, in a particular case, the punishment affixed by the law will fall (as in most general laws it often does) with undue harshness on a less offending individual.[131]

Lushington did not spare adulterous husbands from harsh comment, particularly when adultery was combined with other wrongs:

He first abandons all his duties, and, under false pretenses, and for criminal purposes, absents himself from his wife and family.[132]

In a case where the husband was found to have committed adultery with his wife's sister, Lushington described the connection as 'disgusting', and added:

All reasons unite to convince me that the justice of the case requires that the wife should be removed entirely from the control of the husband who has so repeatedly sinned and offended against her.[133]

Three principal defences were recognized to a divorce suit based on adultery: connivance, condonation, and recrimination. In considering these defences it must be borne in mind that the consequences of a divorce, despite – or rather, because of – the fact that it did not dissolve the marriage, were very serious. A sentence of divorce against a wife left her without property, unable to remarry, and with no right of maintenance from her husband, a set of circumstances described by Lushington in the case of a young wife as 'utter ruin'.[134] A sentence of divorce against a husband was less likely to be ruinous, but meant that he was bound to maintain his wife so long as she chose to live apart from him. Divorce proceedings were, therefore, potentially oppressive, and the defences were then an essential restraint on the unfair use of the court. In permitting a wife to plead that her husband had introduced her to a woman of bad character (a kept mistress of a third person) he said:

---

[128] *Phillips* v. *Phillips* above, *Harris* v. *Harris* (1829) 2 Hagg Ecc 376, affd ibid. 511.
[129] *Morgan* v. *Morgan* (1841) 2 Curt 679, 1 Not Cas 23.
[130] 2 Curt 690. *Notes of Cases* has 'quasi-license'.
[131] 1 Not Cas 33.
[132] *Fraser* v. *Fraser* (1846) 5 Not Cas 11, 48.
[133] *Turton* v. *Turton* (1830) 3 Hagg 338, 356.
[134] *Morgan* v. *Morgan* above.

It would go to sap the foundations of all morality if a husband might introduce to his wife persons of bad character, and when she follows the example held up to her, he be permitted to come to this court and ask for a separation.[135]

However, in a case where connivance was alleged against a wife, who suspected her husband of adultery with her sister, Lushington was less strict, saying that 'I must not judge her conduct . . . with too much severity . . . Mrs Turton was placed in a situation of painful difficulty.'[136] In the case of condonation, also, Lushington held that a distinction should be made in favour of women. He considered that 'the doctrine of condonation when applied to the wife is totally different from the doctrine when applied to the case of the husband'.[137] The reason for the distinction was the difficulty faced by the wife whose duty was to obey her husband, but who might lose her legal rights if she did so:

The court must consider the safety of the wife; a continuance to share the husband's bed may not, under certain circumstances, in the least degree prove that she was not afraid of renewed violence, or that the husband repented his past cruelty and intended to treat her with conjugal kindness.[138]

The danger of uncertainty was outweighed by considerations of fairness:

I am well aware how much doubt and uncertainty may arise from such a relaxation but I am conscientiously convinced that the peculiar nature of the bond which unites husband and wife, the extraordinary cases that may occur of continued connubial intercourse under circumstances which no-one can foresee; the power of the husband in cases of cruelty over the wife, and many times the helplessness of her condition – all these considerations compel me to say, that the risk attending the relaxation of the principle would be less than the mischiefs resulting from its rigorous enforcement.[139]

Recrimination (counter-accusation of adultery) may seem, at first sight, the strangest of the defences, and it clearly became anomalous in the present century, where the legal and social environment was

[135] *Graves* v. *Graves* (1842) 3 Curt 236, 240–1.
[136] *Turton* v. *Turton* above 354–5.
[137] *Angle* v. *Angle* (1848) 1 Rob Ecc 634, 641, 6 Not Cas 192.
[138] *Snow* v. *Snow* (1842) 2 Not Cas Supp i, xviii.
[139] Ibid. See also *Simmons* v. *Simmons* (1847) 1 Rob Ecc 566, 5 Not Cas 324, 332 ('it is difficult to say when the cup of sorrow overflows'). But in *Campbell* v. *Campbell* (1857) Deane 285, Dr Lushington refused an application by a wife for a delay in order to enable her to establish condonation.

quite different, and adultery by both parties was seen as strengthen-
ing, not weakening, the case for dissolving a marriage. In Lushington's time, the matrimonial courts were not, as has been seen, in the
business of enhancing the welfare of the litigants – still less of dissolving marriages that had broken down. In an environment where a
sentence of divorce had ruinous consequences, it was perceived as
wrong that such a remedy should be obtained from a court of justice
by a husband who had been as guilty as the wife whom he accused:

Many arguments have been urged as to the hardship that Sir Jacob Astley will
incur from the refusal of a sentence of separation; but this is an inconvenience
which he has brought upon himself, and which the law imposes upon him . . .
It is also to be remembered that the wife will equally suffer inconvenience if a
sentence is given against her, and she be turned loose upon the world.[140]

In giving the judgment of the Privy Council on an appeal, he held that
a wife could adduce evidence of her husband's adultery even after
sentence of divorce had been pronounced against her by the lower
court – a case where considerations of finality might well have been
thought to cut in the other direction.[141] Condonation was at issue in
Lady Byron's case, in 1816, and connivance and recrimination both
formed a part of Lushington's arguments in defence of Queen Caroline, in 1820.

Lushington repudiated the notion that a husband could take the law
into his own hands. In a case where, after three years' *de facto*
separation, the husband entered his wife's house by force, he said:

I think this proceeding wholly unjustifiable; I know of no right which, under
the circumstances, a husband possesses to take the law into his own hands, to
supersede the established tribunals, and to attempt to do himself what he
thinks justice by force of arms. If such measures are permitted, suits for the
restitution of conjugal rights may at once be abolished, and the ipse dixit of
the husband substituted for the decree of a court of justice, the husband being
his own judge and executing his own sentence. One of the most certain
consequences of such proceedings might be a breach of the peace.[142]

A duty that Lushington was assiduous in enforcing against husbands was the duty of support. A husband was bound to support his
wife during matrimonial litigation, and to pay her costs, from day to

[140] *Astley* v. *Astley* (1828) 1 Hagg Ecc 714, 722.
[141] *Anon* (1855) 9 Moo PC 434.
[142] *Lockwood* v. *Lockwood* (1839) 2 Curt 281, 301.

day, win or lose. In awarding alimony *pendente lite* (interim alimony) in a nullity suit, he said

Alimony follows as a matter of course except where the wife has a provision of her own sufficient for her condition in life and proportionate to the means of her husband.[143]

Where a husband, having been found guilty of cruelty, objected to the debts incurred by his wife pending the lawsuit, Dr Lushington was unsympathetic:

It is not alleged that during that period the husband furnished the wife with any means of subsistence whatever, and it is now established by the decree of this court that by reason of his cruelty the wife was justified in separating herself from him. Under such circumstances I will not enter into a consideration of whether the expenses were extravagant or not; the whole is at the door of the husband; he compelled her to leave his house, and left her without the means of subsistence, and so situated it might be difficult for her to get credit and live economically.[144]

Even where Lushington had no power to allot alimony, he went out of his way to make provision for the wife by extraordinary means. In a case where an insolvent husband had instituted a divorce suit, Lushington stayed the proceedings 'until some small sum by way of maintenance is afforded to the wife'.[145] In another case, where the marriage had not yet been proved (a prerequisite to alimony), and the wife was left without support during the long vacation, she sought an order 'as a favour, not as a right'. Lushington saw to it that some payment was made. The reporter records that

Dr Haggard, on the part of the husband, stated that he was willing to allow a guinea a week, but the court considered it too little, advised compliance with its recommendation (25 s.) and intimated that, in the event of non-compliance, the husband would have reason to regret it when the formal allotment of alimony pendente lite came before the court after the long vacation.[146]

These cases illustrate Lushington's very flexible and informal use of judicial power, in order to achieve results that he considered just. Similar attitudes are to be seen in his decisions in the Admiralty

---

[143] *Miles* v. *Chilton, falsely calling herself Miles* (1849) 1 Rob Ecc 684, 700, 6 Not Cas 636.

[144] *Harmer* v. *Harmer* (1857) Deane 282, 284.

[145] *Bruere* v. *Bruere* (1837) 1 Curt 566. The cause papers include an allegation of faculties alleging that the husband was heir to an estate worth at least £7,000 per annum, GLRO DL/C AC 7377 57/1.

[146] *Mitchell* v. *Mitchell* (1853) 1 Sp 102.

Court, discussed below, in marked contrast to the more structured approach of the common-law courts to legal rights and obligations.

The amount of alimony *pendente lite* was generally based on income, but Lushington included, in his assessment of the husband's wealth, reversionary interests,[147] and shares, even though not producing income. Of the shares, he said:

Although it might be true that [the shares] might not be available as income, yet if the Court were to allow this exception, a husband might so invest his income as to evade all claims upon him for the support and maintenance of his wife.[148]

The amount allotted, in this case, was more than the usual proportion of the husband's income, Lushington's reason being that 'she must have the means of furnishing herself with a decent subsistence'.[149]

In a remarkable case, a wife, having obtained a divorce on the ground of adultery, and an order for permanent alimony, took her children abroad in defiance of an order of habeas corpus issued by the common-law court. The husband sought to withhold the alimony, but Lushington held that he was bound to continue it, showing little sympathy with the prevailing law of child custody:

I am at a loss to know why I should, by starving an innocent wife, compel obedience to the orders of other tribunals to render up to the guilty husband the offspring of that union, the obligations of which he has grossly violated.[150]

In nullity cases, Lushington asserted the importance of upholding the stability of marriage in the public interest, particularly in the interests of children (on whom a decree of nullity had the disastrous effect of making them illegitimate), even though annulment might conduce to the happiness of the particular parties before him:

It may be true that, on this occasion, if the marriage could be set aside it might be productive of happiness and comfort to all parties concerned; but true it also is that I am to decide the question as if no such considerations belonged to it, and as if it involved also the legitimacy or illegitimacy of the children.[151]

I must not lose sight of this, that, although in this case the lady avails herself of the law for her protection, that law, if not administered with caution,

---

147 *Stone* v. *Stone* (1843) 3 Curt 341.
148 (1828) 1 Hagg Ecc 351, 353.
149 Ibid. The husband's income was £250. The alimony awarded was £75. The usual proportion was one fifth; see *Hawkes* v. *Hawkes* 1 Hagg Ecc 526.
150 *Greenhill* v. *Greenhill* (1836) 1 Curt 462, 467. See the common law custody decision in *R* v. *Greenhill* (1836) 4 Ad & E 627.
151 *Ray* v. *Sherwood* (1836) 1 Curt 173, 192, revd id. 193.

might, under similar circumstances, have been wrested against her and against the innocent offspring of the marriage.[152]

But where Lushington's sympathies were strongly engaged, he showed himself willing to depart from strict adherence to rules. His sympathies were so engaged in cases of nullity sought by a woman on grounds of the man's impotence, where the prevailing medical opinion was that there was risk to the woman's health – menorrhagia[153] – and where the legitimacy of children could not be in issue. It had been a rule of the ecclesiastical courts, derived from the canon law, that the parties must, unless the man's defect were apparent on inspection, cohabit for three years in order to establish the permanence of his incapacity. In a case where the cohabitation fell just short of the three-year period Lushington avoided the rule by the common judicial technique of appealing to the reason behind it:

> The cohabitation of the parties falls short by two months of the term usually required by law. What then am I to do? I have a choice, it is true, either to refuse, or to grant the wife's prayer ... The melancholy state of the wife's health is distinctly established[154] ... I am of opinion that a *triennial* cohabitation is not an *absolutely binding* rule ... I am not aware that there is any magic in *three* years; I conceive that the object of the rule is to provide that sufficient time may be afforded for ascertaining, beyond a doubt, the true condition of the party complained of.[155]

Nullity cases on grounds of impotence were not common, but it happened that Lushington had another case pending at the same time which raised the same question. There, the period of cohabitation was two years and a half. Again, Lushington annulled the marriage:

> The ordinary rule, applicable to such a case as this, is that there must have been a triennial cohabitation ... Within the strict letter of the rule mentioned this case then certainly does not come. But upon what principles, I will inquire, is this rule founded? ... Admitting as I do the general rule to be a

---

[152] *Dormer falsely called Williams* v. *Williams* (1838) 1 Curt 870, 879.

[153] See *B—n* v. *B—n* (1854) 1 Sp 248, 260 (JCPC, per Dr Lushington), *N—r* v. *M—e* (1853) 2 Rob Ecc 625 (Rochester Consist Ct), *S* v. *E* (1863) 3 Sw & Tr 240, W. B. Bell, *Principles of Gynaecology* (London, 1910), 201: 'The effect of sexual abstinence with the stimulation of sexual desire may cause menorrhagia'.

[154] The fourteenth article of the libel includes the following: 'The health of the said G. H. Unwin otherwise Ffolkes visibly and gradually sank under the distressing circumstances of her cohabitation', *Unwin falsely called Ffolkes* v. *Ffolkes*, GLRO DL/C AC 7377 13/2.

[155] *U—n* v. *F—s* (1853) 2 Rob Ecc 614, 617–18.

triennial cohabitation may there not be occasions on which the Court would be justified in departing from the letter of the rule? I think there may be . . . I am of opinion . . . that I am not under the necessity of compelling this lady to return for the purpose of completing the triennial cohabitation. I think that so to do would not only be a useless, but might be a very mischievous application of a technical rule, which I think, in its spirit, does not apply to this case. I think I have no right to expose this lady to the humiliation and possible injury to her health, which might be the effect of a further trial.[156]

In a case decided in the following year, where there had been a cohabitation of only three months, Lushington, in pronouncing for the nullity, showed how heavily the danger to the woman's health weighed with him. He said that:

he could not think of sending the lady back to renew cohabitation, though he could have wished that it had been more distinctly stated that her health had suffered, and was liable to suffer, by such cohabitation.[157]

That the rule of triennial cohabitation was by no means universally considered obsolete may be demonstrated by its strict reassertion, by the secular court, ten years later.[158]

In other cases, also, Lushington asserted a need for flexibility, declaring that 'there can be no rule of practice, in this or any other Court, so strict as to defeat the ends of justice',[159] and that 'all rules of law depend upon the principles of common sense'.[160]

Where a husband sought a decree of nullity on the ground of the wife's incapacity, the question arose, in two cases, of whether a long period of cohabitation ought to bar the husband's remedy. In *B—n* v. *B—n*,[161] giving the judgment of the Privy Council, Lushington said that a long period of cohabitation, though not in itself a bar, might operate as a bar if the husband could not account satisfactorily for the delay, or were found to be 'insincere', i.e. if his motive were something other than objection to the wife's incapacity. He was able, thus, to relieve the wife from harsh consequences:

That very lapse of time may be most injurious to the wife. The consequences of the dissolution of the marriage bond to the wife, unconscious of her own

---

[156] *N—r* v. *M—e* above, at 640.
[157] *G—s* v. *T—e* (1854) 1 Sp 389, 390.
[158] See *M* v. *H* (1864) 3 LJPMA 159, distinguishing the two earlier cases of Dr Lushington's as cases where other evidence satisfied the court of the impotency 'beyond a doubt'.
[159] *Turton* v. *Turton* (1840) 3 Hagg 338, 352.
[160] *Collett* v. *Collett* (1843) 3 Curt 726, 1 Not Cas 504, 512.
[161] *B—n* v. *B—n* (1854) 1 Sp 248.

defect, as is most frequently the case, are necessarily most painful; a proclamation of that defect is made to the world, her *status* is destroyed, and should
unnecessary delay occur, not only are these consequences aggravated, but
parents and relations may have died in the interim, who, had the suit been
brought earlier, would have sustained her in her trials, and secured to her a
home.[162]

But when the question arose in a subsequent case, he found that there
was a price to be paid for flexibility:

If I consider the question of time, I do not find that any period has been fixed.
If I look to other circumstances I am still in the dark. I am not aware of any
authority which has attempted to define them. I know nothing more painful
than to have to exercise a judicial discretion without landmarks to guide the
judgment.[163]

Lushington's matrimonial decisions contain many references to the
desirability of expediting the proceedings in the interests of reducing
delay and expense. He often appealed to these principles in rejecting
interlocutory applications (i.e., proceedings on points collateral to the
main issue),[164] though the same principles led him to defend the
practice of preliminary objection to the admissibility of pleadings, as
likely to save expense by enabling a point of law to be determined
without the need to call evidence.[165] He frequently rejected attempts
to introduce exceptive allegations, that is, evidence on collateral
matters designed to discredit witnesses, while recognizing that such
evidence might, in some cases, 'by possibility tend to the elucidation
of the truth'.[166] But even if admission of such evidence conduces to
the discovery of truth in individual cases, 'by incurring the expense
and delay in all, [it] denies real justice to the great burthen of those
whom necessity or circumstances call to judicial tribunals'.[167] For
these reasons he said that he would 'rigidly adhere to the rule so
established'.[168] But, as he found elsewhere, rigidity sometimes exacts

---

[162] 1 Sp 260.   [163] *Anon.* (1857) Deane 295, 298.

[164] *Phillips* v. *Phillips* (1844) 3 Curt 796, 801 ('instead of tending to elucidate the truth
it would tend to choke it'), *Morse* v. *Morse* (1828) 2 Hagg Ecc 608, *Campbell* v.
Campbell (1857) Deane 285.

[165] *Croft* v. *Croft* (1830) 3 Hagg Ecc 310 ('one of the most wholesome and beneficial
usages which can prevail in any court').

[166] *Lambert* v. *Lambert* (1834) 1 Curt 6, 8.

[167] *Trevanion* v. *Trevanion* (1836) 1 Curt 406, 447, affd 1 Curt 486.

[168] *Sergeant* v. *Sergeant* (1834) 1 Curt 3, 6.

too high a price, and in one of his last reported matrimonial cases, he did reluctantly admit allegations by a wife defending a divorce suit excepting to (i.e., seeking to discredit) the evidence of one of the husband's witnesses:

It appears to me, with all my reluctance to admit exceptive allegations, that I have no power, looking at the rules and practice which have governed this Court, to reject that article . . . It is a complete contradiction [of the witness] and pertinent to the issue . . . Looking at the whole of [a second] allegation, I regret to say that I feel myself under the necessity of admitting this allegation.[169]

Lushington showed himself, on many occasions, sensitive to the plight of individual litigants, particularly of women. Proof of adultery against a wife, he held, must meet a burden heavier than that usual in civil litigation, because a divorce suit 'is, as concerns the wife, not a civil but in effect a criminal proceeding; if there be any doubt, she is entitled to the benefit of it'.[170] A wife alleging misconduct was in a favoured position as a defendant and not, in a husband's suit for restitution 'held precisely to the same strictness of proof'.[171] In admitting proof of a husband's pre-marital misconduct, he said that 'it would be contrary to all proceedings of justice to exclude the wife from the benefit of the exception' (i.e. the exception to the general rule excluding proof of pre-marital misconduct).[172]

In a short biographical sketch, published in 1894, the anonymous writer said, referring to *Dysart* v. *Dysart*[173]

'Her duty is submission', 'The path of duty is often beset with thorns', and so on. Dr Lushington might require police protection from the fair sex if he uttered these sentiments now.[174]

That this comment is as dated as the matter commented on must serve as a warning of some of the difficulties attending an attempt to assess the role of the ecclesiastical courts, and the state of matrimonial law in

---

[169] *Davidson* v. *Davidson* (1856) Deane 132, 167.
[170] *Dillon* v. *Dillon* (1842) 1 Not Cas 415, 443, 3 Curt 86.
[171] *Bramwell* v. *Bramwell* (1831) 3 Hagg Ecc 618, 619 (Rochester Consist Ct).
[172] *Weatherley* v. *Weatherley* (1854) 1 Sp 193, 195–6. See also *Turton* v. *Turton*, above, *Cocksedge* v. *Cocksedge* (1844) 1 Rob Ecc 90, *King* v. *King* (1850) 2 Rob Ecc 153, 7 Not Cas 396.
[173] *Dysart* v. *Dysart* (1844) 3 Not Cas 324, revd 5 Not Cas 194, 1 Rob Ecc 105.
[174] *Law Times* 1894, 336.

Lushington's time. From one perspective, Lushington's view was conservative: as has been seen, he made no excuses for adultery, in either sex, and he asserted a wife's duty to obey her husband, taking a narrow view of cruelty.[175] On the other hand, he was not always consistent, and many of his decisions operated, in practice, in favour of women. Extra-judicially, it will be recalled, he favoured equal access for women to the process of parliamentary divorce, but signed the 1853 report that introduced a formal inequality between the sexes in the grounds for divorce.

Inconsistency in judicial decision-making is partly to be explained by tensions that affect all judges. Lushington's inconsistencies were caused by acute consciousness of the harsh consequences to individual litigants of applying rigid rules. The stretching of principles, or the departure from rules, usually, though not always, operated in favour of women, whom Lushington perceived as weaker parties, and whom he often described as placed in situations of difficulty or helplessness. Consistency is a desirable judicial characteristic, but a lack of it from these causes is not wholly to be condemned.

Inconsistency in Lushington's attitude towards the status of women is another question. The appearance of such an inconsistency springs largely, it may be suggested, from the application of later perspectives. It is not plausible to suggest that Lushington's decisions and opinions, when they operated in favour of women, were motivated by a desire to ameliorate their general social condition: there is no evidence, in his parliamentary career, of support for women's political rights. But it is equally implausible to suggest, with the writer of 1894, that those of his opinions that were later perceived to have operated against the interests of women were motivated by opposition to women's rights. Lushington accepted the prevailing opinions of his time as to the status of women generally, but he was very strong for effective enforcement by individuals, including women, of their rights under the existing law. Hence, his support for procedural rules that favoured women litigants, and his dislike of a parliamentary procedure that virtually excluded women petitioners, with his suggestion that any distinction should be in favour of the wife as the 'weaker party'.[176] These views sprang rather from a lawyer's sense of balance and fair process, than from a reformer's desire to effect social change.

---

175 The fact that Lushington was reversed in *Dysart* v. *Dysart* may suggest that his views were conservative, even by the standards of his own time.

176 See text at note 95, above.

PROBATE OF WILLS

Until 1837, there was a distinction between the requirements for disposition, on death, of real and personal property. A devise of real property (i.e. land) had to be signed by the testator and attested by three witnesses;[177] determination of its validity was by the common-law courts, subject to interference on various grounds by the Court of Chancery.[178] Few formalities were required for wills of personal property,[179] validity being determined by the ecclesiastical courts.[180] Various explanations have been adduced of the link between the Church and proof of wills in mediaeval times,[181] but, by the nineteenth century, the jurisdiction was 'purely Civil, and in name only Ecclesiastical'.[182] The Ecclesiastical Courts Commission, of whose report Lushington was the principal draftsman, recommended in 1832 that the distinction between wills of real and personal property should be abolished, with all wills required to be in writing, signed, and attested by two witnesses.[183]

The reasons supporting this recommendation were simplification of the law by unifying the formalities required for the disposition of real and personal property, the avoidance of conflicting decisions in different courts, the abolition of disputes relating to the validity of informal documents, and the encouragement of due deliberation on the part of the testator. The Commission expressly recognized that the introduction of a formality would involve a sacrifice of 'the occasional benefits resulting from the latitude which the law at present allows'.[184]

In a draft memorandum to the Commission during the course of its deliberations, Lushington strongly advocated these points. On the question of the price (loss of flexibility) to be paid for the benefits of formality, he said:

---

[177] Statute of Frauds, 29 Car. II c.3, s.5.
[178] Report of Ecclesiastical Courts Commission, PP 1831–2, xxiv, 26.
[179] E. V. Williams, *Treatise on the Law of Executors and Administrators* (London, 1832), 54. Oral (nuncupative) wills were possible, ibid., 58–64, but rare, Report of Ecclesiastical Courts Commission, PP 1831–2, xxiv, 30.
[180] Ibid., 25, 30.
[181] See Blackstone's *Commentaries*, ii, 32, Hansard, 3rd ser., lxvi, 313 (9 Feb. 1843; Sir J. Nicholl).
[182] Report of Ecclesiastical Courts Commission, PP 1831–2, xxiv, 25.
[183] Ibid.
[184] Report of Ecclesiastical Courts Commission, PP 1831–2, xxiv, 32.

Is it too much to require of an individual on whom the municipal law not for his but the public advantage confers the right of making a will that he should do so solemn & important an act with some care & deliberation so as to prevent litigation & waste of property to those who come after him.[185]

In his evidence to a Select Committee of the House of Commons, in 1833, he emphasized the expense, and delay, of litigation in two separate courts to determine the validity of a will, and the uncertainty inherent in the practice of admitting informal documents.[186] In a letter to Brougham, of the same year, he described these reforms as 'a great public benefit', because they would reduce litigation, not by making it more expensive, but 'by the removal of the causes of litigation & the introduction of certain & fixed rules instead of leaving matters in the discretion of the Judge'.[187]

In Parliament, he expressed similar views, calling for reforms by which 'an end may be put to unnecessary litigation – or, where litigation may be necessary, to render justice speedy, certain, and inexpensive'.[188] He rejected a proposal for the recognition of holograph wills of personal property, on the ground that it would perpetuate the distinction between real and personal property, with all its attendant difficulties.[189] He thought that the reforms proposed would benefit 'the humbler classes' by making the law more certain.[190]

In 1837 the reforms that Lushington favoured were enacted. The Wills Act of that year provided that a will must be 'signed at the foot or end thereof by the testator' and that 'such signature shall be made or acknowledged by the testator in the presence of two or more witnesses present at the same time; and such witnesses shall attest and shall subscribe the will in the presence of the testator . . .'[191] It turned out that this provision did not usher in quite the era of simplicity and clarity that its proponents had anticipated, and it fell to Lushington, in his judicial capacity, to struggle with some of the difficulties.

---

[185] Draft memorandum on Ecclesiastical Courts, Lushington Family Papers, ff. 19–20. See pp. 18–19, above.

[186] Select Committee on the Admiralty Courts, PP 1833, vii, 379, 435 (q. 556).

[187] Lushington to Brougham, 5 Oct. 1833, Brougham Papers, University College, London, 4160.

[188] Mirror of Parliament 1835, 283–4 (11 Mar.).

[189] Hansard, 3rd ser, xxvii, 1289–90 (20 May 1835). It was conceded by the proponents of this proposal that formalities would be retained for devises of real property; see Nicholl, ibid., 1287.

[190] Hansard, 3rd ser, xxxviii, 1666 (27 June 1837).

[191] 1 Vic. c.26, s.9.

Lushington did not, as a judge, hear a large number of probate cases. The London Consistory Court had a probate jurisdiction, but only where there were no goods outside the diocese exceeding £5 in value: where there were such goods, the Archbishop had a prerogative jurisdiction.[192] Important cases, therefore, were usually disposed of by the Prerogative Court of the Province, which had 'not less than four-fifths of the whole *contentious business*, and a very much larger part of the uncontested'.[193] Lushington sat, on several occasions, in the Prerogative Court, while the judge (Jenner Fust) was indisposed.[194] On the last occasion, when Jenner Fust was dying, the reporter comments that 'Dr Lushington disposed of a vast amount of cause business, which had fallen into arrear'.[195] He also decided some cases, after the appointment of Jenner Fust's successor (Sir John Dodson), in which Dodson had been involved as counsel.[196] Lushington also sat in 108 of the 126 testamentary cases heard by the Privy Council between 1838 and 1858.[197] About fifty of his probate decisions are reported.

The price of every legal formality is a loss of flexibility, which means, in this context, the invalidating of wills where the intention of the testator is clearly manifested, but the formality is not complied with. That there was such a price to be paid was, as has been shown, known in advance, but it is a hard judge who does not feel some discomfort in actually exacting the price. The judge's position is unenviable, for if he takes a strict view, he defeats the clear intention of the testator, impoverishes deserving beneficiaries, and enriches undeserving heirs-at-law; but if he stretches the meaning of the statutory words, he introduces complexities and uncertainties perhaps worse than those that the statute was designed to eliminate.

Lushington suffered some discomfort on account of this tension. In one case in 1844, he asserted and defended a strict approach:

It may possibly be said, that the intentions of the Testator will be defeated by this decision; and if so we may lament it; but we sit here, not to try what the

---

[192] Such goods were called *bona notabilia*, in respect of which the Ecclesiastical Courts Commission commented that the law was 'extremely complicated and ill defined', Report, PP 1831–2, xxiv, 23.

[193] Report of Ecclesiastical Courts Commission, PP 1831–2, xxiv, 12.

[194] See 1 Rob Ecc 2 (1844), and 705 (1849), and 2 Rob Ecc 419 (1852).

[195] 2 Rob Ecc 419n.

[196] Ibid.

[197] Return of Ecclesiastical Appeals (Privy Council) PP 1866, lv, 51 (includes two cases of estate administration).

Testator may have intended, but to ascertain, on legal principles, what testamentary instruments he has made; and we must not be induced by any considerations of intent or hardship, to relax the provisions of a statute (perhaps the most important of modern times) for the disposition of property.[198]

In a decision in the Prerogative Court, in the same year, he held to be invalid a will where the witnesses had not actually seen the testator's signature, even though the latter expressly stated that it was his will. 'That an honest will must thereby be rendered null' he said 'I know and lament, but this same argument, if of any avail, would tend to emasculate all the provisions of the statute.'[199] But when, in a subsequent case, it was argued that a will was invalid because the witnesses, though they saw the testator write, could not be sure that he was writing his signature, Lushington upheld the will. He said that his only duty was to construe the statute 'without regard to the consequences', but he showed himself not entirely blind to consequences, when he added that 'it would be ridiculous' to interpret the statute so as to require proof that the witnesses had actually seen the testator's hand forming the letters of his name.[200]

The cases just mentioned demonstrate that the apparently simple words 'shall attest and shall subscribe' are not free of difficulty. Even more trouble was caused by the apparently equally simple phrase 'at the foot or end thereof'. A digest published in 1849 refers to seventeen cases on this point,[201] and in 1852, the statute was amended to relax the requirement.[202] In Lushington's one reported decision on this question, he upheld the validity of a will that included blank spaces in its body, but not immediately above the signature, though it might be supposed that the object of the statutory requirement was to avoid the possibility of blank spaces being filled up after execution. Lushington held, that on a literal interpretation of the statute, the will was valid, and it was for the legislature, not the court, to add to the stringency of the requirements, if that were desirable.[203] In 1850, he perhaps recognized that the statute had not fulfilled all his original expectations of it, when he said that he considered it no part of his duty 'to

[198] *Croker* v. *Hertford* (1844) 4 Moo P.C. 339, 368.
[199] *Hudson* v. *Parker* (1844) 1 Rob Ecc 14, 40 (Prerogative Court).
[200] *Thomson* v. *Hall* (1852) 2 Rob Ecc 426, 431, 435 (Prerogative Court).
[201] A Waddilove, *Digest of Cases decided in the Court of Arches etc.* (London, 1849), 342–4, and notes.
[202] 15 & 16 Vic. c. 24.
[203] *Corneby* v. *Gibbons* (1849) 1 Rob Ecc 705 (Prerogative Court).

raise obstacles and make the Wills Act more difficult of compliance than it is already'.[204]

Dr Lushington's decisions on probate show that reforms of the law do not always match their framers' expectations, even when interpreted by the framers themselves. The decisions illustrate also the tension, experienced by every conscientious judge, between competing conceptions of justice: a fair result in the case at hand, or the establishment of principles that will benefit the community in the long run.

[204] *In the goods of Swindin* (1850) 2 Rob Ecc 192 (Consistory Court), where the disputed words were interpolated at the bottom of a page. The decision is queried in Jarman, *A Treatise on Wills* 8th edn (1951), 175n.

6

THE ADMIRALTY COURT

SALVAGE

Salvage is the branch of maritime law that rewards those who save property at sea. A case from the middle of Lushington's time as Admiralty Court judge will illustrate the kinds of facts and legal issues with which he had to deal. In 1853, *The Orbona*, a 300-ton sailing ship, was damaged in a collision at night with *The Actaeon*. The master and nine of the eleven-man crew escaped onto *The Actaeon*, leaving only two men on board *The Orbona*. Those on board *The Actaeon* expected *The Orbona* to sink, but she was still afloat at daylight, when a third ship, *The Poictiers*, came up in response to a distress signal. The master of *The Poictiers* 'desired his crew to volunteer' their services, 'being reluctant to give an order in consequence of the danger to which he apprehended they would be exposed'. Volunteers were found, and four men of *The Poictiers* (the salvors) boarded *The Orbona*, by jumping together from a boat, at the top of a wave, and catching hold of the rigging – an obviously dangerous and difficult operation. *The Actaeon* then came up, and hailed *The Orbona* (which was by this time under sail) to heave to, so that her master and crew could retake possession of her – no doubt desiring to minimize any subsequent salvage award – but the salvors ignored the signals, and conducted *The Orbona* into port, reaching safety on the afternoon of the same day. The salvors then sued in the Admiralty Court for a salvage award, and Dr Lushington, having held that they had 'an undoubted right' to retain possession of the ship in the circumstances, gave what he called an 'adequate award' for a 'most meritorious service', of £700, on a salved value of £5,000.

The simple facts of this typical case illustrate the nature and effects of salvage law. £700 was a very substantial sum of money, and, even when divided among the crew of *The Poictiers* (thirty-one hands) would supply a handsome supplement to the wages of an ordinary seaman. The burden on the owners of *The Orbona*, of having to pay fourteen per cent of her value, was correspondingly substantial, as reflected in the ineffective efforts of her master to regain possession. A salvage case was, in one aspect, a dispute between private parties, but it had also a public dimension: the role of the Admiralty Court was to maintain rewards at a sufficiently high level to encourage volunteers, as in this case, to undergo hardship and danger in saving the lives and property of others.[1]

It was for this reason that, in 1861, Lushington called salvage 'a mixed question of private right and public policy'.[2] This is an interesting statement for a judge to make about any area of the law in an era when private rights were clearly identified and strictly enforced, and when public policy was an unruly horse and dangerous to ride. A few years earlier a common-law judge had said that it was not the province of the judge 'to speculate upon what is best, in his opinion, for the advantage of the community'.[3] Lushington's salvage decisions are almost all plainly influenced by his opinion of what is for the advantage of the maritime community.

A treatise on the law of salvage appeared in 1870,[4] three years after Lushington's retirement from the bench. The author cites some American and Irish cases, and the comparatively few English cases decided before 1838 and after 1867, and the few Privy Council decisions on the subject, but the great bulk of the work consists more or less of a digest of Lushington's decisions, with copious quotations from his judgments. The law of salvage, as it stood at that date, could be said to have been largely Lushington's work. About 250 of Lushington's decisions on salvage have been reported. The total number of salvage cases instituted during Dr Lushington's tenure as judge was about 3,000, representing about a quarter of the business of the High

---

[1] *The Orbona* (1853) 1 Sp 161. A version of the first part of this chapter has been published: 'Dr Lushington's Contribution to the Law of Maritime Salvage', *Lloyd's Maritime and Commercial Law Quarterly* 1989, 59.
[2] *The Albion* (1861) Lush 282, 284 (attributing the saying to Mr Justice Story).
[3] *Egerton* v. *Brownlow* (1853) 4 HLC 1, 123, per Parke B.
[4] E. Jones, *Law of Salvage* (London, 1870).

Court of Admiralty.[5] Decisions appear to have been rendered in about 750 cases.[6]

It is always a matter of interest to one studying the work of a judge, to know to whom the judge perceived himself as speaking in his judgments. There is no doubt that Lushington expected to be listened to by the profession. The phrases 'I wish it to be understood'[7] and 'I wish it to be distinctly understood'[8] occur frequently as a means of conveying Lushington's practice directions to what Dickens called the 'uncommonly select audience' at Doctors' Commons.[9] He expected the audience to pay attention: 'I stated upon a former occasion, and I did not expect to be called upon to repeat that opinion ...'[10] In administering a reprimand to a proctor for having refused to reveal the names of his principals, Lushington described the proctor's conduct as 'a matter of deep regret with the Court', and continued:

It has been said that there is no precedent for the course which I am about to pursue. I am thankful that there is none, and I trust that this case is and will continue to be an isolated case.[11]

Lushington perceived a wider audience also. In one case, in which he had found cause to regret the exaggerated claims made by salvors as to the fishing profits they had allegedly lost, he added, in depriving them of their costs, that 'The next time salvors come before me with statements as to the herring fishery I think they will have reason to remember it.'[12] He spoke of the principles of salvage law as 'not only well known here, but by the public at large'.[13] The manner in which

5 Figures derived from H. C. Rothery, *Memorandum on the Jurisdiction and Practice of the High Court of Admiralty of England*, PP 1867, lvii, 1 and 24, with tables showing numbers of salvage, damage and other cases instituted between 1841 and 1866 inclusive. (Salvage cases: 2,653; total cases: 9,994.)
6 Figure derived from the list of salvage decisions between 1839 and 1860 digested in the *Law Times* (1859–65) 33–40 LT (587 cases). Rothery's figures show that final decrees were made in about one third of the total number of cases instituted in the Admiralty Court.
7 *The Emu* (1838) 1 W Rob 15, 16 (Dr Lushington's first reported salvage case), *The Ocean* (1842) 1 W Rob 334, 335.
8 *The Purissima Concepcion* (1850) 7 Not Cas 503, 505; *The Dosseitei* (1846) 10 Jur 865, 867; *The Nicolai Heinrich* (1853) 17 Jur 329, 330.
9 *David Copperfield*, ch. 23.
10 *The Tritonia* (1847) 2 W Rob 522, 526.
11 *The Wilhelmine* (1842) 1 W Rob 335, at 342.
12 *The Hedwig* (1853) 1 Sp 19, 24. Dr Lushington expressed similar sentiments a month earlier in *The Nicolai Heinrich* 17 Jur 329, 330, and evidently felt the need to reinforce the message.
13 *Silver Bullion* (1854) 2 Sp 70, 74.

he described the policies that shaped the substance of salvage law, a matter to be discussed below, shows that he anticipated that the judgments of the Court would have a significant effect on the behaviour of salvors, and potential salvors.

The mid-nineteenth century was a time when common-law judges were more apt to talk of law than of justice. Lushington, in contrast, manifesting the informality and flexibility of the civilian tradition, constantly spoke of his task as to do justice,[14] and, in many cases, he spoke of justice and equity.[15]

He was anxious that there should be the least possible delay and expense in resolving salvage disputes. The procedure, he said, should be 'summary, expeditious, and inexpensive'.[16] 'It is my duty to avoid leading the parties into expense.'[17] Proceedings should be conducted with 'the least possible delay and expense'[18] and should 'combine precision with economy and expedition'.[19]

He often expressed regret at the litigation of small claims, where 'the expenses are so large, that the advantage obtained is not commensurate with the expense of the proceeding'.[20] Where two sets of actions were brought where one would have done, Lushington expressed his regret at the increased expense.[21] He sought to minimize the introduction of collateral issues, saying that 'it is of the greatest importance to adhere as strictly as possible to the main issue'.[22] Rejecting an allegation of misconduct, on the part of the salvors, after completion of the salvage service, he spoke of 'expensive and protracted litigation which ... it has ever been the policy of the Court to avoid'.[23] On similar grounds, he rejected legal arguments that he considered too sophisticated because they 'would in many cases lead to intricate litigation and to questions of great nicety, which it would be

---

[14] *The Neptune* (1841) 1 W Rob 297, 302; *The Aurora* (1842) 1 W Rob 322, 325; *The Prince of Wales* (1848) 6 Not Cas 39, 43; *The Resultatet* (1853) 17 Jur 353, 354; *The Johannes Christoph* (1854) 2 Sp 93,100; *The Mary Pleasants* (1857) Swab 224, 225; *The Elise* (1859) Swab 436, 441; *The Alpha* (1865) 13 W Rep 927.
[15] *The Peace* (1856) Swab 115, *The Spirit of the Age* (1857) Swab 209, 210.
[16] *The Wilhelmine* (1843) 2 Not Cas 213, 219.
[17] *The Harriott* (1842) 1 W Rob 439, 447.
[18] *The Neptune* (1841) 1 W Rob 297, 302.
[19] *The Haidee* (1842) 1 Not Cas 594, 597.
[20] *The Harriett* (1857) Swab 218. Similar sentiments appear in *The Medora* (1853) 1 Sp 17, *The Rosehaugh* (1854) 1 Sp 267, *The Argo* (1856) Swab 112.
[21] *The Nicolina* (1843) 2 W Rob 175; *The Charles Adolphe* (1856) Swab 153.
[22] *The Fielden* (1862) 11 W Rep 156.
[23] *The Hopewell* (1855) 2 Sp 249, 251.

exceedingly difficult for the Court to adjust'.[24] He had no doubt of the need to weigh the expense of litigation. In a passage that would not be out of place in a modern speech on the administration of justice, he said:

We must ever remember that, though truth and justice are the aim and end of all Courts, still they must not be sought through the aid of too expensive machinery. The true principle is, not to adopt that system which, in special cases, may best arrive at the truth, regardless of delay and expense, but to choose that course which, on the whole, will best administer justice with a due regard to the means of those who seek it.[25]

It is of the nature of salvage disputes that the opposing parties seek to put sharply differing complexions on the facts, one portraying as an epic of the sea what to the other is a routine towage service. In the early part of Lushington's tenure, the discrepancy between the rival versions of the facts was exacerbated by the practice of the Admiralty Court, which, like the other civilian courts, did not hear oral evidence. The Admiralty Registrar commented, in 1867, that under this procedure 'the Evidence was consequently in great Measure worthless'.[26] Dr Lushington's own opinion was that oral examination and cross-examination in open court was 'best calculated to elucidate the truth',[27] but, though this was permitted by a statute of 1841,[28] it did not become common until 1855, after a practice change introduced by Lushington himself.[29]

Lushington several times commented on the discrepancy in presentation of the facts by the opposing parties. At times he appeared to accept it as inevitable, saying that 'the Court is well accustomed to meet with statements and evidence which cannot altogether be reconciled'.[30] His usual practice was to make allowances for some shading of the truth short of actual perjury:

[24] *The Emma* (1844) 2 W Rob 315.
[25] *The Resultatet* (1853) 17 Jur 353, 354.
[26] Rothery, *Memorandum*, 3.
[27] *The Harriott* (1842) 1 W Rob 439.
[28] 3 & 4 Vict. c. 65, s. 7.
[29] Rothery, *Memorandum*, 5. The practice change, introduced by Rule under Dr Lushington's name, confirmed by Order in Council, 7 Dec. 1855, required that 'the witnesses instead of being examined as heretofore in private, and upon interrogatories prepared beforehand, should be examined openly in the presence of the parties or their proctors, and upon questions prepared at the time' (Rothery's summary, id., 4). The actual terms of the Order appear as an appendix to Swabey's Reports, 1860.
[30] *The Martha* (1859) Swab 489, 490.

In such cases the Court arrives at the best conclusion it can, without absolutely discrediting the evidence on either side . . . But on the present occasion all attempts to reconcile the evidence are obviously vain.[31]

He spoke in another case of 'softening the description down, as we are generally accustomed to do, when strong statements are made'.[32] He was suspicious of evidence that was too precise, or too good to be quite true. Honest witnesses do not usually remember, in identical terms, the precise words used in the course of an emergency. In a case where he found it necessary to reject a deposition, he described the evidence as 'so strong that its very strength destroys its effect and credibility'.[33]

At times his attitude verged on the cynical. He spoke in one case of the 'usual exaggerations of the merit of the service'.[34] In another, he said that 'all these facts are proved – if anything can be proved in a salvage case – which some, who have great experience, may doubt'.[35] At other times he punished excessive claims by condemnation in costs, saying, in one such case that 'the salvors have seen the whole case through a magnifying glass'.[36] In another case he seemed to be genuinely distressed:

The Court has much to lament in this case . . . It has to lament the great multitude of affidavits which have been made on both sides; and it views with great sorrow the contradiction that prevails between them.[37]

Lushington's approach to expert evidence is of interest. Though nautical questions were often of vital importance, he firmly excluded expert evidence:

It has been an universal rule not to receive these affidavits; for were they to be received the inevitable consequence would be this: the Court would be inundated with the opinions of nautical men on the one side and opposite opinions on the other, to the great expense of suitors and great delay in the hearing of the cause, and with no benefit whatever.[38]

There was a difficulty, however, because questions such as the degree of danger to which a ship was exposed, or the proper methods of

---

[31] Ibid. [32] *The Orbona* (1853) 1 Sp 161, 163.
[33] *The Towan* (1844) 2 W Rob 259, 270. Similar comments appear in *The Graces* 2 W Rob 294, and *The Charles Adolphe* (1856) Swab 153, 157 ('I am a little doubtful of evidence that goes to such minutiae').
[34] *The Orbona* (1853) 1 Sp 161.
[35] *The Minerva* (1854) 1 Sp 271, 273.
[36] *The Paris* (1854) 1 Sp 289.
[37] *The Medora* (1853) 1 Sp 17.
[38] *The No* (1853) 1 Sp 184.

navigation, or of assisting a ship in danger, were often crucial. Lushington's favoured solution was to make use of nautical assessors, senior members (known as Trinity Masters, or Elder Brethren) of the ancient corporation called Trinity House, which had charge of pilotage and lighthouses on the English coast. The assessors sat with the judge, read the evidence, and heard the arguments. Lushington directed them on the points on which they were to advise, and sometimes a decision in their own words is reported.[39] Assessors were very extensively used in collision cases, and it is in one such case that Lushington gives the fullest explanation of their role, explaining (as must not always have been apparent) that their role was advisory only.[40] Though they appeared more rarely in salvage cases, Lushington often recorded his opinion of the assistance they gave, saying in a salvage case that they were 'fully as necessary in this case as, if not more so than, in most cases of damage'.[41] Either party could apply for the appointment of assessors, and Dr Lushington indicated that he favoured such applications, and that, in their absence, the parties would have only themselves to blame if they had reason to complain of a wrong conclusion on nautical questions.[42] On occasion, assessors were engaged at the court's own suggestion.[43]

In two cases, Lushington indicates that there was another way in which he obtained evidence, namely, by instituting his own enquiries. In an 1842 case, he said:

But I was reluctant to leave such a question as this upon the mere comparison of weight and credit due to statements so conflicting on such a subject, and more especially as local knowledge and nautical skill might throw light upon it, and enable me to adjudicate between the parties with greater security and more to my own satisfaction. I therefore caused inquiries to be made as to the nature of the ground itself, with reference to the given circumstances already stated, of the wind, tide, distance, and draught; and I am perfectly satisfied, from the result of these inquiries, made of persons who have great local experience, and knew nothing of this case, nor the purposes for which the questions were asked, that the weight of the evidence in the cause and the truth coincide, and I am enabled with confidence to say, both with regard to

[39] *The Neptune* (1841) 1 W Rob 297.
[40] *The Speed* (1844) 2 W Rob 225, 230.
[41] *The Nimrod* 7 Not Cas 570, 578. Similar sentiments were expressed in *The James Dixon* (1860) 2 LT 696, *The Houthandel* (1853) 1 Sp 25.
[42] *The Princess Alice* (1849) 3 W Rob 138.
[43] *The Ranger* (1845) 3 Not Cas 589.

the evidence itself and such local information as I have been enabled to obtain, that this vessel was not in any danger whatever.[44]

In a later case, where he again made extra-judicial enquiries, he said:

To assist my judgment, but not to govern it, I have sought for information as to the local position, and from persons not only competent to afford it, but who could, by no possibility have any bias, nor indeed communicate with each other, nor know what the object of my inquiries might be.[45]

There is an uneasiness here, in the explanation of the procedure used, and in the insistence, in both cases, that the conclusion was also supported by evidence. There are, of course, drawbacks to a procedure that does not reveal to the parties the identity of the persons consulted, nor the precise questions put to them, nor the precise content of their replies, and that relies on statements not made on oath, and not subject to cross-examination. The methods favoured by Lushington for the obtaining of expert knowledge are significant indications of his determination to keep the proceedings in his court informal, inexpensive, and expeditious. When assessors were used, and also when Lushington instituted his own enquiries, he remained firmly in control, asking just such questions as he wished, and cutting off the process when he thought fit.

The other superior courts, in the mid-nineteenth century, placed heavy emphasis on stability, certainty, and predictability.[46] In marked contrast, Lushington's emphasis in salvage cases was upon flexibility, and justice in the individual case. This attitude was reflected in his approach to precedent. The only court whose decisions were binding on points of admiralty law was the superior court of civil law, viz., before 1833, the High Court of Delegates, and afterwards the Judicial Committee of the Privy Council. Since the High Court of Delegates gave no reasons for its decisions, and there were no reports of admiralty cases, even in the lower court, until the nineteenth century, Lushington commenced his duties, in 1838, almost free from binding authority. Lushington had a virtual monopoly in the field, deciding every important English salvage case between 1838 and 1867. The common-law courts had no jurisdiction. There was no intermediate court of appeal between the High Court of Admiralty

[44] *The Wilhelmine* (1842) 1 Not Cas 376, 378–9.
[45] *The Lockwood* (1845) 9 Jur 1017, 1018.
[46] In *Mullings v. Trinder* (1870) LR 10 Eq 449, 455, Romilly MR said that it was 'a great scandal to the public and the profession generally that there should be a case in which a Court of Law is not able to determine what the law is'.

202 Law, politics and the Church of England

and the Privy Council. Appeals to the Privy Council (of which Lush-ington himself was a member throughout his tenure in the Admiralty Court) were, of course, binding on him, but there were few salvage appeals, and the Privy Council was avowedly reluctant to reverse the judge of first instance on questions of quantum,[47] or on nautical questions.[48]

The few reported decisions of Lushington's predecessors were persuasive, especially those of Lord Stowell, to whom Lushington always referred with deference. He referred also, with great respect, to American judges, particularly Mr Justice Story, but he considered himself bound by none of them. Though he said on one occasion that 'least of all should I be disposed to depart from any judgment of Lord Stowell on a matter of principle',[49] he did, on several occasions, depart from Lord Stowell's views (though whether on matters of 'principle' might, no doubt, be debated).

Lushington's judgments include very sparse reference to decided cases. In his last reported salvage case, he said, in rejecting a claim by salvors who had themselves wrongfully caused the damage that necessitated the service:

I don't seek for authorities, but I look to the principle which ought to govern the case. In my mind, the principle is this, that no man can profit by his own wrong.[50]

Not one salvage case contains what could be called a technical legal discussion, appeal being made throughout to general principle rather than to particular precedent.

On a number of questions, Lushington brought about what he expressly recognized as changes in the law as laid down by his prede-cessors. Early cases had given very little by way of salvage reward to the owner of the salving vessel in his capacity as owner.[51] The concept was of reward to individual seamen for personal service. In the new era of steamships, where the principal agency of a rescue was the motive power of the steamship, the old rule was incompatible with what Lushington perceived as an important social objective, namely,

---

[47] *The Neptune* (1858) 12 Moo PC 346, 351; *The Carrier Dove* (1863) Br & Lush 113; *The Fusilier* (1865) Br & Lush 341; *The Scindia* (1866) LR 1 PC 241; *The True Blue* (1866) LR 1 PC 250. But contrary is *The Medora* (1845) 5 Not Cas 156, where an award of Dr Lushington's was doubled by the Privy Council.
[48] *The Julia* (1861) Lush 224; *The Minnehaha* (1861) Lush 335.
[49] *The Vrede* (1861) Lush 322, 326.
[50] *Cargo ex Capella* (1867) LR 1 Ad & E 356.
[51] The old approach is reflected in *The Charlotte* (1848) 3 W Rob 68.

the holding out of strong incentives to the owners of steamships to rescue ships in danger. He said, in 1859, 'I cannot shut my eyes to the great change which has taken place with regard to salvage services by the introduction of steam power.'[52] In another case decided two years earlier, he expressly referred to a change from former practice.[53] In many other cases he spoke of the desirability of offering powerful incentives to steamships, on the ground of their great efficiency in performing rescue services.[54]

Another point on which Lushington perceived a change to have occurred was in respect of the old rule that salvors of a derelict vessel were entitled to a reward of half its value. Though he himself said, in 1843, that he was 'bound' to give a moiety,[55] in many subsequent cases he departed from that position, saying in one case that the court was 'relieved from the ancient rule'.[56] In a later case, he made clear his preference for a flexible concept of justice:

Remembering that the judgment of the Court must be guided by justice, I lay out of consideration old rules; I never think of a moiety or any other such sum; I endeavour to give a reward proportionate to the services.[57]

On procedural questions there were necessary limits to such a philosophy. In refusing leave to amend pleading to introduce new matters at a late stage, which he said would potentially be 'an act of injustice' to the other party, he said:

The Court is at all times anxious to show indulgence when it can do so with propriety, but looking to the facts set forth in the plea now under consideration, I must hold that in admitting them I should violate all the principles of pleading.[58]

The court had power to reduce, or to remove entirely, an award that had been earned, in order to mark its disapproval of misconduct on the part of the salvors. Lushington again favoured flexibility:

[52] *The Martha* (1859) Swab 489, 490.
[53] *The Spirit of the Age* (1857) Swab 286, 286–7.
[54] *The General Palmer* (1844) 5 Not Cas 159n; *The Monkwearmouth* (1845) 9 Jur 72; *The Santipore* (1854) 1 Sp 231; *The Alfen* (1857) Swab 189; *The Princess Helena* (1861) Lush 190; *The Martin Luther* (1857) Swab 287, 290; *The Spirit of the Age* (1857) Swab 286, 287; *The Otto Herman* (1864) 33 LJPMA 189; *The Andalusia* (1865) 12 LT 584.
[55] *The Watt* (1843) 2 W Rob 70.
[56] *The Genessee* (1848) 12 Jur 401.
[57] *The Minerva* (1854) 1 Sp 271, 274.
[58] *The Aurora* (1842) 1 W Rob 322, 325–6.

204 Law, politics and the Church of England

If the charge [of misconduct] be made, and it is proved that the property, from the misconduct of the salvors, has experienced great deterioration, the perfect forfeiture is the result. But there may be a medium ... If I did [find the charge proved] I should not entirely reject their claim for salvage, although it would be a wrong thing in itself.[59]

Lushington's dislike of technical legal rules appears clearly in a collision case, in which he admitted into evidence a lightship log (technically, hearsay), without requiring the evidence of the person who made the entries:

These logs are official books, kept under authority, and deposited in official custody. I know that in strictness they are not admissible in evidence *per se*; but this Court, for reasons of public policy, allows of several relaxations in the rules of evidence observed in the Courts of Common Law.[60]

Lushington's preference was for an approach that was sensible, non-technical, and administratively convenient. Requiring the actual attendance of the lightship keeper would be none of these things.

Another example, which may remind the reader that Lushington was also an ecclesiastical-court judge, concerns the service of legal process on a Sunday. Service of the process 'might not be improper' in a case of urgency, but it ought to be done 'with the greatest possible decorum that circumstances will allow'.[61] He even went on to explain what these might be:

Instead of being done in the open street, it would have been much more proper had [the clerk] written to Mr Chapman and requested him to accept it on that day ... If the weather had permitted the vessel to be visited from the shore, it might have been served on board.[62]

Lushington's rejection of rigid rules, and his preference for finding a workable balance between conflicting interests on a case-by-case basis is not unlike the approach of some modern administrative tribunals.

Lushington attempted, in giving reasons for his decisions, not to tie himself too closely in respect of future cases. But it is impossible for

---

[59] *The Charles Adolphe* (1856) Swab 153, 155–6. A partial deduction was made in *The Perla* (1857) Swab 230.

[60] *The Maria das Dores* (1863) Br & Lush 27, 28. The reporters' note indicates that, in response to a representation from Trinity House, Dr Lushington in a subsequent case permitted a further relaxation, by dispensing with the attendance of a Trinity House officer, and allowing proof by examined copy.

[61] *The Cumberland* (1845) 9 Jur 191. The service of any writ or process on a Sunday was prohibited by the Sunday Observance Act, 1677, s. 6.

[62] 9 Jur 192.

any decision-maker, in seeking to give persuasive reasons, mostly unwritten, in hundreds of cases, always to avoid occasions where former statements come back to exert an unwelcome influence. Lushington recognized this inevitability, and, in one case, congratulated himself on a narrow escape:

I am exceedingly glad, though I confess I am somewhat surprised, that I should have expressed myself with so much caution on that occasion, because, when delivering a judgment, without its being previously written, it does not always happen that it is expressed in terms so guarded as these.[63]

In another case, where he had stretched a point in favour of a salvage claim, he said, probably without complete confidence, that he wished 'it to be distinctly understood that this case must not be drawn into a precedent'.[64] In a case where he did feel bound by past practice to allow (in part) a kind of claim by salvors of which he disapproved (for loss of fishing profits), he announced that, in the future, he would only allow claims for loss of profits in cases of imminent danger – a kind of prospective overruling.[65]

On a number of occasions[66] Dr Lushington appears to have ignored previous decisions of his own. Such cases naturally tend to attract criticism,[67] and it appears to a modern reader that it is more satisfactory for a judge to state openly that he or she has found it necessary to depart from a former decision, than to pass it over in silence. No doubt Lushington could have explained the discrepancies – probably by appealing to a principle of greater generality than the rules apparently in question – but the fact that he felt no need to do so is, itself, of interest, and indicates something of his, and of the Civilian, attitude to legal rules.

---

63 *The Kingalock* (1854) 1 Sp 263.
64 *The Purissima Concepcion* (1850) 7 Not Cas 503, 505.
65 *The Nicolai Heinrich* (1853) 17 Jur 329.
66 The derelict cases have been mentioned. *The Purissima Concepcion* (1849) 3 W Rob 181 seems hard to reconcile with *The Lively* (1848) 3 W Rob 64. In *The Deveron* (1841) 1 W Rob 180 he said that the effect of deviation on the salvor's insurance was to be disregarded, but seems to have spoken to different effect in *The Aletheia* (1864) 13 W Rep 279, and *The Sir Ralph Abercrombie* (1867) LR 1 PC 454. In *The Little Joe* (1860) Lush 88, he said it was doubtful whether giving advice was a salvage service, but in *The Eliza* (1862) Lush 536, he said that it was. Some other dicta are hard to reconcile, but it would be astonishing if, in a series of hundreds of oral judgments over a thirty-year period, not always accurately reported, there were no such cases.
67 See F. L. Wiswall, *The Development of Admiralty Jurisdiction and Practice since 1800* (Cambridge, 1970), 68–73, commenting on a number of inconsistencies in non-salvage cases.

The natural consequence of the approach that has been described, and, in a sense, the inevitable price to be paid for the advantages of flexibility, was that it became very difficult to predict the result of salvage claims. Lushington himself recognized this, describing salvage law as 'loose and indefinite',[68] as 'rough justice',[69] to be administered 'with something of a rough hand',[70] as a *'rusticum judicium'*[71] and as having 'no definite rule'.[72] In allowing a claim for the costs of defending a salvage suit as damages in a collision case, he said:

> I apprehend there is nothing more difficult, even with the best advice that can be procured from proctor or counsel, than to determine the amount of the tender . . . I say that a prudent man in many cases acts much more wisely in taking the judgment of the Court than in making the tender.[73]

Where appeals from salvage awards were in question, the appellate court often expressed reluctance to interfere 'upon a question of mere discretion'.[74] This view was repeated in other cases.[75] In Lushington's later years as judge, jurisdiction in small salvage cases was transferred from the High Court of Admiralty to magistrates, and Lushington himself had appellate jurisdiction.[76] In rejecting an appeal on a question of amount he said:

> The amount of salvage reward due is not to be determined by any rules; it is a matter of discretion, and probably in this, as in any other case, no two tribunals would agree.[77]

However, as in modern times, appellate courts find it difficult to be quite faithful to such a creed when a decision comes before them that seems seriously wrong. Thus, Lushington, stating that 'under ordinary circumstances' the amount of the award was 'a mere matter of discretion'[78] did on a number of occasions allow appeals where the justices' awards were 'entirely insufficient',[79] in 'extreme cases',[80] and where there had been a 'gross miscarriage'.[81]

[68] *The William* (1847) 2 W Rob 521, 522.
[69] *The Samuel* (1851) 15 Jur 407.
[70] *The Glory* (1850) 14 Jur 676.
[71] *The Norma* (1860) Lush 124, 127.
[72] *The Otto Herman* (1864) 33 LJPMA 189.
[73] *The Legatus* (1856) Swab 168, 170.
[74] *The Neptune* (1858) 12 Moo PC 346, 351 (the phrase is repeated).
[75] See note 47, above.
[76] Merchant Shipping Act, 1854, 17 & 18 Vic., c. 104, s. 464.
[77] *The Cuba* (1860) Lush 14, 15.
[78] *The Messenger* (1857) Swab 191.
[79] Ibid.   [80] *The Andrew Wilson* (1863) Br & Lush 56, 57.
[81] *The Harriett* (1857) Swab 218.

The difficulty of predicting the outcome of salvage suits had an effect on the administration of the rules governing costs. The Admiralty Court, like the common-law courts, recognized the principle that, if the respondent made a formal offer in response to the promoter's claim (a 'tender'), and the promoter rejected it, and subsequently recovered a lesser sum, the promoter could be compelled to pay the respondent's costs. The purpose of the rule is to encourage settlements. Lushington said in one case, in condemning the salvors in costs, 'I wish to encourage liberal tenders'.[82] However, he refused to bind himself always to award costs against the salvors in such circumstances, saying that 'leniency and relaxation' were required in salvage cases in order to encourage salvors.[83] Making an express comparison with common-law practice, he said:

In the practice of other courts I apprehend the principle of the rule is carried out to the fullest extent. I have considered with some care how far in the proceedings of this Court it is desirable that this rule should be generally and uniformly applied. The result of the consideration is that I should feel great reluctance in applying the rule with full rigidity in all cases; and for this reason, viz. that there is something loose and indefinite in the very nature of all salvage transactions, which renders it difficult for the best constituted minds, when judging of their own merits, to determine with nicety the real value and extent of their services . . . In the present case, although I am clearly of the opinion that the tender ought to have been accepted, yet at the same time, looking at the value of the property and at all the circumstances of the case, I do not think I ought to deprive the salvors of all reward, which I should in effect do by condemning them in the costs of these proceedings.[84]

In several cases he indicated that only where the tender was 'amply' sufficient[85] or where the salvors were 'to blame'[86] or 'unreasonable'[87] in not accepting the tender would costs be imposed. Even in such

---

82 *The Iodine* (1844) 3 Not Cas 140, 144.
83 *The Princess Alice* (1849) 3 W Rob 138, 143, and see *The Shannon* (1847) 11 Jur 1045 ('costs are never [in case of adequate tender] given against the owners, and in some cases the owners would be entitled to costs against the salvors').
84 *The William* (1847) 2 W Rob 521, 521–2. The tender was £100, on a value of £3,820, the services lasting two and a half hours in fine weather. A similar comparison with the common-law practice appears in *The Paris* (1854) 1 Sp 289, where, with expressions of reluctance, the salvors were ordered to pay costs.
85 Ibid., and *The Emu* (1838) 1 W Rob 15, 16.
86 *The Queen* (1853) 1 Sp 175n.
87 *The Batavier* (1853) 1 Sp 169.

cases Lushington sometimes condemned salvors to pay only part of the owner's costs.[88]

More generally, Lushington used his power to award costs in a large variety of ways in order to express his approval or disapproval of various kinds of conduct at sea,[89] and during litigation.[90] He quite often reduced the award of costs by a proportion[91] or by allowing a fixed sum *'nomine expensarum'*.[92] In a case where the claimants had run risk and expended effort, but, as it turned out, unnecessarily, he ordered the owners, though successful in their defence, to pay the claimants' costs.[93]

Excessive claims by salvors were regularly penalized by deprivation of costs.[94] More unusual was the power of the Admiralty Court, asserted in several cases,[95] to compel promoters of salvage suits that were wholly unreasonable, to pay damages to the owners. At first sight it seems an oddity to make the unsuccessful promoter of civil litigation liable for more than the defendant's costs. However, when it is recollected that the promoter of a suit in Admiralty had the power to arrest the defendant's ship pending the litigation, it becomes apparent that this is a process that, if unrestrained, would put an extortionate power into the hands of the promoter. There are parallel practices in the other courts.[96]

The history of the High Court of Admiralty was, to a large extent, the history of the limits of its jurisdiction. By Lushington's time the competition between the courts was at an end, and the jurisdiction of the Admiralty Court had been enlarged by statute in some respects, though reduced, as has been mentioned, in respect of small salvage

---

[88] *The Endeavour* (1847) 6 Not Cas 56, affd 6 Moo PC 334.

[89] *The Little Joe* (1860) Lush 88 (salvors responded to an ambiguous signal where there was in fact no danger).

[90] *The Commodore* (1853) 1 Sp 175n; *The Chancellor*, ibid.; *The Persia* (1842) 1 W Rob 327; *The Wilhelmina* 1 W Rob 335; *The Sarah* (1849) 6 Not Cas 677; *The Felix* (1853) 1 Sp 175n.; *The Bartley* (1857) Swab 198; *The Spirit of the Age* (1857) Swab 209.

[91] *The Albatross* (1853) 1 Sp 175n.

[92] *The Endeavour* note 88 above.

[93] *The Ranger* (1845) 3 Not Cas 589.

[94] *The Red Rover* (1850) 3 W Rob 150; *The Hedwig* (1853) 1 Sp 19; *The Earl Grey* (1853) 1 Sp 180; *The Hopewell* (1855) 2 Sp 249.

[95] *The Nautilus* (1856) Swab 105; *The Gloria de Maria* (1856) Swab 106, *The Kate* (1864) Br & Lush 218.

[96] See R. J. Sharpe, *Injunctions and Specific Performance* (Toronto, 1983), 196–232.

claims.[97] Nevertheless, jurisdictional limits occasionally caused problems, as in one case where, in declining to make an order against the consignees of a cargo, Lushington said:

I cannot, for want of power to reach all concerned, do justice, and I might work injustice.[98]

In other cases, he appeared to reach beyond the strict limits of his jurisdiction, ordering recompense to claimants despite their ineligibility for salvage.[99] In one case, where the services in question were performed on shore, he reacted with indignation to a defence based on lack of jurisdiction:

But the first question which I should naturally put to myself is – if this be so, if I am to acknowledge myself bound hand and foot, and totally helpless to do justice on the present occasion, who is to do it?[100]

Salvage law, as has been said, contains a large ingredient of public policy, the court seeking not only 'to do that which is just and right for [the salvors'] interests', but also for 'the interests of the public, which is to encourage them and give that amount of salvage reward which is due to them'.[101] The reward is given 'not merely to remunerate the effort made to save the ship, cargo, and lives of the person on board, but also to encourage others to make similar attempts'.[102]

Some might be inclined to hope that motives of humanity or of generosity, or the conventions of the sea, would be sufficient to induce the rendering of assistance to fellow mariners in distress. Lushington, despite, or, more probably, because of, his experiences as a judge of the ecclesiastical court, had no illusions on this score, saying that 'so long as human nature remains human nature' there would be an indisposition, on the part of naval vessels, to undertake the rescue of British merchantmen in distress.[103] Even the discipline of the Royal Navy was not so effective an incentive as the hope of reward:

[97] Dr Lushington dealt with jurisdictional questions in this context in *The Leda* (1856) Swab 40, *The John* (1860) Lush 11, *The William & John* (1863) Br & Lush 49, and *The Louisa* (1863) Br & Lush 59.
[98] *The Johannes Christoph* (1854) 2 Sp 93.
[99] *The Watt* (1843) 2 W Rob 70; *The Undaunted* (1860) Lush 90; *The Favorite* (1844) 2 W Rob 255; *The E. U.* (1853) 1 Sp 63.
[100] *The Rosalie* 1 Sp 188, 192.
[101] *The Magdalen* (1861) 31 LJPMA 22, 24.
[102] *The William Hannington* (1845) 9 Jur 631, 632. Similar statements appear in *The Albion* (1861) note 2 above, *The Ocean* (1843) 2 W Rob 91, *The Swan* (1839) 1 W Rob 68.
[103] *The Iodine* (1844) 3 Not Cas 140, 144.

Say what you will, so long as human motives operate on conduct, unless you give a reward, you must take away all incitement to service. It is all very well to talk of the abstract question of fulfilling duty and obeying commands; and I have no doubt that, so long as men can execute the duty and perform the commands entrusted to them, they will do so; but in cases of doubt or difficulty, and where great and extraordinary exertions have to be made, reward according to human exertions is the only great stimulus to their performance.[104]

He had no doubt of the beneficial effect of salvage law, describing it as 'of the utmost importance to the safety of shipping',[105] and 'absolutely necessary'.[106] 'If the reward given to small vessels was not sufficient to compensate them for their services it would tend to discourage all those who labour to save cargoes on the coasts of this kingdom.'[107] Particularly were steamships to be encouraged by adequate awards.[108] In allotting shares in the award, he was prepared to recognize particular merit in individual seamen.[109]

Lushington often showed an inclination towards generosity to salvors, giving them the benefit of what seems to have been considerable doubt in cases where they were accused of looting (salvors are entitled to maintain themselves and 'it is impossible for the Court to look into minutiae'[110]) and when accused of excessive expenses ('they would, upon landing, expect to receive hospitable treatment at whatever public house they resorted to'[111]). In a number of cases where one set of salvors had worked hard but to little effect, and another set of salvors had eventually saved the ship, Lushington rewarded the first set, although it would seem that the owner had received little or no real benefit from their services.[112]

On the other hand, salvors were not always meritorious, and Lushington did not hesitate to impose a reduction or a forfeiture in order to mark his disapproval of misconduct, even where substantial benefits had been conferred on the owners:

---

[104] *The Rosalie* (1853) 1 Sp 188, 189.
[105] *The Albion* (1861) note 2 above.
[106] *The Neptune* (1858) 12 Moo PC 346, 350.
[107] *The Harriett* (1857) Swab 218, 219.
[108] See note 54, above.
[109] *The St Nicholas* (1860) Lush 29.
[110] *The Houthandel* (1853) 1 Sp 25, 29. Similarly, *The Louisa* (1842) 7 Jur 182.
[111] *The Hebe* (1844) 2 W Rob 246, 250.
[112] *The Genessee* (1848) 12 Jur 401; *The Pickwick* (1852) 16 Jur 669; *The E. U.* (1853) 1 Sp 63; *The Santipore* (1854) 1 Sp 231. In *The Magdalen* (1861) 31 LJPMA 22, the first set of salvors were allowed their expenses.

It is an established rule of this Court, and one I shall never depart from, that however valuable a service may be, salvors may forfeit their just reward if they are guilty of misconduct.[113]

He was particularly incensed at cases where a second set of salvors had forcibly dispossessed salvors already in possession. The incentives created by salvage law were working rather too well when they encouraged this kind of piratical competition:

I go the whole length of laying down this principle, that where salvors are on board a ship in distress, and their services have been accepted by the master, if, before they have done one stroke of work, they are forcibly dispossessed (without the concurrence of the master) by any persons who in any manner salve the ship or cargo, or part of the same, the alleged second set of salvors can earn nothing for their own benefit, but every act done and every service performed by them must enure to the benefit of the original salvors.[114]

In a case where the salvors had removed part of the cargo and resisted the owner's claim to possession, Lushington described the salvors' conduct as 'most censurable' and condemned them in costs, as well as forfeiting their reward.[115]

Salvors in possession were, however, to be encouraged to call in the aid of more competent or better equipped salvors if such were at hand:

But I wish it to be distinctly understood, and to be well known, that the Court always will, and in another case probably may, visit with great severity conduct on the part of salvors who do not avail themselves, in cases of danger, of any proferred assistance to bring a vessel into perfect safety.[116]

Where salvors had been convicted, under statute, of improperly interfering with a ship in distress, Lushington felt bound to deny any award for fear that 'the case would be reduced to the absurdity of the same men being punished in one court and rewarded in another for the very same act'.[117] In cases of accidental error, he proportioned the penalty to the gravity of the error, sometimes deducting an amount

---

[113] *The Lady Worsley* (1855) 2 Sp 253, 256.
[114] *The Fleece* (1850) 3 W Rob 278, 281. To similar effect is *The Samuel* (1851) 15 Jur 407.
[115] *The Barefoot* (1850) 14 Jur 841.
[116] *The Dosseitei* (1846) 10 Jur 865, 867. To the same effect: *The Glory* (1850) 14 Jur 676, *The Martha* (1859) Swab 489.
[117] *The Wear Packet* (1855) 2 Sp 256, 258.

equal to the loss caused by the error,[118] sometimes of a greater amount,[119] and sometimes of a lesser amount.[120]

Strong as were Lushington's assertions of the importance of supplying adequate incentives to salvors, he was almost equally forceful in declaring that awards must not be excessive, fearing that 'there would be a disinclination on the part of the masters of vessels to accept the assistance of salvors, even in a case of danger to life, if the cost of salvage service was likely to be very great'.[121] Again, he said:

It is consistent with every day's experience that the masters of foreign ships are most reluctant to accept salvage assistance, unless they ascertain previously the extent of payment to which they will be subjected. On the other hand, salvors are very reluctant to make agreements, and seldom assent to doing so unless compelled.[122]

He realized that owners, as well as salvors, would govern their conduct by their perception of salvage law, saying, in one case, that 'the Master must have weighed the chance of the four tugs coming against the chance of a suit in the Admiralty Court'.[123]

Unreasonably high demands at the time of the service were to be discouraged,[124] as were excessive claims afterwards.[125] Lushington was ready to protect the owners 'wherever the Court sees that salvors pursue a line of conduct which is harassing to the owners, and for the purpose of exacting a larger amount of salvage than they are fairly entitled to'.[126] Where necessary he would see that 'salvors must be restrained within the bounds of the law'.[127]

Questions of contract law arose from time to time in salvage cases, as it was not uncommon for agreements to be made, before and after the service, affecting the amount of the reward. On many occasions Lushington showed himself to be lacking in the faith, widely held in the other courts, that enforcement of contracts was in the public interest. His attitude was plainly revealed in a case in which he dis-

118 *The Magdalen* (1861) 31 LJPMA 22.
119 *The Cape Packet* (1848) 3 W Rob 122.
120 *The Perla* (1857) Swab 230. In *The Minnehaha* (1861) Lush 335, and *The Atlas* (1862) Lush 518, the Privy Council proved more lenient than Dr Lushington on this question.
121 *The Inca* (1858) Swab 371, 373.
122 *The Arthur* (1862) 6 LT 556.
123 *The Persia* (1853) 1 Sp 166, 169.
124 *The Elizabeth* (1844) 8 Jur 365, *The Nimrod* (1850) 7 Not Cas 570.
125 *The Eleonore* (1863) 9 LT 397.
126 *The Cumberland* (1845) 9 Jur 191.
127 *The Lady Katherine Barham* (1861) 5 LT 693.

agreement between the salvors and a third party, saying 'that it has been the practice of this Court not to allow agreements barring salvage, in order that the spirit of enterprise should not be interfered with'.[128]

He quite often said that contracts should be enforced if 'fair and equitable', but had some tendency to see contracts as unfair and inequitable when they departed markedly from the result that the court would otherwise have decreed. In a case where, after a service, the salvor had signed a receipt for a small sum (11 shillings) in full payment, he said, exhibiting little of the deference to the sanctity of contractual documents manifested in the common-law courts at the time:

Now, I have always a certain suspicion of these papers. I do not mean to say that this receipt was not honestly obtained, but the inclination of the court is to look at the circumstances of the case, and not to allow a paper to operate as a bar; and upon that principle I shall continue to act.[129]

There was, certainly, an element of paternalism here, out of keeping with the individualistic spirit of the age, but consonant with the attitude of the Admiralty Court to seamen's wage claims. 'Ignorant persons of this description,' he said, speaking of the salvor who had settled his claim for 11 shillings, 'are not competent judges.'[130] To allow salvors to encumber their claims, he held, 'would be detrimental to the interests of salvors themselves, particularly to mates and seamen'.[131]

There are indications in several cases that Lushington did not much approve of salvors who attempted to bargain too keenly in their own interests,[132] or to exclude the rights of co-salvors.[133] He placed a heavy onus of proof on proponents of agreements.[134]

---

[128] *The Pensacola* (1864) Br & Lush 306, 310–11. The decision rested primarily on another ground. Also *The Arthur* (1862) 6 LT 556.

[129] *Silver Bullion* (1854) 2 Sp 70, 75.

[130] *Silver Bullion*, above, 74–5.

[131] *The Louisa* (1848) 3 W Rob 99.

[132] In *The Henry* (1851) 16 LT (OS) 553, 15 Jur 183, where an agreement was enforced against salvors although the master of the salved vessel had understated the value of the cargo, Dr Lushington made comments strongly disapproving of the salvors' attempts to strike an advantageous bargain before performing the service.

[133] *The Atlas* (1862), note 120 above, where Dr Lushington was reversed by the Privy Council.

[134] *The British Empire* (1842) 6 Jur 608; *The Graces* (1844) 2 W Rob 294; *The William Lushington* (1850) 7 Not Cas 361; *The Resultatet* (1853) 17 Jur 353; *The Armonia* (1853) 17 Jur 354n.

On a number of points of contract law Lushington differed from the view generally prevailing in other courts at the time. Thus, he held in several cases that there was a positive duty, before a contract was entered into, to disclose material facts. In 1854 he said;

An agreement to bind two parties must be made with a full knowledge of all the facts necessary to be known by both parties; and if any fact which, if known, could have had any operation on the agreement about to be entered into is kept back, or not disclosed to either of the contracting parties, that would vitiate the agreement itself. It is not necessary, in order to vitiate an agreement, that there should be moral fraud; it is not necessary, in order to make it not binding, that one of the parties should keep back any fact or circumstance of importance, if there should be misapprehension, accidentally or by carelessness; we all know that there may be what, in the eye of the law, is termed equitable fraud.[135]

Again, in 1866, he said that 'if, though unintentionally, there was a concealment of a fact so material that it ought to invalidate the agreement, I should not enforce it'.[136]

On the question of taking account of unexpected events subsequent to the contract, Lushington took quite a different view from that of the common-law courts, where the terms of contracts were strictly enforced. The problem generally arose in cases where a towage or pilotage contract had been made for a fixed sum, and performance became unexpectedly onerous on account of a change in the weather. In a towage case relief was given from the contract:

I think that I should be laying down a very dangerous doctrine if I were to hold that, where a person agrees to perform the simple duty of towing from the Nore to London, if, from stress of weather, from an accident happening to the ship, or other circumstances of a like nature, it should so happen that other and different services have to be discharged, the original agreement is binding on the parties.[137]

Near the end of his career, he said:

When an engagement is made – a contract – for a specific time, that contract must be adhered to, and is not to be broken hastily, unless it be shown that

[135] *The Kingalock* (1854) 1 Sp 263, 265.
[136] *The Canova* (1866) LR 1 Ad & E 54, 56. Qualifying these cases must be considered *The Henry* (1851), note 132 above, where the value of the cargo salved, and *The Jonge Andries* (1857) Swab 226, where minor damage to the ship, were held to be immaterial facts.
[137] *The William Brandt Jr* (1842) 2 Not Cas Supp lxviii.

circumstances have occurred which could not have been within the contemplation of the parties, and that such is the state of circumstances that to insist upon the contract and hold it binding would be contrary to all principles of justice and equity ... If the tugs were merely ordinarily delayed in performing the service they must not have additional remuneration; but if the delay was unexpected, and beyond all contemplation, they must have something additional.[138]

In a case of danger 'services rendered were beyond the scope of the contract to tow'.[139] He did not hesitate to modify a contract rather than discharge it totally, holding that in case of unexpected danger the obligation to render services continued, but at salvage rates, not contract rates.[140] He differed again from the common-law courts, both in perceiving the question as one of justice (and not of mere interpretation) and in the flexibility of modifying rather than abrogating a contract on this account. Probably such an attitude was easier for a judge dealing with a limited area of the law; Lushington was confident of the Court's ability to do justice in all salvage cases, and he did not have to concern himself with the wide range of contracts that were litigated at common law.

Another area of interest to a student of contract law is Lushington's willingness to set aside agreements that he considered unfair. In stating that contracts should be enforced, he frequently added the words 'if just and equitable' or if 'fair and equitable' or words to the same effect.[141]

The danger of extortion by salvors strikes the modern reader as the obvious case of potential unfairness, but Lushington had few such cases. There is no doubt, however, that he would have set aside such extortionate agreements. In one such case he described the salvors' demand as 'exorbitant, and such as no Court of Justice would be justified in carrying into effect'.[142] In the same case he said that the

---

138 *The White Star* (1866) LR 1 Ad & E 68, 70–1.
139 *The Pericles* (1863) Br & Lush 80. Also *The Galatea* (1858) Swab 349.
140 *The Saratoga* (1861) Lush 318; *The Hebe* (1844) 2 W Rob 246, 247–8 (pilotage); *The Black Sea* (1855) Pritch Dig 337. But contracts were enforced in *The Betsey* (1843) 2 W Rob 167, and in *The Jonge Andries* (1857) Swab 226 with a warning of the danger of too readily disregarding contracts, and in *The True Blue* (1843) 2 W Rob 176, and *The Cato* (1866) 35 LJ Ad (though services unexpectedly onerous).
141 *The Arthur* (1862) 6 LT 556; *The Crus V* (1862) Lush 583; *The Helen & George* (1858) Swab 368; *The Enchantress* (1860) Lush 93; *The Resultatet* (1853) 17 Jur 353; *The Firefly* (1857) Swab 240; *The British Empire* (1842) 6 Jur 608; *The Henry* (1851) 16 LT (OS) 553, 15 Jur 183.
142 *The Theodore* (1858) Swab 351, 352.

'court would be just as ready in favour of salvors to set aside an agreement if satisfied that it was wholly inequitable',[143] and there are more cases of this latter kind. The concern in such cases is not with the salvors' taking undue advantage of the emergency, but with the owners taking undue advantage of the inability of ordinary seamen to protect their own interests.[144] On similar lines, settlements made by the owner or master of the salving ship were held not to bind the crew. If an owner had been rash enough to settle in this way, he would have to pay again, despite the hardship:

> It is to be observed that a still greater hardship will be inflicted upon the crew of the Fortitude, whose meritorious services are not denied, if the aid of the Court should be refused them, and their services should be altogether unrewarded.[145]

Lushington was very vigorously opposed to agreements whereby crew members gave up potential salvage claims in advance of the service. Holding such an agreement to be 'highly prejudicial to the public interest' on the ground that it 'would take away motives of enterprise and energy', he added:

> Until therefore I am compelled by superior authority, I never will consider articles of this nature made previous to the performance of the salvage service, binding and conclusive upon my judgment.[146]

In other cases he described such agreements as 'against equity and public feeling',[147] contrary to all justice,[148] and 'inequitable'.[149]

Salvage law, as has been said, rests on a mixture of private and public considerations, and it has proved resistant to easy

---

[143] Ibid.
[144] *The Enchantress* (1860) note 141 above, *Silver Bullion* (1854) note 129 above, *The Phantom* (1866) LR 1 Ad & E 58. But contracts were enforced, as consistent with equity, in *The True Blue* (1843) 2 W Rob 176, *The Resultatet* (1853) 17 Jur 353, *The Firefly* (1857) Swab 240 ('though it seems a hard bargain'), *The Helen & George* (1858) Swab 368, *The Cato* (1866) 35 LJ Ad 116. Dicta in *The Repulse* (1845) 2 W Rob 396, to the effect that the only defences to contract are fraud, misrepresentation, and agreed cancellation, seem inconsistent with the frequent references to inequity in this context.
[145] *The Britain* (1839) 1 W Rob 40.
[146] *The Louisa* (1843) 2 W Rob 22, 23. Also *The Pensacola* (1864) Br & Lush 306.
[147] *The Colombine* (1843) 2 W Rob 186.
[148] Ibid.
[149] *The Pride of Canada* (1863) Br & Lush 208.

classification; there has been much debate about its juridical basis.[150] It is clear that salvage law was not, in Lushington's view, founded on contractual principles. No request for a salvage service was necessary[151] and Lushington's treatment of express contracts plainly shows that he did not ground the source of the obligation to pay salvage in any agreement, express or implied.

As has been seen, Lushington often referred to public policy. If this were the source of the obligation, then one would expect that merit would be rewarded, regardless of success. However, one of the principal characteristics of salvage law has been that merit alone is insufficient. The principle of salvage was 'the rescuing of a ship and cargo from some impending danger or distress':[152]

However meritorious the exertion of alleged salvors may be, if they are not attended with benefit to the owners they cannot be compensated in this Court; salvage reward is for benefit actually conferred in the preservation of property, not for meritorious exertions alone.[153]

The reason was that some property must be actually in the custody of the court to give it jurisdiction.[154]

There is a further, and stronger aspect of this matter. Lushington said that 'human life is more valuable in the sight of God and man than any property'.[155] If, therefore, the roots of salvage law lay in public policy one would expect it to reward the saving of life. But, on the contrary, until modified by statute in 1846[156] no salvage reward was available for the saving of life.[157] The saving of life might enhance a reward if some property were also saved,[158] but for the saving of life alone the Admiralty Court could do nothing. In 1854 Lushington

150 R. Goff and G. H. Jones, *The Law of Restitution* 3rd edn (London, 1986); D. W. Steel and F. D. Rose (eds), *Kennedy's Law of Salvage* 5th edn (1985), paras 25–7. Lord Wright, *Legal Essays and Addresses* (Cambridge, 1939), 55, noting with approval the omission of the subject from the American Law Institute's Restatement, Birks, *An Introduction to the Law of Restitution* (Oxford, 1985), 304–8.
151 *The Annapolis* (1861) Lush 355. The derelict cases also show that no request is needed.
152 *The Mary* (1842) 1 W Rob 448.
153 *The India* (1842) 1 W Rob 406, 408. Similarly, *The Lockwood* (1845) note 45 above, *The E. U.* (1853) note 112 above, *The Undaunted* (1860) supra (but see text at note 99 above), *The Edward Hawkins* (1861) 31 LJPMA 46, affd PC, Lush 515.
154 *The Chieftain* (1846) 2 W Rob 450.
155 *The Florence* (1852) 16 Jur 572 See also *The E. U.* (1853) note 112 above, *The Johannes* (1860) Lush 182.
156 Wreck and Salavage Act, 9 & 10 Vic. c. 99.
157 *The Zephyrus* (1842) 1 W Rob 329; *The Fusilier* (1864) Br & Lush 341.
158 See *The Bartley* (1857) Swab 198; *The Fusilier*, above, 344.

described this state of affairs as a 'gross anomaly',[159] and it had been, by that time, modified by statute, but still, where the statute did not apply, there was no power in the Court to reward life salvage, despite recognition that 'the saving of human life is a much higher service than the rescuing from destruction of any property, however valuable, and deserves the most ample reward'.[160] Lushington added, referring as he more often did in non-salvage cases, to international maritime law:

I do not know that by the general maritime law of Europe, either in ancient or in modern times, a contrary doctrine has been maintained.[161]

Moreover, it should be noted in this context that the very case in which the Admiralty Court gave the highest reward (traditionally a half of the value salved) was in the case of derelict, where the saving of life was not in question. These cases go far to show that the roots of salvage law lie primarily in the notion of a benefit conferred by the service on the owner of the property salved, with reward for merit on public policy grounds as an additional feature where convenient.

It is true that Lushington spoke often of a reward for meritorious service, but he also spoke often of 'remuneration',[162] recompense,[163] compensation[164] and 'what the services were worth'.[165] A primary factor was 'a due regard to the benefit received'.[166] In giving a large reward for a brief but efficient service Lushington said that 'It is not the mere time occupied; it is not the mere labour, but the real value of the services rendered.'[167] Many other of his expressions are fully consistent with an attempt to measure the award by the value of the services.[168]

A large value salved was always apt to increase the award. This is not inconsistent with measurement by value of service, since all valuation supposes a hypothetical bargain, and a reasonable owner

---

[159] *Silver Bullion* (1854) note 129 above. Also *The Coromandel* (1857) Swab 205.
[160] *The Johannes* (1860) Lush 182, 187.
[161] Ibid.
[162] *The Inca* (1858) Swab 371; *The Harriett* (1853) note 107 above, *The Undaunted* (1860) note 99 above.
[163] *The Syrian* (1866) 14 LT 833.
[164] *The Rajasthan* (1856) Swab 171, *The Mary Pleasants* (1857) Swab 224.
[165] *The Mary Pleasants* (1857) above, *The Africa* (1854) 1 Sp 299 ('reward for services rendered'), *The Otto Herman* (1864) 33 LJPMA 189 (payment 'for services').
[166] *The Fusilier* (1864) note 47 above.
[167] *The General Palmer* (1844) 5 Not Cas 159n. Also *The Andalusia* (1865) 12 LT 584.
[168] See *The Otto Herman* (1864) note 165 above (salvors to be 'paid for their services'), *The Jan Hendrik* (1853) 1 Sp 181 (the underwriters 'ought to be thankful to pay the sum I am now about to allot').

would naturally pay more for salvage of more valuable property. Less readily reconcilable with a compensatory theory is the suggestion, appearing in two cases, that a large salved value enabled the court in effect to overpay in those cases in order to offset the many cases where awards were smaller than merit deserved.[169] But in a later case he appeared to rule out cross-subsidization of this sort:

> In dealing with the present case the court also bears in mind that there is a large amount of property salved; but for the single purpose of remembering that it is enabled out of an ample fund fitly to remunerate meritorious services well performed; and the Court does not hold the large value of the property salved as a ground for attempting to extort from the owners of that property or from the underwriters . . . more than the full recompense for such services.[170]

It would be idle to attempt to show that all Lushington's dicta are consistent on this point, and equally idle to attempt to reconcile salvage law in all respects with common-law ideas. Lushington himself felt no need to do such a thing. Indeed, the administration of salvage law in a separate court, and (until 1858) by a separate profession, made it natural that it should possess distinctive features.

PRIZE LAW

Prize law rewards those who, in wartime, capture enemy ships, or neutral ships that contravene the rules of neutrality. Disputes as to the legality of captures were adjudicated by the Admiralty Court, acting under a commission as a Prize Court. A tribunal of this sort was generally essential to the validity of the capture in international law.[171] The outbreak of the Crimean War, against Russia, in 1854 caused a revival, after a lapse of forty years, of this prize jurisdiction. Prize cases had made some of Lushington's predecessors wealthy,[172] but, as a consequence of the abolition in 1841 of payment of the judge by fees, Lushington had no longer a personal financial interest in the outbreak of war.[173] The war was of comparatively short duration, and

---

[169] *The Earl of Eglinton* (1855) Swab 7; *The Henry* (1851) 15 Jur 183, 184.

[170] *The Syrian* (1866) 14 LT 833, 834.

[171] A. D. MacNair, *International Law Opinions* (Cambridge, 1956), iii, 61–78.

[172] See evidence of Sir John Nicholl to the Select Committee on Admiralty Courts, PP 1833, vii (qq. 98–9), and Brougham's law reform speech, 7 Feb. 1828, in which he pointed out that the admiralty judge, with a regular salary of only £2,500, could expect fees of seven or eight thousand pounds in wartime, H. Brougham, *Speeches* (Edinburgh, 1838), ii, 355.

[173] Fees were abolished by 3 & 4 Vic. c. 66, s. 18.

produced 214 prize cases for Lushington's adjudication,[174] of which about fifty are reported,[175] almost all dealing with the seizure by British warships of neutral merchant ships.

It is even more difficult, in wartime prize law, than in other fields of law, to draw a clear line between judicial and political functions. Lushington in fact played a direct political role in the establishment of the law he was to administer. As a member of the Privy Council, he signed the Order in Council granting reprisals against Russian ships,[176] and he advised the Government on the drafting of orders to enforce the blockade, writing, in April 1854, to Lord Granville, the President of the Privy Council:

I send you some memoranda on the subjects discussed yesterday. Lord Clarendon complains that he has no advice. You will perceive by the inclosed that I have endeavoured to form an opinion on three points:

1. Not to allow British ships to trade with the enemy
2. To permit British merchants to trade with Russia
3. Not to grant Licences, unless necessity requires[177]

The terms of the order of 15 April conform to this advice,[178] prohibiting British ships from visiting Russian ports, but otherwise permitting British trade to continue, thereby substantially relaxing the law as then understood.[179] Even with the permissive terms of the Order,

[174] Index of Russian War Prize Cases. PRO HCA 33/44. PRO List, 9/15.
[175] Mainly reported in 1 and 2 Sp, Sp PC, and Moo PC.
[176] Sp PC, appendix, i–ii.
[177] Lushington to Lord Granville, 5 April 1854, Granville Papers PRO 30/29/23/4. See also Lushington to Lord Clarendon, 11 June 1854, Clarendon Papers, Bodleian Library, Oxford, MSS Clar dep. C 19, 376–7. Greville records that Lushington was a member of a committee of the Privy Council on questions relating to shipping and trade restraints, *The Greville Memoirs*, ed. L. Strachey and R. Fulford (London, 1938) vii, 31, 23 April 1854.
[178] See Sp PC, appendix v, Order in Council of 15 April 1854: 'and it is hereby further added that, save and except as aforesaid, all the subjects of Her Majesty . . . may, during and notwithstanding the present hostilities with Russia, freely trade with all ports and places wheresoever situate which shall not be in a state of blockade, save and except that no British vessel shall . . . be permitted . . . to enter . . . any port . . . in the possession . . . of Her Majesty's enemies'.
[179] J. Harding, the Queen's Advocate, gave, as his opinion on 3 April 1854, that, under the then existing law, all trade with Russia was illegal, Foreign Office, Confidential Prints, 3576, no. 55. Greville, *Memoirs*, 24 April 1854, comments: 'When we went to war, the Government, I believe very wisely, resolved to relax belligerent rights and give all possible latitude to trade, with no more restrictions and reservations than were essentially necessary for carrying on the war.' See O. Anderson, *A Liberal State at War* (London, 1967), 252–4.

there was a flood of requests for exemptions, and Lushington assisted the Government in dealing with them.[180]

Lushington advised Lord Granville on more than strictly legal questions. Granville had been criticized for admitting Russian nationals to the Travellers' Club. Lushington advised that enemy aliens should be well treated, adducing a mixture of humanitarian and pragmatic considerations:

I am of opinion that you ought to take high ground in this matter both as a Cabinet Minister & as a Peer of Parliament. Indeed when acting in your latter capacity & in a mere private matter it is sheer impertinence to question your conduct, but I admit that as Minister it may be open to examination. I would openly avow & maintain that in all that relates to private society it is fully justifiable to treat with civility & kindness the subjects of a state at war with Great Britain. During the last war naval officers on their parol in England were received & courteously treated . . . but apart from the instances I would avow the principle & defend it:

1st. Because such intercourse does not in the remotest degree tend to strengthen the enemy or weaken belligerent measures.
2d. Because it is in the interest of the whole civilized world that the evils incidental to warfare should be mitigated as much as possible. Because civility shewn to Russian subjects here tends to insure good treatment to British subjects still in Russia. Because the Emperor by his Proclamation promises kind treatment & there is no reason to suppose he has not kept his word.
3d. That British connexions are to be found in every part of the Globe & the course of events shews that such admixture must increase, it is therefore both wise & just to maintain a line of conduct in private life which may in case of war tend to the comfort of British connexions abroad & of course to that of their friends at home . . . The Law of Nations during war was a state of barbarity, unchristian & inhuman; as the world has become more civilized the earliest practices have been discontinued, for instance, not only as to the treatment of prisoners, but as to not seizing enemies' property on Land. That the feelings of mankind clearly run in this sense & that there ought to be *no limit* to the *relaxation* of the rigours of warfare, provided such relaxation does not tend to weaken the exertion of the Nation & therefore postpone the chance of peace. May you not safely ask, what the Travellers' Club has to do with such matters?[181]

---

[180] Greville, *Memoirs*, 24 April 1854: 'With the help of . . . Dr Lushington . . . they have contrived to scramble through the business.'
[181] Lushington to Granville, 19 July 1854, Granville Papers, PRO 30/29/23/4.

The attitude to war, revealed here, reflects the liberal views to be seen in other aspects of Lushington's career, and the confidence, general at the time, in the progress of civilization.

British interests lay, generally, in the preservation of the reputation of the Prize Court as 'notoriously impartial and entirely beyond the control of the Government'.[182] In particular cases, however, there might be a strong national interest in a result favourable to the Crown, and Lushington clearly took this into account. It is unusual, to say the least, for a judge in an ordinary case to consult privately with one of the parties to litigation, while the decision is pending, but Lushington did not regard prize cases as ordinary. He wrote to Lord Clarendon, the Foreign Secretary, on the subject of an important prize case[183] pending at the end of 1854, summarizing the legal problem and inviting Clarendon to adduce further argument:

My dear Ld Clarendon, I have now before me in the court of Admiralty the cases which have arisen from the Blockade of the Baltic, & a new question has lately arisen & I doubt not with the authority of the Danish Minister, which may be of some importance. It is contended on the part of the Danish claimants, that the Treaty made between Denmark & England in 1670 is in force (there was a similar Treaty with Sweden in 1665) & in proof thereof reference was made to the Instructions sent to the Court of Admiralty in 1793 on the breaking out of that war. These Instructions certainly make exception in favor of Denmark & Sweden & tend to shew that there was some secret Treaty in force. On the part of the Captors it is alleged that this Treaty with Denmark was cancelled by the Convention with Russia in 1801 to which Denmark acceded.

So stands the matter at present & unless I can obtain further information on such material I must form my judgment; but as the question is of consequence not only as relates to captures already made but also to inforcing Blockades for the future I venture to trouble you. I think that it would be desirable that search should be made in the Foreign Office to discover, if practicable, whether any thing has passed since 1793 between the Governments of England & Denmark as to the Treaty of 1690 & especially whether any thing occurred on the subject when Denmark acceded to the convention of 1803 or when peace was subsequently made with Denmark.

Sweden appears to be in the same position but that question has not yet been mooted.

The circumstances I have stated will I trust be a sufficient excuse for my

182 J. Harding (The Queen's Advocate), Foreign Office, Confidential Prints, 3576, no. 195, 5 Oct. 1854.
183 *The Franciska* (1855) 2 Sp 113, argued 20 Dec. 1854, judgment 27 Jan. 1855, revd, JC, on grounds not relating to the treaties, Sp PC 287, 10 Moo PC 37.

troubling you with this communication. I shall be glad of any information you can procure for me.[184]

The point was crucial, in Lushington's mind, to the legality of the blockade, because he held that an exception in favour of Sweden and Denmark would be 'repugnant to the just rights of other neutral nations'.[185] Probably he did not receive any useful response to his letter to Lord Clarendon,[186] because, though deciding the case against the Danish claimant, he rested his conclusion, not on any amendment or abrogation of the treaty, but on a – somewhat strained – construction of its terms.[187]

It has been demonstrated, in a recent study of Lord Stowell's prize decisions, that, though Stowell asserted that prize law was an international law, neutrally applicable to all nations, he manifested some inclination towards British political interests.[188] The same can be said of Lushington, who himself said, in giving evidence to a Select Committee in 1833 that

to a great extent every Judge of the High Court of Admiralty must be a political Judge. When I use the term 'Political Judge' I mean to say he must administer the prize law with reference to the relations this country holds towards other countries.[189]

In his prize cases, Lushington frequently referred to the Law of Nations,[190] and asserted the 'just rights of belligerents',[191] but this latter phrase, while even-handed in sound, was, in the circumstances of the cases before him (disputes between the British Crown and owners of merchant ships) synonymous with British interests.

In condemning a cargo, along with a ship, and refusing opportunity to the cargo owner to demonstrate innocent intent, he made it clear that prize law did not attempt to balance the interests of the parties in quite the same way as ordinary litigation:

---

184 Lushington to Clarendon, dated 25 Dec. 1854, Ockham Park, Ripley, Surrey, Clarendon Papers, MSS Clar dep. c. 19/376.

185 *The Franciska* (1855) 2 Sp 113, 154.

186 On the question of construction, he said, 'I have used my best endeavours to obtain information, but I must candidly acknowledge that I am unable to refer to any auxiliary information of this description', 2 Sp 150.

187 Ibid., 150–7.

188 H. J. Bourgignon, *Sir William Scott, Lord Stowell* (Cambridge, 1987), 219, 223.

189 Report of Select Committee on Admiralty Courts etc., PP 1833, vii, 379, 428–9.

190 e.g., *The Leucade* (1855) 2 Sp 228, 248, *The Aline and Fanny* (1856) Sp PC 322, 325, *The Benedict* (1855) Sp PC 314, 316, *The Baltica* (1855) Sp PC 264, 276, *The Nina* (1855) id., 276, 280, *The Franciska*, note 183 above, 115, 227, *The Ionian Ships* (1855) 2 Sp 212, 214.

191 *The Nina*, above, 281, *The Leucade*, above, 243.

I am forbidden to make an exception which, if once admitted, would in all cases of blockade call on the court to consider the guilt or innocence of the owners of the cargo, a proposition which Lord Stowell declared to be fraught with danger; indeed, I believed it to be utterly impossible to enforce the belligerent rights of this country except upon general principles, and that all attempts to go upon purely equitable principles, particular decisions and particular cases, without regard to the great principles, can only have the effect of destroying the right, and rendering it no longer worth the exertion which Great Britain used in times past for the purpose of protecting it.[192]

'We all know,' he said, in another case

that one of the most efficacious means in the possession of Great Britain to carry on this war, and that which is universally allowed by the law of Nations, was the capture of the mercantile navy of the enemy. The present scheme [a sale in contemplation of war] was a crafty device intended to defeat that right when it should arise.[193]

'The great desideratum of a Court of Prize,' he said, was to

preserve, undiminished, the rights of the subjects of neutral states without derogating from rights equally sanctioned by the Law of Nations – the rights of belligerent powers; and so reconcile the abstract principles of justice with practicability.[194]

'Practicability' meant, in effect, that British interests would not be subordinated to the interests of individual claims, even those that might, in particular cases, happen to be honest claims.

When it was argued that, under the terms of the Order in Council that he himself had signed, only Russian, and not neutral,[195] ships were liable to be condemned, he reacted forcefully:

If this were the true construction of the Order in Council, it would go to show that the Court has no power to condemn neutral vessels committing a breach of blockade, or carrying articles contraband of war, because they did not belong to subjects of the Emperor of Russia. Certainly no Judge who ever occupied this chair before was so tied, nor have I any intention to place such manacles upon my own hands.[196]

[192] *The Panaghia Rhomba* (1857) 12 Moo PC 168, 179–80, affd JC, ibid.
[193] *The Baltica* (1855) Sp PC 264, 276, revd 11 Moo PC 141.
[194] *The Leucade*, above, 248.
[195] The Order referred to 'all such ships, vessels and goods, as shall belong to the Emperor of all the Russias, or his subjects, or to any others inhabiting within any of his countries, territories or dominions', 1 Sp 355.
[196] *The Primus* (1854) 1 Sp 353, 355.

'What would become of belligerent rights,' he said in another case, rejecting a claim of neutral ownership of a Russian ship,

> if, when you search vessels under hostile colours, you are to be told 'This is not a Russian vessel; it is neutral, or nine-tenths is neutral. You are quite mistaken; it is entitled to restitution at the hands of the Court'. It is manifest that the right of search, under these circumstances, would be destroyed. It is clear that the whole trade of an enemy might be carried on with perfect impunity, and all the naval force of France and Great Britain would never be able to carry into execution those rights which they are undoubtedly justified in exercising by the law of nations.[197]

That an inclination in favour of the Crown was perceived in his own time may be suggested by the fact that Lushington was reversed in seven of the eleven reported appeals from his decisions, reversal being, in every case, in favour of the claimant, and against the interests of the Crown. In one case, where the Judicial Committee, in reversing a decision, ventured, very courteously, to suggest that Lushington had been mistaken in his view of Lord Stowell's practice,[198] Lushington, who was one of the few living persons to have a personal recollection of Stowell's prize decisions, was stung, and, when the opportunity arose, he made an elaborate defence of his own prior opinion, while somewhat ostentatiously avowing his duty as a judge to submit to the wisdom of the superior court.[199] In a later case, commenting on the same issue, he used language which would earn a place in any collection of rebukes addressed by inferior to superior tribunals:

> I will not again be tempted to consider what the principles were or what practice prevailed in former cases. I may indeed on this question have much to learn, and perhaps even more to unlearn; but my own task now is to understand and apply the judgment of the Privy Council . . . to the best of my skill and ability.[200]

As elsewhere, Lushington asserted the importance of flexibility and freedom from technicalities, claiming a particular freedom in these respects for the Prize Court:

> This is a broad distinction, which I consider not only indispensable to Prize Law, but to be one of the most honourable distinctions which exist between a prize and a municipal Court; that a Prize Court looks to that which is *bona fide*

---

[197] *The Industrie* (1854) 1 Sp 444, 447.
[198] *The Ostsee* (1855) 9 Moo PC 150.
[199] *The Leucade*, note 190 above.
[200] *The Fortuna* (1855) Sp PC 307, 313.

true, while a Court of Law is sometimes bound by formality, which prevents real justice in the case.[201]

In matters of evidence, he held similar views:

I believe the practice to have been, not to entertain objections to the admissibility of the evidence offered, but to receive all that might be tendered; and certainly we have in this case the license of evidence of every kind and description which could well be offered to the consideration of the Court. I apprehend that this, so far as I know, the universal practice of the Court, was founded on several reasons. *First*, because the Prize Court being not a Municipal Court . . . was not restrained by those rules which are applicable to questions of municipal law. *Secondly*, it would be most difficult, even if possible, to have laid down any rules of evidence; because this Court, having to concern itself with the transactions of various nations, could never construct a code in conformity with all their various rules . . . *Thirdly*, because of the extreme difficulty in procuring what we are accustomed to call the best evidence, when such evidence is to be obtained from distant countries. *Fourthly*, because, though the Court may receive all, it will form its own judgment . . . of the weight to be attributed to each species of evidence . . . *Lastly*, though not least, because as all its judgments may be exposed to the test of an appeal, the Superior Court may, with greater facility, correct any error arising from too great force being attributed to any species of testimony, than it could remedy an evil arising from exclusion.[202]

Judicial notice (i.e., acceptance of facts without proof) could be taken of facts established in earlier cases – a practice that might be objectionable to a party who did not have the opportunity of arguing the prior case, but which can well be seen to be convenient to a single judge deciding many cases raising such a question as whether a blockade were in effect at a certain date. Lushington asserted that 'it is the custom of the Court when information has been acquired in one case to use it in others'.[203]

He recognized the tension, more apparent in prize law even than in other fields, between adherence to general principle, and justice in individual cases:

Lord Stowell administered the Prize Law on great and comprehensive principles; his object was that on the whole equal justice should be done to the

[201] *The Ocean Bride* (1854) 2 Sp 8, 20. See also *The Benedict*, Sp PC 316.
[202] *The Franciska* (1855) 2 Sp 113, 141–2.
[203] *The Rapid* (1854) Sp PC 80, 81. The issue in this case was the connexion between certain commercial firms. But see *The Aline and Fanny* (1856) Sp PC 322, 332, where he said that, as to facts concerning a particular ship, the court 'ought to know nothing but the evidence before it'.

rights of the belligerent, and the just claims of natural nations, but he did not seek in each particular case to do the most perfect justice.[204]

In many cases, as some of the passages quoted show, Dr Lushington asserted his loyalty to the decisions of Lord Stowell, though, on at least one occasion, he expressly departed from one of his dicta.[205] His personal knowledge of the earlier era must have made argument before him a little difficult at times:

That case I perfectly well remember having argued, and I have had recourse to the original papers to see whether my memory failed me or not . . . My own notes, for I have gone through them all, furnish but very meagre information, and, for the best of all possible reasons – that such questions were not discussed – the practice was known to all who practised here . . . I have not, I regret to say, been able to find the name of that case, but I have a perfect recollection of the fact within my own knowledge – I was present at the time.[206]

In one of his last reported prize decisions, he said:

If, in pronouncing this judgment, therefore, I have erred, I have either misunderstood the judgments of Lord Stowell, or they no longer have the force of law. In all cases which it has fallen to my lot to decide during this war, those judgments have been my guide, and in this, probably the last decision[207] I may have to pronounce upon a question of prize law, they will be my guide also. I have endeavoured not only to uphold and maintain the principles enunciated by that great Judge, but also, what is little less important, to carry out the practical application of them.[208]

These passages well illustrate the highly personal, intimate, and somewhat loose deference to past practice that characterized the use of precedent in Doctors' Commons.

In November 1861, five years after the end of the Crimean War, an incident occurred that might have affected the outcome of the American Civil War. A British mail and passenger steamer, *The Trent*, was stopped by a United States warship, and two envoys of the confederate states, Mason and Slidell, and their secretaries, were taken off by force. Britain demanded reparation. *The Times*, then at the height of

204 Ibid., 236, 240.
205 *The Aline and Fanny* (1856) Sp PC 132.
206 *The Leucade* (1855) 2 Sp, 233, 235, 237.
207 There was a later case: *Cargo ex Katharina* (1860) Lush 142.
208 *The Panaghia Rhonda* (1857) 12 Moo PC 168, 180.

its political power,[209] in a long series of bellicose leading articles, predicted war.[210] Orders were given to reinforce British troops in Canada, and to prepare the Navy for war.[211] Anthony Trollope, the novelist, who was in Washington at the time, was told to be prepared to leave at an hour's notice. He considered the threat of British intervention to be the severest danger that the Northern cause encountered during the war.[212] The United States Government, however, in January 1862, admitted that the seizure was irregular (on the ground that *The Trent* had not been brought into port for prize adjudication), the envoys were released, and the conflict with Britain was avoided.[213]

The Admiralty Court judge was a natural source of expertise on the international law of blockade, and Lushington was consulted by the British Government. On 11 March, three days, in fact, after *The Trent* had been stopped, but before the news had reached England, Palmerston, the Prime Minister, summoned a meeting in anticipation that another United States ship, known to be cruising near the English coast, might intercept *The Trent*. Palmerston wrote an account of the meeting, which was attended by 'the Chancellor, Dr Lushington, the three law officers, Sir G Grey, [and] the Duke of Somerset'. The advice received was that 'a belligerent has a right to stop and search any neutral not being a ship of war, and being found on the high seas, and being suspected of carrying enemy's despatches, and that consequently this American cruiser might, by our own principles of international law, stop the West India packet, search her, and if the Southern men and their despatches and credentials were found on board, either take them out, or seize the packet and carry her back to New York for trial,' and, on the basis of this advice, Palmerston 'determined to do no more than to order *The Phaeton* frigate to

---

209 See Sir E. Cook, *Delane of The Times* (London, 1916), passim, and quoting (p. 94) Abraham Lincoln (1861) to the effect that *The Times* was one of the greatest powers in the world.

210 Leading articles of 28 Nov., 29 Nov., 30 Nov., 2 Dec., 4 Dec., 9 Dec., 11 Dec., 26 Dec., 27 Dec., 28 Dec., 30 Dec.

211 C. P. Stacey, *Canada and the British Army 1846–71* (Toronto, 1963), 120–3; J. P. Baxter III, 'The British Government and Neutral Rights', *American Historical Review* 34 (1928–29) 16; Cook, *Delane of The Times*, 130–1; H. Maxwell, *Life and Letters of the Earl of Clarendon* (London, 1913), ii, 249–50.

212 A. Trollope, *Autobiography* (London, 1883), Worlds Classics edn, 150–1.

213 Accounts of the case appear also in J. G. Ridley, *Lord Palmerston* (London, 1970), 552–4, E. D. Adams, *Great Britain and the American Civil War* (London, 1925), 207–9, T. L. Harris, *The Trent Affair* (Indianapolis, 1896), N. B. Ferris, *The Trent Affair* (Knoxville, 1977).

drop down to Yarmouth Roads and watch the proceedings of the American within our three mile limit of territorial jurisdiction'.[214] Palmerston's letter includes reference to 'the principles of international law laid down in our courts by Lord Stowell', which strongly suggests that Lushington's opinion dominated; the letter indicates that the opinion had a direct effect on British policy. Since Palmerston's correspondent was the editor of *The Times*, it may also be taken to have had an indirect effect on public opinion.

The written opinion of the law officers, dated 12 November, stated that

The United States ship of war may put a prize-crew on board the West India steamer, and carry her off to a port of the United States for adjudication by a prize court there

adding, however, in contrast to the report in Palmerston's letter, that 'she would have no right to remove Messrs Mason and Slidell and carry them off as prisoners leaving the ship to pursue her voyage'.[215] The possibility envisaged in this last paragraph was precisely what had occurred, and so the law officers' opinion of 12 November led to the conclusion that the United States action was illegal, not on the ground that the search was unlawful, but on the ground that *The Trent* had not been taken for adjudication by a US prize court. This opinion was repeated on 28 November, after the facts were known.[216] From a political point of view, this offered a weak ground for protest. Any sense of outrage to the British flag[217] must be diluted if the only

---

[214] A. I. Dasent, *John Thadeus Delane, editor of 'The Times': his life and correspondence* (New York, 1908), ii, 36, reprinted in Adams, *Great Britain and the American Civil War*, 207–8. See also A. C. Benson and Viscount Esher (eds), *Letters of Queen Victoria: a Selection from Her Majesty's Correspondence*, iii, 593.

[215] MacNair, *International Law Opinions*, iii, 276–8 (12 Nov. 1861). Palmerston's account to the Queen, dated 13 Nov., again mentioning Lushington's name, and the Law of Nations as laid down by Lord Stowell, stated that the advice given to him was that the Northern Union was entitled to stop and search the steamer, and, if despatches were found, to proceed against her for condemnation. *Letters of Queen Victoria*, iii, 593.

[216] MacNair, *International Law Opinions*, 278–9. Palmerston's letter to Queen Victoria dated 29 Nov. mentions the presence at a cabinet meeting of the law officers and Dr Phillimore. Dr Lushington is not mentioned. The cabinet's conclusion was that a 'gross outrage and violation of international law has been committed, and that your Majesty should be advised to demand reparation and redress'. *Letters of Queen Victoria*, iii, 595. A further opinion of the law officers, dated 21 Dec., notes that no legal difference had been recognized between postal packets and other merchant vessels. Reports of Law Officers of the Crown, Microfilm, No. 88/334, 310 (21 Dec. 1861).

[217] *The Times*, 29 Nov. 1861.

ground of objection were that the United States had not arrested the ship, thereby causing vastly greater inconvenience to the passengers, and greater delay to the mail.

Lushington, no doubt on account of his anti-slavery views, was, in contrast to the general opinion in England,[218] strongly sympathetic to the Northern Union.[219] It is impossible to say to what extent these views may have influenced him in giving his opinion to Palmerston on 11 November. The law officers evidently did not dissent from his opinion at that time.[220] But later, in January 1862, they gave a very different opinion, that the envoys, and their despatches, were not contraband, adding a reference to the importance of allowing mail-packets to proceed unmolested, and strongly implying that a seizure of the steamer for adjudication would not have been lawful.[221] Whether Lushington shared this opinion in January is not known; but, at the critical time in November, he did not.

THE BANDA AND KIRWEE BOOTY CASE

Almost at the end of his judicial career, Dr Lushington had to decide a case on the law of booty, that is, enemy property seized on land, the military equivalent of maritime prize law.[222] This is not, strictly speaking, the leading case, since it is the only case, on the law of booty. It is of interest to a student of the judicial process, for it required Lushington to set out, on an issue previously regarded as political, and without the assistance of any judicial precedent, what

---

218 See Dasent, *John Delane*, ii, 35, Cook, *Delane of The Times*.
219 Lushington's opinion on this point is recorded by Holman Hunt, who stayed at Ockham in 1862 while painting Lushington's portrait. W. Holman Hunt, *Pre-Raphaelitism and the Pre-Raphaelite Brotherhood* (London, 1905), ii, 219–20.
220 But see the qualification in the written opinion of 12 Nov., text at note 215, above.
221 MacNair, *International Law Opinions*, 279–87 (15 Jan. 1862). Subsequent legal commentaries on the *Trent* incident were not unanimous on this question. See H. Wheaton, *Elements of International Law*, first English edn. (1878), 151 (condemning the US action, but on the ground that the steamer was not brought in for adjudication); J. B. Moore, *Digest of International Law* (Washington, 1906), vii, 1239–69; R. Phillimore, *Commentaries upon International Law* 3rd edn (London, 1882), cxxxA; L. F. L. Oppenheim, *International Law* 5th edn, ed. Lauterpacht (London, 1937), 693, 702; W. E. Hall, *A Treatise on International Law* 2nd edn (Oxford, 1884), 634–7; T. Twiss, *The Law of Nations* 2nd edn (Oxford, 1875), 39–40; M. Bernard, *A Historical Account of the Neutrality of Great Britain during the American Civil War* (London, 1870), 233–4.
222 *The Banda and Kirwee Booty Case* (1866) LR 1 Ad & E 109.

considerations should count as proper to be judicially taken into account. Coming at the end of his long career, it amounts to a considered view of the nature of the judicial function. This is rare, but what is practically unique is to find such a view expressed in a context that demands its immediate application.

In the course of the suppression of the Indian Mutiny of 1857, valuable booty, worth about £700,000, fell into the hands of British forces. The question at issue was how widely the booty should be distributed, in particular, whether soldiers under the command of General Whitlock, whose force had actually taken possession of the booty, should have an exclusive claim, or whether other troops, especially those under the command of Sir Hugh Rose, who had fought gallantly with little reward, should share. Booty belongs to the Crown, which, by long practice, had distributed it to the actual captors. Questions of distribution had formerly been dealt with as political questions, and the Government initially proposed a scheme of distribution that included Sir Hugh Rose's army.[223] This provoked dissent, and a commission of inquiry was set up, which recommended that the question be referred to the High Court of Admiralty, as was envisaged by an otherwise unused section of the Admiralty Courts Act of 1841.[224] The reference to Dr Lushington was made, accordingly, and argued for twenty-six days[225] by no fewer than thirty-seven counsel, including most of the leading figures at the bar. The costs were later estimated at £50,000.[226]

Lushington declined an invitation to consider himself completely unfettered, suggesting that one of the characteristics distinguishing a judicial decision was attention to former precedent and practice:

> But I have been invited by some of the counsel to decide the conflicting claims upon what has been called the broad principle of justice and equity, that is, to lay down once for all a new code of rules of joint capture according to my own discretion, irrespective of precedent and practice. I disclaim having any such authority; such is not my task; my duty, I apprehend, is to make a judicial, not an arbitrary, decision. I have to ascertain the true principles on which claims to joint capture depend . . . and in doing so I am not at liberty to treat the subject as a tabula rasa, and to shut my eyes to all that has been done in past times in the naval and military services. I am bound, not only to exercise

---

[223] See *Law Magazine* 23 (1867), 69; LR 1 Ad & E 115.
[224] 3 & 4 Vic. c. 65, s. 22.
[225] LR 1 Ad & E 117.
[226] (1866) 41 LT 728. The costs were paid out of the fund: LR 1 Ad & E 268.

my own reasoning on the subject matter, but to borrow all the light I safely can from the decisions in cases of prize, and from the usage in cases of booty.[227]

He then listed matters that he thought to be extraneous. First, he disclaimed altogether the possibility of giving a reward 'on the sole ground of meritorious service'. Unless the claimant could also show that he had actually assisted in the capture, he must be excluded, 'however severe his sufferings'.[228] The reason for this exclusion was the practical impossibility of administering a criterion of pure merit on a basis likely to satisfy judge or litigants of fairness and consistency:

It would not be possible to prescribe bounds to the admission of claims founded upon such extraneous grounds, or, admitting them, to observe any practice consistent or satisfactory.[229]

He declined an invitation to divide the property on the basis that not all was, in the strict sense, booty, for this would have been to evade the responsibility that had been placed upon him – a particular temptation to judges in reference cases.[230]

Next, he declined to take into account the value of the property, because a principled ground of decision must lead to the same result, however large the sum in question, saying that 'the principles of joint capture must be the same, whether the sum is small or large'.[231]

Lastly, he rejected arguments and statements extraneous to the proceedings before him. A judge's duty was to exercise his own judgment, not to defer to those in political power:

Further, the reference being to my judicial decision, I have deemed it my duty to form my judgment independently of all that took place relative to the distribution of this booty before the matter came to this court; independently, that is, not only of statements advanced post litem motam by any of the claimants, however distinguished, but also of the various opinions expressed by the high authorities, civil and military, who previously had the subject under their consideration.[232]

He then directed himself to what he perceived as the key question, that is, the proper application of decisions on naval prize law. His approach to these decisions illustrates the power of reasoning by analogy, and also its weaknesses. Lushington said:

[227] LR 1 Ad & E 131–2. [228] Ibid., 132. [229] Ibid.
[230] Ibid. [231] Ibid. [232] Ibid., 132–3.

I do not consider that I am to be absolutely governed by any decision in naval prize. Those decisions are not properly precedents, that is, judgments by a competent court possessing the same jurisdiction as myself, and consequently commanding the course I should pursue. But be it not supposed that I shall disregard those decisions altogether. On the contrary, I think them of great value, if properly used, if used, that is, to illustrate the general principles applicable to the distribution of property taken from the enemy. All I wish to insist upon is, that there is an essential distinction between naval prize and booty from the fact of the one capture being on land and the other at sea. This is a distinction pervading every case. The particular way in which the distinction operates I shall be in a better position to explain after I have reviewed the naval decisions, and stated their result.[233]

Legal reasoning by analogy requires identification of the principle underlying the asserted analogy, identification of the issue in the instant case, and then an application of the principle to the issue. But it is evident that these steps are by no means mechanical, and so an analogy can never be logically compelling. It might be said, and it was evidently argued by Sir Hugh Rose, that the purpose of prize law was to reward valour. Rose's army was valorous, and it would follow that it should be rewarded. But Lushington declined to discern such a broad principle in the prize cases, though admitting that this was the original purpose:

The purpose of the Sovereign, ceding prize to the takers, may have been originally to reward successful valour. But captures are made under all circumstances, and by the nature of the case are as often the result of careful vigilance or even fortuitous finding as of actual combat; and accordingly the system of ceding prize to the takers is not limited, either in purpose or effect, to this primary object, the rewarding of successful valour. It may now, I think, be regarded as providing a stimulus to the performance of every kind of duty, by furnishing certain gratuities as incidental to certain services. Another result of the cession of prize, and that by no means unimportant, is, that it restrains pillage. That property captured at sea should be preserved intact is to the interest of all parties: of neutral and friendly powers, that, if not prize, it may be restored; and of the captors, that, if prize, it may be legally distributed.[234]

Rose's argument then was that his army should be considered as joint captors: though not actually present at the moment of seizure, they were engaged with Whitlock's troops in a joint venture. The use of fictions in legal reasoning is, perhaps, inevitable. What is actual

[233] Ibid., 133.   [234] Ibid., 134–5.

capture: who could be said to have actually taken the treasure? At one extreme this might be the single soldier who opened the door of the treasury. At the other, it would be the whole British army, which all, in a sense, assisted in making the capture possible. The problem, very frequently encountered in legal reasoning, is how to draw the line at a point that can be rationally defended:

> The rule of actual capture, if pushed to an extreme, produces the very results to prevent which is the primary object of having a rule at all. To confine the enjoyment of booty to those who have actually laid hands upon the property would be simply to give legal sanction to lawless plundering. On the other hand, to distribute it indiscriminately would be to discourage personal efforts, and in many cases to dissipate the booty till it became insignificant. The line has to be drawn somewhere, and should not be drawn arbitrarily.[235]

Lushington then adverted to another characteristic of legal reasoning: distinctions recognized by law must be practically workable, as well as theoretically sound:

> It is plain, therefore, that the rule which attributes the capture to the ship rests, not on principle, but on practical convenience. The fact is, that the line must be drawn somewhere; in the distribution of prize it is impossible to make nice distinctions, and there are obvious reasons why no distinctions should be allowed within the limits of a ship's company. The ship itself is a home which includes all the crew, and excludes all others; the crew are an organized body of men, living together in the ship, united in strict discipline under one commander, daily performing regulated and associated duties. If any portion of the crew is detached, they are still under the commander of the ship; they still belong to the ship, and in due time will return to the ship ... To admit distinctions between the members of the same ship's crew in the distribution of prize would greatly increase the difficulty of making out a prize roll; would be invidious, and agreeable neither to the discipline nor welfare of the service.[236]

He then considered the principles governing joint capture at sea, concluding that only ships that were closely associated or that co-operated actively in the capture were entitled to share the prize.

The next problem was the strength of the analogy between naval and land warfare. Lushington recognized several distinctions, and concluded that, on account of the ease of communication by land, a wider application must be made of the notion of joint capture.

---

[235] Ibid., 180.   [236] Ibid., 135–6.

He then considered at very great length the practice of the Crown in previous cases of booty, readily accepting, as perhaps not all judges would, the relevance of past administrative practice: though not strictly speaking, precedents, a course of usage 'ought to command the attention of the court'.[237] On the basis of this practice, he excluded the notion that association in a common enterprise was sufficient to allow the whole army to share. Again, he stressed the need for a principle that should be workable, and applicable to future cases:

To allow two or more divisions to be joint captors, if associated under the same immediate commander, but not otherwise, seems to be a legitimate expansion on the same principles of the general rule that all detachments of the same division share in common as actual captors, and that (in ordinary circumstances) separate divisions share separately. Association so defined has an intelligible, not a vague or constructive meaning. It is elastic enough for practical purposes, being equally applicable to temporary expeditions, and to long-continued operations; to the case of two divisions meeting in the field, and passing under the command of the senior officer, and to the case of a whole army, containing any number of divisions, all under the immediate command of the same commander-in-chief.[238]

Similarly, he rejected a wide view of co-operation on a ground familiar to students of legal reasoning: it would set one on a slippery slope, with no logical stopping point before consequences agreed to be unacceptable:

In a certain sense, every British regiment, every British soldier, co-operates with every other, not only in India but throughout the world. In a certain sense, the successes, the very existence of any British troops, if only known, occasion encouragement to the friend and intimidation to the enemy, wherever the friend and enemy may be. But such co-operation cannot, it is manifest, be admitted as a title to joint sharing of booty, without a total abandonment of the general rule that booty should be awarded to the actual captors. Regard for the principle which underlies the naval prize decisions, and deference to what has been the main usage of the army, alike require me to hold that the co-operation which is necessary is a co-operation directly tending to produce the capture in question.[239]

At the opposite end of the argument, he excluded, on the basis of past practice and future predictability, the notion of subdividing a military division, for purposes of entitlement.

[237] Ibid., 132.   [238] Ibid., 182–3.   [239] Ibid., 184–5.

After a minute examination of the campaign (the law report occupies 160 pages and is accompanied by a fold-out map) he concluded that the association between Rose's forces and Whitlock's was too weak, and the co-operation too remote, to entitle Rose's troops to share. Other claims were similarly dismissed. But the Commander-in-Chief and his staff, who were distant from the scene of action, and some of whom had made no claim at all, were permitted to share, on the analogy of an Admiral sharing in prizes captured by ships under his command.

The judgment was praised by *The Law Magazine*,[240] but outside legal circles it met with criticism. *The Times*, in a leading article, stressed the inequity of excluding Rose's army, questioning the analogy between naval and land warfare, and doubting the supposed bad consequences of throwing all booty into a common fund.[241] A historian of the Indian Mutiny wrote that the result of the decision was to exclude Sir Hugh Rose's army, which had (in the historian's judgment) mainly caused the capture of the booty, and to include the Commander-in-Chief and his staff, who were hundreds of miles away, and whose actions did not influence the capture.[242]

Such comments focus on what seems reasonable in the particular case. One could readily construct the sort of judgment that those critics would have themselves given, by taking each of Lushington's points, and departing from them: the case was unique, and the issue was simple, so let us not be troubled with complex hypotheticals; past cases of booty were different, and naval prize cases more so; Rose had virtually been promised a share; the booty was large enough to include Rose and still leave enough for Whitlock, who, in any case, had had other pieces of good fortune; Rose had rendered meritorious service, and should be rewarded; other divisions recognized Rose's claim, and would not complain very loudly if excluded. A decision supported on such grounds looks to a pragmatic solution for the particular case; this has its merits (not the least being the reduced cost of argument), if there is no need to justify the implications of the reasons given, and no prospect of the reasons coming back to trouble the decision-maker in future cases. The notable feature of Lushington's perception of judicial reasoning is continuity, with a presumed need for regularity in

---

[240] *Law Magazine* 23 (1867), 66. *The Law Times* described it as 'very elaborate and learned', 41 LT 612.
[241] *The Times*, 3 July 1866.
[242] G. B. Malleson, *History of the Indian Mutiny* (London, 1880), iii, 202.

decision-making over an extended period of time. Reasons must be sought that both explain past decisions, and will provide a theoretically satisfactory and practically workable basis of a series of decisions that is implicitly envisaged stretching into the future.

The same view of the legal process is reflected in his matrimonial, probate, and admiralty decisions, and in his approach to law reform. Legal decisions must not only solve a particular dispute between individual litigants, but must be regularized and generalized. A parallel, and related, object was that the law should be not only theoretically sound, but expressed in a form capable of predictable, consistent, and reasonably inexpensive application. It is, perhaps, ironic that Lushington's most detailed elaboration of these principles should be upon a question that, legally speaking, seems to have had neither a past, nor a future.

7

THE PRIVY COUNCIL

In 1833, the Judicial Committee of the Privy Council was established as the final court of appeal from the civilian courts, replacing the High Court of Delegates. The statute constituting the Committee included the Admiralty Court judge,[1] and Lushington was sworn a member of the Privy Council on 2 November 1838.[2] During the succeeding twenty-nine years he was one of the most active members of the Committee, sitting more often than any other member but one, and drafting more judgments than any other.[3] Between his appointment, and 1858, when he became Dean of the Arches, he sat on 153 of the 182 ecclesiastical cases heard by the Committee.[4] The Judicial Committee, in addition to replacing the High Court of Delegates, had taken over also the hearing of Indian and Colonial appeals, and at these too Lushington was frequently in attendance, though they involved questions outside his professional experience.[5]

It was not uncommon for judges in the House of Lords to sit on appeal from their own decisions, and Brougham asserted a right to do so in the Privy Council,[6] but Lushington avoided this practice. The Minute Book[7] records that he withdrew when cases that he had

[1] Act for the Better Administration of Justice in His Majesty's Privy Council, 3 & 4 Wm IV c. 41, s. 1.
[2] Minute Book, Privy Council Office, London.
[3] P. A. Howell, *The Judicial Committee of the Privy Council 1833–1876* (Cambridge, 1979), 146, 223, and appendix (Lushington sat on 605 days, exceeded only by Kingsdown's 704).
[4] Return of Appeals in Ecclesiastical Causes made to the Queen in Council etc., PP 1866, lv, 51 (cases instituted between 16 June 1838, and 2 Feb. 1858; these are the first and last cases in the list showing Lushington in attendance).
[5] He heard 129 of 266 cases reported in Moore's *Indian Appeals* during his active membership of the Judicial Committee (1838–67).
[6] *The Greville Memoirs*, ed. L. Strachey and R. Fulford (London, 1938) ii, 226–7, 8 Dec. 1831. Greville indicates no surprise at the suggestion that Jenner should sit on appeal from a judgment of his own, *Memoirs*, iii, 210 (21 June 1835).
[7] Privy Council Office, London.

decided came before the Committee. This meant that he was absent from practically all English Admiralty appeals. Two apparent exceptions among the ecclesiastical cases prove, on examination, to confirm the general practice. In *Harrison* v. *Harrison*, on appeal from the Court of Arches varying a decision of Lushington's in a nullity case, he is reported by Moore to have been present.[8] But the Minute Book expressly states that the 'judge of the High Court of Admiralty withdrew' before the case was heard, and a printed list of ecclesiastical causes also indicates his absence.[9] It seems likely, therefore, that Moore's report is in error. The other case is *B—n* v. *B—n*, also a nullity case decided at first instance by Lushington in the Consistory Court,[10] where Lushington did not hear the appeal from his own judgment, which was on an interlocutory point,[11] but sat as part of the panel which afterwards heard the case on its merits, as appellate ecclesiastical courts had power to do after an interlocutory appeal.[12]

In 1860, a crucial procedural point arose on an appeal from Lushington's judgment in a highly controversial ecclesiastical case.[13] There was no other civilian member of the Committee at this date, and Lushington was consulted on the point, and his advice was followed. He must have responded promptly to the Committee's request, for his advice is transcribed into the Committee's Minute Book for the day the point was argued and decided.[14] The Committee's desire for expert guidance is understandable: it must have seemed to be the only sensible course to consult a knowledgeable colleague. Such informality, however, may give rise to difficulties. In fact, Lushington's advice was in favour of the appellant, but had it been the other way, it might have appeared as an attempt to protect his own judgment from attack. There is other evidence of informal judicial collegiality in the practice of the Committee. In a testamentary case, in which Brougham and Lushington sat as members of the Committee, Lushington mentioned in a letter to Brougham that he had consulted the judge from whom the appeal was brought.[15]

---

[8] (1842) 4 Moo PC 96.   [9] Ibid., 60.

[10] *B—n* v. *M—e* (1852) 2 Rob Ecc 580 (Consist Ct), *B—n* v. *B—n* 1 Sp 248 (JC).

[11] See 2 Rob Ecc 594.

[12] The cause was 'retained' rather than 'remitted'.

[13] The *Essays and Reviews* case, discussed in chapter 10, below.

[14] Judicial Committee of the Privy Council, Minute Book, Privy Council Office, entry for 19 June 1863. See 2 Moo PCNS 375.

[15] Lushington to Brougham, 9 Aug. 1842, Brougham Papers, University College, London, 32,350, quoted in text at note 20, below.

Even more objectionable than a judge hearing an appeal from his own decision, is the case of a appellate judge having been counsel to one of the parties in the very litigation in issue, for there the judge may be privy to confidential information. The possibility arose in a testamentary case in 1841.[16] Lushington had been counsel for one of the parties at an earlier stage in the litigation. Brougham selected him to sit on the case,[17] but Lushington, in response to objection by counsel, withdrew, explaining that he had only attended with reluctance, on the possibility that there might be no objection.[18] What is more surprising than the result is that the possibility of Lushington's sitting should have been contemplated in the first place, by himself or Brougham, and even pressed by Brougham over counsel's objection.[19]

Correspondence between Lushington and Brougham throws light on the internal workings of the Judicial Committee. The cases were argued among the judges by letter. In one testamentary case, Lushington wrote:

As to Chambers & Wood I have conversed with Jenner & he has again looked over the Papers. He remains quite stedfast to his original opinion. Having again & again considered the case I retain my conviction that the judgment is right & looking to the Mode in which similar cases have always been considered in Doctors Commons I think that the reversal of the judgment would be attended with great mischief.[20]

Lushington's attempts at persuasion were unsuccessful, for the judg-

---

[16] *Wood* v. *Goodlake* (1841) 1 Not Cas 144. See Howell, *Judicial Committee*, 121–2.
[17] Report of Select Committee of the House of Lords on the Jurisdiction of the Judicial Committee of the Privy Council. See HL Sess Pap 1844, xix, 323, 407, Howell, *Judicial Committee*, 121.
[18] 1 Not Cas 145.
[19] 1 Not Cas 145, complaining of the lateness of counsel's objection, and insisting on an affidavit that counsel (Sir F. Pollock) was speaking the truth when he told the Board that he had no prior notice of Lushington's presence. In his evidence to the House of Lords Select Committee on the Jurisdiction of the Privy Council, Brougham gives a different impression: 'when we met, it turned out that . . . Dr Lushington had been counsel in the cause, and could not attend', Report, HL Sess Pap 1844, xix, 407. Reeve, at 377, implied a practice of regular exclusion in such cases. See also Howell, *Judicial Committee*, 191.
[20] Lushington to Brougham, 9 Aug. 1842, Brougham Papers 32,350. The case referred to is probably *Chambers* v. *Wood* (1843) 2 Not Cas 481 (Cottenham, Campbell, Lushington, Knight Bruce, Wigram, Brougham absent for judgment); judgment (Cottenham) 27 Nov. 1843.

ment was reversed.[21] He tried again to persuade Brougham in another appeal from the same judge, where he favoured reversal:

The case of Cooper v. Bockett was argued before yourself, Knight Bruce, Ld Wharncliffe & myself. The question was whether certain unattested alterations should be admitted to probate. Jenner thought that the circumstances of the case warranted him in decreeing probate of the paper *with* the alterations & gave no opinion as to the presumption of law where there was no evidence. You at the hearing expressed no decided opinion as to the law but thought there was no evidence either for or against the alteration; that is, to prove they were made before or after the execution. Knight Bruce is strong for affirming the judgment, even if there be no evidence. I think that there is no evidence, & that the legal presumption is against the alterations & therefore am for reversal. If the legal presumption is to be determined in this case it is one of great importance. How do you propose to deal with it.[22]

This is persuasion, not by a claim to superior expertise, but by so setting out the issue as to invite the conclusion desired. It was successful, as Jenner's judgment was reversed, Knight Bruce's dissent being signified.[23]

Revisions were incorporated into the draft judgments in the course of correspondence:

This morning my judgment came back from Parke. I send it to you with his note annexed. His first suggested alteration is noted & I have written it in. To the second at Folio 4 I request your attention. I have some difficulty in making the judgment clear & consistent, if all notice of security *subsequently* acquired be omitted. [Detailed explanation follows of the intention of Lushington's original draft.][24]

The practice of the Judicial Committee was to give a single judgment only,[25] and though, in the early years, the fact of a dissent, and

---

21 *Chambers* v. *Wood* (1843) 2 Not Cas 481. Lushington's dissent was not signified; Brougham was absent.

22 Lushington to Brougham, 17 May 1846, Brougham Papers, 8148. The reference is probably to *Cooper* v *Bockett* (second appeal argued before Wharncliffe, Brougham, Knight Bruce and Lushington) (1846) 4 Moo PC 419, argument 7 Feb. 1846; judgment (Brougham) 1 Aug. 1846.

23 4 Moo PC 452.

24 Lushington to Brougham, 18 July 1842, Brougham Papers, 32,349. The case is probably *Bank of Bengal* v. *Radakissen Mitter* (1842) 4 Moo PC 140 (Brougham, Parke, Knight Bruce, Lushington and two assessors), argument, 28 June; judgment (Lushington) 28 July 1842. Reference appears in the letter, but not in the judgment, to a decision of Lord Eldon, from which it would seem that Lushington revised his draft as Parke had proposed.

25 See D. B. Swinfen, 'The Single Judgment in the Privy Council, 1833–1966', *Juridical Review* 1975, 153.

the names of the dissenters, were not infrequently disclosed,[26] separate dissenting reasons did not come into use until the present century. The search for unanimity, therefore, demanded co-operation in drafting the judgments. Brougham, perhaps because he had played the leading role in establishing the Committee, took it upon himself to give advice; he wrote to Lushington, on one occasion, perhaps intending Lushington to circulate the letter to the other judges:[27]

As I am writing to you at any rate I add a few lines instead of troubling Pemberton Leigh with a letter. My opinion is quite confirmed after reconsidering the case – i.e. differing from my first impression which was strongly in favor of the judgment below. But in revising the greatest care must be taken as to the way in which we express ourselves as to partnerships & as to bodies of various kinds, & body of one kind – but incorporated in various ways. So I trust each of you who are among your books will examine carefully the terms used – laying down the draft after a first perusal & first suggestion of alterations & then some time after giving it a second. This is the only way to make sure work.[28]

In some cases, the preliminary opinions and comments of the various judges were printed for circulation, but it appears that this was a rare practice, and that most drafts were settled in the manner illustrated here.[29]

The British practice of leaving local laws in place in many parts of the Empire faced the Judicial Committee of the Privy Council, as the

---

[26] Howell, *Judicial Committee*, 201–3.

[27] This is suggested by the phrase 'each of you who are among your books'. But it seems not to have been done, as the letter is intact among the Lushington Family Papers. The passage quoted is on a separate sheet of paper, which suggests that it was intended for circulation, but one sentence, added in the top margin, appears to be addressed to Lushington alone.

[28] Brougham to Lushington, with letter dated 24 Dec. 1847, Lushington Family Papers. The case referred to is probably *Bank of Australasia* v. *Breillat* 6 Moo PC 152 (Brougham, Langdale, Campbell, Lushington and Pemberton Leigh), argued 10, 11, 13, and 14 Dec. 1847; judgment (Pemberton Leigh) 15 Feb. 1848. One of the issues was whether directors of a joint stock banking company had the same powers as partners in a banking partnership. In the top margin, apparently added as an afterthought, appear the following words (last few illegible): 'My working with the Bk of Australasia case prevented my writing before on [Slavery Trade...].'

[29] See Howell, *Judicial Committee*, 198. An example is preserved in the *Essays and Reviews* case, on appeal from Lushington's judgment in the Court of Arches, Tait Papers, Lambeth Palace Library, 291/246 (London), 261 (Canterbury), 267 (York) 270 (Chelmsford), 273 and 294 (Kingsdown), 276 (Cranworth), 284 and 289 (Lord Chancellor) but this was an exceptional, and highly notorious case. See chapter 10, below.

imperial Court of Appeal, with a task that many would consider insuperable. Lushington's experience had been confined to English ecclesiastical and admiralty law. Now, in addition, he had to deal with all areas of English law, together with French (old Coutume, and modern), Dutch, Spanish, Muslim, and Hindu law.[30] Lushington was one of the members of the Committee who felt keenly the daunting nature of this task. Writing to Brougham, he said:

I am really vexed to trouble you with so odious a case as that of Janokey Doss, but you will I know agree that judgment ought to be given before the long vacation. I send you all I can write upon the subject, but I must pray you carefully to read it & add the conclusion, if you do not reject it altogether. In a matter of Chancery Practice I should want common sense if I did not doubt my judgment on every step & more especially in Indian Chancery Practice & in a case so frightfully voluminous & complicated. I have had more trouble & anxiety with it than with any 20. My object has been to avoid deciding difficult and abstruse points of Hindoo law; indeed whatever I might have thought I should scarcely have ventured to do so as neither you nor Parke expressed any opinion.[31]

In dealing with Indian appeals, the same themes appear as in Lushington's judgments in the ecclesiastical and admiralty courts: a desire to effect speedy and substantial justice, and an impatience with legal technicalities. He spoke of the duty to 'look to the broad principles of justice and equity ... and to discourage mere technical objections which affect not the merits of the case'.[32] To adopt such a principle might, in the Privy Council, have the appearance of making a virtue of necessity, in view of the difficulty, or rather the impossibility, of mastering the technical rules of legal systems entirely foreign to the judges:

In reviewing the proceedings in India, whence the appeal is brought, the Courts where the Hindoo and Mohammedan laws are the rule, and where the forms of pleading are wholly different from those in use in Courts where the law of England prevails, this Court must look to the essential justice of the

30 See Moore's evidence, Report of Select Committee of the House of Lords on the Jurisdiction of the Privy Council, HL Sess Pap 1844, xix, 393, adding Manx, Jersey, Guernsey, 'and I apprehend now we shall have Chinese' law.
31 Lushington to Brougham, 14 June 1846, Brougham Papers, 8147. The case is probably *Baboo Janokey Doss* v. *Bindabun Doss* (1846) 3 Moo IA 175, (Brougham, Parke and Lushington), argued 23, 24, and 25 Feb. 1843; judgment (Lushington) 1 Aug 1846. The report indicates that the case involved complex questions of Hindu law, but was decided on the basis that an interested person had not been made a party.
32 *Zemindar of Ramnad* v. *Zemindar of Yettia-Pooram* (1859) 7 Moo IA 441, 474–5.

case, without considering whether matters of form have been strictly attended to.[33]

Expedition was desirable. In allowing an objection to an interlocutory decision that might have been appealed separately at an earlier stage, he said:

> We cannot conceive that anything would be more detrimental to the expeditious administration of justice than the establishment of a rule which would impose upon the suitor the necessity of so appealing whereby on the one hand he might be harassed with endless expense and delay, and on the other inflict upon his opponent similar calamities. We believe that there have been very many cases before this tribunal in which their lordships have deemed it to be their duty to correct erroneous interlocutory orders, though not brought under their consideration until the whole cause had been decided and brought hither by appeal for adjudication.[34]

On the other hand, expeditious adjudication sometimes had to give way to considerations of fairness:

> Looking at the whole of these proceedings, they [their lordships] do not think that it would be consonant with justice at once to reverse the Decree of the Court below and to affirm the Decree of the Provincial court; they think that the parties have unfortunately lost their way, and on that mistake and misapprehension it would be going too far finally to dispose of the case now.[35]

He accepted that English law was not in every respect suitable for transplantation everywhere:

> With regard to the admissibility of evidence in the Native Courts in India, we think, that no strict rule can be prescribed. However highly we may value the rules of evidence as acknowledged and carried out in our own courts, we cannot think that those rules could be applied with the same strictness to the reception of evidence before the Native courts in the East Indies ... We must look to their practice, we must look to the essential justice of the case, and not hastily reject any evidence, because it may not be accordant with our own practice.[36]

Similarly, he declined to transplant English ecclesiastical and matrimonial law into India. Interpreting a provision of the Bombay

[33] *Ghirdharee Sing* v. *Koolahul Sing* (1840) 2 Moo IA 344, 349–50, and see Howell, *Judicial Committee*, 233.
[34] *Maharajah Moheshur Sing* v. *Bengal Government* (1859) 7 Moo IA 283, 302.
[35] *Srimut Moottoo Vijaya Raghanadha Gowery Vallabha Peria Woodia Taver* v. *Rany Anga Moottoo Natchiar* (1844) 3 Moo IA 278, 294.
[36] *Unide Rajaha Raje Bommarauze Bahadur* v. *Pemmasamy Venkatadry Naidoo* (1858) 7 Moo IA 128, 137.

Charter that ecclesiastical law should apply 'so far as the circumstances of the . . . people shall admit or require', he said:

> We must remember that the English ecclesiastical law is founded exclusively
> on the assumption that all the parties litigant are Christians; we are aware
> that, under particular circumstances, the Ecclesiastical Courts in England
> have exercised jurisdiction with respect to Jewish marriages, ascertaining
> their validity by Jewish laws; but the very great difficulties attending such
> investigation, and the almost absurd consequences to which they lead, would
> not induce us to follow those precedents further than strict necessity requires
> . . . What might be the remedy by Parsee law we think it wholly unnecessary to
> inquire, because, from the religion the Parsees profess, it cannot be the
> remedy the Court Christian would afford, nor would such relief be adminis-
> tered by Ecclesiastical law.[37]

It would indeed have been an irony to force upon the Parsees a
Christian system of matrimonial law that was just about to be abolished in England.

Two cases raised the question of whether the Judicial Committee
should entertain criminal appeals. In the earlier case, interpreting
another provision of the Bombay Charter, providing for an appeal by
'any person . . . aggrieved by the Judgment or determination of the
Supreme Court . . . at Bombay', where a literal interpretation would
certainly include criminal cases, Lushington held that criminal
appeals were impliedly excluded on the ground that 'it is not probable
that the Crown, in granting this Charter, intended to make so extraordinary a deviation from the ordinary practice'.[38] In the later case, he
held that there was no general right of appeal to the Privy Council
from a criminal conviction:

> Whenever punishment was likely to ensue there would follow an appeal to Her
> Majesty in Council, and consequently not only would the course of justice be
> maimed, but in very many instances it would be entirely prostrated . . . Their
> lordships are of opinion that they cannot, under the existing circumstances,
> advise Her Majesty to admit this right of appeal, but they doubt not that
> justice will be done, because they would suggest that an application should be
> made to the constituted authorities who have a power to afford a remedy,
> though in a different way. They doubt not that when it is represented to those
> authorities that this suggestion emanates from the Judicial Committee, they
> will not be loth to examine into the circumstances of the case, and to do that
> which justice may require.[39]

37 *Ardaseer Cursetjee* v. *Perozeboye* (1856) 10 Moo PC 375, 415, 416, 418.
38 *R.* v. *Eduljee Byramjee* (1846) 5 Moo PC 276, 289.
39 *R.* v. *Joykissen Mookerjee* (1862) 1 Moo NS 272, 298.

246 Law, politics and the Church of England

Commenting on this last case, describing Lushington's judgment as
extraordinary, and emphasizing his old age, a modern historian has
observed that there is no easy equation between progressiveness in
politics and in law.[40] No doubt there is truth in this comment, but it
may be doubted whether that truth is illustrated by this case. As
Lushington emphasized in the earlier case, there was no general right
of appeal in England against a criminal conviction; this was not
introduced until the present century.[41] At a time when expedition was
taken to be essential to the administration of criminal justice, the
reluctance of the Judicial Committee to encourage criminal appeals
from distant parts of the Empire can readily be understood. Moreover, the judgment might be said to illustrate an aspect of Lushington's liberalism in that he went out of his way to suggest an executive
remedy for what he considered to be an injustice in the individual
case. Clearly the Committee expected the executive to respond, and
the India Office Records reveal that it did so.[42] The judgment had the
effect of allowing the appeal in the particular case, while denying a
right of appeal in the future. In contemplating the question of what is
progressive, it may also be relevant to note that, when the Privy
Council did 'at last' allow an appeal in an ordinary criminal case, in
1867, it was in favour of the Crown, setting aside an order for a new
trial, and restoring a conviction and capital sentence.[43]

Apparently more extraordinary, it may be suggested, are comments, in several cases, on the unreliability of Indian witnesses:

Among other arguments urged for the respondent it was said that, with regard
to instruments of this kind, considering the habits and customs of the native
inhabitants of India, their well-known propensity to forge any instrument
which they might deem necessary to their interest, and the extreme facility
with which false evidence can be procured from witnesses, that the probability or improbability of the transaction formed a more important consideration in ascertaining the truth of any transaction relied upon. With this
argument we agree...[44]

40 Howell, *Judicial Committee*, 147.
41 Criminal Appeal Act, 1907. 7 Ed. VII c. 23.
42 Government of India to Sir Charles Wood, 3 Mar. 1863, India Office Records, L/P
    & J/3/302/75, Judicial No. 12 of 1863: 'You will perceive that the Lieutenant-
    Governor of Bengal has remitted the remainder of the punishment of imprisonment
    accorded to Joykissen Mookerjee and ordered his immediate release.'
43 *A-G for New South Wales* v. *Bertrand* (1867) LR 1 PC 520. The earlier case of
    Falkland Islands Co. v. *R.* was regarded as, in substance, civil; see Howell, *Judicial
    Committee*, 106-7.
44 *Bunwaree Lal* v. *Maharajah Hetnarai Sing* (1858) 7 Moo IA 148, 155.

In support of the genuineness of the document relied on, is the evidence of witnesses against whose veracity no solid objection has been raised beyond the general observation that oral evidence in India is untrustworthy.[45]

In another case, he spoke of the 'lamentable disregard of truth prevailing among the native inhabitants of Hindostan',[46] though adding that the caution against accepting oral evidence must not be carried to an extreme length. Elsewhere he spoke of the 'litigiousness that generally prevails among the natives of India'.[47] These comments are surprising when compared with Lushington's strong assertions of racial equality in the anti-slavery context.[48] The explanation is probably that Lushington's opinion of Indian witnesses – very widely held by British observers at the time[49] and earlier[50] – rested not on any assumption of racial inequality, but on an expectation of progress in India on the British pattern,[51] and a disappointment in its slow advance.

It is easy to forget, looking back on the history of the Judicial Committee, that it was not only the colonial court of appeal, but also a court of English civil law: one of the principal moving forces behind its foundation, in 1833, was the creation of a new civilian court of appeal.[52] Until 1858 it heard appeals in all areas of civil law,[53] retaining admiralty jurisdiction until 1875,[54] and jurisdiction over church discipline cases into modern times.[55] In the first thirty-five years of

---

[45] Ibid., 167.
[46] *Mudhoo Soodun Sundial* v. *Suroop Chunder Sirkar Chaudry* (1849) 4 Moo IA 431, 441.
[47] *Government of Bengal* v. *Mussumat Shurruffutoonnissa* (1860) 8 Moo IA 226, 236.
[48] See pp. 70, 92 above.
[49] J. Mill, *The History of British India* 4th edn (London 1840), i. 467, repeated in 5th edn (1858) i, 324, 'Judicial mendacity is more than common; it is almost universal'. See also C. E. Bernard (ed.), *G. Campbell, Memoirs of My Indian Career* (London, 1893), i, 20. Lushington's eldest son was a magistrate in India: *Guy's Hospital Gazette*, 5 Dec. 1898, 548.
[50] Sir William Jones, a judge in India, well-disposed towards the Indians, and a leading expert on India, spoke of the 'frequency of perjury . . . committed by the meanest and encouraged by some of the better sort . . . with as little remorse as if it were a proof of ingenuity, or even a merit'. 'Address to the grand jury at Calcutta, 1787', Sir W. Jones, *Works* (London, 1799), iii, 21–2.
[51] See Lushington's support of Buxton's project for the civilization and Christianization of Africa, discussed at p. 87 above, and G. W. Stocking, *Victorian Anthropology* (London, 1987), 17, 36, 44, and passim.
[52] Howell, *Judicial Committee*, 18–20.
[53] Howell, *Judicial Committee*, 60. Defamation was removed in 1855.
[54] Judicature Act, 36 & 37 Vic. c. 66, s. 18
[55] Diminished, but not removed, by the Ecclesiastical Jurisdiction Measure, 1963.

the Committee's existence, Lushington was the principal representative on it of Doctors' Commons, sitting on about three times as many days as the three other civilian judges, who were members during that period, put together.[56]

[56] Howell, *Judicial Committee*, appendix.

8

CHURCH RATES

No more significant issue affected the relationship between church and state in mid-nineteenth-century England than the controversy about church rates. The issue raised, in acute form, the conflict between the notion of a national church to which all, in a sense, owed a kind of allegiance, and the individualistic principle that religion was each person's own private concern, religious organizations relying for support on volunteers.

The church rate question was the greatest of the Dissenters' grievances against the Church of England in the forty-year period between the repeal of the Test and Corporation Acts, and the eventual abolition of compulsory rates in 1868.[1] The dispute brought into play law, politics, and religion, nowhere so clearly intertwined as on this matter. The central figure on the legal side was Lushington, whose career as an ecclesiastical court judge spanned almost precisely the forty-year period just mentioned. As judge of the London Consistory Court, and later Dean of the Arches, he decided most of the legally significant cases; he committed to prison John Thorogood, the best known of the 'Church Rate Martyrs';[2] he decided, at first instance, the twin cases, litigated over a sixteen-year period, that became the test cases of the legal aspects of church rates, and the result of which sounded the death-knell of the compulsory rate.

Lushington, unusually for a judge, has left us much more than his judicial record. He was, until 1841, a member of the House of Commons, and, though himself a staunch churchman, was a constant critic, from a liberal political perspective, of compulsory rates. He

[1] The political aspects of the controversy are discussed in G. I. T. Machin, *Politics and the Churches in Great Britain 1832–1868* (Oxford, 1977), and in J. P. Ellens, 'The Church Rate Conflict in England and Wales, 1832–1868', PhD thesis, University of Toronto, 1983.
[2] Lord Stanley, *The Church Rate Question Considered* (London 1853), 20, said that 'Church-rate martyrdom has almost passed into a proverb'.

249

spoke in the House about his conduct in committing John Thorogood to prison. He gave evidence to a Parliamentary Commission on Church Rates, in which he explained his view of the law, and its deficiencies. Attention to his role, therefore, not only casts a unique light on the controversy itself, but supplies a range of perspectives that is seldom available in respect of any legal controversy. Lushington's career contained a striking contrast: as an ecclesiastical court judge he embodied the legal privileges of the Church, and was the chief instrument of the enforcement of rates; as a member of Parliament, he was active in seeking their abolition.[3]

The church rate was a tax, primarily for the maintenance of the nave of the parish church,[4] to which all residents in the parish were liable. Church rates had existed in England from the thirteenth century, and perhaps longer.[5] Yet, until the 1830s, no serious legal or political challenge was made to them.[6] Though Quakers had refused to pay voluntarily, they had not resisted enforcement by execution against their property.[7] But in the 1830s the increased political power of the Dissenters, combined with the individualistic spirit of the age, made a challenge inevitable.

Lushington, in presenting the Dissenters' case in Parliament, never failed to make it clear that he himself favoured the established Church.[8] He considered, however, that dissent should be unfettered. He said that 'On all matters of religion a man must decide for himself', and that 'he had no right to impose his opinions on another'.[9] Such a view practically demanded the removal of those of the Church's

---

[3] He presented the petition for the redress of the Dissenters' grievances in 1834 (Hansard, 3rd ser., xxii, 2–3). The grievances listed in the petition concerned registration of births, solemnization of marriages, burial of the dead, exclusion from the universities, 'and their liabilities to the payment of rates and other compulsory levies for the maintenance of the Established Church'.

[4] But also for purchasing requisites for carrying on worship – a small expense, but a large objection in principle from the Dissenters' viewpoint.

[5] In *Smith* v. *Keats* (1833) 4 Hagg Ecc 275 at 278–9, Dr Lushington said 'from time immemorial'. In *Veley* v. *Gosling* (1842) 2 Curt 253, at 293, he said: 'I know not the origin of Church Rates, nor any authority which fixes a date. The earliest case on the subject is in the year-book of Edward 3.' In *Veley* v. *Burder* (1841) 12 Ad & E 265, at 302, Tindal CJ said that they were already defended then (in 1370) as 'a custom from time immemorial'.

[6] Rates were refused earlier because of objection to their application to particular uses. See Machin, *Politics and the Churches*, 19.

[7] See Lushington's evidence to the Select Committee on Church Rates, PP 1851, ix, 1, qq. 2367–8.

[8] See for example, Hansard, 3rd ser., xxii, 3 (11 Mar. 1834).

[9] Hansard, 3rd ser., xxxvii, 378 (13 Mar. 1837).

privileges that imposed direct or indirect burdens on Dissenters; church rates imposed a very direct burden.

His other main argument was that the Church would be strengthened by the removal of just causes of complaint against it. 'Unless the abuses of the Church were remedied,' he said,

it must be undermined and would fall. The Church of England would only gather strength by divesting itself of all those matters which placed it in an adverse position to the people ... He should support [a proposal for the Abolition of Church Rates] because he saw no other remedy for the existing evils, and because he thought that, whilst it remedied those evils, it would tend to strengthen the Established Church, and promote the great objects to accomplish which it was founded and preserved.[10]

If the Church were not reformed, it would be laid 'bare to the obloquy of the public'.[11] He warned prophetically of the dangers of elitism in the Church:

The Church of England ought to be a national Church, it ought to strive to gather around it the hearts and the respect of the people: the fact however was notorious that it had too long lived in the smiles of the rich and landed gentry, whilst it had been daily losing ground amongst the middle classes of society. Whilst it retained the nobility of the land in its ranks it was satisfied: let it take care that even these did not drop off from it by degrees ... He was of opinion, as he before said, that the Church stood by the will of the majority; when the majority was in its favour it reigned paramount, but as the minority who were against it began to increase in number, so it must decline in power, and if it did not give way to their wishes would run a risk of being overturned. The Church of England was like a besieged city; whilst its garrison was staunch and strong it might defy the enemy, but eventually, as the number of its assailants increased, and the courage and unanimity of its defenders began to flag, it must be subverted.[12]

In his last parliamentary speech on the subject, he said that the settlement of the question, 'so far from injuring, would benefit the Church, in proportion as it tended to uphold it in the opinions, feelings, and affections, of the people'.[13]

Whether the Church of England was strengthened by the loss of its privileges is a question that might probably be debated on more than one level. It might be maintained that, without some reform, the

[10] Hansard, 3rd ser., xxxvii, 380–1 (14 Mar. 1837).
[11] Hansard, 3rd ser., xlvii, 538 (25 April 1839).
[12] Hansard, 3rd ser., xxxvii, 380 (14 Mar. 1837).
[13] Hansard, 3rd ser., lviii, 797 (25 May 1841).

establishment itself would have fallen.[14] But Lushington seems to have expected that, stripped of its privileges, the Church would be more popular. As an actual prediction, this expectation seems, in retrospect, to have been implausible. But its attraction, to churchmen of Lushington's political opinions, is clear. It enabled community interests and liberal political principles to coincide: given a free choice, the people would perceive the merit of the established church. Thus the Church, the individual, and the community all stood to gain by reform.

As early as 1833, Lushington drew attention to the need for a political solution. Writing to Brougham, Lord Chancellor in the first government of the reformed Parliament, he foresaw that the ancient machinery of the ecclesiastical courts would not work smoothly in the political context of the nineteenth century:

> You must make up your mind as to what you will do on the subject of Church Rates. You must of course be aware that in some of the great towns the Vestries have refused to make Rates at all. So in Bishopsgate. I saw the Bishop of London this week; he seems to be in some alarm at the consequences, but I advised him in the present state of the law not to have recourse to the Ecclesiastical Court; the remedy would be most uncertain, and the irritation very great.[15]

The truth of these last propositions was shortly to be demonstrated.

The appropriate kind of reforming action, however, was not obvious. A newspaper called the church-rate question 'a perfect political hedgehog'.[16] Outright abolition was seen as subverting the principle of the establishment,[17] and might leave some churches without necessary support. Even Lushington had reservations about that:

> But if the provision of [a bill introduced in 1841] should have a tendency to leave the Church unprovided with the means of maintaining and repairing the edifices, or of continuing the service as it has been accustomed to be carried on, then there would be reasons for my ultimately voting against the measure.[18]

---

[14] Ellens, 'Church Rate Conflict', at several points discusses the political forces in play on this question.

[15] Lushington to Brougham, 5 Oct. 1833, Brougham Papers, University College, London, 4160.

[16] *Morning Chronicle*, 22 June 1854, quoted by Ellens, '*Church Rate Conflict*', 282.

[17] See Stanley, *Church Rate Question Considered*, at 39.

[18] Mirror of Parliament 1841, 1918a; Hansard, 3rd ser., lvii, 796–7 (25 May).

Proposals to maintain churches out of general state revenues had the effect of transferring the burden from the local taxpayer to the national taxpayer, and were unacceptable to the Dissenters;[19] Lushington pointed this out in respect of a proposal along these lines advanced in 1834[20] Proposals to divert other sources of church revenue for the expenses formerly met from rates were denounced by churchmen as confiscatory. Lushington supported a proposal along these lines in 1837, and it obtained a second reading in the House of Commons, but it was perceived as an anti-establishment measure,[21] and was abandoned by the government.[22]

Another line of thinking was that some system might be devised to allow Dissenters to opt out of the obligation to pay. The obvious objection to this plan was that it would create an incentive to churchmen to declare themselves Dissenters.[23] Another was that it would reintroduce religious tests as a basis of civil rights and obligations. Lushington opposed such proposals on both grounds:

[the proposal] was . . . open to this objection, that it would reintroduce a test similar to that which rendered the Corporation and Test Acts so exceptionable. They were told that they might safely appeal to the consciences of dissenters – that for 5s. 6d. no man would represent himself to be a Dissenter when he really was a member of the Church of England. But let the House recollect, that 5s. 6d. was not the *maximum* amount of church-rates paid by individuals. Some might pay 5*l* – nay some large farmers might be liable for 50*l* and that too at a period of distress. Would anyone say that such a temptation ought to be thrown in the way of any man? The principle was in itself absurd and iniquitous. A man might make the declaration required under the proposed bill, he might still retain his pew in the Church, he might use it and lock it, and might throw upon his neighbours the burden of paying church-rates.[24]

Another set of proposals contemplated the possibility that the burden of the rates could be transferred to actual church attenders, through pew rents, or otherwise. The objections to this sort of proposal were that it would create an incentive to stay away from church,

---

[19] See Machin, *Politics and the Churches*, 44.
[20] See Hansard, 3rd ser., xxxvii, 378 (13 Mar. 1837).
[21] See Machin, *Politics and the Churches*, 61.
[22] O. Chadwick, *The Victorian Church* (London, 1966) i, 146–7.
[23] 'A project, of course, the most effectual that can be conceived for the multiplication of Dissenters, and the extinction of Churchmen', *Christian Observer*, July 1855, 491, in a review of R. B. Hone, *Church Rates etc.*
[24] Hansard, 3rd ser., lii, 112–13 (11 Feb. 1840).

and might exclude the poor altogether. As has been seen, Lushington thought that there were social, as well as individual benefits to religious belief and practice.[25] In giving evidence to a Parliamentary Committee in 1851, Lushington said, in response to a suggestion that repairs might be paid for out of pew rents:

I have thought of that question very much indeed, and I will not hesitate to answer it to the best of my belief ; I have not the slightest objection to tax the occupants of pews who are capable of paying, but I never would assent to any system that should leave the poor of England without a place to go to church.[26]

Eventually, the simplest political solution – outright abolition of compulsory rates – was the one adopted, but not until 1868, after the conclusion of Lushington's judicial career.[27]

The opponents of the rates resorted to a weapon that has been used frequently, before and since, in political controversy, namely, civil disobedience. As has been seen, Lushington advised the Bishop of London not to use the ecclesiastical court, but several of the Dissenters were determined to force the hand of the court. These were the 'Church Rate Martyrs', of whom the most influential was John Thorogood. Thorogood was assessed for a church rate of a very small amount – 5s 6d – which he refused to pay. In respect of claims under £10, the ecclesiastical court had no jurisdiction unless there were a dispute about the validity of the claim; a magistrate could order seizure of the ratepayer's property to enforce the rate. This was similar to the procedure under which the Quakers had, for many years, allowed the rates to be enforced without their active co-operation.[28] But it would not serve the political purpose of causing a direct confrontation between the law and the recalcitrant ratepayer. Accordingly, Thorogood availed himself of a procedure that took the case into the ecclesiastical court. The object of the procedure was to enable a *bona fide* objection to the validity of the rate to be determined by the proper court. Thorogood certified that he intended, in good faith, to dispute the validity of the rate. He served a notice on the

25 See pp. 33–8, above.
26 Select Committee on Church Rates, PP 1851, ix, 1, q. 2601.
27 Compulsory Church Rate Abolition Act, 31 & 32 Vic. c. 109. See J. P. Ellens, 'Lord John Russell and the Church Rate Conflict: the struggle for a Broad Church, 1834–1868', *Journal of British Studies* 26 (1987), 232.
28 See Lushington's evidence to the Select Committee on Church Rates, PP 1851, ix, 1, qq. 2367–8.

magistrates listing a number of legal grounds on which he said that he proposed to challenge the rate, concluding:

And I hereby give you notice, that it is my *bona fide* intention to dispute the validity of the said rate in the proper ecclesiastical court. And I also give you notice, in consideration of the premises, to forbear giving judgment upon the complaint against me.[29]

When Thorogood was cited to appear in the London Consistory Court, he refused to respond, and Lushington, as judge of the Consistory Court, certified that he was in contempt,[30] with the consequence that he was imprisoned until the contempt should be purged, that is, until he should agree to appear in response to the citation.[31] Thorogood called on his friends not to pay the rate on his behalf, saying that he counted his life as nothing 'compared to the idolatry of paying to what I believe a most unchristian Church'.[32] This created a legal impasse, because Lushington held, on the interpretation of a statute empowering him to release a person committed for contempt when his contempt was purged,[33] that he had no power to release Thorogood otherwise. Since Thorogood staunchly declared that he would never submit, it looked as though he might be imprisoned for life for failure to pay 5s 6d. This was excellent fuel for the campaign against the rates, and Thorogood, and his supporters, made the most of it.[34] Eventually, in August 1840, a special Act of Parliament was passed empowering the judge to release a person after six months' imprisonment, on payment of the amount claimed, and costs,[35] even though

[29] Quoted by Lushington, Hansard, 3rd ser., lii, 111 (11 Feb. 1840).
[30] The ecclesiastical courts did not, technically, have power to imprison on their own authority. The procedure was for the ecclesiastical court to certify to the Court of Chancery that a person was in contempt. The actual order of committal was an order of the latter court. See H. C. Coote, *The Practice of the Ecclesiastical Courts* (London, 1847), 817, 828–31.
[31] The procedure is to be found in Coote, *Practice of the Ecclesiastical Courts* 830–1. The prisoner had to appear before a surrogate of the ecclesiastical court and take an oath 'that he will in future obey the lawful commands of the ordinary'.
[32] Quoted in Ellens, 'Church Rate Conflict', 155, from *The Sun*, 14 Nov. 1840.
[33] The Act is 53 Geo. III c. 127. Dr Lushington's explanation of his interpretation is in Hansard, 3rd ser., lv, 1256 (4 Aug. 1840).
[34] See Machin, *Politics and the Churches*, 104, Chadwick, *Victorian Church*, i, 130 (Thorogood held court at the gaol, issued petitions, and addressed crowds from his window).
[35] Costs were, of course, out of all proportion to the amount claimed. The costs in the ecclesiastical court were £16 13s 8d. Two applications had been made to the Court of Queen's Bench, with costs of £75. Dr Lushington held that the Act of 1840, in requiring payment of costs, referred only to costs in the ecclesiastical court. See *Baker* v. *Thorogood* (1840) 2 Curt 632.

his contempt had not been purged.[36] On 10 November 1840, after
Thorogood had spent almost two years in prison, Lushington ordered
his release in accordance with this statute.[37]

It was ironic that it should have been Lushington, one of the
principal opponents of church rates in the House of Commons, who
was the instrument of Thorogood's imprisonment, though, since
these events ultimately contributed to the abolition of the rate, it
might perhaps be said that Lushington acted a significant part –
though not one that he had chosen – in the political movement he
supported. He defended his conduct in the House of Commons on
several occasions. He stressed the fact that Thorogood had voluntarily
brought himself within the court's jurisdiction in order to defy it:

Hence it was clear that Mr Thorogood was the means of bringing himself into
the ecclesiastical courts ... Thus the House must see, that Thorogood
brought himself within the jurisdiction of the ecclesiastical court, and no
power on earth short of his own free will could have produced that effect. He
had been cited before that court, and he refused to appear; he voluntarily
placed himself in contempt.[38]

Lushington asserted also that he himself had no choice in the matter,
and had acted against his own inclinations:

The hon. member ... had spoken of a man committed to Chelmsford gaol for
five [shillings][39] by the ecclesiastical court in London. It was he who sentenced that man; he regretted it, but he could not help it. He put if off as long
as possible, but he had to do his duty at last. He regretted it; but his answer to
all attacks on him for it was, 'amend the law'.[40]

When Lushington says that 'he could not help it', he does not mean
that he could not have refused to certify Thorogood's contempt. Of
course, he could, as a matter of actual fact, have refused to do so. The
real meaning is that he considered that it was desirable to uphold the
process of the court, even at the cost of imprisoning Thorogood, and
enforcing what he considered personally to be a bad law:

In such circumstances the court must assert its own jurisdiction. The cause
might have been one between husband and wife, where the validity of their
marriage was the question in dispute. It might have related to a will, in which

[36] 3 & 4 Vict. c. 93 (enacted 10 Aug. 1840).
[37] *Baker* v. *Thorogood* (1840) 2 Curt 632.
[38] Hansard, 3rd ser., lii, 110–11 (11 Feb. 1840).
[39] Hansard has 'years' but 'shillings' must be intended. The Mirror of Parliament omits
this passage.
[40] Hansard, 3rd ser., xlvii, 538 (25 April 1839).

the defendant had the will in his pocket and 100,000*l* also. How could the court, in such circumstances, avoid committing a party guilty of a contempt?[41]

He also made the point that, as a judge, 'he had no choice'. If he had refused to commit Thorogood 'he would have subjected himself to proceedings in other courts, for the purpose of making him do his duty, and also the censure of the public'.[42] How likely such proceedings were it is difficult to say, but they were probably not out of the question. The ecclesiastical courts were subject to control by the common-law courts, and there were supporters of church rates who were willing, as the subsequent litigation in the *Braintree* case showed, to spend enormous sums of money to establish the legal principle they favoured.

Another theme in Lushington's speeches about Thorogood touched on a difficulty that he must have felt very acutely in view of his active opposition to church rates, that is, the line between law and politics. He said that 'he was not on the bench to make laws, but to administer them'.[43] In another speech, he asked what he was 'bound to do in virtue of his oath', and answered that 'he was bound to administer the law as it stood, without the slightest reference to any other consideration'.[44]

A judge, when called upon to decide a politically controversial case, often cannot avoid the appearance of taking one side or the other. As the defensive tone of his speeches shows, Lushington was conscious that he was accused of siding with Thorogood's oppressors; but it can safely be said that he would have been more stringently criticized, at least in his own professional circles, for taking sides, if he had refused to commit a person openly defying the due process of his court. A refusal to commit Thorogood, taken in conjunction with Lushington's known views on the matter, would have been perceived, by the legal profession, and by himself too, as an impermissible interference of political opinion in the judicial process.

The opponents of the rates developed another line of attack that involved testing key legal questions in the courts. Church rates were set periodically in each parish, by a vote at a meeting of parishioners called the vestry meeting. In some parishes, the opponents of rates

---

[41] Hansard, 3rd ser., lii, 111–12 (11 Feb. 1840)
[42] Hansard, 3rd ser., lv, 1256 (4 Aug. 1840).
[43] Hansard, 3rd ser., xlvii, 538 (25 April 1839)
[44] Hansard, 3rd ser., lv, 1256 (4 Aug. 1840).

could muster a majority in the vestry, and could vote down any proposed rate. The legal position in such a case was wholly uncertain. Church rates had existed for six hundred years without this point having been tested, and it is a significant indication of the novelty of nineteenth-century political and religious circumstances that these issues were raised then for the first time.

Each parish was bound to repair the nave of the parish church, and church rates were undoubtedly a lawful means of discharging this obligation. But what happened if a parish declined to repair the church? The ancient remedy was to lay the whole parish under an interdict,[45] but this was absurd in the context of the nineteenth-century dispute: the notion of interdict was obsolete as a means of compulsion, and, in any case, it would damage only those who wished to attend the parish church, and to receive the sacraments. The same objection applied to excommunicating the individual parishioners.[46] Possibly the court might order the parishioners individually 'to concur in those means which were necessary to have the church repaired',[47] and commit them to prison for contempt if they refused, until a majority was obtained in the vestry, but, since the procedure had not been used for hundreds of years, it was (to say the least) unlikely to operate smoothly in the political climate of the mid-nineteenth century.[48] When this suggestion was put to Lushington, he said:

I believe that the ecclesiastical court has the power to do it; but considering that these proceedings have been obsolete now for 150 or 200 years, there is a very great chance that there may be a miscarriage in some point of form, so that the power of the ecclesiastical courts would never be called into perfect effect.[49]

There would be insuperable difficulties in defining precisely what conduct constituted contempt, and in selecting the individuals to be imprisoned on this basis. Any attempt to follow this line would have

---

[45] See Dr Lushington's evidence to the Select Committee of the House of Commons on Church Rates, PP 1851, ix, 1, q. 2341.

[46] In Ayliffe's *Parergon* it is stated that 'the Spiritual Court may even now compel the Parishioners to repair their Parish Church . . . and may excommunicate every one of them severally till the greater Part of them do agree to assess and levy a Tax for the Repairs thereof.' J. Ayliffe, *Parergon Juris Canonici Anglicani* (London, 1726), 455. 'Even now' implies obsolescence in 1726.

[47] Select Committee on Church Rates, PP 1851, ix, 1, q. 2341.

[48] Ibid. q. 2342.   [49] Ibid. q. 2342.

created a whole army of church-rate martyrs. As Lord Stanley said, in a pamphlet published in 1853:

A proceeding 'obsolete for 150 to 200 years', complicated in its nature, taken before a tribunal probably soon to be abolished, and altogether opposed to the public opinion of the day, is hardly to be relied on. And a fresh obstacle is stated to exist, in the possible length and cost of the litigation ... It need scarcely be remarked that fanatics, bent on suffering for conscience sake, and resisting the law to the utmost, would be certain to put into operation this machinery of delay, supposing it possible that an attempt were made to coerce a refractory parish into the performance of its legal duties.[50]

It the church were in a state of disrepair, the churchwardens could be ordered to take steps to repair it. This meant summoning a vestry meeting and proposing a rate. But if the wardens summoned a vestry, and the vestry refused to make a rate, the legal position was unclear. Some thought that the wardens could be made personally responsible, and, from this, it was sought to deduce that the wardens could themselves make a rate, without the concurrence of the vestry. This reasoning was convoluted and tenuous, and Dr Lushington indicated, later, that he rejected its premise, i.e., that the wardens could be made personally liable if, having summoned a vestry, the vestry refused the rate.[51] If this were right, the consequence would be that there was no way of making a rate in a parish where active opponents formed a majority of the vestry. But it was not clear that it was right: there was a very even division of legal opinion. This was the question that was tested in the two *Braintree* cases, with litigation in eight courts over a period of sixteen years.[52]

In the first *Braintree* case, a vestry was summoned, which refused to make a rate. The churchwardens then purported to make a rate on their own authority, and proceeded against one of the principal opponents of the rate, Joseph Burder. The case came before Lushington in the London Consistory Court, in November 1837. Only one relevant precedent was found, a decision of the Court of Arches in 1799, in which it had been held that the wardens could make a valid rate after a refusal by the vestry. This case, *Gaudern* v. *Selby*, had not been reported (there being no published reports of ecclesiastical cases

[50] Stanley, *Church Rate Question Considered*, at 26–7.
[51] Select Committee on Church Rates, PP 1851, ix, 1, q. 2346.
[52] Consistory Court (twice), Arches, Queen's Bench (twice), Exchequer Chamber (twice), House of Lords. The total number of judge sittings was thirty-eight, since many of the judges heard both cases, and the second case twice.

at that time), but had been recorded in notes taken by counsel.[53] The notes contained an obvious error in the dates. The libel did not correspond with the facts proved.[54] The judge did not refer to any authority for his conclusion. The circumstances of the dispute were wholly different; a sentence in *Gaudern* v. *Selby* suggests that it was only by chance that a majority opposed to the wardens was present at the vestry meeting; the judge is noted as saying:

On the whole, as I think the Churchwardens have been justified in what they did, and there has been a combination against them by some individuals, for I cannot call it a parish act . . .[55]

There was really no comparison with the social and political context of the dispute in the *Braintree* case, where the dispute was part of a national controversy, and the whole parish knew what was at stake.

Lushington said of *Gaudern* v. *Selby* that it had been quite unknown in the profession until lately discovered:

That case came with the appearance of surprise upon the whole profession. It was not known to the Ecclesiastical Commissioners, or at least it was not recollected by any of the members of the Commission;[56] and during the thirty years that I have been in this court I never heard the case adverted to, nor was I aware that there was such a case in existence, till very lately.[57]

He went on to say that, 'as to the case itself, it is certainly one in which, not to use too strong a term, there appears to be a good deal of eccentricity'.[58] Nevertheless, he held himself to be bound by the case, it being a decision of a superior court.

Lushington gave his decision immediately, without reserving the question for consideration. It might have been expected that, in such an important and controversial case, he would have reserved. He explained that, as he considered himself absolutely bound by *Gaudern* v. *Selby* there was no need to reserve: 'delay . . . being unnecessary, the sooner I deliver my judgment the better'.[59] The case of *Gaudern* v. *Selby* had not come upon Lushington wholly unexpect-

[53] Sir C. Robinson's note of the case is printed in 1 Curt 394.
[54] The libel was the statement of the case of the party commencing the suit. It alleged that the majority of the vestry had consented to the rate, but the evidence showed that they had disallowed it. See 1 Curt 392.
[55] 1 Curt 397.
[56] This was the commission of 1830–1, of which Dr Lushington was the most active member.
[57] 1 Curt 391.   [58] Ibid.   [59] 1 Curt 387.

edly in the course of argument. There had been a flurry of pamphlets on the question published in 1837, of which he must have known, in which the case was discussed at great length.[60] It seems clear that he must have made up his mind that (unless something new came up in argument) he would hold himself to be bound by *Gaudern v. Selby*. The principal reason he gave for this decision was the conventional one that binding precedent must be maintained in the interest of certainty:

I apprehend, that obedience to a superior court is one of the first duties that an inferior judge has to perform, as the presumption of law is, that the Judge of the superior court is not only superior in rank and station, but in judgment also, and ability; and the evil which would arise from uncertainty, if any judge were to allow himself to be let loose from precedents, and to give his judgment according to his own impression of each individual case, would overwhelm and be destructive of the best interests of the people, for the great interest of all people is, that the law should be certain, and that all should know by what rules they should govern themselves. Upon these principles I have always endeavoured to regulate my own conduct, even under circumstances where my own private opinion might lead me to a different result.[61]

In a later case, he said that he had followed *Gaudern v. Selby* 'against my own conviction of what really was the law, but I stated at the time that though I obeyed I did not concur'.[62]

The reader cannot avoid asking whether the effect of *Gaudern v. Selby* really was so stringent as this implies. The report of the case was inadequate, and contained obvious errors: it had been wholly unknown for nearly forty years; it cited no authority whatever; the reasoning was very brief; the circumstances surrounding the dispute were entirely different. It would not take a great deal of judicial ingenuity to find here sufficient reason to depart from the case. This consideration directs attention to comments indicating that Lushington was content that the matter should appear to be out of his own control:

[60] Sir J. Campbell, *Letter to the Right Hon. Lord Stanley on the Law of Church Rates* (1837); R. Baines, *Letter to Sir John Campbell on the Law of Church Rates* (1837); E. E. Deacon, *Another Letter to the Rt Hon. Lord Stanley etc.* (1837); W. Hale, *The Antiquity of the Church Rates System Considered* (1837); J. Nicholl, *Observations on the Attorney General's Letter to Lord Stanley* (1837); R. Swan, *The Principle of Church Rates etc.* (1837); J. Manning, *Letter to Earl Fitzwilliam upon the power of Compelling the Assessment of Church Rate etc.* (1837).
[61] 1 Curt 390.
[62] *Westerton v. Liddell* (1855) Bayford 18.

I may, however, observe that there are other reasons for not entering into the merits of the case, though those I have stated are satisfactory. I think, that upon a question of such great importance, and which I suppose, from what fell in the course of argument, will be carried to another tribunal, it would be better that it should go there in no way affected by my judgment, in one way or the other.[63]

As with the committal of Thorogood, Lushington, known to be politically active against church rates, was in a difficult position as a judge. He must have been acutely conscious that a decision against the validity of the rate would lay him open to an accusation that he had been improperly influenced by political considerations. It was not inconvenient for him, therefore, to find himself able to make a decision, against what might be supposed to have been his own inclinations, on the ground that he had no discretion, as a judge, to act otherwise.

An appeal lay from the Consistory Court to the Court of Arches, and from there to the Privy Council, but, since the ecclesiastical courts were subject to control by the common-law courts, the latter courts had power to invalidate the rate. Instead of appealing, therefore, the respondent moved immediately in the court of Queen's Bench for a prohibition, a device for controlling the ecclesiastical court when it exceeded its jurisdiction. The prohibition was granted by the Queen's Bench, which rejected *Gaudern* v. *Selby*,[64] and the churchwardens appealed to the Court of Exchequer Chamber. The Court, while dismissing the appeal, suggested that the rate might have been valid if made, not by the wardens alone, but by a minority at a duly constituted vestry meeting. The suggestion was based on the argument that the parishioners were bound to keep the church in repair, and a refusal to cast a vote as a person was legally bound to do might be treated as throwing away the vote. The court did not pursue the matter, as it did not arise in the particular case, but it suggested that *Gaudern* v. *Selby* might be explained and defended on this basis.[65]

Instead of appealing, as they might have done, to the House of Lords, the churchwardens next followed up this suggestion. A vestry meeting was held, in July 1841, at which the majority voted against the proposed rate, but the churchwardens and several other members

[63] 1 Curt 393.   [64] *Burder* v. *Veley* (1840) 12 Ad & E 233.
[65] *Veley* v. *Burder* (1841) 12 Ad & E 265.

of the minority purported to approve the rate. The case came back to Lushington in the form of proceedings against another of the dissenters, John Gosling. Lushington, pressed again with *Gaudern* v. *Selby*, said that the case:

has been expressly disclaimed as an authority by the Court of Queen's Bench; that having lost its original authority it was not set up by the Court of Exchequer Chamber, for that court having disclaimed giving any opinion upon the present question neither did nor could pronounce any opinion as relating to this question of *Gaudern* v. *Selby*.[66]

The question in issue in the second *Braintree* case was this: assuming that the churchwardens could not make a rate on their own, could they do so as part of the minority at a vestry meeting? The difficulty in relying on *Gaudern* v. *Selby* at this stage was that that case had held that the wardens alone could make a rate (a point not now in issue) and had said nothing at all about the significance of a minority vote at a vestry meeting. For these reasons, Lushington, after what the reporter calls a 'minute examination of the case of *Gaudern* v. *Selby*'[67] declined to be bound by the case. His position is understandable: the alternative would have been to hold himself bound by a proposition that was not in issue and had not been asserted in the earlier case.[68] He pointed out that the question now at issue had been expressly left open by the Exchequer Chamber, and he concluded that he was bound to decide it according to his best judgment.

There is much force in this line of reasoning, but the point shows how elusive is the doctrine of precedent. For it might, with equal force, he said that the Exchequer Chamber had rejected the repudiation of *Gaudern* v. *Selby* by the Queen's Bench, and had implied that the case was rightly decided. This was the opinion of the Dean of the Arches, who reversed Lushington's decision on appeal.[69]

Lushington's concern was again to avoid the appearance that his personal opinions influenced the result, and he was fortunate, from this point of view, in that the proposition supported by the churchwardens contained serious weaknesses, which Lushington did not hesitate to expose. The argument was, in some ways, weaker than in the first *Braintree* case. It was plausible to argue that, since repair of

---

[66] 3 Curt 279.
[67] The record of the case in the Peterborough Consistory Court was examined; it is reproduced as a footnote in 3 Curt 272–8.
[68] 3 Curt 278.
[69] (1843) 3 Curt 304, at 330.

the church was required by law, the churchwardens alone might lay a rate for that purpose, and a vestry meeting was unnecessary; it was rather less plausible to argue that, though a meeting was necessary, the voting at it was irrelevant. The purpose of having a vestry meeting, Lushington said, must be to enable the majority opinion to prevail; if a minority were sufficient, there would be no point in requiring a meeting, as it might be a minority consisting of the churchwardens and one other, or, indeed, as he later suggested, the churchwardens alone, or even one of the churchwardens.[70] If the meeting were really a mere empty formality, he continued, in a style exceeding the forceful and verging on the sarcastic, it was surprising that this very convenient truth should have been so long concealed:

If this new doctrine be the law, it is a matter to me of extreme wonderment, that in the usage of centuries, when so many cases must have called for its application, when so many powerful minds have dedicated to the question their learning and ingenuity, it should first have been discovered in the year 1841; and more especially am I moved to astonishment, when I recollect that this doctrine, if tenable, would have taken away all necessity for interdict, excommunication, all ecclesiastical process, all interposition; on the part of the High Commission. A more easy remedy for the disease, a surer preventive against its re-occurrence, a more efficient substitute for severer and harsher remedies which were used, could not, I think, have been devised, yet, till the year 1841, though the necessity for the use of it so often must have occurred, there is in all the books in all the reports, ecclesiastical or common law, *altum silentium* respecting this panacea.[71]

It was urged that new means of enforcement were required, since the old were obsolete. Here, Lushington was at pains to separate the judicial from the political role:

But if I were at liberty to pronounce the ancient remedies insufficient or obsolete, could I invent a new one? Could I usurp the office of the Legislature, and, *jus facere non dicere*?[72]

In a striking concluding paragraph, he entered a defence of his judicial function, seeking again to distance himself from political considerations, in answer to critics who should accuse him of deliberately undermining church rates in accordance with his own views:

---

[70] Select Committee on Church Rates, PP 1851, ix, 1, q. 2361.
[71] 3 Curt 301–2.   [72] 3 Curt 302–3.

I am well aware of the heavy responsibility, which has attached upon me in the
discharge of this arduous duty, – I well know how many evil consequences, or
supposed evil consequences, may be attributed to my miscarriage, if I have
failed to discover the legal truth; but this I know also, that I have industri-
ously, earnestly, and fearlessly done my best to ascertain the law. Once
convinced as to what the law is, I never will be induced to resort to subtle and
ingenious refinements to defeat the law. Whatever may be, in the opinions of
others, the pernicious consequences of adhering to it, I am well persuaded,
from the history of this country, that the continuance of bad laws, and the
prevention of good laws, have, in no small measure, been occasioned by the
laudable, though mistaken endeavours to wrest the law to particular notions
of justice and expediency, and by the intervention of subtle distinctions, to
ward off evil and injurious results, which, if they be the effects of the law,
ought to be remedied, not by Judges, but by the Legislature.[73]

Since, as no one knew better than Lushington, legislation *strengthen-
ing* church rates was politically impossible, this amounts to saying
that, as there was not the political will to patch up the leaks, church
rates should be permitted to sink.

Lushington conceded that a judge (if willing to wrest the law) could
find a plausible legal ground for upholding the rate, and the subsequent history of the case shows that this was indeed so. Lushington
said that his own best judgment was that the arguments in favour of
the rate were fatally flawed, and it is not necessary to doubt his
sincerity. In reversing his judgment, the Dean of the Arches, Sir
Herbert Jenner Fust, in a remark that conjures up the collegial
atmosphere of Doctors' Commons, actually said that he remembered
that Lushington had long been of the same opinion:

If my recollection serves me, I always understood, that, although the point
was doubted, the better opinion was, that such a rate was a good and valid
rate, but I well remember, that at an early period of my communication on the
subject with the learned judge of the Consistory Court, he entertained a
different view of the law.[74]

It is, however, permissible to doubt whether the flaws would have
been so fatal in the eyes of a judge who thought church rates an
essential feature of a desirable establishment.

The Dean of the Arches, reversing Lushington, shows how convincing arguments can be marshalled in the opposite direction: *Gaudern* v. *Selby* was applicable, and, so far from discredited, was
impliedly approved by the Exchequer Chamber; the obligation to

[73] 3 Curt 303–4.   [74] 3 Curt 331.

repair churches was admittedly mandatory, and there must be an effectual means of enforcing it, or churches would fall into ruins; votes cast against a necessary rate were, therefore, illegal and void.

Lushington's fear of criticism from supporters of church rates was well founded, as was promptly shown by a charge to his clergy by the Archdeacon of Maidstone, delivered very shortly after Lushington's judgment.[75] The Archdeacon accused Dr Lushington of disregarding the law, plainly implying that he had allowed his personal views to affect his decision:

I have not adverted in these remarks to a judgment delivered within the last few days by Dr Lushington, directly adverse to the view just stated, as taken by the common-law judges ... It shows that the learned judge himself still retains the opinions he had before expressed, and that the weight of authority has less influence upon his mind than it might perhaps have been reasonable to anticipate.[76]

Lushington's opinion did eventually prevail in the courts, but only after the Court of Arches, reversing him, had been upheld by the Queen's Bench (four judges, unanimous)[77] and the Exchequer Chamber (majority of four to three)[78]. Gosling then appealed to the House of Lords, where all the judges were summoned to give opinions, as was the practice in important cases.[79] Ten attended, who divided five to five, and Lord Truro (who had already heard the case, and dissented in the Exchequer Chamber) decided against the rate. Lord Brougham concurred.[80] It points up the anomalous – indeed, bizarre – nature of the appellate jurisdiction of the House of Lords at this

[75] W. R. Lyall, *A Charge delivered to the Clergy of the Archdeaconry of Maidstone, in May 1842; Containing some Remarks on the Judgment Pronounced by Dr Lushington in the Consistory Court of London, 6 May 1842*. Lyall says the judgment was 'delivered within the last few days' (p. 16). In an appendix, he attempts to take account of a more careful reading of the judgment, admitting that he overstated his criticism in the main body of the text.

[76] Ibid. at 16.

[77] *Gosling v. Veley* (1847) 7 QB 406.

[78] *Gosling v. Veley* (1850) 12 QB 328.

[79] See PP 1856, 1, 7 (return showing number of times the judges were summoned between 1846 and 1855).

[80] *Gosling v. Veley* (1853) 4 HLC 679. The Lord Chancellor (Cranworth, who happened to be the husband of Lushington's sister-in-law, and who had also heard the case, and dissented, in the Exchequer Chamber) said that he had not heard the argument, but indicated that he agreed with Lord Truro, and reported Lord Brougham's concurrence (4 HLC 813–14).

time,[81] that after fifteen separate judgments had been given on the case by nineteen judges (not to mention the judgments in the first case), it should, in the end, be decided by two retired Whig politicians, both, as it happens, former close associates of Lushington,[82] one of whom had actually dissented in the court appealed from.[83] In evidence given to a committee of the House of Lords in 1856, on the appellate jurisdiction of the House, Roundell Palmer, later himself Lord Chancellor, acknowledged, with implicit reference to the *Braintree* case, an inevitable influence of political opinion:

Experience shows that upon questions of that kind [church rates or tithes] it naturally happens that the most high minded men bring certain general principles to their consideration, which have a great influence upon the determination to which they come. In four or five semi-political cases which occur to my mind, if you were to trace the circumstances of the different cases, and see what opinions had been given by judges upon them, you would generally find that the judges have arrived at those conclusions which might have been expected from the known complexion of their political views.[84]

In 1851, Lushington, by this time no longer himself a Member of Parliament, gave lengthy evidence to a select committee of the House of Commons on church rates. Again he felt the need to separate the legal from the political. When asked his opinion on reform, he made suggestions for simplifying the law, on the assumption, expressly stated, that the principle of universal rates was to remain. He favoured legal rules that should be simple, effective, and inexpensive to interpret and enforce, and on these grounds he proposed the exclusion of the ecclesiastical courts altogether. This was the kind of reform that he considered it proper to propose, and it was similar to proposals

---

81 See evidence given to Select Committee of the House of Lords on Appellate jurisdiction HL Sess Pap 1856, xxiv, 1, 4–5, 10, indicating that it was common for cases about this period to be decided by two lords who disagreed, or by the Lord Chancellor alone, or by Lord Brougham alone. Lay peers, chatting or writing letters, were often present in the House to form a quorum (three peers). The law peers would come and go during argument, and judgments were delivered in the style of parliamentary speeches. See also D. E. C. Yale, 'Note' (1970), 86 LQR 311.

82 Brougham, Wilde (Lord Truro) and Lushington were all counsel to Queen Caroline in 1820; Lushington and Wilde were the executors of the Queen's will; Lushington and Brougham were fellow founders of the Society for the Diffusion of Useful Knowledge, and a considerable correspondence between them is preserved at University College, London.

83 It was not unique for a case to be determined in the House of Lords by the judge appealed from. See evidence of Malins to the House of Lords Committee on Appellate jurisdiction, HL Sess Pap 1856, xxiv, 1 at 38.

84 HL Sess Pap 1856, xxiv, 1 at 66 (q. 404).

made by the Ecclesiastical Courts Commission, of which Lushington was a member, in 1832.[85] His professional and judicial experience justified him in saying that the existing law was inefficient, expensive, troublesome, and divisive. But, on the underlying assumption – that it was desirable to retain a universally binding system of rates – he firmly refused to be drawn, evidently considering that, having with-drawn from the House of Commons, it was no longer appropriate for him to take a political position:

> With great deference, that is asking me to give you an opinion upon a great legislative principle, which must be decided not by any legal tribunal, but by the House of Commons and the House of Lords.[86]

Lord Stanley, in the pamphlet of 1853, already referred to, reflected the perceived propriety of this reticence, when he wrote:

> But the weightiest evidence, both in regard of the personal character and official station of the witness, is that of Dr Lushington, Judge of the Admir-alty and Consistory Courts. His acknowledged ability – his judicial experience – and his absolute withdrawal from the field of political controversy – give to the expressions of opinion which follow an authority such as those of no other person possess.[87]

Church rates continued to be a fruitful source of litigation until their abolition in 1868. During the nine years in which Lushington sat as Dean of the Arches (1858–67) church rate cases formed the largest class of cases in the Court of Arches.[88] The volume of the Law Reports reporting Lushington's judgments in his last year on the bench includes six ecclesiastical cases, of which four are church rate cases.[89]

Lushington's role in this prolonged controversy offers a perspec-tive, not only on the controversy itself, but on the interaction among law, religion, and politics. The judge's duty, Lushington said in the second *Braintree* case, is to declare the law, not to make it. But the almost equal division of judicial opinion,[90] in both the ecclesiastical and the common-law courts, shows that declaring the law is not a

---

[85] PP 1831–2, xxiv, 1.
[86] Select Committee on Church Rates, PP 1851, ix, 1, qq. 2528, 2540. Similar refusals are at qq. 2582 and 2585.
[87] Stanley, *Church Rate Question Considered*, 9.
[88] Seventeen of fifty-two cases were church rate cases. Court of Arches Assignation Book, Lambeth Palace Library.
[89] (1867) LR 1 Ad & E.
[90] Twenty judges heard the second case. One died before giving judgment. A total of ten found the rate to be valid, and nine found it invalid.

simple or mechanical task. Lushington sought to set aside his own opinions, but the very fact that he felt the need to be so emphatic about this objective may suggest that he had not wholly attained it. This is not to say that the influence of his opinions on his decisions was a simple one, or that its effect was predictable. In the *Braintree* cases, his opinions, if influential, carried him in two opposite directions. There is little sign, in Lushington's other decisions, of a general hostility to church rates.[91] Most of his reported decisions as Dean of the Arches were in favour of churchwardens.[92]

There are few manifestations of shared community values more powerful than a national religion. But a strong national religion, that makes a claim to the active allegiance of all, necessarily imposes burdens on those who dissent from it. Church rates were seen, by both sides, as a test of whether the national church could assert a claim on the whole nation. In the end, the burden proved intolerable to the liberal and individualistic spirit of the mid-nineteenth century. Lushington was strongly predisposed by personal religious inclination, and by professional connections, to favour the established Church. Yet, the force of political liberalism prevailed in his mind, as, ultimately, it did in the national polity.

[91] One decision, *Gough* v. *Jones* (1862) 1 New Rep 107, 7 LT 566, 9 LT 610, 3 Moo. PC NS 1, 7, holding valid a rate that excluded residents in a part of the parish incorporated into a new parish, particularly alarmed opponents of church rates, as it implied that new parishes could lay their own rates. See Ellens, 'Church Rate Conflict', at 437. However, in *Smith* v. *Billington* (1852) 8 Moo PC 179, he gave the judgment of the Privy Council (reversing the Court of Arches) holding a rate invalid on the ground of inadequate notice.

[92] Several cases are reported in the *Law Times Reports* (New Series) vols 1–15. All four cases in (1867) LR 1 Ad & E are in favour of churchwardens.

9

THE HIGH CHURCH

The business of the ecclesiastical courts did not, by the nineteenth century, have any very close connection with the affairs of the Church, probate and matrimonial work forming the bulk of the cases. Even on the ecclesiastical side, most of the disputes dealt with by the courts had nothing to do with theology; they concerned such questions as church rates, tithes, pew rents, faculties, with an occasional case on brawling in church, or the moral conduct of a clergyman. Doctrinal disputes were virtually unknown.[1]

In the period after 1840, however, a number of theological issues agitated the Church, and the relationship between Church and State was still such that what agitated the Church, agitated the nation. The ecclesiastical courts suddenly found themselves called upon to determine some questions of deep theology.

In 1865, a volume was published, containing a collection of the judgments of the Judicial Committee of the Privy Council in ecclesiastical cases relating to doctrine and discipline, with the object, as stated in the Preface by the Bishop of London (Tait), of enabling churchmen to come to an informed opinion on the very controversial questions of the constitution and legitimacy of the Judicial Committee as a final court of appeal in ecclesiastical matters.[2] The volume includes fifteen cases that reached the Privy Council between the years 1840 and 1864, all the cases judged by the editors to involve questions of

[1] A report to the House of Commons on Appeals in Doctrine and Discipline to the High Court of Delegates, PP 1867–8, lvii, 75, xxi, says that not more than seven cases, in the whole records of the High Court of Delegates over 300 years 'even remotely involved any question of doctrine' (introduction by H. C. Rothery, the Registrar of the Admiralty Court, pointing out also that the early records were incomplete, and that the High Court of Commission may have dealt with such cases before 1641).

[2] G. C. Brodrick, and W. H. Fremantle, *A Collection of the Judgments of the Judicial Committe of the Privy Council in Ecclesiastical Cases relating to Doctrine and Discipline* (London, 1865).

doctrine. The membership of the Judicial Committee varied very considerably over this twenty-four-year period, but Lushington was involved in every one of those cases, either as a member of the Judicial Committee, or at an earlier stage in the proceedings.

Of the fifteen cases, four arose more or less directly out of the revival of Catholic doctrine associated with the high-church party, or were of vital importance to that party, and these are discussed in the present chapter.

GORHAM

The *Gorham* case involved the theology of the sacrament of baptism. Gorham, a clergyman of forty years standing, a holder of evangelical views, incurred the displeasure of his bishop, Phillpotts, of Exeter, by describing the Church of England as a 'National Establishment' and advertising for a curate who should be 'free from Tractarian error'.[3] When, in 1847, Gorham was presented to another benefice in the same diocese, Phillpotts refused to institute him without an examination of the soundness of his doctrine concerning baptism. The bishop was entitled (by the canons[4]) to examine those presented to benefices, but an extensive examination was unusual, especially in the case of a clergyman of Gorham's age and standing. The bishop eventually found Gorham's theology wanting, and refused to institute him. Gorham commenced proceedings in the Court of Arches for a remedy against the bishop. So rare were such cases, that 'for some time no precedent could be found for the forms of pleading',[5] but at last one was discovered in a proctor's office. Gorham failed in the Court of Arches, but appealed successfully to the Judicial Committee of the Privy Council.

Lushington sat as a member of the Judicial Committee. He was an experienced judge,[6] and the most experienced member of the Committee, in the sense that he had, at the time of the hearing, sat more frequently in the Committee than any other member.[7] He was the

[3] E. F. Moore, *The Case of the Rev. G. C. Gorham against the Bishop of Exeter* (London, 1852), 141 (Jenner Fust).
[4] Canon 39 (1603).
[5] Moore, *Gorham against the Bishop of Exeter*, 184 (Turner's argument).
[6] Consistory Court Judge for the diocese of London from 1828, and Admiralty Court Judge from 1838.
[7] P. A. Howell, *The Judicial Committee of the Privy Council, 1833–1876* (Cambridge, 1979), 234–5.

only civilian member of the Committee, and so the only member claiming a professional expertise in ecclesiastical law. Indeed, the Dean of the Arches (Jenner Fust) indicated that he would have sought Lushington's assistance himself had it not been anticipated that he would be hearing the appeal. He is reported as saying to Gorham's proctor, when informed that there would be an appeal from his judgment:

that he fully expected that an appeal would be made against his decision. He did not wish the burden of finally deciding so important a case to remain upon his shoulders. Had he not expected that an appeal would be made, he should have requested the assistance of the Chancellor of the Bishop of London [Lushington]; but he had not done so, as he was aware that he would be called upon to give his assistance as a member of the Judicial Committee of the Privy Council.[8]

The case aroused enormous public interest. Over 140 pamphlets were published on it.[9] Dire consequences were threatened whatever the decision should be. If Gorham lost, the evangelicals would be driven out of the Church; if he won, widespread defections to Rome of the Tractarians were predicted. In fact a number did defect to Rome as a result of the Privy Council decision, of whom the most distinguished was Archdeacon, later Cardinal, Manning.

Baptism, the Christian rite of initiation, took the usual form, in the nineteenth-century Church of England, of a ceremonial sprinkling with water of infants. The dispute between Gorham and Phillpotts was essentially a conflict between what may be called a 'low', or Protestant view of the sacrament, and a 'high', or Catholic view. There were many shades of Protestant and Catholic opinion on these matters, but probably the general nature of the controversy can be sufficiently explained by saying that the 'high' view tended to emphasize the objective effect of the ceremony duly administered, while the 'low' view insisted on the need for faith on the part of the recipient (afterwards, in the case of infant baptism), or emphasized the autonomy of God's act in conferring grace, independent of any human

---

[8] *British Magazine and Monthly Register etc.*, 36 (1849), 447–8. This remark addressed to the proctor does not appear in Moore's or Robertson's reports.
[9] S. C. S. Nias, *Gorham and the Bishop of Exeter* (London, 1951), appendix.

agency. The importance of the question, and the public interest it aroused, were stressed by the Dean of the Arches in his judgment.[10]

The extensive nature of the theological arguments addressed to the courts was extraordinary. Gorham's examination by the Bishop lasted for fifty-two hours, over eight days, and required answers to 149 questions. The full transcript of the examination was before the courts. The addresses of counsel in the Privy Council were extensive. Badeley (Phillpotts' counsel) published his argument as a substantial book.[11] The arguments were subtle, confusing, and complex, and, even from the perspective of 1850, antiquarian. The views of many theologians, written over the course of the preceding 300 years, were quoted at a length that would be likely to deter even a dedicated professional theologian. The arguments before the Judicial Committee took four days,[12] and, as reported by Moore, occupy 277 pages. One can, perhaps, detect a plea for sympathy in Lord Langdale's reference to the theology that had been 'discussed before us at such great length and with so much learning'.[13]

It was not surprising, then, that the Judicial Committee sought to avoid deciding questions of theology. Greville, the clerk of the Privy Council, records in his diary, that when, at a conference of the judges after the argument, the Bishop of London said he hoped the judgment would not condemn Phillpotts' doctrine

they all exclaimed that they would take care that nothing of the kind was done; they would steer as clear as possible of any declaration as to doctrine, and found their judgment on this, that it had not been proved to them that Gorham had put forth any doctrine so clearly and undoubtedly at variance

---

[10] 'The nature of the question, the vast body of learning . . . and the important result to which the decision may possibly lead, have created in the mind of the public, a more than ordinary interest, and, as may be imagined, in the mind of the Court, a corresponding anxiety and sense of responsibility.' Court of Arches, Moore, *Gorham against the Bishop of Exeter*, 131.

[11] E. Badeley, *Substance of a Speech Delivered before the Judicial Committee of the Privy Council on Monday the 17th and Tuesday the 18th of December, A.D. 1849, upon an Appeal in a Cause of Duplex Querela Between the Rev. George Cornelius Gorham, Clerk, Appellant and the Right Rev. Henry Lord Bishop of Exeter, Respondent, with an Introduction* (London, 1850), (xxviii and 215 pp.).

[12] 11, 12, 14, 17, Dec. 1849; Minute Book, Privy Council Office.

[13] Moore, *Gorham against the Bishop of Exeter*, 474. At one point in his argument Badeley said (after ninety-seven pages): 'I shall, therefore, my lords, endeavour to trace this matter historically' and added, as though fearful of impatience in his audience, '(it will not take so very long a time as your Lordships might possibly suppose).' *Speech*, 98.

with the Articles and formularies as to warrant the Bishop's refusal to induct him.[14]

Lord Langdale, giving the judgment of the Committee, said that the question was not whether Gorham's opinions were 'theologically sound or unsound' but whether they were contrary to the expressed requirements laid down in the formularies of the Church of England. In a passage that formed the basis for all the subsequent decisions of the ecclesiastical courts he said:

> This question must be decided by the Articles and the Liturgy; and we must apply to the construction of those books the same rules which have been long established, and are by law applicable to the construction of all written instruments. We must endeavour to ascertain for ourselves the true meaning of the language employed, assisted only by the consideration of such external or historical facts as we may find necessary to enable us to understand the subject-matter to which the instruments relate, and the meaning of the words employed.[15]

At the end of the judgment, he said:

> The case not requiring it, we have abstained from expressing any opinion of our own upon the theological correctness or error of the doctrine held by Mr Gorham which was discussed before us at such great length and with so much learning.[16]

But it proved not to be such an easy task to separate law and theology into watertight compartments. The form of procedure before the Court of Arches, on which the Judicial Committee commented severely,[17] had not required the Bishop to state precisely what he alleged Gorham's doctrine to be, or precisely which of the Church's formularies he alleged to be contradicted. So the Judicial Committee, like the Court of Arches, had before it, on the one hand, Gorham's unedited answers to 149 questions, and, on the other hand, the Articles of Religion (a set of doctrinal propositions adopted by the Church of England in the sixteenth century, also known as the Thirty-nine Articles) and the Prayer Book. Gorham was an intelligent and knowledgeable man. His answers to Phillpotts' questions had been carefully given, and he had avoided any form of words that directly

[14] *The Greville Memoirs*, L. Strachey and R. Fulford (eds) (London, 1938), vi, 193, (16 Jan. 1850).
[15] Moore, *Gorham against the Bishop of Exeter*, 462.
[16] Ibid., 474.   [17] Ibid., 461.

contradicted anything in the formularies. It was not easy for his accusers to pick out a heretical passage.

Another major difficulty was that the formularies themselves did not speak clearly on the question. The Articles were Protestant in tone, and in general tendency, but they were drawn up with the express object of accommodating a number of different views on the theological controversies of the sixteenth century, and when carefully read, they stopped short, in many cases, of expressly condemning Catholic doctrine.[18] On the sacraments they were decidedly ambiguous. Protestant views are suggested by Article XXV, which says, of the sacraments, that 'in such only as worthily receive the same, they have a wholesome effect or operation', and by Article XXVII, which says that they that receive baptism 'rightly' are grafted into the Church. On the other hand, Article XXV had abandoned an earlier version, where the Catholic doctrine of the sacraments had been condemned in express words;[19] it asserted that sacraments were 'not only badges or tokens of Christian men's profession, but rather be certain sure witnesses and effectual signs of grace'; Article XXVII stated that 'Baptism is not only a sign of profession, and mark of difference whereby Christian men be discerned from others that be not Christened, but it is also a sign of Regeneration or new Birth', drawing an analogy with a legal instrument 'signed and sealed'; the assertion that infant baptism was to be retained also favoured the Catholic view. The liturgical sections of the Prayer Book, containing expressions implying that baptism effected regeneration, tended also to support the Catholic view.

The problem before the court, like many legal problems, was not soluble by the perusal of words, nor could the implicit views of the judges on theology, and on the effects of their decision on the welfare of the Church, be excluded. The judges could not ignore at least the following known or assumed facts: many churchmen of undoubted respectability had, for hundreds of years, held views very similar to Gorham's;[20] if the condemnation of Gorham were upheld, the implications would be not only that he would lose the vicarage to which he had been presented, but that he, and every clergyman holding similar

---

[18] See O. Chadwick, *The Victorian Church* (London, 1966–70) i, 183–4.

[19] The 1552 Article expressly described as superstitious the doctrine, later defined at the Council of Trent, that the sacraments worked '*ex opere operato*', i.e. objectively. This sentence was abandoned in the 1562 version.

[20] Greville says that this point was stressed at the judicial conference by the Archbishop of Canterbury (Sumner). Greville, *Memoirs*, vi, 192.

views, could be driven out of the benefices they actually held;[21] and proceedings could possibly be instituted, not only by bishops, but by individuals,[22] opening the door to the distasteful prospect of a witch-hunt organized by the Tractarians on a national scale.

It might safely be deduced from other evidence that Lushington would be anxious to avoid such consequences, but the fact is confirmed by another passage in Greville's diary:

> Lushington said he had written out his opinion, but had not brought his paper with him. He made, however, a short speech, very good indeed, in which he pronounced a strong opinion against the Bishop, commenting in severe terms upon the nature of the examination, and setting forth the great danger to the peace of the Church which would result from a judicial declaration on their part that Gorham's opinions were clearly proved to be heretical.[23]

This account is of interest in illustrating Lushington's approach to his judicial function, as well as giving an insight into the methods of decision-making in the Judicial Committee. It is evident from Greville's account that Lushington did not, in the privacy of the judicial conference room, think first of what a strict interpretation of words might require; on the contrary, if Greville's account is complete, he relied almost entirely on the policy implications of a decision against Gorham.

Of course, it was urged on the other side that support of Gorham would drive the Tractarians out of the Church.[24] On this point, it might be deduced from what is revealed, by later decisions, of Lushington's views, that he would not greatly have deprecated this consequence. But this was not put to the test in the *Gorham* case, because a decision in favour of Gorham could be supported on liberal, rather than Protestant principles. The issue was whether those of Gorham's

---

21 'My Lords, I cannot also forget, that upon your decision may depend the actual livelihood of many members of that Church; men, who, whatever opinion may be entertained of their doctrines, it cannot be denied are, and have been, zealous ministers in the discharge of their duties', Moore, *Gorham against the Bishop of Exeter*, 181 (argument of Turner).

22 Lushington, in the Denison case, held that the bishop had no discretion, under The Church Discipline Act, to refuse to institute proceedings. *Proceedings against the Archdeacon of Taunton etc.* (Bath and London, 1857), 130.

23 Greville, *Memoirs*, vi, 192–3.

24 'I believe that there [are] . . . thousands of members of the Church of England, both of her clergy and her laity, who will regard the reversal of this judgment by your lordships, as a sentence of the highest tribunal in the land, declaring that the Church of England has in fact betrayed her trust; that she has ceased to hold that Catholic doctrine, that Apostolic truth, which is at once her profession and her boast', Badeley, *Speech*, 214–15.

view could have a place in the Church; an affirmative answer might
rest on the premise that Gorham's view was a permissible view; it did
not necessarily imply that the contrary view was not also permissible.
Liberal principles of another sort also tended to support Gorham.
Although Gorham was the promoter of the proceedings in the Court
of Arches, it was easy to cast the Bishop in the role of prosecutor, and
even of persecutor. He had intervened to stop a perfectly ordinary
move from one parish to another, to which Gorham's right would
ordinarily have been unchallengeable. The examination was a considerable imposition upon a man of Gorham's age and standing.
Greville says that Lushington commented 'in severe terms upon the
nature of the examination'. The Bishop did not specify Gorham's
offence in precise terms. Greville records that Lushington stressed
this point also:

> Lushington said he had the greatest difficulty in making out what Gorham's
> doctrine really was, and he was much struck with the fact that in no part of the
> Bishop's pleadings did he say explicitly with what he charged him.[25]

In the criminal-law context, an accused person has a right not to
answer questions, a privilege against self-incrimination, and a right to
know against what law he is alleged to have offended, and in what
respect. It is true that Gorham was not charged with a criminal
offence, but his livelihood was at stake, and it is understandable that
liberally minded judges would object to the procedures used against
him. Gorham's appeal was allowed, with one judge (Knight Bruce)
and one bishop (Blomfield) dissenting. Greville records also that
Lushington, with Lords Langdale and Campbell, was in favour of
allowing costs to Gorham, but eventually agreed to say nothing about
costs.[26]

The speech of Badeley before the Judicial Committee, in support of
Phillpotts, was published in book form, including the judicial inter-
ventions. Lushington intervened several times in Badeley's argument, with considerable effect. Badeley had been arguing that
baptism, duly performed, always effected regeneration. Lushington's
questions compelled him to admit that some element of intention was
a part of 'due performance'.[27] This led on to a more serious question.

[25] Greville, *Memoirs*, vi, 193.
[26] Greville, *Memoirs*, vi, 210–11 (9 Mar. 1850).
[27] Badeley, *Speech*, 69–70.

Lushington asked about the significance of the words in the Article, quoted above, 'they that receive Baptism rightly'. He wanted to know whether Badeley's submission was that 'rightly' referred only to the outward performance of baptism. Badeley had no satisfactory answer. Even more damaging was this question:

> DR LUSHINGTON – I must put this case to you. Take the Baptism of an adult, who has neither faith nor repentance, and he afterwards has faith and repentance, would you say that regeneration would take place then?
> MR BADELEY – Regeneration, I should say, would take place then. [The context shows that this means at the time of the baptism]
> DR LUSHINGTON – According to the doctrine of the Church, even without 'faith and repentance'?[28]

This is an astute question. Badeley's difficulty was that, if he said that regeneration occurred at baptism, he denied the need for faith and repentance, generally conceded to be necessary for receipt of grace in baptism of adults; if he admitted that regeneration was postponed, he abandoned the main point of his argument on the efficacy of baptism. He was driven to suggest that the baptized unfaithful adult would receive regeneration in the baptism, but not remission of sin. This is a very weak answer, which established what one writer (sympathetic to the Catholic view) has called 'a purely arbitrary distinction'.[29]

A central question, and one that disturbed the Tractarians as much as, if not more than, the substance of the decision, was the constitution of the Judicial Committee. It was a shocking thought to many that a secular court, composed of judges appointed by the Crown, having no connection with the Church, should be the ultimate authority upon questions of Church doctrine; this seemed irreconcilable with the claim of the Church of England to be a part of the universal church. The Church Discipline Act provided for Bishops to be members of the Judicial Committee in proceedings under that Act, but Gorham's case was not brought under that Act. The two Archbishops (Sumner and Musgrave) and the Bishop of London (Blomfield), who dissented, attended the hearings, and expressed their opinions at the judicial conference described by Greville, in January

[28] Ibid., 99.   [29] Nias, *Gorham and the Bishop of Exeter*, 86.

1850, but they were not members of the Judicial Committee, as, in giving judgment, Lord Langdale emphasized.[30]

Lushington, as it happens, had been personally involved on two previous occasions with this question, his activity tending in opposite directions. He was a member of the Committee that had originally proposed, in 1831, that the Judicial Committee of the Privy Council should become the final court of appeal in ecclesiastical cases,[31] and, in 1847, he drafted a bill introduced by the Bishop of London in the House of Lords,[32] to increase the ecclesiastical presence in the court. A court was contemplated that comprised not only bishops and judges, but also professors of divinity.[33]

Until 1832, the court of appeal was the High Court of Delegates, which had replaced the appeal to Rome in the reign of Henry VIII.[34] In 1832, when the Privy Council was made the ultimate ecclesiastical court of appeal, the focus of attention was on reform of the court that should hear appeals in probate, matrimonial, and admiralty matters; very little thought was given to whether the court would be well constituted to decide questions of ecclesiastical doctrine. The Commission issued its report on the new proposed court of appeal as a separate short report, before its main report on ecclesiastical courts in general, and although the second report mentions false doctrine as a cause for discipline of clergy, there is no evidence that this was in the minds of the commissioners when they issued their first report.

Probably, as Professor Chadwick says, even if thought had been given to the question in 1832, the relationship between Church and State was then such that no one would seriously have objected to a Crown-appointed court.[35] But by the 1840s there is some evidence of embarrassment in respect of the strictly ecclesiastical duties of the Judicial Committee, and the summoning of the three bishops in the

30 See Moore, *Gorham against the Bishop*, 458. '[The case] has been fully heard before us; and by the direction of Her Majesty, the hearing was attended by [the bishops] who are Members of Her Majesty's Privy Council.' He then indicated the assent to the judgment of the Archbishops and the dissent of Blomfield. At the end of the judgment, he says: 'His Honour The Vice Chancellor Knight Bruce, dissents from our judgment; but all the other members of the Judicial Committee, who were present at the hearing of the case . . . are unanimously agreed.'
31 *Special Report on Practice and Jurisdiction of the Ecclesiastical Courts*, PP 1831–2, xxiv, 5–8.
32 See Blomfield Papers, Lambeth Palace Library, 61/24–5, 41–8, 73–6, 79, 90, 95, 101, 125, 131, 135; Hansard, 3rd ser., xcii, 1095–9.
33 Lushington to Blomfield, 14 June 1847, Blomfield Papers, 61/101.
34 See G. I. O. Duncan, *The High Court of Delegates* (Cambridge, 1971).
35 Chadwick, *Victorian Church*, i, 257.

Gorham case may be taken as evidence that the Judicial Committee, at the least, was thought to profit by clerical assistance.[36] A letter from Lushington to Brougham in 1842 commenting on a draft judgment of Brougham's, shows that Lushington was more ready than Brougham to recognize that the Privy Council was still an ecclesiastical court. In the draft, Brougham had evidently said that the Judicial Committee should steer clear of spiritual questions. Lushington replied that the court must, in one sense, interfere with spiritual duties 'as when articles are preferred for holding doctrine contrary to the Church . . . or to compel the Clergyman to perform the service in a more regular mode'.[37]

DENISON

In 1856, Lushington was called upon to consider the other principal sacrament of the Church of England, called, in the Articles, the Supper of the Lord. This is a ceremonial meal, that is also a memorial of the sacrifice of Christ on the cross. Bread and wine consumed by the faithful represent, in some sense, the body and blood of Christ. But in what sense? This was an issue that had divided Catholics and Protestants for centuries. Again, as with baptism, there were several shades of Catholic and Protestant opinion. In general, the Catholic view stressed the objective effect of the sacrament, in this case, the reality of the presence of Christ's body and blood. The Protestant view emphasized the faith of the recipient, the uniqueness of Christ's sacrifice, and the overriding unfettered nature of God's gift of grace.

The Articles were again ambiguous. Article XXV, quoted above, though Protestant in tone, stopped short of condemning the objective view of sacraments. Article XXVIII, on the Lord's Supper, condemned the doctrine of 'Transubstantiation (or the change of the substance of Bread and Wine)', but, it could be and was argued, stopped short of condemning a less literalistic version of the objective view usually called the doctrine of the Real Presence. Article XXIX, much in issue in the *Denison* case, entitled 'Of the Wicked which eat not the body of Christ in the use of the Lord's Supper', said:

[36] Gladstone was much concerned with this question. See M. B. Stephen, 'Gladstone and the Composition of the Final Court in Ecclesiastical Cases, 1850–73', *Historical Journal* 9 (1966), 191.
[37] Lushington to Brougham, 30 June 1842, Brougham Papers, University College, London, 32348.

The wicked, and such as be void of a lively faith, although they do carnally and visibly press with their teeth (as Saint Augustine saith) the Sacrament of the Body and Blood of Christ, yet in no wise are they partakers of Christ: but rather, to their condemnation, do eat and drink the sign or sacrament of so great a thing.

Denison was an aggressive high-churchman, who, along with Manning and others, had signed a protest against the decision of the Judicial Committee in the *Gorham* case. Unlike Manning, Denison remained to fight for his views within the Church of England, and he did not by any means shun the battle. In 1852, in his office of examining chaplain to the Bishop of Bath and Wells, Denison insisted that ordinands should assent to the proposition that an unfaithful communicant would nevertheless actually receive the Body and Blood of Christ.[38] All agreed that the unfaithful communicant received no benefit, but the issue was important, theologically, because it was, in 1855, a test case for the objective efficacy of the sacrament. The legal proceedings were important because, although the leading high-churchmen had little sympathy with Denison's aggressive methods, a legally binding definition of the opposite of Denison's view might drive them out of the Church of England.[39]

Not surprisingly, objections were raised to Denison's conduct, and his opponents were alerted. Denison preached a series of three sermons in Wells Cathedral on the Real Presence, in which he repeated his views, and legal proceedings were instituted against him by an evangelical clergyman, Ditcher. Because Denison's bishop also happened to be the patron of his living, The Archbishop (J. B. Sumner) was designated as the proper person to bring the proceedings under the Church Discipline Act.[40] Sumner commenced proceedings, and then refused to continue them. Ditcher obtained an order from the Court of Queen's Bench requiring Sumner to hear the case, and so the case was heard at Bath in 1856 nominally before Sumner,[41] with three assessors, but, in effect, before Lushington,

---

[38] See *Letter to the Rt Rev. the Lord Bishop of Bath and Wells by the Rt Rev. Bishop Spencer, late Lord Bishop of Madras* (London, 1853), (p. 8, letter from ordinand).
[39] Chadwick, *Victorian Church*, i, 493.
[40] 3 & 4 Vic. c. 86, s. 24.
[41] Of whom Gladstone said that he hedged 'by a reservation of his own liberty to go to sleep daily during the hearing'. Gladstone to Hon. Arthur Gordon, 29 Oct. 1856, D. C. Lathbury, *Correspondence on Church and Religion of W. E. Gladstone* (New York, 1910), i, 373.

who was the only legally trained assessor.[42] The record of the proceedings shows that Lushington alone presided, dealing with all procedural objections, and delivering the judgment.[43]

Unlike Gorham in his answers to the Bishop, Denison, in his sermons, had made no effort to use language that should be readily reconcilable with the Articles.[44] Denison had said, in words that appeared boldly disdainful of any compromise with the twenty-ninth Article:

> That to all who come to the Lord's Table, to those who eat and drink worthily, and to those who eat and drink unworthily, the Body and Blood of Christ are given; and that by all who come to the Lord's Table, by those who eat and drink worthily, and by those who eat and drink unworthily, the Body and Blood of Christ are received.[45]

Lushington delivered a judgment condemning Denison, and depriving him of his benefice. Denison appealed successfully to the Court of Arches, and its decision was upheld by the Judicial Committee of the Privy Council on the technical ground that proceedings had not been commenced within two years of the offence, as required by the Church Discipline Act.[46] The judgment was delivered by Lord Justice Knight Bruce, the judge who had dissented in the *Gorham* case.

Comparison between the *Gorham* case and Lushington's decision in *Denison* is inevitable. There are several parallels, and several important contrasts. Both cases concerned a conflict between Catholic and Protestant sacramental theology; in both cases the Protestant view prevailed. But whereas the *Gorham* decision was inclusive, in the sense that those holding Gorham's views could remain in the church, the *Denison* decision was exclusive, in the sense that it would drive out

[42] The positions of Sumner and Lushington were the reverse of those they occupied in the Gorham case, where Lushington was judge, and Sumner assessor. See C. S. Grueber, *A Letter to the Rt Hon. Stephen Lushington* (London, 1856), 16, where this is pointed out.
[43] G. A. Denison, *Notes of My Life, 1805–1878* (London, 1878), 242, says, of Dr Lushington, 'nominally "Assessor", really "the Court"'. The anonymous author of a pamphlet *A Crisis in the Church* (Bath, 1856) says the other assessors 'never opened their lips during the proceedings, and were apparently mere cyphers'.
[44] See Machin, *Politics and the Churches*, 255.
[45] *Proceedings*, 137.
[46] s. 20.

of the church those holding Denison's views.[47] The personalities of the principal parties were significant. It was easy to see Phillpotts as the aggressor in the *Gorham* case: Gorham, a respected clergyman of seniority and standing was interrupted by Phillpotts in a perfectly ordinary step in his career. On the other hand, Denison had gone out of his way to attract attention; he could not earn sympathy, even among high-churchmen, for his conduct as examining chaplain, or for his deliberately aggressive sermons. *The Law Magazine*, in an article generally sympathetic to the high church position, had 'little sympathy' for him.[48] Gladstone wrote in his diary: .'Saw Phillimore [Denison's counsel] (as usual) on the Bath case. His client is if possible worse than his Judge'.[49] Much often depends, in legal disputes, on the context in which a point arises. If Denison had been a pious and respected clergyman, quietly teaching his views to a sympathetic congregation, making genuine efforts to avoid expressions that contradicted the formularies, and the promoter had sought to interfere without provocation, though the legal issue would have been the same, the attitude of the court might have been different. It was as well for the high-church party that *Ditcher* v. *Denison* eventually went off on a technicality, and that by the time the Privy Council came, in another case in 1871, to deal with the substantive issue, both the facts of the case then in issue, and the temper of the times, favoured a somewhat more sympathetic view.[50]

Lushington felt ill at ease with the theology of the case. During the course of the argument, he wrote to his daughter saying that he found the business 'peculiarly contrary to my taste',[51] and he predicted that his decision would make a stir:

---

[47] Lathbury, Gladstone's editor, says: 'The crisis thus created [by Dr Lushington's decision] was immeasurably more acute than that which had followed upon the Gorham judgment. The one had made it impossible for High Churchmen to turn Evangelicals out of the Church of England; the other made it possible for Evangelicals to turn out High Churchmen.' Lathbury, *Correspondence on Church and Religion*, i, 365.

[48] *Law Magazine* 56 (1857), 139, 145–6.

[49] H. C. G. Matthew (ed.), *Gladstone Diaries* (Oxford, 1978), v, 158 (entry for 1 Sept. 1856).

[50] *Sheppard* v. *Bennett* (1871), Brooke 209. But a passage at 248 shows that Bennett's conduct was not approved by the Court. Phillimore, who had been counsel for Denison, was the Dean of Arches, deciding in favour of Bennett, the accused clergyman; the Denison case was not mentioned in the judgment of the Judicial Committee.

[51] Lushington to Alice Lushington, 25 July [but pm 24 July] 1856, Lushington Family Papers.

I foresee much future trouble & anxiety in this case, but I must put my hand to the plough. It will travel to other courts & make a great disturbance in the Church; decide which way you will, it will be appealed.[52]

The prediction was accurate: about thirty pamphlets appeared,[53] a not insubstantial number, even at a time when pamphlets were a popular medium of debate, for a first-instance decision of an ecclesiastical court in Bath; Trollope referred to the decision in *Barchester Towers*, indicating that his heroine did not favour it;[54] Keble, writing to Pusey, called it 'this miserable judgment of Dr L's';[55] Gladstone was very much agitated, writing 'at once but not in haste':

My mind is quite made up that, if belief in the Eucharist as a reality is proscribed by law in the Church of England, everything that I hold dear in life shall be given and devoted to the oversetting and tearing in pieces such law, whatever consequences, of whatever kind, may follow.[56]

Lushington was subjected to public criticism of a kind that must have been most disagreeable to him. In a pamphlet entitled *A Crisis in the Church*, the author said:

Now, the Doctor's low-Church predilections are visible enough in his judgment in the case of Westerton v. Liddell.[57] We may here ask why was not Lord Wensleydale – a man of higher dignity and larger reputation – appointed, as at first announced? Possibly, the Doctor told his Grace that he felt no need of his assistance ... All concerned, except the unhappy Archdeacon, were of the same theological family; never was there a more complete subversion of the first principles of judicial fairness.[58]

C. S. Grueber published *A Letter to the Right Hon. Stephen Lushington* which ran to seventy-two pages, and consisted of a bitter attack on

---

[52] Lushington to Alice Lushington, 25 July 1856, Lushington Family Papers.
[53] British Library Catalogue, s.n. Denison.
[54] A. Trollope, *Barchester Towers*, ch. 53. 'It must not be presumed that she [Eleanor] has a taste for candles, or that she is at all astray about the real presence; but she has an inkling that way. She sent a handsome subscription towards certain very heavy ecclesiastical legal expenses which have lately been incurred in Bath, her name of course not appearing.' *Barchester Towers* was published in 1857. See E. Jay, *The Religion of the Heart: Anglican Evangelicalism and the Nineteenth-Century Novel* (Oxford, 1979), 107.
[55] 16 Aug. 1865, H. P. Liddon, *Life of Edward Bouverie Pusey* (London, 1894–8), iii, 435.
[56] Gladstone to the Earl of Aberdeen, 13 Aug. 1856, Lathbury, *Correspondence on Church and Religion*, i, 373.
[57] The case is discussed below.   [58] *A Crisis in the Church*, 3.

the judgment, in which Lushington is accused of illiberality, inconsistency with the *Gorham* decision, and unfair conduct of the proceedings. The work ends with a reminder to Lushington of the judgment that he was to face at his own death:

> are you content, that that measure of consideration only that you have meted to another shall be measured to you again, and with what judgment you have judged, that yourself shall be judged?[59]

Almost equally unpleasant – more unpleasant in some ways, because it looks like the judgment of the profession, whereas Grueber was known to be a close friend of Denison[60] – is the following passage from an anonymous writer in the *The Law Magazine*:

> On the mode in which the trial at Bath was conducted, as we can say hardly any thing in praise, we wish to say but little. No one can read carefully the details of the proceedings, without being most unpleasantly impressed with the idea that a strong bias was manifested against the accused. The summary dismissal of some of the objections raised by the Archdeacon's advocate, and the (as it appears to us) insufficient grounds on which others were overruled, is not what we ordinarily see in English courts of justice. But the surprise we might experience at this impression is chastened by the remembrance that Dr Lushington, though an able and accomplished judge, and a respected man, is notoriously imbued with party spirit of the strongest kind, apt to be exhibited on all occasions, and even, we are credibly informed, boasted of as patriotic virtue. Such a man may, without intending to be partial, lean unfairly towards one side of such a dispute as this, and be no less likely to find nothing but heresy in the opinions of a High Church opponent, than he was to discover 'meretricious' qualities in the hallowed emblem of salvation.[61]

Denison himself, in an autobiography published after Lushington's death, accused him, implausibly, of 'eagerness to arrive at the prestige of condemnation by a Court presided over by the Archbishop'.[62]

An examination of these accusations is of interest, not only for the light it throws on the actual dispute, and on Lushington's career, but for what it shows of public attitudes to judicial decisions in areas of high controversy. A full published account of the proceedings enables some assessment to be made of the soundness of the criticisms.

[59] Grueber, *A Letter to Lushington*, 56.
[60] Denison, *Notes of My Life*, 245.
[61] *Law Magazine* 56 (1857), 139, 150. The reference is to a passage in Lushington's judgment in *Westerton* v. *Liddell*, discussed below, p. 293.
[62] Denison, *Notes of My Life*, 242.

As to the actual conduct of the proceedings, the criticisms appear to miss the mark. Gladstone, who evidently had his information directly from Phillimore, Denison's counsel,[63] conceded that 'they [Sumner and Lushington] always consented to hear Phillimore – the Primate only hedging by a reservation of his own liberty to go to sleep daily during the hearing'.[64] The suggestion that due consideration was not given to Phillimore's objections ('summary dismissal') is not borne out by the record. Lushington adjourned the court to consider all the more serious of the objections, and gave reasons indicating that he had fully understood Phillimore's points. It is true that on the second objection raised by Phillimore – that the proceedings were out of time – Lushington was ultimately reversed. But this certainly does not establish any kind of bias, or impropriety; *The Law Magazine* itself said, while disagreeing with Lushington's decision, 'the point is a nice one',[65] and the promoter's advocate adduced some quite persuasive arguments for his view (that the proceedings should be held to have commenced when the Commission was constituted, before the hearing at Bath). The suggestion that Lushington decided all points against Denison is also not borne out by the record. On a number of procedural points, Lushington's decision was in favour of Denison, and one of these turned out to be possibly crucial in Denison's favour, as Lushington must have known that it might be.[66]

A consistent theme of Lushington's critics was the illiberality of his decision, in contrast to the *Gorham* case. Gladstone felt strongly on this point:

That which makes the cup of disgust overflow is the recollection that these worthies had an exactly contrary set of canons and principles of law ready for the case of Gorham, which they have now turned inside out with

63 His diary shows that he was in close contact with Phillimore during this period. The entry for 1 Sept. 1856 shows that Gladstone had little sympathy for Denison personally: 'Saw Phillimore (as usual) on the Bath case. His client is if possible worse than his Judges'. Matthew, *Gladstone Diaries*, v, 158.

64 Lathbury, *Correspondence on Church and Religion*, 373. Phillimore's objections were all heard, and he addressed the court for two days (early adjournment on one day) on the substantive issues.

65 *Law Magazine* 56 (1857), 149.

66 Lushington held that there was insufficient proof of publication of Denison's third sermon, dated 14 May 1854; consequently, the last offence proved was in November 1853; proceedings had to be commenced within two years; it was held by the Judicial Committee that the Bath suit 'was not commenced, was not a "proceeding" begun, before April 1856'. (19 April was the date of the mandamus; the Archbishop's first citation to Denison to appear was dated 5 May 1856; an offence proved on 14 May 1854 might well have been crucial, therefore.)

a rapidity and facility which would be admirable if it were not somewhat execrable.[67]

A reader of the critics might suppose that there was no explanation, other than improper bias, for a distinction between the cases. On this point, Lushington explained his position carefully in his judgment. No specific charges were brought against Gorham; Phillpotts simply claimed the right not to institute him on the ground that he found his doctrine unsound; to rebut this, it was sufficient for Gorham to show that his doctrine was not proven to be inadmissible. But Denison was accused, under a particular statute that prescribed penalties for contradicting the Articles of Religion, of making a specific statement that contradicted a specific provision in the Articles and, in Lushington's view, the charge was made out. What Phillpotts failed to prove against Gorham, Ditcher succeeded in proving against Denison. Not all could be expected to agree, of course, with Lushington's conclusions, but even Denison's supporters would have had to concede that the Articles were more specific on the Lord's Supper than on baptism, and that Denison had gone out of his way to use language that appeared, on its face, to contradict the twenty-ninth Article. As often happens where a judicial decision affects a matter on which emotion runs high, those who disliked the result of the decision were very ready to attribute bias and improper motives to the decision-maker. In short, we see the phenomena that are often present in such cases: oversimplification, polarization, distortion of facts, and attribution to opponents of improper conduct and motives.

Nevertheless, having conceded this point, a critic may still say that Lushington's decision bears indications that it is affected by his own theological opinions. Lushington, following the *Gorham* decision, held that his task was to find the plain meaning of the Article, using ordinary principles of construction of documents. His business was not to be a theologian:

this tribunal is a court of justice and of ecclesiastical law, not a school of theology, and, as a court of justice, bound to administer the law as we find it.[68]

The Articles must be construed 'by their plain and grammatical meaning'.[69] In case of a reasonable doubt, extrinsic evidence was relevant to show how the words had been interpreted in the past. But,

---

[67] Lathbury, *Correspondence on Church and Religion*, 374.
[68] *Proceedings*, 216.   [69] Ibid.

in this case, Lushington found that the meaning of the twenty-ninth Article was clear:

The Article is free from all ambiguity . . . there is no ambiguity, no doubt to be cleared up which would justify a resort to other sources of information for explanation.[70]

Here, surely, there is room for one to ask how Lushington came to be so sure that the words were clear, the whole subject being inherently mysterious. In adjourning the court, on 28 July, after argument, Lushington said:

His Grace the Archbishop desires me to say that, considering the great importance of the question discussed on this occasion, and the abstruse nature of it, as well as the learned arguments of counsel, and the many authorities adduced, he thinks it proper to have further time for deliberation.[71]

This is not readily compatible, as Grueber pointed out in his pamphlet,[72] with the proposition that the Article in question was so free from ambiguity as to exclude all extrinsic explanation. Words do not always have clear and plain meanings, particularly when they are words drawn up, as were the Articles of Religion, 300 years earlier, on a highly controversial subject in order to accommodate a variety of theological views. The suggestion that Lushington was guilty of any crude kind of bias or impropriety can certainly be rebutted. But it would be harder to show that Lushington's interpretation of the Article, and the source of his certainty that it excluded Denison's view, could be entirely dissociated from his own assumptions about the Church of England. Those who were adversely affected by the decision were quick to discern bias; looking back, we may agree that there was a kind of bias, but it is a kind of bias from which, probably, no decision-maker has been entirely free.

LIDDELL

Lushington's decision in *Westerton v. Liddell*, referred to twice by the critics of his decision in the *Denison* case, had been given a few months before the *Denison* case was heard, in December 1855. The case involved church furnishings and ornaments, important questions at the time.

[70] Ibid., 217, 220.   [71] Ibid., 128.   [72] Grueber, *A Letter to Lushington*, 8.

The furniture in issue was in two churches in London. The principal matters in dispute were whether a communion table could be made of stone (instead of wood as had been usual), whether a cross and candles and coloured coverings were permissible on the communion table, and whether a side table, called a credence table, was permissible. As in the two cases previously discussed, the dispute was again between Catholic and Protestant views. The material of which the communion table was made was significant, because a stone altar[73] symbolized the sacrificial aspects of the sacrament emphasized by the high-church party; a wooden table fitted better into the Protestant emphasis on the sacrament as a meal. Decorations on the altar also emphasized a high view of the sacrament. An aspect of the matter important to both sides concerned the relationship of the Church of England to the Roman Catholic Church. The decorations introduced by the high-churchmen tended to make the churches look more like Roman Catholic churches – an association on the whole welcomed by one party and deprecated by the other.

Another important factor was the Gothic revival in architecture generally, and a general nostalgia for things mediaeval. With these there went, very naturally, a sympathy with the restoration of ancient mediaeval churches to their former splendour, and support for the building and furnishing of new churches in the mediaeval style.[74] St Barnabas, Pimlico, one of the churches involved in the case, was a new church, completed in 1850.[75] It is built in the Gothic style, inside and out. An illustration appears in the *Illustrated London News*,[76] showing a Gothic interior, with low-backed pews, chancel screen, and large altar decorated with two candlesticks and a cross (but apparently without any covering). The altar forms the focal point, and dominates the whole church. A watercolour painting also

[73] The word 'altar', though not used in the formularies, was in common use as an alternative to 'communion table'. See Chadwick, *Victorian Church*, i, 496.

[74] One of the best known church architects of the period, A. W. N. Pugin, published a short book in 1841, the thesis of which was that Gothic architecture was the only proper ecclesiastical style, referring to St Paul's Cathedral (p. 5) as 'built in the revived pagan style', A. W. N. Pugin, *The True Principles of Pointed or Christian Architecture* (1841, reprinted 1973).

[75] The building is described in detail in *The Ecclesiologist* 9 (1848), 331–2, and 11 (1850), 110–14, with enthusiastic praise for the furnishings: 'In brief, S. Barnabas' is the most complete, and, with completeness, most sumptuous church which has been dedicated to the use of the Anglican communion since the revival.'

[76] *Illustrated London News* 16 (1850), 428. The chancel screen and exterior are illustrated in *The Illustrated Times*, 27 Dec. 1856, which also has an account of the dispute and of Dr Lushington's judgment headed 'The Religious War in Belgravia'.

survives of Lushington's own parish church, at Ockham, in Surrey, at the same period.[77] The church is filled with high-backed pews that block the line of sight to the chancel. The communion table is a small square table, almost hidden from view by a heavy communion rail, and without any sort of decoration. Although Ockham is a much smaller church, the contrast is quite striking. So successful has been the Gothic revival, in respect of church interiors, that it is easy for a modern observer to forget how radical were the changes introduced in such churches as St Barnabas.[78]

The cases came before Lushington in his capacity as judge of the London Consistory Court, the objectors seeking orders for the removal of the articles of which they disapproved. Lushington began by saying that his duty was to administer the law, not to give effect to his own opinion:

I am not to consider whether, in my own private opinion, this practice or that usage be abstractly right or wrong – convenient or inconvenient; but I am to ascertain, if practicable, what the law of the land enjoins, and obey it . . . My present task is not to investigate and ascertain great principles, but to institute a dry and tedious inquiry into doubtful propositions of positive law.[79]

This statement gives expression to a common opinion on the role of judges; the judge is an interpreter only, not a maker of the law, a humble functionary rather than a powerful lawgiver. Matters of policy are not for the court, but for the legislature. The expression is conventional; what is unusual is to find, a few pages later, what look like personal opinions, on the very points in issue, expressed in the strongest terms.

It is difficult – perhaps impossible – for a judge to exclude entirely his own opinions. But it is surprising that, after such an introduction, Lushington appears to go out of his way to express his own opinions on the relationship between the Church of England and the Church of Rome. He describes the reformers of the sixteenth century as persons 'by whose means under the blessing of Providence, we have been emancipated from the thraldom and corruption of the Church of

---

77 The church was restored in Gothic style in 1875, two years after Lushington's death.
78 See G. W. O. Addleshaw and F. Etchells, *The Architectural Setting of Anglican Worship* (London, 1948).
79 A. F. Bayford (ed.), *The Judgment of the Right Honourable Stephen Lushington . . . in the cases of Westerton against Liddell* (London, 1855), 9–10.

Rome'.[80] He says, with reference to the secessions to Rome associated with the Oxford Movement:

have we not, even in our own day, witnessed a sad example of the danger of endeavouring anew to reform that which the reformers left us, and assimilate our position to the Church of Rome? Have we not seen, what never has before, from the days of Cranmer, been seen in this land, – not less, in a very few years, than 100 clergymen of our Church secede to Rome, and who were, many of them, men of undoubted piety, of great learning, and blameless lives? See the monuments erected to the memory of the martyrs of our own church at Oxford; and read the names of those who took a leading part in that work. How many have seceded from that Church which they sought to preserve by honouring the memory of its first restorers and martyrs? Ought we not then to pause – to doubt our own strength and our own judgment, – when we seek to mend that which they bequeathed to us, consecrated by their own blood? Ought we not to hesitate before we admit any one practice, any one thing, not sanctioned by them, and more especially any one thing which has the remotest leaning to the Church of Rome and her usages, which our reformed faith holds in just abhorrence? Is it not wiser to keep on the safe side, – to omit rather that which may be innocent in itself, even decorous or ornamental, – than run the remotest risk of consequences so much to be deplored?[81]

This is strong language – almost amounting to oratory – from one who, a few pages before, had declared his determination to confine himself to a dry and tedious enquiry. Nor is it an isolated instance. On the question of crosses, he says:

If this reasoning be true [that ornaments, innocent in themselves, should not be prohibited merely because some had used them superstitiously], why should not crosses be put in the same category as crucifixes? Surely I need not waste time in showing that they have been equally perverted to superstitious practices. Indeed, I think no man can travel on the continent, and not see that such is the case, even at this day.[82]

On the question of coloured coverings, Lushington had to interpret a canon prescribing that the communion table should be covered with 'a carpet of silk or other decent stuff'.[83] The practice objected to was the use of colours that varied according to the liturgical seasons of the year. Lushington said, rightly, no doubt, that this practice was copied from that of the Roman Catholic Church. It is not apparent, however,

---

[80] Ibid., 40.   [81] Ibid., 38–9.   [82] Ibid., 42–3.   [83] Canon 82 (1603).

that it was prohibited by a rule prescribing a carpet of silk or other decent stuff. It was conceded that the covering might be of any colour, and that a church might lawfully have two or three of different colours, if they were used at random. Nevertheless, Lushington found that the canon implied a prohibition of the practice in question:[84]

What does [the canon] say? That the table shall be covered with a carpet of silk or other decent stuff. I admit that these words do not necessarily exclude carpets; that the expression in the singular, 'a carpet', does not, *vi termini*, exclude the plural, though it gives no authority for it. But the question is not whether there might not be several cloths, but several cloths of different colours, placed on the communion table at stated periods. For such a practice the canon affords no sanction whatever. If the fact were that three or four different cloths of a description accordant with the canon had been used indifferently for convenience sake, and without particular motive, the whole matter would not have been worth consideration; but this is not the state of things in either church. The fact is, that embroidered and ornamental cloths of different colours are used to cover the communion table, in precise accordance with the usages of the Roman Catholic Church, the colours being emblematic of different periods. What warrant is there for engrafting into our churches this ceremonial of Rome? . . . Then the plain truth is, that, without authority, without reason, this practice of the Roman Catholic Church has been introduced into a place of Protestant worship. What is this but a servile imitation of the Church of Rome? And what is a servile imitation of that Church but a direct violation of all the principles and all the rules established for the regulation of the ceremonies and ornaments of the Church of England.

Then follows a remarkable comparison of the Church of England with that of Rome:

A decorous simplicity is the characteristic of the Church of England. What is lace and embroidery but a meretricious display of fantastic and unnecessary ornament? But look at its accompaniment, – more especially with respect to St Barnabas, – a metal cross, ornamented with jewels, – a rood screen, and brazen gates. Is it to be supposed that all this has no meaning? But I need not speak of that . . . If it be objected to this my judgment that the Court would leave the House of God barren and destitute, I answer, that no such consequences would ensue. Chastity and simplicity are not at variance with grandeur and beauty; but they are not reconcilable with jewels, lace, variegated

---

[84] He appears to realize the weakness of this, as a matter of interpretation (it was summarily reversed by the Judicial Committee), and one passage suggests that he was exercising his own discretion in prohibiting the coverings (Bayford, *Judgment*, 59–60).

cloths, and embroidery, which are better fitted for the gorgeous pageantry of the Church of Rome, than the pure and severe dignity of the Church of England.[85]

The use of the word 'meretricious', the Latin derivation of which Lushington must well have known, in contrast with the word 'chastity' attributed to the Church of England, can hardly be dissociated from the reference in the Book of Revelation to the Whore of Babylon,[86] often associated by extreme Protestants with the Church of Rome. A few paragraphs later, Lushington again voiced his principal objection to the ornaments:

The whole of history, both sacred and profane, shows the proneness of mankind to idolatrous practices. So powerful has this propensity been, that all who profess themselves Protestants admit that even the religion of Christ, in itself the least likely to give rise to so fearful an abuse, yet has been so abased, and therefore in our reformed church every precaution had been taken against so deplorable an error.[87]

These comments are difficult to reconcile with the opening statement about the neutrality and humble functions of the judge. An explanation is required when a senior and highly respected judge, who has just reminded himself of his duties, seems to fall so far short of them. Perhaps, in his enthusiasm, Lushington forgot his opening paragraph, or perhaps the opening paragraph was a mere sham. It seems far more probable, however, that he considered his view of the Church of Rome so self-evidently true, that he did not perceive it as a matter to which the principles of judicial neutrality applied. This was not a matter to be decided, judicially, and therefore neutrally; it was an assumed truth that formed part of the background against which a decision had to be made.

Every decision-maker has to define the question to be decided, and, in doing so, inevitably assumes a background that, for this purpose, is to be taken for granted. As Lushington saw the question, he did decide it neutrally. At an early stage in the judgment he indicated his view of the question:

I cannot refrain, in the very first instance, from expressing, not my earnest hope, but my conviction, that none of the contending parties, however

---

[85] Ibid., 59–60.
[86] Revelation XVII. *Meretrix* is the Latin word for prostitute.
[87] Bayford, *Judgment*, 63.

zealous they may be in support of their own opinions, do for one moment conceive that in the matters now under discussion there is anything of real importance to vital religion, or indeed to true worship, save so far as one party may apprehend that the things complained of may lead to superstitious uses, and the other that they conduce to the more decorous and effectual performance of Divine worship. We must all feel that these things in themselves are utterly immaterial, and derive their importance only from the ideas, connected or supposed to be connected with them; by some considered as indicia of the ancient and decorous worship of our Christian faith; by others as denoting a disposition to return to those abuses from which our Reformed Church has been happily purified.[88]

Lushington evidently saw this as a perfectly fair and neutral statement of the issue, and churchmen of all persuasions might well have agreed with him. The Privy Council said much the same, but in support of the opposite conclusion. It is one thing to say that ornaments are trivial, and therefore they should be permitted; it is another thing to say that ornaments are trivial, and therefore they should be prohibited.[89] In Lushington's mind the point tended in the latter direction: those seeking to use the ornaments had only a trivial interest in doing so, whereas the objectors could point with reason to serious dangers.

Another consideration operating in Lushington's mind was his view of the parochial system. The Church of England was the national church and every Englishman must be at home in his own parish church:

Our parish churches are pre-eminently churches for all who belong to the Church of England, and not for any particular section thereof, – if indeed that term can be properly used. Some portion of the congregation of St Paul's is drawn from places out of the district, – is composed of persons non-resident. It is not their approbation that I am at liberty to consult; for mark the consequences, – I should, if I so erred, give the sanction of the Ecclesiastical Court to the establishment of a mode of worship, peculiar in itself, and fitted, not for parishioners, but for persons who may be collected from all parts of the metropolis, in clear defeasance of our parochial system.[90]

Lushington was perfectly right in thinking that this aspect of the national church was threatened by innovation: within a few years the

[88] Ibid., 15.
[89] Brodrick & Fremantle, *Judgments of the Privy Council in Ecclesiastical Cases*, 125, appear to overlook this difference in a footnote to the Privy Council judgment on this point in which they say 'the same sentiments had been emphatically expressed by Dr Lushington'.
[90] Bayford, *Judgment*, 14.

London churches were competing for non-resident parishioners as though, in a capitulation to the free-market economic system, offering a variety of liturgy to suit every taste, and the demise of the traditional role of the parish church in rural areas as symbolizing the unity of the whole community (perhaps doomed in any event) was hastened. The innovations of the sort considered in *Westerton* v. *Liddell* did, ironically, considering that the Oxford Movement had its origins in a sermon on national apostacy,[91] hasten the demise of the Church of England as a national institution.

Lushington's decision was upheld on all points by the Dean of the Arches (Dodson).[92] The Judicial Committee of the Privy Council upheld the decision as to stone altars, but reversed it in most other respects.[93] The judgment concludes with an indication of satisfaction that, in contrast to the ecclesiastical difference of opinion in the *Gorham* case, the ecclesiastical assessors (Sumner and Tait, Blomfield's successor as Bishop of London) both concurred in the Committee's conclusion.

The published response to Lushington's judgment was, as might be expected, mixed. Several critical pamphlets appeared, including an open letter to Lushington from Phillpotts, which was written in a tone of mild and respectful remonstrance.[94] A full-length book appeared, developing at very great length the high-church position on all the points in issue.[95] Other pamphlets defended Lushington.[96] *The Law Magazine* was extravagant in his praise, portraying him as a bulwark against papal encroachment:

> The reader will see that we have attempted no more than to give a skeleton of this memorable judgment . . . He will there find, not only the whole law of the subject skilfully and admirably elucidated, but abundant passages of rich historical illustration, relieved by the most acute observation and profound

---

91 Inaugurated by Keble's sermon on national apostacy in 1833. O. Chadwick, *Mind of the Oxford Movement* (London, 1960), 33.

92 [1857] JP 100.

93 Br & F 117, Brooke 42, [1857] JP 499.

94 Henry, Lord Bishop of Exeter, *Letter to the Right Hon Dr. Lushington on his judgment in the case of Westerton v. Liddell (clerk)* (1859). See also J. Skinner, *A Plea for the Threatened Ritual of the Church of England* (1865), *Dr. Lushington's Judgment in the Case of Westerton v. Liddell upon Ornaments of the Church considered by a Parish Priest who has not in Use the Articles Complained of* (1855).

95 T. W. Perry, *Lawful Church Ornaments* (London, 1857), (547 pp. and appendix).

96 W. Pearce, *Letter to the Right Rev. the Lord Bishop of Exeter in reference to his Lordship's Letter to Dr. Lushington on his Judgment in the case of Westerton v. Liddell* (1856).

thought. The past year witnessed two striking events, – the Austrian Concordat and this judgment of Dr Lushington. By their aid we may accurately compare the relative states of the two empires; and in reference to ourselves we may exultingly say, 'Happy are the people that are in such a case!'[97]

It is hard to know whether this can be the same judgment that was described in the same journal a year later as indicating that Lushington was 'notoriously imbued with party spirit of the strongest kind' and apt to 'discover "meretricious" qualities in the hallowed emblem of salvation'. Where emotions are so much engaged, as they were in these disputes, there is no common ground for a consideration even of the fitness of the judge, let alone of the merits of the judgment.

Lushington's decision in *Westerton v. Liddell* was the forerunner of a series of legal disputes on church ritual that continued until the end of the century.[98] Lushington retired from the bench in 1867, while the battle over ritual was still in its early stages. Before his retirement, however, he decided important interlocutory points in two cases of clergy charged with using illegal ritual. In each, the decision was, not unexpectedly, against the accused.[99]

One aspect of Lushington's decision in *Westerton v. Liddell* was potentially favourable to the high-church party, though probably Lushington did not realize this when the case was argued. The direction in the Prayer Book, on which the case turned, known as the 'Ornaments Rubric' provided that 'such ornaments of the church and of the ministers thereof . . . shall be retained and be in use as were in this Church of England by the authority of Parliament in the second year of the reign of King Edward the Sixth'.[100] Lushington proceeded on the assumption that the Rubric was legally binding, the whole Prayer Book having been appended to an Act of Parliament.[101] In *Westerton v. Liddell*, the ornaments of the ministers were not in issue (only the ornaments of the church). In 1871 the question of the ornaments of ministers came before the Privy Council, and the high-church party was able to adduce evidence that eucharistic vestments (strongly associated by everyone with the Church of Rome), though out of use since the beginning of Elizabeth's reign, had been in use in

---

[97] *Law Magazine* 55 (1856), 54, 59.
[98] See Chadwick, *Victorian Church*, ii, 308–25.
[99] *Flamank v. Simpson* (1866) LR 1 Ad & E 276, *Martin v. Machonochie* (1867) 36 LJ Ecc 25.
[100] Note preceding the Order for Morning Prayer.
[101] 13 & 14 Car. II c.4 (the Act of 1662).

the second year of the reign of King Edward VI. This was embarrass-
ing, because it suggested that these vestments were not only
permissible, but actually mandatory. The Privy Council, in *Hebbert
v. Purchas*[102] held that the Rubric (as part of the Act of 1662) was to
be read subject to earlier canons (of 1603) which required the use of
other vestments. The reason for this conclusion was, very plainly, not
founded on strictly legal considerations, but on the inconvenience and
upheaval that would be caused by holding the use of eucharistic
vestments to be mandatory. The decision damaged the reputation of
the Judicial Committee, and led to suggestions that its commitment to
the rule of law had yielded to a desire to avoid unpalatable results: the
Ornaments Rubric was law when it favoured one party, and not law
when it favoured the other. Lushington, ironically, was invoked by
the high-churchmen. Gladstone wrote:

> the course and character of the judgments at times has been very unsatis-
> factory, and has tended to compromise the high reputation of our judges . . . I
> might add that, having read the judgment with care, I am unable to follow
> especially that part of the [argument] which repudiates the opinion of Dr
> Lushington on the rubric of 1662.[103]

Lushington was certainly not alone in attracting the accusation that he
allowed his personal religious opinions to affect his judgments.

POOLE

The three cases discussed did not quite exhaust Lushington's involvement in sacramental theology, for he was called upon, in 1859, to
hear a case, as assessor to the Archbishop of Canterbury, on confession. In the 1850s some high churchmen began to introduce the
practice of regular (auricular) confession and absolution. This practice involved a private disclosure by a penitent to a priest of particular
faults, and, frequently, though not necessarily, questioning by the
priest to elicit full disclosure. This practice raised widespread alarm in
the Church of England throughout the second half of the nineteenth
century.[104] The hostile agitation centred on the questioning of women
about sexual practices. Roman Catholic manuals suggested (though

---

[102] (1871) Brooke 162.
[103] Gladstone to Liddon, 26 Feb. 1871, Lathbury, *Correspondence on Church and
Religion*, i, 380. The word 'argument' is given as 'arrangement' in Lathbury.
[104] It was vigorously denounced by W. Walsh, *The Secret History of the Oxford
Movement* (London, 1897), which went through several editions in quick succession (4th edn 1898). See also Jay, *Religion of the Heart*, 113.

in the decent obscurity of the Latin language) some detailed questions that might be asked by a confessor of women penitents, and these manuals began to be used by Church of England clergy. The nature of the agitation, and the tone of the debate may, perhaps, be judged from a speech in the House of Lords in 1877, on the subject of a manual produced for high-church clergy[105]. Tait, at this time Archbishop of Canterbury, and no narrow-minded churchman, as his judgment in the *Essays and Reviews* case[106] shows, said, of the manual:

> The noble Earl [Lord Redesdale] spared us from many details; but at the same time, he read from the book quite enough to show that no modest person can read the book without regret, and that it is a disgrace to the community that such a book should be circulated under the authority of clergymen of the Established Church ... I cannot imagine that any right-minded man could wish to have such questions addressed to any member of his family; and if he had reason to suppose that any member of his family had been exposed to such an examination, I am sure it would be the duty of any father of a family to remonstrate with the clergyman who had put the questions, and warn him never to approach his house again.[107]

What is still the leading criminal-law case on the mental element in obscene publication springs from this controversy. It was there held that a pamphlet written by a low-churchman, quoting (in order to disparage) obscene passages from such a confessors' manual, was itself an obscene publication.[108]

In 1858, this controversy was in its early stages. The Reverend Alfred Poole, a curate at the church of St Barnabas, Pimlico (one of the churches whose ornaments Lushington had condemned in *Westerton v. Liddell*) was in the practice of hearing his parishioners' confessions. Two women alleged that he had asked them improper questions, and a complaint was made to the Bishop of London (Tait), who revoked Poole's licence. The relevant statute[109] provided for an appeal to the Archbishop, and Poole appealed. The Archbishop of Canterbury (Sumner) at first dismissed the appeal by writing a letter, but Poole obtained a mandamus from the Court of Queen's Bench – an order requiring him to give Poole a hearing.[110] In accordance with this

---

105   *The Priest in Absolution*, part II (privately printed).
106   See chapter 10, below.
107   14 June 1877, Hansard, 3rd ser., 1745, 1748.
108   *R. v. Hicklin* (1868) LR 3 QB 360.
109   1 & 2 Vic. c. 106, s. 98 (an Act to abridge the holding of benefices in plurality, and to make better provision for the residence of the clergy).
110   *R. v. Archbishop of Canterbury* 1 El & El 545.

order, the Archbishop heard the appeal at Lambeth Palace. Lushington sat with him, in theory as his assessor, but in substance playing a judicial role. Argument was heard by two counsel on each side; Lushington presided; his 'Report' is, in substance, a judgment, giving reasons in support of a decision[111] dismissing the appeal, the Archbishop speaking only a final formal paragraph.[112]

The practice of hearing confession and giving absolution was not in itself illegal, for it was specifically provided for in the Prayer Book as part of the ministry to the sick. What Tait objected to was the use of the practice on the Roman Catholic model, which he called 'a systematic admission of your people to Confession and Absolution going beyond any thing contemplated by the services or teaching of our church'.[113] The issue before Lushington was whether Poole had been given a fair opportunity to answer the allegations against him, and whether the Bishop had grounds to revoke the licence.

The evidence of the complainants must have been striking. A contemporary pamphlet asserted that 'part of the evidence is omitted as being unfit for publication'.[114] Its general nature, however, is clear enough from the context, and from Lushington's reference, in his Report, to 'gross language', and 'disgusting questions'.[115]

He then asked me . . . He told me not to be ashamed to tell my holy father these things . . . I must not be ashamed to tell him, if I ever had . . .[116]

Poole denied that he had put any improper questions to any of his penitents, and the bishop admitted that the evidence of the women was unreliable.[117] Poole conceded that he had asked such questions as 'appeared to me to be necessary, in order to enable me to give "counsel and advice"'.[118] He demanded to know precisely what impropriety he was alleged to have committed, but the Bishop took the position that Poole's own admissions supplied sufficient ground for revoking his licence.

111 The formal decision is recorded in the Vicar-General's Act Book, Lambeth Palace Library, VB1/17/500 (23 Mar. 1859).
112 *The Rev. Alfred Poole* v. *The Bishop of London: Report*, Lambeth Palace Library, VXIA/3c, 15; *The Times*, 19 Feb. 1859, 10e, 21 Feb. 8c, 24 Mar. 10d–f.
113 R. Liddell, *A Letter to the Lord Bishop of London on Confession and Absolution with Special Reference to the case of the Rev. Alfred Poole* (London, 1858), 45, R. Davidson and W. Benham, *Life of Archibald Campbell Tait, Archbishop of Canterbury* (London, 1891) 226–8.
114 R. Liddell, *Letter to the Bishop*, appendix I.
115 *Report*, pp. 4 and 9, *The Times*, 24 Mar. 1859, 10d.
116 Ibid.   117 Br & Fr 177 (letter from Tait to Poole).   118 Br & Fr 179.

The case against Poole shows how evidence, though theoretically conceded to be irrelevant, may nevertheless be highly prejudicial. Lushington said that Poole ought to have 'stated to the best of his recollection the questions that he did actually put, instead of contenting himself with a general description',[119] indicating that he drew an adverse inference from Poole's silence. Further, the Bishop's grounds tended to shift. What he really objected to was the systematic practice of confession, particularly the questioning by young priests[120] of women on sexual matters. But he could not object to confession itself. Definitions of 'systematic' would raise intractable problems. He could hardly inhibit all discussion of sexual matters by young clergymen. So the bishop said that he objected to improper questions. But of these there was no specific allegation, and no reliable evidence.

Lushington was seventy-seven years of age at the time of the hearing; the Archbishop was seventy-nine. According to Coleridge, who was counsel for Poole, both fell asleep during the argument.[121] It would have been surprising if men of their age and background had been sympathetic to Poole. Lushington's statement of the facts gave support to the inevitable conclusion of the Archbishop. Lushington's report said:

It appears to me that the following will be a true statement. That when women, who had sinned against the seventh commandment, came or were sent to Mr Poole for confession and absolution, he did ... at their own request, put certain questions to them respecting their violation of the seventh commandment, not in the gross language mentioned, but the questions were such as, in the opinion of the Bishop, would bring scandal upon the Church.[122]

On this Report, the Archbishop held that Tait had 'exercised a sound discretion'.[123] An appeal to the Privy Council was dismissed on jurisdictional grounds.[124]

---

[119] *Report*, p. 9, *The Times*, 24 Mar. 1859, 10f.

[120] Lushington, in summarizing the bishop's argument says 'that if Mr Poole be right the whole body of priests of the Church of England, down to the youngest, would have a right to follow his example'. *Report*, p. 9, *The Times*, 24 March 1859, 10f.

[121] E. H. Coleridge (ed.), *Life and Correspondence of J. D. Coleridge* (London, 1904), i, 254. Lushington suffered from insomnia at night, writing, 'nothing yet mends my nights; I am quite sleepless for hours ... I rather fear the going into Court tomorrow', Lushington to Fanny Carr (sister-in-law), 14 Nov. 1860, Lushington Family Papers.

[122] *Report*, p. 9, *The Times*, 14 Mar. 1859, 10f.

[123] Ibid.   [124] (1861) 14 Moo PC 262, Br & Fr 176.

The Bishop was not bound to prove an ecclesiastical offence; all agreed that he had a discretion to revoke a licence for various other reasons. But Lushington accepted that he was bound to conform to what he called, variously, 'justice',[125] 'common justice',[126] 'natural justice',[127] and 'substantial justice',[128] and he said that it was of the essence of justice that the accused person should have an opportunity of knowing what is alleged against him and that natural justice required that the accusation should be 'sufficiently definite to enable the accused to defend himself'.[129] He held that the Bishop had met these requirements, but this does not appear to be so clear. Some of the facts found were not ostensibly, as has been said, made the ground of the Bishop's action. As to the improper questioning, the facts found were that Poole had 'put certain questions' and that these questions 'were such as, in the opinion of the Bishop would bring scandal on the Church'. Precision is strikingly absent here, and one may ask, as Poole did, how, if this were the substantial ground on which the Bishop acted, he could make a full answer and defence unless he knew what the 'certain questions' were. It would be going too far to say that the record of the proceeding establishes impropriety on the part of the Archbishop or his assessor – though it suggests, as is not surprising, that their own views coincided with those of Tait. It does, however, seem apparent that a conclusion favourable to Poole could readily have been reached by another tribunal applying the same principles of 'substantial justice' accepted by Dr Lushington.

The examination of these four cases, in which questions of sacramental theology were directly raised, shows – to say the least – that Lushington had a marked antipathy to high-church ideas and practices. If his task were to decide neutrally between high and low, there would be no avoiding the conclusion that he was biased. But here it becomes apparent that everything depends, in justifying such a conclusion, on the way in which the judicial task is described, and here lies the advantage of a perspective that is disengaged from the merits of the dispute. Lushington was faced with a set of ideas about the church – an integral part, in his mind, of his own polity – that were radically different from his own ideas. Impartial decision-making can never mean that every imaginable idea has, as a matter of fact, an

[125] *Report*, pp. 1, 2, 3.
[126] Ibid., 1.   [127] Ibid., 3.   [128] Ibid., 2.
[129] *Report*, pp. 2–3, *The Times*, 24 Mar. 1859, 10f.

equal chance of success: some propositions must be so extreme as to be, to the judge, 'unthinkable'. If Lushington's task was to hold an impartial balance between high and low, he failed; but if his task was to exclude from the Church of England, after fair consideration, impermissible practices and ideas, one cannot establish that he failed, without establishing also another vision than his of the Church.

10

THE BROAD CHURCH

In 1836, the post of Regius Professor of Divinity at Oxford – a Crown appointment – was offered to Dr R. D. Hampden. The appointment was vigorously opposed by a combination of different ecclesiastical and political interests at Oxford.[1] Ostensibly, the objection was to the theological soundness of a series of lectures delivered by Hampden in 1832, though (as is usual in such cases) many who objected had not read the lectures.[2] R. W. Church, writing from a high-church point of view, gives a not wholly unsympathetic account, suggesting that Hampden was led into difficulties because of a failure to see the implications of his requirement of a scriptural basis for all ecclesiastical doctrine.[3] Hampden was a low-churchman, and was opposed by the Tractarians in 1836, but not exclusively by the Tractarians.[4] Professor Chadwick's assessment is that there was nothing particularly startling in the lectures, and that the bulk of the opposition was based on Hampden's unpopularity for having supported the admission of Dissenters to the University.[5] The Prime Minister (Melbourne) persisted, and the appointment was made. Oxford University then passed a statute depriving Hampden of some privileges associated with the professorship. Lushington gave an opinion

---

[1] O. Chadwick, *The Victorian Church*, 2 vols (London, 1966–70), i, 115
[2] Hampden's supporters seem to have been exceptionally anxious to point out how large was the number of non-readers of his works: R. T. Davidson and W. Benham, *Life of Archibald Campbell Tail* (London, 1891), 133 (Letter of Tait dated 18 Jan. 1848), *The Greville Memoirs*, L. Strachey and R. Fulford (eds) (London, 1938), vi, 3 (1 Jan. 1848), R. W. Church, *The Oxford Movement: Twelve Years 1833–1845* (London, 1891), 146. The present writer must confess to being also among this number.
[3] Church, *Oxford Movement*, ch. 9.
[4] Ibid., at 149. [5] Chadwick, *Victorian Church*, i, 115–16.

(later reiterated, and concurred in by the Attorney-General) that the statute was illegal, but the opinion was ignored.[6] Lushington wrote to Brougham:

Have you noticed the proceedings at Oxford against Dr Hampden; J. Campbell & myself have given an opinion that the proposed Statute is illegal. What a Clatter when the opinion is published in the University. I presume they will forthwith obtain a counter opinion from Wetherall.[7]

In 1847, another Whig Prime Minister (Russell, sympathetic with low-church opinion[8]) nominated Hampden to the see of Hereford. This nomination also was vigorously opposed, and brought into question the supremacy of the Crown, particularly the effect (objectionable especially to high-churchmen) of putting the appointment of bishops into the hands of the Prime Minister. The form by which bishops were appointed was full of anomalies. In the ancient sees, the bishops were elected by the dean and chapter of the cathedral, but the election had been, since the sixteenth century, a mere formality: the Crown nominated the person to be elected, and the chapter was bound to elect that person. The election of a bishop had also to be confirmed by the archbishop, and this was done at a ceremony (called preconization) in Bow Church, in London, the traditional seat of the archbishop's legal business.[9] The ceremony, for Dr Hampden, was to include this announcement (twice):

Oyez! Oyez! Oyez! All manner of persons who shall, or will object to the confirmation of the election of the Reverend Renn Dickson Hampden, Doctor in Divinity, to be bishop and pastor of the Cathedral Church of Hereford, let them come forward and make their objections in due form of law and they shall be heard.[10]

For three centuries, this had been assumed to be a formality, but Hampden's opponents determined to put this assumption to the test.

[6] Chadwick, *Victorian Church*, i, 120.
[7] Lushington to Brougham, 3 May 1836, Brougham Papers, University College, London, 8143. Probably the reference is to Sir Charles Wetherell, standing counsel to the University, and a strong Tory (*DNB*).
[8] See letter of 8 Dec. 1847, in reply to a protest of thirteen bishops, in which Russell pointed out that many of those prominent in condemning Hampden in 1836 'have since joined the communion of the Church of Rome', reproduced in A. O. J. Cockshut, *Religious Controversies of the Nineteenth Century: Selected Documents* (London, 1966), 106.
[9] See R. Burn, *Ecclesiastical Law* 2nd edn (London, 1767), 183–5.
[10] R. Jebb, *A report of the case of the Right Rev. R. D. Hampden D.D. . . . in the Ecclesiastical Courts and the Queen's Bench* (London, 1948), 25. Slightly different wording appears in *The Case of Dr Hampden* (London, 1848), 51.

An ecclesiastical legal controversy in Bow Church was, therefore, anticipated. The church was crowded for the occasion, and a number of ecclesiastical lawyers were present. *The Times* called it 'a regular turn out of Doctors' Commons'.[11] Lushington, as assessor (with Sir John Dodson) to the Archbishop's Vicar-General (Dr Burnaby), presided over the argument and gave the principal judgment determining it.[12] The issue was whether substantive objections to the appointment should be heard. The argument that they should be was based on the wording of the formal announcement: it seemed absurd to invite objectors to speak, and then not to hear them. This was supported by the fact that the bishoprics had been made donative (i.e. in the unfettered gift of the Crown) in the time of Edward VI, but the former practice (requiring election and confirmation) was restored in the reign of Elizabeth.[13] There had been a case in which objection had been attempted, in 1618, but the objection was rejected as being in improper form; the implication was that, if it had been in proper form, the objection would have been heard, and the leading textbook on ecclesiastical law supported this view.[14] The argument on the other side was that the preconization ceremony had become a formality: if objections were to be heard by ecclesiastical lawyers, and could, in principle, be allowed, complex and polemical theological argument would be inevitable, and, more significantly, the right of the Crown to appoint bishops would be subject to at least a temporary veto in Doctors' Commons – a surprising conclusion, to say the least. A further consideration was that rejection of the Crown's nomination might expose all involved (including Dr Burnaby, Sir J. Dodson and Dr Lushington) to the penalties of the ancient Statute of Praemunire (enacted originally to protect the Crown from papal encroachment) – an even more startling conclusion, as the penalties included forfeiture of all property and indefinite imprisonment.[15]

When the invitation to objectors was read, a proctor attempted to appear on behalf of the objectors. The Vicar-General (who was

---

[11] *The Times*, 12 Jan. 1848, 5a.

[12] *The Times*, 12 Jan. 1848, 5d, *Illustrated London News*, 15 Jan. 1848, 20–2, *The case of Dr Hampden*, 37–50, Jebb, *Report of the Case of Dr Hampden*, 25–69. The scene in the church is the subject of an illustration in the *Illustrated London News*, showing the lawyers, in wigs and gowns, seated at a table in the church (p. 22).

[13] See argument of Dr Addams, Jebb, *Report of the Case of Dr Hampden*, 42–5.

[14] Burn, *Ecclesiastical Law*, 207, s.t. 'Bishops'.

[15] Dr Burnaby thought that the statute would apply; Dr Lushington did not rule this out, but found it unnecessary to decide the point. Jebb, *Report of the Case of Dr Hampden*, 55, 69.

officially presiding) seemed about to receive the objections, asking whether the proctor had them in writing, but Lushington intervened at this point, and informed the proctor that he was not permitted to appear. Lushington then consented to hear argument from an advocate, limited to the question of whether or not there was a right to appear. Three advocates were, in fact, heard, and the Vicar-General then gave a short judgment, and Lushington a longer judgment, to the effect that no objections would be heard. Sir J. Dodson concurred without adding reasons.

Lushington's reasons were that the Archbishop was bound by statute 'to confirm the said election, and to invest and consecrate the person so elected to the office and dignity that he is elected unto'.[16] Many of Hampden's critics were high-churchmen, who opposed the subjection of the Church to the secular power. Lushington gave these opinions short shrift, referring to Henry VIII's Act as:

a Statute memorable, no doubt, for all its provisions, and not the less so because it restored to the Crown of Great Britain its undoubted right, and put to sleep for ever the pretensions of the Bishop of Rome.[17]

He conceded that there was an 'inconsistency' in the procedure that invited objections but would not hear them. 'Indeed,' he added,

I think it would be vain to deny that such is the case. But what are the facts? The times when this statute was passed were times when we were emerging from the power of the papacy into the freedom of the Reformation, and when the practice, and I am sorry to say the principles, too, vacillated; and is there any wonder that a sovereign upon this throne, in those times, should be anxious to retain the ancient form, though at the same time anxious to engross into his own hands the real power?[18]

On these reasons, the first obvious comment is that they exhibit strong sympathy with a Protestant and Erastian view of the establishment and royal supremacy. Lushington would have seen eye-to-eye with Russell on these questions, and his inclination is amply confirmed by his decisions in other ecclesiastical cases. On the merits of the point in issue, it certainly did appear odd that objections should be invited, but not heard. On the other hand, the forms of episcopal appointment, like other aspects of the Constitution, were full of anomalies, Lushington was probably right in his interpretation of

[16] 25 Hen. VIII, c. 20, s. 4 (Annates and First Fruits, 1533–4).
[17] Jebb, *Report of the Case of Dr Hampden*, 55.
[18] Ibid., 66–8.

Henry VIII's intentions, there were three hundred years of (almost uninterrupted) precedent on his side, and a full-scale hearing on the alleged heresies of Dr Hampden would have introduced even greater difficulties. It is plain that Lushington's decision did not rest on formal legal considerations. His views of the history and nature of the Church, and what was desirable for it as a matter of policy, were also in play. Greville records, ten days after the confirmation, that he had spoken to Lushington on the matter, who had told him that 'the old law of Edward VI, making the bishoprics donative [must be] restored'.[19] This suggests that Lushington realized that his decision rested on uncertain legal ground.

An article in *The Law Magazine* was critical of Lushington's decision on grounds of ecclesiastical independence from secular control.[20] *The Times*, hostile to Hampden, objected to the appearance the proceedings had of foregone conclusion, saying that 'the Vicar General and Dr Lushington administered the law as gaily as an inquisitor might exhibit the instruments of his profession'.[21] A week later *The Times* reproduced a paragraph from *Punch*, under a heading that sufficiently indicates its import: 'A solemn farce'.[22]

Hampden's opponents moved for an order (a mandamus) to compel a hearing, but the Court of Queen's Bench was equally divided (2–2), and the order was refused.[23]

Ecclesiastical opinion was, of course, also divided. Tait wrote:

If the law really is as Dr Lushington expounded it, then certainly either the old forms of citation etc., ought to be abolished, or new powers granted, to allow objections when made to be entered on.[24]

But the practical considerations in favour of Lushington's conclusion were well put by the theologian, F. D. Maurice, who had no sympathy with either the high- or low-church party:

Each bishop elect will be met at Bow Church by a troop of High Church or Low Church opponents, who will hold him bound to answer according to their maxims; and if he does not, will cause the See to be vacant for some months.[25]

[19] Greville, *Memoirs*, vi, 6–7 (21 Jan. 1848).
[20] *Law Magazine*, New Series, 8 (1848), 233.
[21] *The Times*, 13 Jan. 1848, 4d.
[22] *The Times*, 20 Jan. 1848, 7e.
[23] (1848) 11 QB 843.
[24] Davidson and Benham, *Life of Tait*, 133 (letter dated 18 Jan. 1848).
[25] F. D. Maurice, *Letter . . . on the attempt to defeat the Nomination of Dr. Hampden* (1847), 4.

This is an argument from practicality, which plainly weighed as heavily with Lushington as any formal legal considerations: if it were ever to be seriously proposed that bishops should be examined for the orthodoxy of their opinions, a better manner of proceeding would have to be devised than a tribunal of ecclesiastical lawyers in Bow Church.

HEATH

In 1858, a volume of sermons was published, by D. I. Heath, a clergyman with a living in the Isle of Wight. The sermons expressed views on several doctrines central to the Christian religion, which it will not be necessary to examine in detail. Heath's opinions did not belong to any of the recognized theological parties. F. D. Maurice described them as 'solitary' and 'eccentric', and equally disagreeable to rationalists as to the most orthodox.[26]

Proceedings were commenced against Heath under the statute of 1573 – the same statute under which Denison had been condemned – providing a penalty of deprivation against any holder of an ecclesiastical living who should advisedly maintain any doctrine contrary to the Thirty-nine Articles.[27] The case was heard by Lushington, as Dean of the Arches, at first instance.[28]

A preliminary issue arose as to how specific the charges must be. Lushington held that the promoter was bound to specify which of the Articles of Religion had been contravened, but that he need not specify in what precise respects Heath had contravened them.[29] This was a crucial point, because it is always difficult, where orthodoxy of opinion is in controversy, to establish precisely what requirements orthodoxy imposes, and precisely how the accused party has offended. Lushington, 'with much doubt and difficulty',[30] gave leave to appeal, and Heath's appeal on this point was allowed by the Judicial Committee of the Privy Council.[31] Lord Kingsdown said that 'it is of the essence of justice ... that a person indicted for a breach of the law shall be distinctly informed, before he is called upon to defend him-

---

[26] F. D. Maurice, 'Dr. Lushington, Mr. Heath, and the Thirty-nine Articles', *Macmillan's Magazine* 5 (1861), 153.
[27] 13 Eliz. I, c. 12, s. 2.
[28] It was referred to him by letters of request, under s. 13 of the Church Discipline Act, 1840, 3 & 4 Vic. c. 86.
[29] *Heath* v. *Burder* 15 Moo PC 5 (Order of 6 March 1860).
[30] Ibid., 18.   [31] Ibid., 20.

self, of the nature of the offence with which he is charged'.[32] The long passages that had been cited from Heath's book were held to be insufficient notice of the offences alleged. The charges were reformed (i.e. revised) and were again objected to as insufficiently precise. Lord Cranworth ordered that the charges 'should be reformed by specifying the several doctrines alleged to be affirmed by the Appellant, contrary to any of the Articles of the Church of England'.[33] A further reformation was made, of which Lord Cranworth said, hinting, perhaps, that he was still not entirely satisfied: 'the Appellant did not oppose the pleadings as thus finally settled. It must be assumed, therefore, that the nature of the charge now appears with sufficient distinctness on the pleadings'.[34]

The reformed charges were remitted to Lushington for hearing on the merits. He stated that his duty was 'to endeavour to ascertain the plain grammatical sense of the Article of Religion said to be contravened', to determine the meaning of the writing complained of, and to judge whether there was a contradiction.[35] Where there was ambiguity, the accused should have the benefit of it. Nevertheless, Heath's views were idiosyncratic, and they were expressed in terms that made no attempt to conform to the Articles of Religion. It is therefore not entirely surprising that Lushington, though with repeated expressions of reluctance,[36] condemned him, and concluded by emphatically denying the power of a judge to seek to ameliorate the law:

It is contrary to all sound principles for a Court to seek, as has been by some Judges done formerly, ingenious subterfuges to evade or weaken the law, and that upon a notion of its own power to discover what is best and most convenient. Such a course is not only contrary to principle, but would be most injurious in its effects; for all such attempts to wrest the law according to supposed consequences, invariably tend to postpone a remedy, if there be a real evil. If there be bonds which press heavily on the Clergy, as to which I give no opinion, I repeat that the Legislature imposed them, and the Legislature alone can loose them.[37]

Heath declined to retract,[38] and, as the statute required, was deprived of his benefice. His appeal to the Privy Council was dismissed, and, after he had declined a further opportunity to retract, the

---

[32] Ibid., 22.   [33] Ibid., 33.   [34] Ibid., 81.
[35] Ibid., 45–6.   [36] Ibid., 54, 63, 64.   [37] Ibid., 65–6.
[38] He published a 200-page book defending his theological opinions in a tone of aggrieved remonstrance: D. I. Heath, *A defence of my professional character* (London, 1862).

sentence was confirmed. Lushington's general approach was approved and adopted[39] and his conclusion, with two minor exceptions,[40] confirmed.

Heath's case was not of great importance in itself: he represented no substantial body of academic or popular theological opinion. His book would have been unknown had he not been prosecuted.[41] F. D. Maurice, who was one of the few to protest against the proceedings, took care to dissociate himself from Heath's opinions. The significance of the case lies in its relationship to the much more important case of *Essays and Reviews*, which, as will be seen shortly, was pending before Lushington when the Privy Council gave its judgment.

ESSAYS AND REVIEWS

Essays and Reviews was a book of theological essays, published in 1860, that created an extraordinary agitation in the Victorian church.[42] Documents opposing it were signed by nearly 11,000 clergy and by 137,000 lay persons.[43] The essayists were six clergymen and one layman, all associated with a liberal view of theology, and with the Broad Church. They included Frederick Temple, subsequently Archbishop of Canterbury, and Benjamin Jowett, subsequently Master of Balliol College, Oxford. The book was perceived as an attack on the fundamental truths of the Christian religion, and proceedings were taken against two of the essayists in the ecclesiastical courts. The two were condemned by Lushington, as the Dean of the Arches, on three points each but his judgment was reversed by the Judicial Committee of the Privy Council. The Privy Council decision underlined the anomalous – and to some intolerable – circumstance that a court dominated by laymen (who might not even be churchmen) should have the ultimate power to determine the theological doctrines of the Church of England. Three bishops sat on the Privy

---

[39] Ibid., 78.   [40] Ibid., 94–5
[41] The whole sale up to notice of the prosecution was said to be 150 copies. Heath, *Defence*, 13.
[42] *Essays and Reviews* (London, 1860).
[43] These documents were circulated after the Privy Council decision. The former was a declaration of belief in the inspiration of scripture and the everlasting punishment of the wicked; the latter was a vote of thanks to the Archbishops for their dissent in the Privy Council. See I. Ellis, *Seven Against Christ: a Study of 'Essays and Reviews'* (Leiden, 1980), 193–4.

Council to hear the case but the two senior of them (the two archbishops) dissented, in part, from the decision. The decision had serious effects on the reputation of the Privy Council as the ecclesiastical court of appeal, and was a significant step in loosening the ties between the Church of England and the State.[44]

The book that caused all this trouble had no named editor (though in fact it was assembled by H. B. Wilson)[45] and commenced with an anonymous notice 'to the reader' that

It will be readily understood that the authors of the ensuing essays are responsible for their respective articles only. They have been written in entire independence of each other, and without concert or comparison.

Despite this declaration, the book was, from the beginning, perceived to have a common theme. Frederic Harrison, a non-Christian positivist, in a review that set the stage for the ensuing controversy, treated the book 'as a joint publication, and not as a mere collection of essays, for such, notwithstanding its outward form, it evidently is'.[46] Samuel Wilberforce, Bishop of Oxford, in his subsequent review said that 'to a certain extent we admit the claim [of independent authorship], but to a certain extent only. For the object and intention of the volume as a whole they are all clearly responsible.'[47] The preface expressed a hope that

The volume ... will be received as an attempt to illustrate the advantage derivable to the cause of religious and moral truth, from a free handling, in a becoming spirit, of subjects peculiarly liable to suffer by the repetition of conventional language, and from traditional methods of treatment.[48]

This appeared to be a clear announcement of a common theme, but Williams wrote later that he never saw the preface before it was published.[49] The contributors were selected by Wilson, and obviously not selected at random.[50] All were associated, to a greater or a lesser degree, with liberal theological opinion. Among those invited to

---

[44] In defiance of the Privy Council judgment, the book was condemned in both houses of Convocation. See O. Chadwick, *The Victorian Church, Part II* (2nd edn, 1972), 83–4.

[45] See Ellis, *Seven Against Christ*, 48–52, R. Williams, *Life and Letters*, edited by his wife (London, 1874), ii. 367 ('Wilson was the editor').

[46] 'Neo-Christianity', *Westminster Review* 74 (1840), 293 at 294.

[47] *Quarterly Review* 109 (1861), 248 at 250.

[48] *Essays and Reviews*, preface ('To the reader').

[49] Williams, *Life and Letters*, ii, 366. It is possible that Wilson thought the preface innocuous, and consultation unnecessary.

[50] See Ellis, *Seven Against Christ*, 51.

participate was A. P. Stanley, the natural leader of the broad church, who declined, foreseeing the inevitable association that would be made among the essayists, and the probable reaction.[51]

The principal theme that was perceived in the book was an attack on the truth of the scriptures, belief in which was, for the evangelicals, and to an only slightly lesser extent for the Tractarians, a mainstay of the Christian religion. The same, indeed, was presumed by the vast majority of Christians not attached to any theological party, and by those outside the Church also. Harrison wrote

Of the seven essays, four are wholly occupied in treating of the authority or value of Scripture; two of the other three deal chiefly with the same topic . . . Is it too much to say that a book has appeared which at once repudiates miracles, inspiration, Mosaic history, and the authenticity of the Bible?[52]

Wilberforce took a similar approach. The book must be considered as a whole, and as a whole it must be condemned:

Because, as honest men and as believers in Christianity, we must pronounce those views to be absolutely inconsistent with its creeds, and must therefore hold that the attempt of the Essayists to combine their advocacy of such doctrines with the retention of the status and emolument of Church of England clergymen is simply moral dishonesty.[53]

Harrison and Wilberforce can have agreed on little else in the realm of theology, but they agreed that the essayists were not fit to be clergymen.

It is doubtful whether *Essays and Reviews* would have created such a stir as it did, if it had not followed closely on Darwin's *Origin of Species*, published a few months earlier.[54] There was little in common between the books. The intellectual roots of the essayists lay in textual criticism of the scriptures, not in scientific observations, though, as Professor Chadwick has said, both forms of inquiry tended to flourish in the same favourable intellectual climate.[55] Darwin compelled a reappraisal – some must have thought an abandonment – of the stories

[51] R. E. Prothero, *The Life and Correspondence of Arthur Penrhyn Stanley D. D., late Dean of Westminster* (London, 1893), ii, 21; Ellis, *Seven Against Christ*, at 12, calls *Essay and Reviews* without Stanley *'Hamlet* without the prince'.

[52] Harrison, 'Neo-Christianity', at 294 and 297.

[53] Wilberforce, *Quarterly Review*, 274.

[54] A reference to the book ('a masterly volume . . . which now substantiates on undeniable grounds the very principle so long denounced by the first naturalists – *the origination of new species by natural causes*') occurs in Powell's essay on the Evidences of Christianity, *Essays and Reviews*, 139.

[55] Chadwick, *Victorian Church*, 1–23.

of the Creation and of a universal flood. The essayists added doubts about some of the Old Testament miracles[56] and the authenticity and authorship of parts of the Old and New Testaments.[57] It must have seemed to many that the enemy without had been joined by traitors inside the walls of the Church itself. Harrison, in his article on *Essays and Reviews*, made the connection:

What becomes of the Christian scheme when the origin of man is handed over to Mr Darwin, and Adam and Eve take their seats beside Deucalion and Pyrrha?[58]

The ideas that lay behind *Essays and Reviews* had begun to filter through into the public forum, as is shown by Trollope's novel, *The Bertrams*, published in 1859.[59] The hero of the novel (George Bertram) writes two controversial books, the result of which is that, though not a clergyman, he is compelled to resign a fellowship at an Oxford college. The content was remarkably similar to what was to be alleged against the essayists:

It was acknowledged . . . that all Scripture statements could not now be taken as true to the letter; particularly not as true to the letter as now adopted by Englishmen. It seemed to him that the generality of his countrymen were of opinion that the inspired writers had themselves written in English . . . Their truth was the truth of heaven, not the truth of earth. No man thought that the sun in those days did rise and set, moving round the earth, because a prolongation of the day had been described by the sun standing still upon Gibeon.[60]

Of his second book, it is said that 'he had called the whole story of Creation a myth'.[61] The kind of argument to be made against Dr

---

[56] Wilson in his essay (*Essays and Reviews*, 177) mentioned, among other things that might be accepted literally, or allegorically, or as parable, poetry or legend, the serpent tempter, Balaam's ass, the arresting and reversal of the earth's motion, waters standing in a heap, witches, apparitions, the primeval institution of the Sabbath, the flood, the tower of Babel, and the assumption of Elijah. Williams referred to the story of Jonah as containing 'a late legend': *Essays and Reviews*, 77.

[57] Williams was acquitted by Dr Lushington on charges of denying the traditional authorship of the book of Daniel, and of the Epistle to the Hebrews and the second Petrine Epistle: 1 New Rep 208–9.

[58] Harrison, 'Neo-Christianity', 297. The *Guardian* also linked *Essays and Reviews* with *The Origin of Species*. See Ellis, *Seven Against Christ*, 114–15.

[59] The connexion is pointed out by E. Jay, *The Religion of the Heart* (Oxford, 1979), 76, and by A. O. J. Cockshut, *Anthony Trollope: A Critical Study* (New York, 1955), 78. Cockshut considers the novel marred by the vagueness with which the religious questions are addressed.

[60] A. Trollope, *The Bertrams*, ch. 18 (2 vol. edn, 1859, 287). See also ch. 26.

[61] Ibid. ch. 18 (2 vol edn, 303)

Williams before Lushington, and the general nature of Williams' defence was foreshadowed, with remarkable precision, by Trollope. George Bertram's defence is that he has said nothing heretical, but his accusers say that heresy is to be inferred:

Bertram however denied this [calling the story of Creation a myth]. He had, he said, not called anything a myth. There was the printed book, and one might have supposed that it would be easy enough to settle this question. But it was far from being so. The words myth and mythical were used half a dozen times, and the rabbis declared that they were applied to the statements of scripture. Bertram declared that they were applied to the appearance those statements must have as at present put before the English world.[62]

Trollope proved to be right in suggesting that it would not be easy to settle a question of this sort.

The double condemnation of *Essays and Reviews* by the avowedly non-Christian Harrison, and by the Bishop of Oxford, persuaded many that the views of the six essayists who were clergy were indeed incompatible with their positions, and this feeling induced the evangelicals and the Tractarians – who hardly agreed on any other theological issue (the controversy made several sets of strange bedfellows) – to join forces against the essayists. Stanley supplies a vivid reproduction of the image projected upon the minds of the bulk of clergy and laity through the lenses of hostile reviews:

Seven infidels, in the disguise of clergymen, asserting that the Bible was a fable, denying the truth of Christianity and the existence of God – this was the portent which was supposed to have appeared.[63]

Some official response became inevitable, and, after considerable debate, proceedings were instituted in the ecclesiastical courts, which had power to deprive clergy of office and benefice, though not to degrade them (i.e. to deprive them of their orders). Only two of the essayists held benefices, Williams and Wilson, and accordingly these were the two against whom proceedings were instituted in June and December 1861.

The ordinary ecclesiastical courts of first instance were the diocesan (consistory) courts (in the cases of Williams and Wilson, Salisbury and Ely respectively) but important cases could be, and were usually, transferred at the request of the diocesan bishop to the provincial

---

[62] Ibid. ch. 18 (2 vol edn, 304).
[63] *Edinburgh Review* 113 (1861) 461 at 468.

court.[64] In accordance with this procedure the cases against Williams and Wilson were transferred to the Court of Arches, where they were argued at length. Lushington wrote to his daughter, 'these Essays & Reviews are horrible – a *fresh* prosecution this morning of Mr Wilson',[65] and, after the argument:

> The argument in Essays & Reviews is concluded, having occupied nearly 10 days. The counsel very handsomely returned thanks to me for my so patiently hearing the case. This is consoling but alas my trials now commence for I have to write my judgment.[66]

From these letters, it may be deduced that Lushington was conscious of facing a difficult task. It does seem, to use Stanley's phrase, a 'singular lot' for one of his background and age to be 'called four times over to preside as arbiter of the doctrine and discipline of the Church of England'.[67] Lushington was no theologian. Yet many at the time would have said that his incompetence as a theologian was the very thing that qualified him to perform his judicial tasks.[68] If a new declaration were required by the Church of England of its theological doctrine, a man in Lushington's position, however learned in theology, would never be selected to supply it. If such a thing were possible for the Church of England in the nineteenth century, which is very doubtful, it would have required some sort of synodical assembly with power to lay down doctrine – the sort of body that the critics of the Privy Council judgments in *Gorham* and *Essays and Reviews* imagined – though it may be doubted whether those critics would have liked the probable consequences had such a body been formed. Lushington, as he saw his role, was not called upon to play the part of a theologian but that of a lawyer. The question in issue was

---

64 The procedure was called transfer by Letters of Request. The form can be found in H. C. Coote, *Practice of the Ecclesiastical Courts* (1847), 126.

65 Lushington to Alice Lushington, 19 Dec. 1861, Lushington Family Papers.

66 Lushington to Alice Lushington, 16 Jan. 1862, Lushington Family Papers.

67 A. P. Stanley, *Edinburgh Review*, July 1864, reprinted in *Essays, chiefly on Questions of Church and State from 1850 to 1870*, (London, 1870) 98. See chapter 9, above, for the references probably intended by Stanley.

68 '"There is nothing to laugh at in Dr Lushington", said the Squire [in response to a complaint by a clergyman that he was threatened with legal proceedings in the ecclesiastical court, and describing Dr Lushington as 'the new Council of Trent']. "He gives you justice, at all events, which you parsons never give each other, you know"'. Mrs M Oliphant, *The Perpetual Curate* (London, 1864, reprinted New York and London, 1975), iii, 57. This passage was first published in *Blackwood's Magazine*, June 1864.

the meaning of words – the formularies and the essays themselves – and a determination of whether or not there was a conflict. This was made to appear a simple mechanical task, eminently suited to lawyers, and not at all to theologians. Lushington, in this sense, derived his legitimacy from the very fact that he was not, and did not pretend to be, a theologian. This theme appears very plainly in the judgment itself. 'This is not a court of Divinity; it is a court of ecclesiastical law',[69] he said, echoing the words used by him in the *Denison* case: 'this tribunal is a court of justice and of ecclesiastical law, not a school of theology.'[70]

The reader of Lushington's judgment must ask to what extent this concept corresponds to the reality. First it must be said that the concept did not correspond to the theoretical structure of the ecclesiastical courts. In theory, Lushington was not a purely secular judge: he was appointed by the Archbishop of Canterbury, and he represented the Archbishop in matters falling within the court's jurisdiction. The canons required ecclesiastical judges to be 'well affected, and zealously bent to religion, touching whose life and manners no evil example is had'[71] (though it may be doubted whether religious zeal was of much assistance to an aspiring advocate by the nineteenth century). The formal decrees of the court contained religious language: all commenced 'In the name of God, Amen'.[72] The conception of Lushington as a neutral arbiter outside the Church did not therefore correspond with the legal theory. It may be said that this is a theoretical point only since the ecclesiastical judges were, by this date, in practice quite independent of the episcopate. Nevertheless, there are indications that Lushington saw himself as, in a real sense, speaking on behalf of the Church, as for example in a passage where he said that he should not have hesitated one moment to come to the conclusion that one of the extreme Tractarians was 'no longer fit to be a clergyman in the Church of England'.[73] In a letter to Brougham, in 1842, he had said that the ecclesiastical courts were bound on occasion to decide theological questions.[74]

Turning to another level of practicality, the question arises to what extent Lushington was in fact able to disengage his own theological

---

[69] 1 New Rep 199.   [70] See p. 287, above.   [71] Canon 127 (1603).
[72] See Coote, *Practice of the Ecclesiastical Courts* (1847).
[73] *Burder* v. *Heath* (1862) 15 Moo PC 11.
[74] See p. 280, above.

views in performing his interpretative task. That is, to what extent was he able to live up to his own ideals? It is one thing for a judge to say that his personal views must be set on one side. It is another thing for him to do it. Professor Grote, in a lengthy pamphlet published in 1862, made the point as follows

At present, in our distrust of theologians, all our disposition seems to be to put our theology in the hands of lawyers; as we are pleased to express it, what we want is not theology but 'the plain grammatical sense' of documents. But will grammar and logic do what we want? Are we sure that we shall not get theology, and that it will not be by theological thought that the matter, really and necessarily, is determined, with the disadvantage that it is the thought of one whose training and habit of mind has not been theological, but something different? . . . What he [the judge] must, whether he will or not, call in to help him must be his manner of thinking about theology, a thing he has not been trained to or practised in.[75]

Lord Kingsdown, too, in the Privy Council, was sceptical. In a confidential memorandum to the other members of the Judicial Committee, he doubted the ability of the Court to avoid questions of theology, adding that 'Dr Lushington has laid himself open to observation in some degree in his judgment by professing an ignorance with which he is not justly chargeable'.[76]

The judgment must now be examined and tested by the criteria that Lushington set for himself. He stated these as follows:

I think I shall best consider this objection [that quotations from the scriptures were improperly included in the charges] and at the same time mark out the course of my judgment by stating what are the legal tests of doctrine in the Church of England. This statement is of the last importance, in order that the issue in this case should be clearly settled. What has the court to try? Theological error in its general sense, – i.e., whether Dr Williams is sound or unsound in his theological views; whether he has maintained doctrine inconsistent with the true doctrine of the Christian faith? Certainly not. The issue is, has Dr. Williams promulgated doctrines at variance with the

---

[75] J. Grote, *An examination of some portions of Dr. Lushington's judgment on the admission of the Articles in the cases of the Bishop of Salisbury v. Williams, and Fendall v. Wilson, with remarks upon the bearing of them on the clergy* (Cambridge, 1862), 7. Grote was Vicar of Trumpington, Professor of Moral Philosophy at Cambridge, and younger brother of G. Grote, the historian, Lushington's parliamentary ally on the matter of the secret ballot.
[76] Tait Papers, Lambeth Palace Library (LPL) 291/273.

doctrines of the Church, as declared in the articles and formularies?[77] To use the words of the judgment in the *Gorham* case: 'this court has no jurisdiction or authority to settle matters of faith, or to determine what ought in any particular to be the doctrine of the Church of England. Its duty extends only to the consideration of that which is by law established to be the doctrine of the Church of England, upon the true and legal construction of her articles and formularies'.[78]

The public agitation was an added reason for adhering to strict legal principles:

The court cannot pretend ignorance of the great excitement created by the publication of this volume; but the effect of such excitement on the mind of the court, ought to be this only: to induce me to exercise all the care and vigilance in my power, and to preserve a perfectly equal and dispassionate mind, looking only to ascertain the law, and justly administer it.[79]

Referring to the *Gorham* case, Lushington indicated his guide to the construction of the formularies: 'We seek the plain literal and grammatical sense'.[80]

Lushington went on to exclude the opinions of theologians, however eminent, and to exclude also his own interpretation of scripture, on the ground of the confusion and uncertainty that would be created by judges attempting to weigh apparently conflicting extracts from scripture. His own opinion was to be suppressed.[81]

These repeated references to his role suggest that Lushington felt a little uneasy about it. The concluding paragraph of the judgment reinforces a sense of uncertainty:

I cannot leave these two cases without adding a few words in conclusion. I have discharged my duty to the best of my ability. I am aware that these Judgments will be severely canvassed by the Clergy and by others. Be it so; thereby it may be ascertained whether they are in accordance with Law; and accordance with Law ought to be the sole object of a Court of Justice. It may be, that on the present occasion some may think that, so far from having gone

---

[77] The formularies were usually taken to include the Articles of Religion (1562), the Prayer Book (1662), the Canons (1603), and (possibly) the Homilies (referred to in the Articles). See 6 *Law Times* 727, where Dr Lushington considered the question of the homilies to be open.

[78] 1 New Rep 199.   [79] Ibid.

[80] 1 New Rep 202. The phrase 'literal and grammatical sense' goes back to the Declaration of Charles I attached to the Thirty-nine Articles, and published in every edition of the Prayer Book. Dr Lushington referred to this by saying: 'To the same effect is the higher authority of the King's Declaration'.

[81] 1 New Rep 205.

too far, I have taken too limited a view of the powers intrusted to me, and consequently have failed to provide a remedy where a remedy might seem to be wanted. I can only say that I have shaped my course according to the authority I am bound to follow, – the authority of the Privy Council.[82]

It becomes clear at an early stage that Lushington was not disengaged from the issues before him. He said that 'a more important subject . . . could not be submitted to the consideration of mankind: the question to be determined was, what was sufficient for the salvation of the human race?'[83] In respect of his obligation to determine the ultimate fate of evildoers – a matter on which Wilson's views were condemned – Lushington described the questions he had to resolve as 'of the most momentous character – the future destiny of mankind,' and added, 'to a certain extent I cannot escape the task, and I will not evade it'.[84] 'The salvation of the human race' and 'the future destiny of mankind' are not expressions that fall naturally from the lips of one whose function is the mechanical interpretation and comparison of documents.

Counsel, too, were personally engaged in the dispute. J. F. Stephen, the great criminal law codifier, and later a judge, who appeared for the defence said of the case, 'if I stay 51 years at the Bar, I shall never have another which will interest me so much'.[85] Stephen published his argument in the form of a book.[86] It contains a very vigorous and eloquent plea for freedom of theological enquiry, perhaps a little too vigorous and eloquent. The extravagant peroration at the end suggests that Stephen may have forgotten that Dr Lushington's courts contained no juries.[87] J. D. Coleridge, later Lord Chief Justice, appeared for the Bishop of Salisbury. He wrote, during argument in the case against Williams:

---

[82] *Judgment . . . in the case of the Bishop of Salisbury versus Williams and in the case of Fendall versus Wilson* (London, 1862), 44. The passage does not appear in the New Reports.

[83] 1 New Rep 203–4.

[84] Ibid., 219.

[85] Williams, *Life and Letters*, 51, n.2.

[86] J. F. Stephen, *Defence of the Rev. Rowland Williams in the Arches' Court of Canterbury* (London, 1862), 335 pp.

[87] 'The issue . . . is whether men are to crouch before the Bible as an idol, as an inanimate Pope . . . I am sure that your lordship will look beyond the cynical and ignorant clamour . . . for it is the cause of learning, of freedom, and of reason – the learning of the most learned, the freedom of the freest, and the reason of the most rational church in the world.' Ibid., at 330–1.

I found Arthur Stanley [i.e. A. P. Stanley] quite *hot* upon the subject . . . so I dropped it, but in his view the Church of England shuts up shop if Lushington decides for us. I can't help thinking if *he* is right that she *will* shut up shop. I have been looking tonight at Butler, Cudsworth, Hooker, Horsley, Leighton, Davison, Arnold and S.T.C. [Samuel Taylor Coleridge?], all to my mind *conclusive* against Taffy [i.e. Williams] in the points of influence, inspiration and prophecy.[88]

One of the reasons why modern liberal societies have hesitated to control the expression of opinion, quite apart from the positive value of free speech, is the difficulty of defining offences and proving infractions. If ordinary principles of fairness, as generally applied in the criminal process, are to be observed, a definition will be required of the orthodox opinion so that persons, before they are accused, may govern their conduct in accordance with what the law requires, and, after they are accused, may know what case it is that they have to meet. Convincing proof will also be required that the accused has offended, for no one should be punished unless clearly guilty. Statements of orthodoxy, however, are hard to frame, and proof of offences is also equally difficult to establish, for rarely is the heretic so accommodating to his prosecutors as to write his opinions so that they precisely negative the very words of the orthodox text. Nowhere are these points more clearly illustrated than in *Essays and Reviews* and in the associated case of *Heath*, where the pleadings were three times amended in an attempt to specify the charges with sufficient particularity.[89] In *Essays and Reviews* there was no separate appeal from the admission of the articles of charge but it is clear that the Privy Council, in overturning Lushington's decision, was influenced by the failure of the promoters[90] to specify with sufficient precision the orthodox position and the alleged contradictions in the essays.

It must have surprised those observing the proceedings in 1862 that there should be any difficulty in this respect. The whole world knew that the essayists impugned the inspiration of scripture; the inspiration of scripture was a cardinal doctrine of the Church of England; atheists and bishops agreed that the essayists were unfit to hold office in the Church; the court had only to do its clear duty.

[88] J. D. Coleridge to his father, 5 Jan. 1862, E. H. Coleridge, *Life and Correspondence of J. D. Coleridge Lord Chief Justice of England* (London, 1904), ii, 116.

[89] See pp. 308–10, above.

[90] The promoter was the prosecutor, theoretically 'promoting the office of the judge', but in practice acting independently and at his own expense. See Coote, *Practice of the Ecclesiastical Courts*, 104, 133–4, 148.

But, what the whole world knows does not always sustain a close analysis. It must have seemed astonishing to many that not one of the Thirty-nine Articles of Religion[91] set out the doctrine that the scriptures were divinely inspired, but this was the fact. This may have been because of the difficulty of giving precision to the idea of inspiration; more probably it is because the controversies of the sixteenth century did not necessitate an official statement on this question.

Article VI is entitled 'On the Sufficiency of the Holy Scriptures for Salvation' and commences:

> Holy Scripture containeth all things necessary to salvation: so that whatsoever is not read therein, or may be proved thereby, is not to be required of any man, that it should be believed as an article of the faith, or be thought requisite or necessary to salvation. In the name of the Holy Scripture we do understand those canonical books of the Old and New Testament, of whose authority was never any doubt in the Church. [The Article then specifies the canonical books.]

There is little here that is of help to the promoters. The thrust of the Article is not to establish that the scriptures are inspired, but to deny the necessity of requirements derived from non-scriptural sources. The phrase 'necessary for salvation' is not equivalent to 'inspired', and in any event the Article only says the scripture 'containeth all things necessary to salvation', so, by implication, it presumably contains some things that are not necessary. So, on any reading, the Article does not establish the inspiration of the whole of the scriptures.

Article XX, 'Of the Authority of The Church', is similarly not very helpful. It reads:

> The Church hath power to decree rites or ceremonies, and authority in controversies of faith: and yet it is not lawful for the Church to ordain anything that is contrary to God's Word written, neither may it so expound one place of Scripture, that it be repugnant to another. Wherefore, although the Church be a witness and a keeper of Holy Writ, yet, as it ought not to decree anything as against the same, so besides the same ought it not to enforce any thing to be believed for necessity of salvation.

Again it is plain that the general gist and purpose of this Article is not to establish the importance of scripture but to diminish the power of

---

[91] The Articles of Religion were appended to a statute (13 Eliz. c. 12), required to be subscribed by all clergy (Canon 36), and were printed in every copy of the Prayer Book, which was also annexed to a statute. The difficulties of prosecution were pointed out in an article, 'The Essays and Reviews considered in relation to the legal liabilities of the writers', *Law Magazine* 11 (1861), 1.

the Church to derive requirements from non-scriptural sources. It is true that the phrase 'God's Word written' is used, but this, it appears, is merely an incidental manner of referring to the scriptures, as with the further variation 'Holy Writ' in the next line. If the purpose were to require assent to the proposition that the scriptures were inspired by God, the terms of Article XX would be a very indirect way of achieving it.

Lushington, however, deduced from these Articles a doctrine of inspiration of the scriptures. He said that the expression 'Holy' scripture in Article VI and the phrase 'God's Word written' in Article XX denote divine origin.[92] In the latter phrase, combined with the statement in Article VI that 'the Holy scripture containeth all things necessary to salvation', is 'necessarily implied' (said Lushington) 'the doctrine that in all matters necessary to salvation the Holy Scripture emanated from the extrordinary and preternatural interposition of the Almighty'.[93]

'Necessarily implied', as Professor Grote pointed out in his pamphlet,[94] would seem to be a step or two from 'the plain grammatical sense'. But Lushington has no hesitation in using the latter phrase subsequently in the same paragraph. It is true that all words, even those we call express, have in them elements of implication. Words do not exist in a vacuum, and something of a context is always imported. But to find 'necessarily implied' in the expressions mentioned 'the doctrine that in all matters necessary for salvation the Holy Scriptures emanated from the extraordinary and preternatural interposition of the Almighty' does seem to be giving a large scope to necessity.

Further doubt is cast on the necessity of the implication by the variety of phrases resorted to by Lushington. The following statements can be found of what the Articles require to be believed:

1 In all matters necessary for salvation the Holy Scriptures emanated from the extraordinary and preternatural interposition of the Almighty (quoted above).
2 The Holy Scriptures contain everything necessary to salvation, and that to that extent they have the *direct* sanction of the Almighty.[95]
3 The Bible is an inspired writing and canonical.[96]

[92] 1 New Rep 204.   [93] Ibid.
[94] Grote, *Dr Lushington's Judgment*, 6–7.
[95] 1 New Rep 204 (Dr Lushington's italics).
[96] Ibid., 205.

4 The Scriptures, so far as the salvation of man is concerned, have been written by the interposition of the almighty power of God.

5 The Bible is the written Word of God (elsewhere 'God's Word written').

6 The sacred writers wrote from the influence of a supernatural power to effect a given object, clearly distinct from the ordinary operation of God's omnipotence on the minds of man in its ordinary course.

7 The Bible in matters essential to salvation is the written word of God.

8 The Bible was written by the interposition of the Almighty, supernaturally brought to operate.[97]

9 The scriptures, so far as relates to matters concerning salvation, were written by the divine interposition of God, and that in a manner different from the ordinary agency of providence.

10 The Bible was written by the special interposition of the Almighty for that purpose [i.e. salvation].

11 The Bible was written by the special interposition of the Almighty power.[98]

Some of these formulations are very similar, but on the other hand there are significant differences among them. A clergyman whose livelihood was at stake surely had a right to know to which he must adhere. The variety of formulations that Lushington found to be 'necessarily implied' weakens the case for the necessity of implying any one of them.

The other aspect of the matter is convincing proof of a clear offence. Unfortunately for the promoters neither Williams nor Wilson had stated in precise words the negative of any of Lushington's implied propositions – still less had they expressly negatived the words of the Articles of Religion. The worst that could be found in Williams' essay was this passage:

In the Bible as an expression of devout reason and therefore to be read with reason in freedom he [i.e. the reader of the work that Williams was reviewing] finds a record of the spiritual giants, whose experience generated the religious atmosphere we breathe.[99]

---

[97] The last five phrases occur in 1 New Rep 206.
[98] The last three phrases are at 1 New Rep 215.
[99] *Essays and Reviews*, 60–1.

Lushington condemned Williams for the phrase 'expression of devout reason'. But here too he is on weak ground. Even the most rigidly orthodox did not require a belief that the writers of scripture were (in Williams' phrase) 'passionless machines',[100] i.e. that they wrote without use of their own faith and reason. So, to say that the Bible is an expression of devout reason is fully consistent with the strictest orthodoxy. Lushington seems to read the phrase as though it denied that anything other than human reason was involved. But Williams did not make any such denial. Nor can another phrase for which Williams was condemned in describing the Bible as 'the written voice of the congregation'[101] fairly be taken to deny the possibility of divine inspiration. Tait's handwritten notes made when the case was before the Privy Council, emphasize this point:

I know not where Dr W has asserted that the Bible is not the Word of God or that it does not contain any special revelation of God's truth nor of his dealings with mankind and that it is not the rule of our faith. Greatly as I dislike and object to many of Dr W's statements I find nothing in them to justify this accusation.[102]

The only one of the formulations of the orthodox position that might justify condemnation of these phrases is that the scriptures have the *direct* sanction of the Almighty (Lushington's own word, and his own empahsis).[103] This formulation occurs three pages before the discussion and consideration of Williams' phrases, and Lushington does not again advert to the concept of 'direct', or explain its meaning. The only implicit reference rather suggests that he does not require a belief in – at any rate the crudest sort of – direct intervention when he says:

Whether the sacred writers ought to be called 'passionless machines', that is, if I rightly apprehend the meaning, whether they wrote down what the Divine Power dictated, without thought or understanding, – is a question I do not enter upon.[104]

But if Lushington is not to enter upon that question, surely he owes it to his readers, and to Dr Williams, to explain what he does mean by 'direct' and why the phrases condemned are inconsistent with his reading of the Articles of Religion. The reader might perhaps justly

100 Ibid., 78.   101 Ibid.   102 Tait Papers, 291/179.
103 1 New Rep 204.   104 1 New Rep 206.

say that, whatever may be said of the writers of scripture, the writers of judgments do not always appear to be 'passionless machines'.

Wilson's condemnation on the question of inspiration was based not on an assertion about scripture, but on an expression of opinion about the meaning of the sixth Article. Wilson had pointed out, what was undoubtedly true, that the Article did not itself contain the expression 'Word of God', nor an express declaration of inspiration. Lushington said:

I feel myself compelled to come to the conclusion that, in the passage quoted, Mr Wilson expressing the opinion which he himself holds, denies that the Bible was written by the spiritual interposition of the Almighty power.[105]

But, again, it is only by reading more into the words than is there that such a denial can be clearly extracted from Wilson's actual words. As Professor Grote pointed out, for a writer to say that an Article does not contain some doctrine is not the same thing as for the writer to deny that he holds the doctrine himself.[106] To condemn an expression of opinion on the meaning of an Article makes any commentator on ecclesiastical law write at his peril. For if he should be wrong in his opinion, he will be held himself to have denied the doctrine required to be believed.

Of course, in one sense, Lushington was quite right. The general tendency of the essays, and of the book as a whole, certainly was in the direction of the opinions attributed by Lushington to Williams and Wilson. But this is the nub of the problem: condemning the writers on account of an unspecified general tendency towards theological unsoundness was the very thing that the Privy Council forbade and that Lushington disclaimed.

Two other points may be made about Dr Williams' essay. In form, the essay was a review of a work by Baron Bunsen, and all expressions of opinion and all speculation were attributed to Bunsen (as his opinions, or as what he might say if he should deal with some point). A preliminary question, therefore, was whether Williams could be held personally responsible for opinions attributed by him to Bunsen. Again, it cannot be denied that the *tone* of the essay denoted approval of Bunsen's opinions. On the other hand, if Williams was only to be condemned where he had clearly offended, how could it be said that

[105] Ibid., 215.   [106] Grote, *Dr Lushington's Judgment*, 33–5.

he was guilty in attributing views to another? On this point Lushington was peremptory:

After many perusals of the Essay, after carefully considering the arguments of his counsel, I think this review does prove a general, but not indiscriminate, approval of the opinions quoted from the work of Baron Bunsen, – a general adoption, with particular exceptions; and I come to this conclusion the more readily because, with respect to a very large part of the extracts on which the charges are founded, Dr Williams' counsel have declared that they espouse and defend them. If there be parts as to which the approval of Dr Williams is still left in doubt, surely Dr Williams himself is responsible for that difficulty; surely it was his duty to have taken care that he did not so arrange his quotations and shape his observations, as to leave it in doubt whether he, a clergyman of the Church of England, approved of what may be found to be repugnant to the doctrine as by law established.[107]

One can see the force of this from the point of view of the promoter. As Lushington had said a few lines previously:

Were it otherwise, it would have been possible for a clergyman, under colour of a review, to disseminate, even with the sanction of his name and profession, opinions and arguments directly opposed to the doctrine (as by law established) of the Church.[108]

In other words it would be inconvenient to the promoter if Williams could thus hide behind Baron Bunsen. But the convenience of the promoter ought perhaps not to be weighed quite so heavily. There are difficulties with this part of Lushington's judgment. It is surprising that the opinion of Williams' counsel expressed at the trial over two years after publication should be relevant to the question of what Williams said in the essay.[109] The suggestion that it was Williams' duty not to leave his own opinions in doubt raises further difficulties. It is one thing to condemn a person for what he has said; it is going a good deal further to condemn him for what he has not said on the ground that it was his duty not to leave his opinions doubtful. Such an approach runs the danger of turning the onus of proof on its head: all the promoter has to do is to establish a doubt, and then it is for the defendant to show that he has clearly expressed the orthodox view. Lord Kingsdown, in the Privy Council, felt the force of this point,

---

[107] 1 New Rep 198.   [108] Ibid.

[109] Stephen argued very strenuously that Williams could not be guilty of an offence simply by giving an account of another's views. See Stephen, *Defence of the Rev. Rowland Williams*, 289–96.

saying that 'Dr Lushington lays down the law too strictly when he says that a clergyman must not quote erroneous opinions without stating that he dissents from them'.[110]

A somewhat related point arises in respect of the phrase 'expression of devout reason' discussed above. Lushington said:

With every desire to put upon Dr Williams' words a construction reconcilable with the Article, I must hold that to characterize without qualification the Bible as an expression of devout reason, is inconsistent with the doctrine that it was written by the interposition of God.[111]

The words 'without qualification' point up the weakness of this passage. It was suggested above that, standing alone, the statement that the Bible is an expression of devout reason can hardly be unorthodox. Lushington evidently feels some of the force of this point, and so he introduces the phrase 'without qualification'. It is the absence of qualification that makes this passage in the essay punishable. But what precisely is meant by the expression? What kind of qualification would suffice? Again, it appears that Williams is condemned, in part, for what he has not said, and that a burden is put upon him to establish, if he can, the required orthodox qualification. In point of fact, Williams had written immediately after the second passage in respect to which he was condemned 'we are promised illumination from the Spirit which dwells in them [the sacred writers]'[112] a phrase which the Privy Council read as indicating that Williams had 'plainly affirmed that the Holy Spirit dwelt in the sacred writers of the Bible'.[113] Again, the 'plain' meaning of words is not always (it would seem) found by everyone everywhere to be the same.

On these points Lushington was reversed by a majority of the Judicial Committee of the Privy Council.[114] Williams and Wilson both argued their cases in person, having, apparently, so far lost their faith that they trusted no longer even in ecclesiastical lawyers. The ground of reversal was that the extracts from Williams' essay could not fairly be construed to deny divine inspiration and (in respect of the charge against Wilson) the sixth Article of Religion could not legitimately be read to assert that every part of scripture was inspired. In the one case the offence was not sufficiently proved; in the other the

[110] Tait Papers, 291/273.   [111] 1 New Rep 206.
[112] *Essays and Reviews*, 78.
[113] *Williams v. The Bishop of Salisbury* 2 Moo PCNS 42.   [114] Ibid.

prohibition was not sufficiently clear. Despite the attempt always made by the Privy Council to achieve unanimity,[115] the two archbishops dissented. The Bishop of London (Tait) voted with the majority.

Coleridge, the counsel for the Bishop of Salisbury, was well informed of the pending division of opinion three months before it became public. In November 1863 he wrote to his father:

> I gather that there is a division, but that the majority is for reversing. I gather this from the story that Reeve [the Registrar of the Privy Council] and the Chancellor . . . are urging on the Primates that the judgment must be supposed to be the judgment of the whole court, and that if they do not agree they must yet not say that they differ. Phillimore told me this last night at our Bench, from which, if it be true, I argue that London has ratted, and that the Primates are standing out against the laymen.[116]

Allowing for the unflattering metaphor applied to Tait, this turned out to be an entirely accurate prediction of the result. It suggests that the archbishops must have consulted Phillimore (the leading counsel for the promoters in both cases) on the question of their right to dissent. Confidential printed memoranda were prepared and circulated by each member of the Committee, and no fewer than five confidential drafts of the judgment were printed and circulated.[117]

Scriptural inspiration was regarded by most readers of the essays and by Lushington as the principal point at issue. But the essayists were each condemned also on two other points. Lushington deals with them more briefly, but, nevertheless, they are an important part of the judgment, and require some brief attention.

Dr Williams was condemned for saying that 'propitiation would be the recovery of that peace which cannot be, whilst sin divides us from the Searcher of hearts'.[118] This proposition was held by Lushington to be contrary to the thirty-first Article of Religion, which states:

> The offering of Christ once made is that perfect redemption, propitiation, and satisfaction . . . for all the sins of the whole world.

But the Article does not, in terms, fix any definition of propitiation. The weakness of this condemnation may perhaps be sufficiently

---

[115] See P. A. Howell, *The Judicial Committee of the Privy Council 1833–1876* (Cambridge, 1979), 201–4.

[116] J. D. Coleridge to his father, 14 Nov. 1863, Coleridge, *Life and Correspondence*, 121

[117] Tait Papers, 291, ff. 246–300. See Howell, *Judicial Committee*, 198.

[118] *Essays and Reviews*, 81. 1 New Rep 210–11.

demonstrated by the fact that, during the course of argument (by Williams in person) before the Privy Council, the article of charge on this point was withdrawn, without objection or argument from the promoter.[119]

The third point on which Williams was condemned concerned the doctrine of justification by faith. Article XI states:

We are accounted righteous before God only for the merit of our Lord and Saviour Jesus Christ by faith, and not for our own works or deservings.

Williams had written:

Why may not justification by faith have meant the peace of mind, or sense of Divine approval, which comes of trust in a righteous God, rather than a fiction of merit by transfer? St Paul would then be teaching moral responsibility, as opposed to Sacerdotalism.[120]

This was condemned. But the Article does not expressly set out as an article of faith the doctrine that the merits of Christ are transferred to believers. It does not seem obvious, then, that in calling that doctrine a 'fiction' Williams contradicts the eleventh Article – still less that he contradicts its plain ordinary and grammatical sense. This was the view of the Privy Council.[121]

Wilson was condemned first, as has been stated, on the question of inspiration of scriptures. The second and third points of condemnation in his case both had to do with what is known as universalism, that is, the idea that all, including non-Christians, may eventually achieve salvation. The eighteenth Article states:

They also are to be had accursed that presume to say, That every man shall be saved by the law or sect which he professeth, so that he be diligent to frame his life according to that law, and the light of Nature. For Holy Scripture doth set out unto us only the name of Jesus Christ, whereby men must be saved.

Two passages in Wilson's essay were in issue. In the first he had said:

As to the necessity of faith in a Saviour to these peoples when they could never have had it, no one, upon reflection, can believe any such thing: doubtless they will be equitably dealt with.[122]

The second passage, immediately following, read:

---

[119] Br & Fr 281.   [120] *Essays and Reviews*, 80. 1 New Rep 212.
[121] 2 Moo PCNS 428   [122] *Essays and Reviews*, 153

And when we hear fine distinctions drawn between covenanted and uncovenanted mercies, it seems either to be a distinction without a difference, or to amount to a denial of the broad and equal justice of the Supreme Being.

Lushington held that the first passage did not contradict the eighteenth Article, but that the second did.

To deny any distinction [between covenanted and uncovenanted mercies] appears to me to declare that a man may be saved by the law which he professeth.[123]

In effect Lushington reads the eighteenth Article to postulate the notion of uncovenanted mercy and to require a distinction between it and covenanted mercy. It would be said by many that this is reading into the Article what is not there: not only is a concept discovered (uncovenanted mercy) that is not mentioned in the Article, but the Article is found to lay down the subtleties of a distinction between that and another concept also not mentioned. This was a point that was withdrawn in the course of argument before the Privy Council without objection from the promoter.[124] It is odd that a result that Lushington saw as required by the plain grammatical meaning of words should appear, so soon afterwards, not even to be arguable.

The last point upon which Wilson was condemned is perhaps the point on which the *Essays and Reviews* case is now most remembered, namely the everlasting punishment of the wicked. Wilson, at the very end of his essay, expressed a hope

that there shall be found, after the great adjudication, receptacles suitable for those who shall be infants, not as to years of terrestrial life, but as to spiritual development – nurseries as it were and seed grounds, where the undeveloped may grow up under new conditions – the stunted may become strong, and the perverted be restored. And when the Christian Church, in all its branches, shall have fulfilled its sublunary office, and its Founder shall have surrendered His kingdom to the Great Father – all, both small and great, shall find a refuge in the bosom of the Universal parent, to repose, or be quickened into higher life, in the ages to come, according to His will.[125]

The Articles of Religion do not deal with this question. In the other formularies there are conflicting statements. The Athanasian creed contains these words:

---

[123] 1 New Rep 218.   [124] Br & Fr 280–1.   [125] *Essays and Reviews*, 206.

And they that have done good shall go into life everlasting; and they that have done evil into everlasting fire.

On the other hand the burial service – required to be used for all persons buried by the Church – includes the words, used in reference to the particular person being buried, 'in sure and certain hope of the resurrection to eternal life', words that favoured Wilson's view. Lushington, however, did not quote from the burial service (though he indicated that this was one of the documents that he was called upon to construe):

> I think it would be an unprofitable task to go *seriatim* through every passage cited from the Prayer Book. I will advert to what I deem most important to the present issue.[126]

Lushington then quoted the words just given from the Athanasian creed, added 'I must construe them in their plain literal and grammatical sense' and condemned Wilson accordingly. On this point the Privy Council held – with the concurrence of all three ecclesiastical members of the Committee[127] – that the formularies were not sufficiently clear to require the courts to condemn as penal an expression of hope that even the ultimate pardon of the wicked, who are condemned in the day of judgment, may be consistent with the will of Almighty God.[128] It was this holding that led to the mock epitaph on Baron Westbury, who delivered the judgment, that he had 'dismissed hell with costs and taken away from orthodox members of the Church of England their last hope of everlasting damnation'.[129] Forty-four years earlier, Lushington had linked a belief in hell with 'the general moral condition of the people at large'[130] and it is likely that his view of the relation between religion and society played a part in his condemnation of Wilson.

In discussing Lushington's judgment, emphasis has been placed on the points on which he condemned the defendants. This is natural, for in a real sense the points of condemnation counted more than the

---

[126] 1 New Rep 219. In Dr Lushington's defence it should be pointed out that the Privy Council had adverted to this phrase in the burial service, in the *Gorham* case, and had suggested that it could not be taken literally, W. G. Brooke, *Six Judgments of the Judicial Committee of the Privy Council in Ecclesiastical Cases, 1850–1872* (London, 1874), 30.

[127] But the Archbishop of Canterbury later explained that he had assented to this part of the judgment 'solely on technical grounds'. See Ellis, *Seven Against Christ*, 154.

[128] 2 Moo PCNS 433.

[129] J. B. Atlay, *The Victorian Chancellors* (London, 1908), ii, 264.

[130] See pp. 33–4, above.

points of acquittal. Lushington did, indeed, reject many of the articles of the charges but this was to be expected. In a scatter-gun attack it is the shots that hit that are counted, not those that miss. The promoters included all the charges that were even remotely plausible: in more than one sense they 'threw the book' at the defendants. Nevertheless, due attention must be paid to the points of acquittal, first for the sake of a balanced account of the judgment, and secondly because, since Lushington was reversed on the points of condemnation, it is the points of acquittal that stand, and it is his reasons in support of acquittal that are most often cited and that can be justly said to have had the greatest influence upon future events. The final outcome of the litigation was an acquittal, and an important part of that acquittal and of the reasons in support of it were Lushington's.

The most significant point decided in favour of the defendants had to do with scripture. In the course of the service for ordination of deacons the diaconand is asked: 'Do you unfeignedly believe all the canonical Scriptures of the Old and New Testaments', and answers 'I do believe them'. Dr Lushington put on this answer a construction which, as Stanley said, 'admits the widest latitude that the extremest Essayist ever claimed'.[131] Lushington said:

I think that the declaration, 'I do believe,' must be considered with reference to the subject matter, and that is the whole Bible, the Old and New Testaments. The great number of these books; the extreme antiquity of some; that our scriptures must necessarily consist of copies and translations; that they embrace almost every possible variety of subject, parts being all important to the salvation of mankind, and parts being historical and of a less sacred character, certainly not without some element of allegory and figures – all these circumstances, I say, must be borne in mind when the extent of the obligation imposed by the words 'I do believe' has to be determined.[132]

He went on to say that it was open to a clergyman to represent parts of scripture (though not whole books) as spurious, and to dispute the traditional authorship of any books.

There is something of an oddity in comparing these conclusions with the condemnation of Williams described above. Lushington says:

131 Stanley, *Essays*, 100. The Archbishop of York, in the Privy Council, thought that Dr Lushington had given the deacon's affirmation 'a very strained and unnatural interpretation', Tait Papers, 291/267.
132 1 New Rep 204.

The general averment that the statements of Holy Scripture as to historical facts may be read and understood in a wholly figurative sense, cannot be deemed a violation of the declaration of belief in the truth of Scripture.[133]

If it is open to a clergyman to describe the historical passages of scripture as figurative, or to reject them and their traditional authorship as spurious, it seems odd to condemn one who describes the scriptures as an expression of devout reason. It seems that Lushington has swallowed the camel, but strained at the gnat.

In accordance with the principle of applying only the formularies of the Church, Lushington rejected charges alleging denial of Messianic prophecy, denial of the traditional authorship of Daniel, Hebrews, and II Peter, and of the traditional dating of John and Hebrews, and denial of the historical truth of the Flood. Williams was also acquitted on three charges relating to matters of doctrine (propitiation, baptism and the incarnation).[134]

Wilson was acquitted on charges relating to scripture on similar grounds to Williams. He was also acquitted of a charge of asserting that Christ was a mere moral teacher and reformer.[135] Articles charging that Wilson had asserted that it was lawful to interpret the Articles of Religion in a non-literal sense were rejected, but on the technical ground that inciting disobedience of the canons did not itself constitute an offence against the canon requiring subscription by clergy to the Articles of Religion, and this was all that had been charged. Lushington made it clear that he left open the possibility that Wilson's comments on the Articles of Religion constituted some other offence – indeed, he implied that they did.[136] The points decided in favour of the defendants were substantial. On several of these points there are strong indications that Lushington reached his decision reluctantly and against his own inclinations. There is every reason to take at face value Lushington's repeated statement of his desire to do justice to the defendants. He gave leave to appeal against his judgment of 25 June, admitting the articles of charge,[137] and, as will be seen, he later advised the Privy Council to decide a crucial procedural point in favour of the defendants.[138]

A word must be said about the penalty. Lushington suspended the

---

[133] Ibid., at 210.   [134] 1 New Rep 207–12.   [135] Ibid., 214–15.
[136] Ibid., 217.   [137] Ibid., 212–13.
[138] Minute Book, Judicial Committee of Privy Council, entry for 19 June 1863.

defendants from their benefices for a year. In *The Times* Lushington was reported as saying:

> The sentence he was about to pronounce might be found fault with as too lenient, but he would rather have it so regarded than otherwise.[139]

The account in the *Manchester Guardian*, probably based on Coleridge's notes,[140] includes further reasons that lay heavy stress on deterrence:

> In Dr Williams' case, he [Lushington] said it was necessary for the welfare of the Church that punishment should be awarded against him for the security of the Church, the punishment of the individual being a secondary consideration. It might be thought by some that the sentence he was about to pronounce would be too lenient, but he hoped it would be sufficiently severe to show Dr Williams how seriously he had erred, and be a warning also to other clergymen throughout the country.[141]

Others have also suggested that the outcome was lenient.[142] Compared with the maximum sentence passed on Heath (deprivation) it may perhaps appear so.[143] However, Heath had refused to retract after being invited to do so, and, furthermore, deprivation in those circumstances (under the statute involved in the *Heath* case) was mandatory. On the other hand suspension for a year from office and benefice is a substantial penalty, and would be ruinous to a clergyman with family obligations and no private income. A further significant aspect of this matter is that the promoter had specifically asked for a milder sentence:

> The counsel for the promoter asked the court to suspend the defendant until such time as he should retract his erroneous opinions ... The object of the promoter in bringing these proceedings was not to visit with any severity of punishment the individual, but to secure the Church from pernicious and false teaching.[144]

---

[139] *The Times*, 16 Dec. 1862, 10d.

[140] Coleridge, *Life and Correspondence*, 118, 16 Dec. 1862.

[141] *Manchester Guardian*, 16 Dec. 1862, 3b. The report in the *Law Times* is to similar effect: 7 LT 474.

[142] See, for example, Ellis, *Seven Against Christ*, 185.

[143] The *Manchester Guardian* made the comparison, 18 Dec. 1862, 2 d, e, as did Dr Lushington himself, according to the *Law Times*, 7 LT 474.

[144] 1 New Rep 213.

A retraction was offered through counsel for Williams, but Dr Lushington said 'he could not take into account a verbal retraction'.[145] Nor did he give any opportunity for a formal retraction:

He [Lushington] thought it would be wrong to suspend the defendant until he had retracted, as that judgment might cause a retraction which did not come from the heart.[146]

It must be said that, if this is an accurate report of Lushington's words,[147] there is apparent here a determination to do that which the promoter himself had disclaimed, i.e. to inflict punishment upon the defendants. An informal retraction was rejected; opportunity for a formal retraction was denied because it might not 'come from the heart'. This goes far to deprive the concept of retraction of meaning. It may be doubted to what extent a retraction should be required 'from the heart'. Lushington had earlier said that the court had no business to punish opinion, but only to control its expression. It would be perfectly possible for Dr Williams, in good faith, to retract the expressions in the essay that had been judged contrary to law, and to promise not to repeat them, without altering his own private opinion. But even allowing that an element of altered opinion should be required, it would seem unfair to assume its absence in advance of the fact, and to deprive Dr Williams of the opportunity of demonstrating it. The point has added significance since the promoter of the case against Williams, the Bishop of Salisbury, stated as a reason for proceeding under the general ecclesiastical law (rather than under the statute under which Heath was prosecuted) that the defendant 'if found guilty would not be deprived of a locus penitentiae [i.e. room for repentance]'[148] – an ironical mistake, for the statute under which

---

[145] Ibid. See slightly different wording in 7 LT 473, adding: 'Such a retraction must be in writing, submitted to the consideration of the court, and for the approval of the party prosecuting'. In Williams, *Life and Letters*, ii, 81, a letter from Stephen to the *Spectator* is reprinted, in which Stephen says that Williams only offered to retract two passages on justification and propitiation, and 'the court did not entertain this offer, because the prosecutor's counsel were not satisfied with it'.

[146] New Rep 213. The *Law Times* report does not contain these words, but gives: 'I feel an objection to continuing the period of any suspension I may pronounce till a recantation is made which might appear to be enforced by depriving a man of his means of livelihood'. 7 LT 474.

[147] The *Law Times* report differs.

[148] See Br & F 251n, referring to a letter to the Archdeacons of his diocese printed in the appendix to his Charge of 1864.

Heath was prosecuted expressly provided for the possibility of retraction and required the court to afford the necessary opportunity.[149]

The explanation of Lushington's attitude to this question may lie in a comment published by Williams after the date of the judgment admitting the articles, and before the sentence. Williams had written:

My counsel will best teach me how legal fictions are to be met. I do not like the idea of calumniating myself; or of giving to persecutors the barren semblance of a triumph: but if I were technically to withdraw every expression reserved by the Court, in the sense which the Court has technically affixed to it, I should not thereby retract a particle of my meaning, or imply any modification of opinion.[150]

These are very rash words for a convicted offender to publish, while sentence is pending. He accuses the court of fictions and technicalities, and announces in advance that he will go through the motions of compliance with any order of retraction without intending to retract a particle of his meaning. A judge would hardly be human, if he did not find here a temptation to deny the opportunity of such a retraction as this.

The relationship between the *Essays and Reviews* case, and the *Heath* case, is of interest. The cases, though in vital respects very different, were made to appear similar from a legal point of view. There can be little doubt that both the Privy Council, and Dr Lushington, in giving their respective judgments in the *Heath* case, had in mind the far more significant case that they knew was about to follow.

The cases were similar in that each involved accusations against a clergyman of stating false doctrine, but they were quite dissimilar in their theological and public significance. Heath was a little-known clergyman who held idiosyncratic theological views. His book would have passed unnoticed but for the suit against him. On the other hand the authors of *Essays and Reviews* were leading figures in the ecclesiastical and academic world whose ideas were, rightly, taken to be representative of a growing and powerful school of thought that would have a profound effect on academic and on popular theology. It is odd

---

[149] 13 Eliz. I c. 12, s. 2 provides that 'if any person Ecclesiastical ... shall advisedly maintain or affirm any doctrine directly contrary, or repugnant to, any of the thirty-nine Articles, and being convened before the Bishop of the Diocese, or the Ordinary, shall persist therein and not revoke his error; such maintaining or affirming shall be just cause to deprive such person of his Ecclesiastical promotion'.

[150] R. Williams, *Persecution for the Word, with a Postscript on the Interlocutory Judgment and the present State of the Case* (London, 1862).

that cases that are from every other point of view so different should appear, from a legal point of view, to be so similar.

The suit against Heath was commenced in February 1860.[151] *Essays and Reviews* was published in the following month. The first review of *Essays and Reviews* appeared on 7 April.[152] On 16 April the *Heath* case was argued before Lushington on the question of the degree of specificity required in the charges – a crucial point in both cases. Lushington gave judgment on 25 April, holding that the promoter was not bound to specify the precise formularies alleged to have been infringed. The appeal was allowed on this point by the Privy Council on 9 July, and after a further reformation of the articles by the Privy Council on 9 February 1861, the case was remitted to Lushington for a decision on the main question, which was argued on 17 and 18 June. By this time it had become clear that Lushington would be called upon to judge *Essays and Reviews*, the proceedings against Dr Williams having been commenced two weeks earlier, on 5 June. Lushington gave judgment in *Heath* on 2 November.[153] Lushington laid down the principles that he later attempted to apply in *Essays and Reviews*, making a significant reference to 'all causes in which charges of false doctrine are preferred',[154] strongly suggesting that *Essays and Reviews* (to be argued a month later) was present in his mind. The *Essays and Reviews* case was argued before Lushington in December 1861 and January 1862. Lushington reserved judgment, as he specifically said,[155] until the judgment of the Privy Council in the *Heath* case should be delivered (Privy Council 6 June; Court of Arches 25 June 1862).

The fact that Lushington deliberately postponed his decision shows that he considered the *Heath* case highly relevant. No doubt the Privy Council had in mind *Essays and Reviews* when it gave judgment. The case had received enormous publicity, and Lushington's judgment was, as everyone knew, immediately pending. No doubt, also, Lushington knew all this, and saw the judgment in the

---

[151] Dates are from the Assignation Book of the Court of Arches in Lambeth Palace Library, the Minute Book of the Judicial Committee of the Privy Council, and the printed reports of the cases.

[152] See Ellis, *Seven Against Christ*, 104.

[153] F. D. Maurice, in a letter to *Macmillan's Magazine* ('Dr Lushington, Mr Heath, and the Thirty-nine Articles', *Macmillan's Magazine* 5 (1861), 153), regretted that Dr Lushington had not followed his own 'lay instincts', which Maurice took to favour acquittal.

[154] 15 Moo PC 42.   [155] 1 New Rep 198.

Heath case (upholding the condemnation of Heath though not on every point) as something of a green light for a similar result in *Essays and Reviews*. The *Heath* case did not reveal the difficulties that lay ahead, though there was perhaps a hint in the Privy Council's suggestion there that the articles of charge were still open to dispute as not sufficiently specific, even after two attempts at reformation. *Heath* appeared as an easy case because Heath's opinions were very idiosyncratic and expressed in language that made no attempt to avoid inconsistency with the Articles of Religion. Lushington accepted the *Heath* case as binding on him, and he thought that it required him to condemn the defendants. By the time *Essays and Reviews* reached the Privy Council, *Heath*'s case had come to appear much less persuasive: indeed it was not even mentioned in the Privy Council judgment.

The perception of Dr Lushington's judgment in *Essays and Reviews* has been predominantly that it was a liberal judgment, and represented a victory for the essayists. J. S. Mill, replying to a correspondent, not having read the judgment, said he was 'glad to hear that it is on the whole favourable to latitudinarianism and satisfactory to Dr Williams' friends'.[156] Jowett, one of the essayists, wrote:

I am satisfied and pleased with the judgment of Dr Lushington on the whole. A great step has been gained in freedom for the Church of England.[157]

Williams himself, striking a curiously jubilant note for a losing litigant, wrote:

The practical result is that no clergyman will again be prosecuted in England for refusing to misrepresent the origin of the Book of Daniel and of the Psalms, for abstaining from distortion of Hebrew Prophecy, and from calumny of the Hebrew race. Hence literary misrepresentation is so far checked that although bishops will still make it a passport to their favour, they can no longer enforce it by law. Glory be to God ... My Master has done by me a work which will abide.[158]

While Lushington's decision was pending, Williams had preached a sermon on the text, from Psalm CXIX, 'Princes have persecuted me without a cause; but my heart standeth in awe of thy words'.

---

[156] F. E. Minetra and D. N. Lindley (eds), *Later Letters of John Stuart Mill 1849–1873* (Toronto, 1972), 786 (Letter 544, 21 July 1962, to H. Fawcett).

[157] E. Abbott and L. Campbell, *Life and Letters of Benjamin Jowett* (London, 1897), 301.

[158] Letter to the editor, *Daily News*, 28 June 1862, 3f. Similar sentiments are expressed in his *Life and Letters*, ii, 69 and 181.

Immediately after the judgment admitting the articles, Williams published this sermon, under the portentious title 'Persecution for the
Word', and added a postscript, dated 8 July 1862, on the judgment. In
it Williams rejoices in the freedom of biblical investigation conceded
as permissible, but, while emphasizing his respect for Lushington
personally, criticizes (he says from a moral not a legal point of view)
the conclusions adverse to the defence.[159] J. W. Colenso, the Bishop
of Natal, who was himself later prosecuted for denying the historical
accuracy of the Bible, welcomed Lushington's judgment, particularly
the passage quoted above on the Deacon's declaration, as removing an
intellectual difficulty.[160] Monsignor (later Cardinal) Manning
commented:

> I cannot omit to say that the judgment of the Court of Arches cleared the way
> for Dr Colenso. What Dr Lushington decided it was lawful to do, Dr Colenso
> did.[161]

Lushington was to play a part in the *Colenso* case, too, for Colenso
appealed to the Privy Council from his condemnation by a South
African ecclesiastical tribunal, and Lushington sat as a member of the
Judicial Committee that decided in Colenso's favour on jurisdictional
grounds.[162]

The general reaction to the judgment (that it was favourable to the
essayists) is borne out by that of Coleridge, counsel for the Bishop of
Salisbury, who was displeased:

> Dr Lushington's judgment given the other day has satisfied neither party, and
> strikes me as by far the most mischievous judgment any English ecclesiastical
> judge ever delivered, and I am vexed that the Bishop has acquiesced in it.[163]

The leading article in *The Times* of 27 June 1862 (after publication
of the judgment admitting the articles of charge, but before the
sentence) described the decision as reasonable, moderate, and liberal.
The writer added:

---

[159] Williams, *Persecution for the Word*.
[160] See P. B. Hinchliff, *John William Colenso* (London, 1964), 94–5.
[161] H. E. Manning, *The Crown in Council on the Essays and Reviews: a letter to an
Anglican friend* (1864), 19–20.
[162] 3 Moo PCNS 115.
[163] J. D. Coleridge to E. Yarnall, 28 July 1862, Coleridge, *Life and Correspondence*,
23. Coleridge had advised the Bishop to appeal against the aspects of the decision
favourable to Williams. Coleridge later referred to the judgment as an 'absurd
judgment'. J. D. Coleridge to his father, 16 Dec. 1862, ibid., 118.

Unless the Dean of Arches had declared, in defiance of their own distinct obligation, that the Articles of Religion were not binding on the clergy, we know not how he could have given a more favourable judgment.[164]

The writer made the point that, since there must be some limits to what clergymen could say while continuing to hold office, there must be some tribunal to judge when the limits were transgressed, and no fairer and more reasonable criteria could be devised than those set out by Lushington. The *Manchester Guardian* commented (after the sentence) that 'the enemies of free inquiry called upon the Court for its anathema, and the Court replied by pronouncing its blessing'.[165]

The more thoughtful comments, however, gave attention to the points decided against the essayists. Stanley said that the judgment was a document deserving of warm admiration and serious attention, but he qualified this praise by his immediately preceding words 'considering the great age and multifarious avocations of the judge' and, indeed, by the whole of the rest of his essay, which indicated his concurrence with the reversal of the judgment by the Privy Council.[166] Professor Grote's pamphlet has been several times referred to; though emphasizing, repeatedly, a personal respect for Lushington, the pamphlet was very critical, not so much of Lushington personally, as of the system that required him to judge such questions. 'Let me not be understood,' Grote wrote, 'as imputing any fault to the tribunal or the judge; the judge does but what he must do; it is the fault of the law.'[167] F. D. Maurice, the most distinguished and original theologian of his era, who had been himself driven from his Chair at King's College London[168] on the very issue of eternal punishment for which Wilson was condemned, was on the point of resigning his benefice in consequence of the judgment. He wrote, to Charles Kingsley,

I know well that my dear and honoured friend Dr Lushington, whom I love as much as almost any man of his age that I know, has no purpose of working this mischief or any mischief to the Church or to mankind. He will be a worker of good, as he ought to be, if his simple blunders lead to the result I have supposed. To provoke the result by any means I am sure is a clear duty.

[164] *The Times*, 27 June 1862. A contemporary novel reflects a similar view; see note 68 above.
[165] *Manchester Guardian*, 18 Dec. 1862, 2e.
[166] Stanley, *Essays*, 191.
[167] Grote, *Dr Lushington's Judgment*, 24.
[168] See A. R. Vidler, *The Church in an Age of Revolution* (London, 1961), 85–6.

[Maurice supposed that by resigning he would focus opposition and inspire action.][169]

Maurice was dissuaded from resigning by his bishop, Tait, who wrote to Maurice, on hearing of his decision after all not to resign, that 'the best members of the Church of England will thank God as I do for the result'.[170]

Tait later sat on the Privy Council and concurred in the reversal of Lushington's judgment (departing in this respect from the opinions of the two archbishops). Tait cannot have been oblivious to the knowledge that if the judgment were affirmed men like Maurice would be driven out of the Church.

Almost all those expressing criticism of the judgment went out of their way to indicate their personal respect for Lushington.[171] Generally his critics have taken at face value his own belief that he had only followed, as he was bound to, the course that the law set for him. A letter written twenty-six years later said that 'my dear friend Dr Lushington grieved that he was compelled by the words of the Athanasian Creed to condemn Mr Wilson'.[172] Perhaps now, a hundred years later still, the compulsion does not seem to have been quite so stringent.

This case, in which theology and law met, illustrates some of the unanswered questions that each must face. Professor Chadwick wrote that 'Lushington's judgment posed the problem of the modern Church in a stark form'.[173] The problem is how to reconcile the unchanging truths of religion with the changing perceptions of the world; in another aspect the problem is how to reconcile the Church's mission to propagate the truth with the freedom of inquiry demanded by academic theologians and by an intelligent laity; in yet another aspect it is how to enforce Church discipline in a way that is effective for the Church while being fair to the individual. All the questions raised, for the Church of England, the problems of a national Church. A religion for the whole nation is a difficult concept in an age of

[169] F. Maurice, *Life of Frederick Denison Maurice, chiefly told in his own letters* (1884; 4th edn London, 1885), ii, 427 (12 Oct. 1862).
[170] Ibid., 434 (30 Oct. 1862).
[171] An exception is H. B. Wilson who wrote: 'Throughout the whole of the judgment in the Court of Arches there ran a strong feeling of personal disapproval', *Westminster Review* (1870), 468. See Ellis, *Seven Against Christ,* 192.
[172] Robert Jenkins to Dean Farrar, 9 Oct. 1888, Farrar Papers, Box 8, f. 34, Canterbury Cathedral Library.
[173] Chadwick, *Victorian Church*, 82.

individualistic liberalism. The intertwining of ancient ecclesiastical and secular institutions added to the difficulties.

The questions for the law are scarcely easier. Lushington's reputation as a judge was unexcelled. He was held in very high regard even by those adversely affected by his decision. It cannot be doubted that he set out in good faith to achieve his object – construing and applying the plain meaning of words. An analysis of his judgment must lead us to ask why he failed. Is the object unattainable, or unattainable in respect of certain kinds of questions? If so can these be identified? Or is it that judges – even the best judges – have weak points? If so, can these be identified in advance? Or is it that none can escape the influence of deeply held opinions and beliefs?

Lushington's judgment was reversed by the Judicial Committee of the Privy Council, a body on which Lushington himself was an active member and where he had sat on almost 600 occasions (he sat on eleven days in the Privy Council while the judgment in *Essays and Reviews* was pending). Lushington did not sit on the panel hearing the appeal from his own decision, but the minutes of the Judicial Committee show that, in June 1863, he advised the Privy Council on a crucial procedural point that had arisen in the *Essays and Reviews* case in the course of argument. Wilson, attempting to argue his case in person, was met with a technical legal argument from the Queen's Advocate (Phillimore) to the effect that, by not appealing from Dr Lushington's interlocutory judgment, Wilson had lost his chance to argue the points that could have been raised then. This argument has some weight; the substance of it is the principle of finality: the question had been finally adjudicated between the parties. But acceptance of the argument would have resulted in a dismissal of the appeals at the outset, on a technicality, and would have astonished all who expected the Privy Council to deal with the matter. The Judicial Committee was evidently puzzled by the point, and applied to Lushington for his advice. Since the panel of the Judicial Committee included no ecclesiastical lawyer, and the Queen's Advocate was engaged as counsel for the promoters, Lushington was a natural source of advice. Nevertheless, the procedure manifests an informality that would be surprising in modern times. Lushington's opinion must have been dictated or written immediately, and is transcribed into the Minute Book of the Judicial Committee for the day the point was argued and decided, 19 June 1863. Lushington's opinion occupied a page and a half, and concluded that it would be unfair to Wilson to put him in a worse position than if he had not opposed the articles at the interlocutory stage.[174]

The Judicial Committee constituted for the appeal consisted of the Lord Chancellor (Baron Westbury), two former Chancellors (Lords Cranworth and Chelmsford), Lord Kingsdown, a longtime active member of the Committee,[175] and three members of the episcopal bench (the Bishop of London and the two Archbishops). As has been said, no civilian (i.e. ecclesiastical lawyer) was present. The Bishop of London joined with the majority in reversing Lushington on all points; the two Archbishops dissented on the question of scriptural inspiration.

The decision of the Privy Council adds some interesting dimensions to the legal questions just raised. Lushington said that he was compelled by the plain meaning of words to reach his conclusion, and almost all contemporary commentators implicitly accepted this view of his function. But the decision of the Privy Council shows that the question can hardly be characterized as a technical legal matter on which all judges were bound to agree. Lushington was reversed on the basis of argument by non-lawyers[176] and two points were actually abandoned by the promoters without argument. The only members of the Privy Council who agreed with Lushington (and then only on one question) were not lawyers but clerics. A commentator may say that Lushington was simply wrong in law. 'If I have erred [in defining and applying the proper principles],' he said in the *Heath* case, 'the judgment of a superior court will correct me.'[177] Perhaps this is what happened in *Essays and Reviews* but it hardly seems a full explanation to say that the Privy Council was compelled by logic to its conclusion, though those who favour the result may tend to see it so, as, for example, did Jowett's biographer.[178] An alternative is the explanation that Lushington was right, and was mistakenly reversed by less expert non-civilian judges. But is the difficulty perhaps not so much in determining which was the legally right answer as in determining what is meant by right and wrong answers in this context? The

---

[174] Minute Book, Privy Council Office. See also 2 Moo PCNS 375.
[175] See Howell, *Judicial Committee*, appendix.
[176] Wilson's speech was published: *Speech of H. B. Wilson before the Judicial Committee*, 1863.
[177] *Burder* v. *Heath* 15 Moo PC 65.
[178] G. C. Faber, *Jowett* (London, 1957), 274.

Privy Council decision has often received implicit praise from those
writing from a liberal perspective. The judges supported the principles of free speech and free inquiry, and stood against the establishment, and against overwhelming public opinion,[179] in order to
vindicate the rights of the two persecuted clergymen. Most modern
readers will tend towards this view, and this may be because they are
themselves disengaged from the controversy. Even those who might
lean towards a Biblical fundamentalism are hardly likely to favour
enforcement of that doctrine in modern times by tribunals constituted
as were the ecclesiastical courts of Victorian England. But it is salutary
to recall that the contemporary reaction to Lushington's judgment
was that it was fair, just, moderate, and reasonable, and to the Privy
Council's that it was narrow, technical, legalistic, and subversive of
the interests of the community. Gladstone, then Chancellor of the
Exchequer, wrote to Tait that 'the spirit of the judgment [of the Privy
Council] establishes a complete indifference between the Christian
faith and the denial of it'.[180] Thus Tait, who had been severely
censured by his broad-church friends for joining in the earlier episcopal condemnation of the book,[181] now incurred the censure of the rest
of the Church. The vote of thanks to the two archbishops, with its
137,000 signatures, and the declaration signed by 11,000 clergy,
were, in effect, votes of censure upon Tait.[182]

For one who is interested in Lushington as an individual, other
questions are posed by *Essays and Reviews*. Lushington was a liberal
in politics, a supporter of extensive social and political reform, and a
leader in the anti-slavery movement. He had vigorously supported the
rights of Dissenters, Catholics, and Jews to follow their consciences in
matters of religion. How did he come to deny the same freedom to
clergymen of his own Church? Stephen, in his argument for Williams,
appealed expressly to Lushington's liberal principles:

[179] In his defence of Williams, Stephen said: 'In the present case, I fear that by an
inversion of English sympathies hardly ever witnessed before, public feeling is
against the accused,' *Defence of the Rev. Rowland Williams*, 330.
[180] D. C. Lathbury, *Correspondence on Church and Religion of W. E. Gladstone* (New
York, 1910), 83 (26 April 1864).
[181] Tait was criticized by Stanley, Jowett, and Temple, see Vidler, *Church in an Age of
Revolution*, 127, D. L. Edwards, *Leaders of the Church of England 1828–1944*
(London, 1971), 110–11.
[182] Tait's notes on the declaration show that he calculated the number of clergy who
had not signed it (13,899; 10,906 had signed). Tait Papers, LPL, 291/325.

Photograph of Lushington with his family on the lawn at Ockham, c. 1870.

My Lord, it is with all the greater confidence that I look up to you, for I am quite sure that if your Lordship could be warped at all from the straight line, it would not be in the tyrannical direction.[183]

Can it be the same Lushington, who always held that punishment should be restricted to the minimum necessary, who went out of his way to inflict a greater punishment on these two clergymen than was sought by the promoter? Is it that Lushington changed with age? Or did he act out of character? Or did this case reveal an aspect of his true character that formerly lay concealed? Or is it that we have so far lost Lushington's perspective on the Church that we cannot perceive that, within that perspective, he did adhere to his principles?

Lushington continued as Dean of the Arches for another five years, though no case comparable to *Essays and Reviews* troubled his court in that time. He lived on in retirement for another five years, and met his death as the result of bronchitis contracted in consequence of making a journey from his home at Ockham in Surrey to Oxford, in December, 1872, in order to cast his vote for A. P. Stanley as Select Preacher for Oxford University.[184] Stanley was Dean of Westminster and had incurred hostility on account of the liberal theological views he had expressed in that office and in particular for views expressed in February 1872 on the Athanasian creed and eternal punishment, the point on which Wilson was condemned by Lushington.[185] Stanley's name was put forward and approved by the Vice-Chancellor for the office of Select Preacher, but his opponents forced a debate (a most unusual procedure) in Convocation, a body in which all MAs, resident and non-resident, were entitled to vote. Stanley's principal opponent described him as:

The advocate of the Westminster Abbey's sacrilegious communion; the patron of Mr Vance Smith the unitarian teacher; partisan of Mr Voysey the infidel; the avowed champion of a negative and cloudy Christianity, which is really preparing the way for the rejection of all revealed truth.[186]

The election was thus a test – though not a crucial test – of the strength

[183] Stephen, *Defence of the Rev. Rowland Williams*, 331.
[184] See *The Times*, 12 Dec. 1872, 9b, f, 21 Jan. 1873, 9 f. *Surrey Advertiser*, 25 Jan. 1873.
[185] Prothero, *Life of Stanley*, 222–5.
[186] Ibid., at 266. The committee appointed to revise the Authorized Version of the Bible included a Unitarian scholar, Dr Vance Smith, who in 1870 received communion with the other members of the committee in Westminster Abbey at Stanley's invitation. The hostile reaction was intense. Voysey was a clergyman who was prosecuted for heresy in 1869. Stanley subscribed for his defence, and explained his motives in a letter to *The Times*. See Prothero, *Life of Stanley*, 216–25, 375.

of liberal theology. Lushington's vote was one of the 349 that formed a majority in favour of Stanley (287 votes were opposed). Lushington returned to Ockham on the same day, fell ill, and died four weeks later.

A brief account of Lushington's life published in 1894 suggests that he can be said to have died a martyr to the cause of religious toleration.[187] At first sight it seems extravagant to attribute the death of a man in his ninety-second year to martyrdom to any cause. But on second thoughts, the journey to and from Oxford on 11 December does suggest some sort of gesture, and it was so perceived at the time:[188] the total travelling time cannot have been less than seven hours. And all this was to cast a vote for an honorary post: Stanley's livelihood was not at stake. If Lushington's journey was a gesture, it was reciprocated, for Stanley travelled from London to Ockham to officiate at Lushington's funeral on 20 January 1873.[189] I have found no record of the sermon, if one was preached on that occasion, but two weeks later, preaching at the University Church in Cambridge, Stanley paid handsome tribute to Lushington in words recalling his earlier prominence as a reformer and anti-slavery campaigner, describing him as:

the venerable judge whose career . . . was fired from first to last by a generous sympathy with human suffering, by noble indignation against wrong, by a firm persuasion of the indissoluble bond between what was highest in religion and what was greatest in morality.[190]

There is, in this comment, an apt reminder that Lushington's ecclesiastical decisions cannot be judged only from a legal perspective, for they represented his view of the place and shape, in his society, of religion, which in turn was an integral aspect of the social and political reform that distinguished his early career.

[187] *Law Times*, 10 Feb. 1894, 335. A letter to Vernon Lushington written on Dr Lushington's death by Lord Justice James (20 Jan. 1873, Lushington Family Papers) struck a similar note: 'Your father's last public act may have accelerated his death – but it will always be an agreeable memory for his family and his friends that it was an act of great public duty, well closing his life in vindication of those great principles of liberty to which throughout that long life he had shown so zealous and unswerving an attachment.'

[188] A letter, dated 14 Dec. 1872, congratulates Lushington on having 'summoned courage to go and fight those miserable bigots at Oxford', W. Rothery (the Admiralty Registrar) to Lushington, Lushington Family Papers.

[189] Prothero, *Life of Stanley*, 415.

[190] A. P. Stanley, *Purity and Light. A sermon preached before the University of Cambridge, Feb 2, 1873* (London, 1873). This passage is also reported (with slight variations) in *Surrey Advertiser*, 1 Feb. 1873.

APPENDIX

Ecclesiastical Courts Commission, 1831–2. Commission appointed to inquire into the Practice and Jurisdiction of the Ecclesiastical Courts in England and Wales.

Church Building Commission, 1831–45. Commission appointed by virtue of an Act of Parliament, passed in the fifty-eighth year of the Reign of His Majesty King George III, c. 45 intitled 'An Act for Building and Promoting the Building of Additional Churches in Populous Parishes'.

Ecclesiastical Revenue Commission, 1832–5. Commission to inquire into the Revenues and Patronage of the Established Church in England and Wales.

Ecclesiastical Commission, 1841–67 (*ex officio* as Admiralty Court Judge).

Anglo-French Commission on the Slave Trade, 1845.

Law of Marriage Commission, 1847–50. Commission on the State and Operation of the Law of Marriage as relating to the Prohibited Degrees of Affinity, and to Marriage Solemnized Abroad, or in the British Colonies.

Canada-New Brunswick Boundary Commission, 1851. Commission appointed by Her Majesty to Investigate and Report upon the Respective Claims of Canada and New Brunswick to the Territory Ceded to Great Britain by the Treaty of Washington.

Divorce Commission, 1852–3. Commission Appointed by Her Majesty to Enquire into the Law of Divorce, and more Particularly into the Mode of Obtaining Divorces *a vinculo matrimonii*.

Commission appointed to inquire into the State of the Several Dioceses of Canterbury, London, Winchester and Rochester 1857–8.

PARLIAMENTARY COMMITTEES OF WHICH LUSHINGTON
WAS A MEMBER

Select Committee on Admiralty Courts, 1833. Select Committee appointed
to inquire into the Office and Duties, the Appointment, Salary and Emoluments of the Judges of the Prerogative Court, and of the High Court of
Admiralty, of the Dean of Arches, and of the Judge of the Consistory Court of
London.

Select Committee on Prisons, 1822. Select Committee appointed to consider
the Laws Relating to Prisons.

Select Committee on Crime, 1827. Select Committee appointed to inquire
into the cause of the Increase in the number of Criminal Commitments and
Convictions in England and Wales.

Slavery Committee, 1832. Select Committee appointed to consider and
report upon the measures which it may be expedient to adopt for the purpose
of effecting the extinction of slavery throughout the British Dominions, at the
earliest period compatible with the safety of all classes in the colonies, and in
conformity with the Resolutions of this House on 15th May, 1823.

BIBLIOGRAPHY

MANUSCRIPT SOURCES

Aberdeen Papers, British Library
Admiralty Court Records, Public Record Office, London
All Souls College Archives, All Souls College and Bodleian Library, Oxford
Anti-Slavery Papers, Rhodes House Library, Oxford
Bedford Journal, Friends' House Library, London
Blomfield Papers, Lambeth Palace Library, London
Brougham Papers, University College, London
Buxton Papers, Rhodes House Library, Oxford
Clarendon Papers, Bodleian Library, Oxford
Consistory Court Cause Papers, Greater London Record Office, and Guild-
    hall Library, London
Earl Grey Papers, University of Durham
Ecclesiastical Court Commission Minute Book, Office of Church Com-
    missioners, London
Glynne-Gladstone Papers, Clwyd Record Office, Hawarden
Granville Papers, Public Record Office, London
Gurney Papers, Friends' House Library, London
Hobhouse Diary, Berg Collection, New York Public Library
Hobhouse Diary, British Library, London
Houghton Papers, Trinity College Library, Cambridge
India Office Records, London
Judicial Committee Minutes, Privy Council Office, London
Liverpool Papers, British Library, London
Lovelace-Byron Papers, Bodleian Library, Oxford
Lushington Family Papers, in private ownership. The collection includes 133
    letters from Lushington, mainly to his family, and 52 letters to Lushington
Records of Doctors' Commons, Lambeth Palace Library, and Public Record
    Office, London
Records of High Court of Delegates, Public Record Office, London
Tait Papers, Lambeth Palace Library, London

Abbott, E., and Campbell, L., *Life and Letters of Benjamin Jowett*, London, John Murray, 1897

Ackermann, R., *Microcosm of London, or, London in Miniature*, 3 vols, London, R. Ackermann, 1908–11

Adams, E. D., *Great Britain and the American Civil War*, London, Longman, Green, 1925

Addleshaw, G. W. O., and F. Etchells, *The Architectural Setting of Anglican Worship*, London, Faber and Faber, 1948

Adolphus, J. (ed.), *A Correct, Full, and Impartial Report of the Trial of Her Majesty Caroline, Queen Consort of Great Britain, Before the House of Peers on the Bill of Pains and Penalties*, London, Jones, 1820

African Institution, Nineteenth Report of Directors, 1825, Anti-Slavery Society Office

Alumni Oxonienses: the Members of the University of Oxford, 1715–1886, 4 vols, Oxford, Parker, 1888

Anderson, O., *A Liberal State at War*, London, Macmillan, 1967
'The Wensleydale Peerage Case and the position of the House of Lords in the mid-nineteenth century', *English Historical Review* 82 (1967), 486–502

Anderson, S., 'Legislative Divorce: law for the aristocracy?' *Law, Economy and Society, 1750–1914: Essays in the History of English Law*, edited by D. Sugarman and G. Rubin, Abingdon (Oxon), 1984

Anstey, R., '"Capitalism and Slavery"; a Critique', *Economic History Review* 21 (1968), 307
'The Pattern of British Abolitionism', *Anti-Slavery, Religion and Reform*, edited by C. Bolt, Folkestone (England), W. Dawson, 1980

Arnould, J., *Memoirs of Thomas, first Lord Denman formerly Lord Chief Justice of England*, London, Longman Green, 1873

Aspinall, A. (ed.), *Letters, 1812–1830* by George IV, King of Great Britain, Cambridge, Cambridge University Press, 1938

Atlay, J. B., *The Victorian Chancellors ... with Portraits*, 2 vols, London, Smith, Elder & Co., 1908

Ayliffe, J., *Parergon Juris Canonici Anglicani*, 2nd edn, London, Printed for Thomas Osborne, 1726

Badeley, E., *Substance of a Speech Delivered before the Judicial Committee of the Privy Council on Monday the 17th and Tuesday the 18th of December, A. D. 1849, Upon an Appeal in a Cause of Duplex Querela Between the Rev. George Cornelius Gorham, Clerk, Appellant and the Right Rev. Henry Lord Bishop of Exeter, Respondent, with an Introduction*, London, John Murray, 1850

Baines, R., *Letter to Sir John Campbell on the Law of Church Rates*, London, 1837

Brougham, H., *Life and Times of Henry, Lord Brougham*, 3 vols, London, W. Blackwood & Sons, 1871

Speeches, Upon Questions Relating to Public Rights, Duties, and Interests, Edinburgh, Adam, 1838

Broughton, Lord (John Cam Hobhouse), *Recollections of a Long Life*, edited by Lady Dorchester, 4 vols, London, John Murray, 1909–10

Brown, F. K., *Fathers of the Victorians: the Age of Wilberforce*, Cambridge, Cambridge University Press, 1961

Buckingham & Chandos, Duke of, *Memoirs of the Court of George IV 1820–30*, London, Hurst and Blacknett, 1859

Burke, *Peerage and Baronetage*, 105th edn, 1970

Burn, R., *Ecclesiastical Law*, 4 vols, 2nd edn, London, A. Millar, 1767

Burnett, T. A. J., *The Rise and Fall of a Regency Dandy: the Life and Times of Scrope Berdmore Davies*, London, John Murray, 1981

Buxton, C. (ed.), *Memoirs of Sir Thomas Fowell Buxton*, 3rd edn, London, H. Longstreth, 1849

Campbell, G., *Memoirs of my Indian Career*, London, Macmillan, 1893

Campbell, J., *A Letter to the Right Hon. Lord Stanley on the Law of Church Rates*, 2nd edn, London, J. Ridgway & Sons, 1837

Carlton, W. J., *Charles Dickens, Shorthand Writer*, London, Cecil Palmer, 1926

The Case of Dr Hampden . . ., London, Bell, 1848

Chadwick, O., *The Mind of the Oxford Movement*, London, A. & C. Black, 1960

The Victorian Church, 2 vols, London, A. & C. Black, 1966–70, 3rd edn 1971

Chamberlin, D., *Smith of Demerara*, London, Livingstone Press, 1924

Church, R. W., *The Oxford Movement: Twelve Years, 1833–1845*, London, Macmillan, 1891

Cobbett, J. M., and Cobbett, J. P. (eds), *Selections from Cobbett's Political Works*, 6 vols, London, Ann Cobbett, 1835

Cockshut, A. O. J., *Anthony Trollope: A Critical Study*, New York, New York University Press, 1955

Religious Controversies of the Nineteenth Century: Selected Documents, London, Methuen, 1966

Cole, G. D. H., *The Life of William Cobbett*, London, W. Collins, 1927

Coleridge, E. H. (ed.), *Life and Correspondence of J. D. Coleridge Lord Chief Justice of England*, London, W. Heinemann, 1904

Colvin, C. (ed.), *Maria Edgeworth: Letters from England, 1813–1844*, Oxford, Clarendon Press, 1971

Cook, E., *Delane of The Times*, London, Constable, 1916

Coote, H. C., *The Practice of the Ecclesiastical Courts, with forms and tables of costs*, London, Butterworth, 1847

A Crisis in the Church! Bath, S. Hayward, 1856

Cruise, W., *A Treatise on the Origin and Nature of Dignities etc.*, 2nd edn, London, Joseph Butterworth & Son, 1823

Dasent, A. I., *John Thadeus Delane, editor of 'The Times': his life and correspondence*, New York, Scribner, 1908

Davidson, R. T., and Benham, W., *Life of Archibald Campbell Tait, Archbishop of Canterbury*, London, Macmillan, 1891

Deacon, E. E., *Another Letter to the Rt Hon Lord Stanley M.P. on the Law of Church Rates*, London, J. Hatchard & Son, 1837

De Burgh-Edwardes, S. B., *The History of Mauritius (1507–1914)*, London, East and West, 1921

Decisions in the High Court of Admiralty during the time of Hay and Marriott, 1776–1779, London, 1801

Denison, G. A., *Notes of My Life, 1805–1878*, London, James Parker & Co., 1878

Dickens, C., *The Personal History and Experience of David Copperfield*, London, Bradbury and Evans, 1850
   Sketches by Boz, London, John Macrone, 1836

Disraeli, B., ed. W. Hutcheson, *Whigs and Whiggism*, London, John Murray, 1913

Dr. Lushington's Judgment in the Case of Westerton v. Liddell upon Ornaments of the Church Considered by a Parish Priest who has not in Use the Articles Complained of, London, 1855

Dod, C. R., *Electoral Facts, 1832–1853*, London, Whittaker, 1853
   Parliamentary Companion, London, Whittaker, 1833–1840

Duncan, G. I. O., *The High Court of Delegates*, Cambridge, Cambridge University Press, 1971

Edwards, D. L., *Leaders of the Church of England 1828–1944*, London and New York, Oxford University Press, 1971

Ellens, J. P., 'Lord John Russell and the Church Rate Conflict: the struggle for a Broad Church, 1834–1868', *Journal of British Studies* 26 (1987), 232–57

[Ellis, G. J. W. Agar], *A few observations on All Souls College Oxford*, 1819

Ellis, I., *Seven Against Christ: a Study of 'Essays and Reviews'*, Leiden, E. J. Brill, 1980

Ellis, Sarah, *The Wives of England: Their Relative Duties, Domestic Influences and Social Obligations*, London, Fisher Son & Co., 1843

Eltis, D., 'Dr Stephen Lushington and the Campaign to Abolish Slavery in the British Empire', *Journal of Caribbean History* 1 (1970), 41–56

Elwin, M., *Lord Byron's Family: Annabella, Ada and Augusta, 1816–1824*, London, John Murray, 1975
   Lord Byron's Wife, London, Macmillan, 1962

Endelman, T. D., *The Jews of Georgian England, 1714–1830: Tradition and Change in a Liberal Society*, Philadelphia, Jewish Publication Society of America, 1979

Essays and Reviews, London, John Parker, 1860

Eversley, W. P., *The Law of Domestic Relations*, London, Stevens & Haynes, 1885

Faber, G. C., *Jowett. A Portrait with Background*, London, Faber & Faber, 1957

Ferris, N. B., *The Trent Affair: A Diplomatic Crisis*, Knoxville, University of Tennessee Press, 1977

Fitzmaurice, E., *Life of Granville George Leveson Gower, Second Earl Granville K G 1815–1891*, London, Longman, Green, 1905

Forster, J., *Life of Charles Dickens*, London, Palmer, 1928

Fox, J. C., *The Byron Mystery*, London, G. Richards, 1924

Fulford, R., *Trial of Queen Caroline*, New York, Batsford, 1967

Gash, N., *Mr Secretary Peel: the Life of Sir Robert Peel to 1830*, London, Longman, 1961

   Reaction and Reconstruction in English Politics 1832–52, Oxford, Clarendon Press, 1956

   Sir Robert Peel: the Life of Sir Robert Peel after 1830, London, Longmans, 1972; 2nd edn 1986

Gaunt, W., *The Pre-Raphaelite Tragedy*, rev. edn, London, Cape, 1975

George, M. D., *Catalogue of Political and Personal Satires ...* London, British Museum, Department of Prints and Drawings, 1952

Georgian Era: Memoirs of the Most Eminent Persons ..., London, Vizetelly, Branston, 1832–4

Goff, R., and Jones, G. H. *The Law of Restitution*, 3rd edn, London, Sweet and Maxwell, 1986

[Grant, J.], *Random Recollections of the House of Commons*, London, Smith Elder, 1836

Greenwod, A., *Lives of the Hanoverian Queens of England*, London, G. Bell, 1911

Grote, J., *An examination of some portions of Dr Lushington's judgment on the admission of the Articles in the cases of the Bishop of Salisbury v. Williams, and Fendall v. Wilson, with remarks upon the bearing of them on the clergy*, Cambridge, Deighton, Bell & Co., 1862

Grueber, C. S., *A Letter to the Rt Hon. Stephen Lushington*, London, 1856

Gunn, P., *My Dearest Augusta: A Biography of the Honourable Augusta Leigh, Lord Byron's Half-Sister*, London, Bodley Head, 1968

Hale, W., *The Antiquity of the Church Rates System considered*, London, 1837

Halevy, E., *History of the English People in the Nineteenth Century*, 6 vols, 2nd edn, London, E. Benn, 1949–52

Hall, W. E., *A Treatise on International Law*, 2nd edn, Oxford, Clarendon Press, 1884

Hare, A. J. C. (ed.), *The Life and Letters of Maria Edgeworth*, London, E. Arnold, 1894

Harris, T. L., *The Trent Affair*, Indianapolis, Bowen-Merrill & Co., 1896

Harrison, F., 'Neo-Christianity', *Westminster Review* 74 (1860), 293

Heath, D. I., *A defence of my professional character*, London, Tallant, 1862

Helmholtz, R. H., *Select Cases on Defamation to 1600*, London, Selden Society, 1985

Henriques, U., *Religious Toleration in England 1787–1833*, Toronto, University of Toronto Press, 1961

Henry, Lord Bishop of Exeter, *Letter to the Rt Hon. Dr. Lushington in his judgment in the case of Westerton v. Liddell (clerk)*, 1855

Herbert, A. P., *Holy Deadlock*, Garden City, N.Y., Doubleday, 1934

Hibbert, C., *George IV: Regent and King, 1811–1830*, London, Allen Lane, 1973

Hinchliff, P. B., *John William Colenso*, London, Thomas Nelson, 1964

Holcombe, L., *Wives and Property: Reform of the Married Women's Property Law in Nineteenth-Century England*, Toronto, University of Toronto Press, 1983

Holdsworth, W. S., *History of English Law*, 16 vols, London, Methuen, 1909–66
  Some Makers of English Law, Cambridge, Cambridge University Press, 1938

Houston, J. C. C., *Cases in the Arches 1858–67*, Lambeth Palace Library

Howell, P. A., *The Judicial Committee of the Privy Council 1833–1876*, Cambridge, Cambridge University Press, 1979

Huish, R., *Memoirs of Her Late Majesty Caroline, Queen of Great Britain*, London, T. Kelly, 1821

Hunt, W. H., *Pre-Raphaelitism and the Pre-Raphaelite Brotherhood*, 2 vols, London, Macmillan, 1905

Jarman, T., *A Treatise on Wills*, 8th edn, London, Sweet and Maxwell, 1951

Jay, E., *The Religion of the Heart: Anglican Evangelicalism and the Nineteenth-Century Novel*, Oxford, Clarendon Press, 1979

Jebb, R., *A Report of the case of the Right Rev. R. D. Hampden D. D., Lord Bishop Elect of Hereford, in Hereford Cathedral, the Ecclesiastical Courts and the Queen's Bench*, London, Benning, 1849

Johnson, J. F., *Proceedings of the General Anti-slavery Convention, 1843*, London, 1843

Jones, E., *Law of Salvage*, London, Stevens and Haynes, 1870

Jones, Sir William, *Works*, London, 1799

Judgment . . . in the case of the Bishop of Salisbury versus Williams and in the case of Fendall versus Wilson, London, Butterworths, 1862

Klingberg, F. J., *The Anti-Slavery Movement in England: A Study of English Humanitarianism*, New Haven, Yale University Press, 1926

Knight, G. W., *Byron and Shakespeare*, London, Routledge and Kegan Paul, 1966

Lord Byron's Marriage: the evidence of the asterisks, London, Routledge and Kegan Paul, 1957

Kriegel, A. D. (ed.), *The Holland House Diaries*, London, Routledge and Kegan Paul, 1977

Lady Byron and the Leighs, London, privately printed, 1887

Laqueur, T. W., 'The Queen Caroline Affair: Politics as Art in the Reign of George IV', *Journal of Modern History* 54 (1982), 417–66

Lathbury, D. C., *Correspondence on Church and Religion of W. E. Gladstone*, New York, Macmillan, 1910

Laughton, J. K., *Memoirs of the Life and Correspondence of Henry Reeve*, London, Longman, 1898

Lean, E. T., *The Napoleonists: a Study in Political Disaffection, 1760–1960*, London, Oxford University Press, 1970

Liddell, R., *A Letter to the Lord Bishop of London on Confession and Absolution with Special Reference to the Case of the Rev. Alfred Poole*, London, 1858

Liddon, H. P., *Life of Edward Bouverie Pusey*, 4 vols 4th edn, London, Longman, 1894–8

Lindsay, J., *Charles Dickens, a Biographical and Critical Study*, London, Dakers, 1950

Longford, E. H. P., *Byron*, London, Hutchinson, 1976

Lushington, S., *The Foundation Stone: a Hymn*, Newcastle, privately printed, 1850

Lyall, W. R., *A Charge delivered to the Clergy of the Archdeaconry of Maidstone, in May 1842; Containing Some Remarks on the Judgment Pronounced by Dr Lushington in the Consistory Court of London, May 6, 1842*, London, 1842

Machin, G. I. T., *Politics and the Churches in Great Britain 1832–1868*, Oxford, Clarendon Press, 1977

McCalmon, I., 'Unrespectable Radicalism: Infidels and Pornography in early Nineteenth-Century London', *Past and Present* 104 (1984), 74–110

MacCoby, S., *English Radicalism, 1736–1832*, 6 vols, London, Allen and Unwin, 1935–61; vol 1, 1955

McGowan, R., 'The Image of Justice and Reform of the Criminal Law in Early Nineteenth-Century England', *Buffalo Law Review* 32 (1983), 89

McGregor, O. R., *Divorce in England: a Centenary Study*, London, Heinemann, 1957

McGuffie, K. C. (ed.), *Kennedy's Civil Salvage*, 4th edn, London, Stevens, 1958

MacNair, A. D., *International Law Opinions*, 3 vols, Cambridge, Cambridge University Press, 1956

Malleson, G. B., *History of the Indian Mutiny 1857–1858 . . .*, 3 vols, London, Allen, 1878–88

Manchester, A. H., 'The Reform of the Ecclesiastical Courts', *American Journal of Legal History* 10 (1966), 51

Manning, H. E., *The Crown in Council on the Essays and Reviews: a letter to an Anglican friend*, London, 1864

Manning, J., *Letter to Earl Fitzwilliam upon the Power of Compelling the Assessment of Church Rate etc*, London, James Ridgway & Sons, 1837

Marchand, L. A., *Byron: a Biography*, New York, Knopf, 1957
   Byron: a Portrait, London, John Murray, 1971
   Byron's Letters and Journals: the complete and unexpurgated text of all the letters available, 12 vols, London, 1973–82

Matthew, H. C. G. (ed.), *Gladstone Diaries*, Oxford, 1978

Mathieson, W. L., *British Slavery and its Abolition, 1823–1839*, London, Longman, Green, 1926
   British Slave Emancipation, 1839–1849, London, Longman, 1932
   English Church Reform 1815–1840, London, Longman, Green, 1923
   Great Britain and the Slave Trade, 1839–1865, London, Longman, Green, 1929

Maurice F. D., *The Life of Frederick Denison Maurice, chiefly told in his own letters*, 2 vols, London, Macmillan, 1984; 4th edn, 1885
   Letter . . . on the attempt to defeat the Nomination of Dr. Hampden, London, 1847
   'Dr. Lushington, Mr. Heath, and the Thirty-nine Articles', *Macmillan's Magazine* 5 (1861), 153–6.

Maxwell, F. H., *The Creevey Papers: a Selection from the Correspondence and Diaries of Thomas Creevey*, 3rd edn, London, Murray, 1905

Maxwell, H., *Life and Letters of the Earl of Clarendon*, London, Arnold, 1913

May, T. E., *Constitutional History of England since the Accession of George III, 1760–1860*, 2 vols, London, 1861

Megarry, R. E., 'Lay Peers in Appeals to the House of Lords', *Law Quarterly Review* 65 (1949), 22

Melville, L., *An Injured Queen: Caroline of Brunswick*, 2 vols, London, Hutchinson & Co., 1912

Milbanke, R. G. N., Earl of Lovelace, *Astarte: a Fragment of truth Concerning Lord Byron*, London, Chiswick Press, 1905
   Lady Noel Byron and the Leighs, London, W. Clowes & Son, 1887

Mill, J., *The History of British India*, 7 vols, 4th edn, London, Madden, 1840–5

Minetra, F. E., and Lindley, D. N. (eds.), *Later Letters of John Stuart Mill 1849–1873*, Toronto, 1972

Moore, D. L., *Ada, Countess of Lovelace: Byron's Legitimate Daughter*, London, John Murray, 1977
The Late Lord Byron: Posthumous Dramas, London, John Murray, 1961
Lord Byron: Accounts Rendered, London, John Murray, 1974

Moore, E. F., *The Case of the Rev. G. C. Gorham against the Bishop of Exeter*, London, 1852

Moore, J. B., *A Digest of International Law*, 8 vols, Washington DC, US Government Printing Office, 1906

Moore, T., *Letters and Journals of Lord Byron, with notices of his life*, 2 vols, London, John Murray, 1831

Muscott, E., *The History and Power of Ecclesiastical Courts*, London, 1846

New, C., *Life of Henry Brougham to 1830*, Oxford, Clarendon Press, 1961

Nias, S. C. S., *Gorham and the Bishop of Exeter*, London, SPCK, 1951

Nicholl, J., *Church Rates. Observations on the Attorney General's letter to Lord Stanley*, London, 1837

Nicolas, H., *A Letter on the propriety and legality of creating Peers for life*, 3rd edn, London, 1834

Nightingale, J. (ed.), *Memoirs of the Public and Private Life of Queen Caroline*, London, J. Robins & Co., 1820; edited by C. Hibbert and reprinted, London, Folio Society, 1978

Northcott, W. C., *Slavery's Martyr: John Smith of Demerara and the Emancipation Movement, 1817–24*, London, Epworth Press, 1976

Oliphant, M., *The Perpetual Curate*, 1864, reprinted, New York and London, Garland Publishing, 1975

Oppenheim, L. F. L., *International Law*, 2 vols, 5th edn edited by Lauterpacht, London, Longman & Co., 1935

Paley, W., *The Principles of Moral and Political Philosophy*, London, R. Faulder, 1785

Parry, E. A., *Queen Caroline*, London, Ernest Benn, 1930

Paston, G. E., and Quennell, P., *To Lord Byron*, London, John Murray, 1939

Patterson, M. W., *Sir Francis Burdett and his Times, 1770–1844*, London, Macmillan, 1931

Peacock, T. L., *Crotchet Castle*, London, T. Hookham, 1831

Pearce, W., *Letter to the Right Rev. the Lord Bishop of Exeter in reference to his Lordship's Letter to Dr. Lushington on his Judgment in the case of Westerton v. Liddell*, 1856

Percival, J., *The Society for the Diffusion of Useful Knowledge, 1826–1848: Handlist of Correspondence and Papers*, London, University College, 1978

Perkin, J., *Women and Marriage in Nineteenth-Century England*, London, Routledge, 1988

Perry, T. W., *Lawful Church Ornaments*, London, 1857

Phillimore, R., *Ecclesiastical Law of the Church of England*, 2 vols, London, 1873–6

Commentaries upon International Law, 4 vols, 3rd edn, London, Butterworth, 1879–89

Thoughts on the Law of Divorce in England, London, Sweet, 1844

Phillips, R., *Putting Asunder: A History of Divorce in Western Society*, Cambridge and New York, Cambridge University Press, 1988

Phillpotts, Henry, Lord Bishop of Exeter, *Letter to the Right Hon Dr Lushington on his Judgment in the Case of Westerton v. Liddell (clerk)*, London, 1856

Pinney, T. (ed.), *Letters of T. B. Macaulay*, Cambridge, Cambridge University Press, 1974

Pollock, F., *The Law of Torts*, London, Stevens & Sons, 1887

Pool, V. (ed.), *The Croker Papers, 1808–1857*, London, 1884; new edition, London, Batsford, 1967

Port, M. H., *Six Hundred New Churches; a study of the Church Building Commission, 1819–1856...*, London, 1961

The Priest in Absolution, London, 1866

Proceedings against the Archdeacon of Taunton..., Bath, Hayward & Payne, London, Joseph Masters, 1857

Proceedings of the General Anti-slavery Convention ... held in ... 1840, London, 1841

Prothero, R. E., *Letters and Journals of Lord Byron*, 6 vols, London, Murray, 1898–1901

The Life and Correspondence of Arthur Penrhyn Stanley DD, late Dean of Westminster, 2 vols, London, Murray, 1893

Pugh, P. M., *Calendar of the Papers of Sir Thomas Fowell Buxton*, London, List and Index Society, 1980

Pugin, A. W. N., *The True Principles of Pointed or Christian Architecture*, 1841; reprinted London, Academy Editions, 1973

Radzinowicz, L., *A History of English Criminal Law and its Administration from 1750*, 5 vols, London, Stevens, 1948–

The Reply of Dr Lushington in support of the Bill for the Better Regulation of Chimney Sweepers ... 20th April..., London, 1818

Report of the Committee of the Society for the Mitigation and Gradual Abolition of Slavery, etc., read at the General Meeting of the Society..., 1824

Report of the Proceedings in the House of Lords on the Bill of Pains and Penalties against the Queen, Edinburgh, 1820

Report on the Manuscripts of Earl Bathurst, London, HMSO, 1923

Ridley, J. G., *Lord Palmerston*, London, Constable, 1970

Robson, J. M. (ed.), *Collected Works of J. S. Mill*, 27 vols, Toronto, University of Toronto Press, 1963–

Roper, R. S. D., *Treatise of the Law of Property arising from the Relation between Husband and Wife*, new edn by Jacob, London, 1841

Rose, G., *The Struggle for Penal Reform: The Howard League and its predecessors*, London, Stevens, 1961

Roth, C., *A History of the Jews in England*, 3rd edn, Oxford, Clarendon Press, 1964

Rowell, G., *Hell and the Victorians: a Study of the Nineteenth-Century Theological Controversies Concerning Eternal Punishment and Future Life*, Oxford, Clarendon Press, 1974

Russell, J. (ed.), *Memoirs, Journals, and Correspondence of Thomas Moore*, 8 vols, London, Longman, 1853–6

Sharpe, R. J., *Injunctions and Specific Performance*, Toronto, Canada Law Book, 1983

Shelford, L., *A Practical Treatise on the Law of Marriage and Divorce etc.*, London, 1841

Skinner, J., *A Plea for the Threatened Ritual of the Church of England*, London, 1865

Smith, H., *The Society for the Diffusion of Useful Knowledge, 1826–1846*, London and Halifax, Nova Scotia, Dalhousie University School of Library Science, 1974

Society for the Diffusion of Useful Knowledge, *Discourse of the Objects, Advantages and Pleasures of Science*, London, Baldwin, Cradock and Joy, 1827

Speech of Dr. Lushington, delivered at a General Meeting of the Society for the Abolition of Slavery throughout the British Dominions etc., 1831

Speech of Dr Lushington in support of the Bill for the better regulation of chimney sweepers and their apprentices and for preventing the employment of boys in climbing chimneys . . . 13 March . . ., London, 1818

Spencer, G. J. T., *Letter to the Rt Rev. the Lord Bishop of Bath and Wells by the Rt Rev. Bishop Spencer, late Lord Bishop of Madras*, London, 1853

Squibb, G. D., *Doctors' Commons: A History of the College of Advocates and Doctors of Law*, Oxford, Clarendon Press, 1977

Stacey, C. P., *Canada and the British Army 1846–71*, Toronto, University of Toronto Press, 1963

Stanley, A. P., *Edinburgh Review* 113 (1861), 461
  Essays, chiefly on Questions of Church and State from 1850 to 1870, London, John Murray, 1870
  Purity and Light. A sermon preached before the University of Cambridge, Feb. 2, 1873, London, 1873

Stanley, E. H. S. (Lord), *The Church Rate Question Considered*, London, 1853

Steel, D. W. and Rose, F. D. (eds.), *Kennedy's Law of Salvage*, 5th edn, London, Stevens, 1985

Stephen, G., *Anti-Slavery Recollections*, London, Thomas Hatchard, 1854

Stephen, J. F., *Defence of the Rev. Rowland Williams in the Arches' Court of Canterbury*, London, 1862

History of the Criminal Law of England, 3 vols, London, Macmillan, 1883

Stephen, M. D., 'Gladstone and the Composition of the Final Court in Ecclesiastical Cases, 1850–73', *Historical Journal* 9 (1966), 191–200

Stevens, R. B., *Law and Politics: The House of Lords as a Judicial Body, 1800–1976*, Chapel Hill, North Carolina, University of North Carolina Press, 1978

Stevenson, J., 'The Queen Caroline Affair', *London in the Age of Reform*, Oxford, Blackwell, 1977

Stewart, R., *Henry Brougham, 1778–1868: his Public Career*, London, Bodley Head, 1986

Stocking, G. W., *Victorian Anthropology*, London, Collier Macmillan, 1987

Strachey, L. and Fulford R. (eds.), *The Greville Memoirs, 1814–1860*, London, Macmillan, 1938

Substance of the debates on the bill for abolishing the Slave Trade ... passed into law on the 25th March 1807, London, 1908

Substance of the Speeches of S. Lushington ... and J. Sydney Taylor ... on the resolution relative to the punishment of death, London, 1831

Surrey Archaeological Society Collections

Swan, R., *The Principle of Church Rates etc.*, London, 1837

Swinfen, D. B., 'The Single Judgment in the Privy Council, 1833–1966', *Juridical Review* 1975, 153

Tallack, W., *Howard Letters and Memories*, London, Methuen, 1905

Taylor, D. C., *People of Cobham: the Pyports Connection*, Buckingham, 1985

Temperley, H., *British Antislavery, 1833–1870*, London, Longman, 1972

Thomas, M. W., *The Early Factory Legislation*, Leigh-on-Sea, Thomas Bank Publishing Co., 1948

Thompson, E. P., *The Making of the English Working Class*, London, Gollancz, 1980

Thorne, R. G., *The House of Commons 1790–1820, History of Parliament* vol 4, London, Secker and Warburg, 1986

Trevelyan, G. M., *Lord Grey of the Reform Bill*, London, Longman Green, 1920

Trollope, A., *An Autobiography*, London, World's Classics edn, 1923

The Bertrams: a Novel, Leipzig, B. Tauchnitz, 1859

Barchester Towers, 1857

Tuberville, A. S., *The House of Lords in the Age of Reform*, London, Faber and Faber, 1958

Turney, C., *Byron's Daughter: a Biography of Elizabeth Medora Leigh*, New York, Scribner, 1972

Twiss, H., *Public and Private Life of Lord Chancellor Eldon*, London, John Murray, 1844

The Law of Nations Considered as Independent Political Communities . . ., 2nd revised edn, Oxford, Clarendon Press, 1875

Vidler, A. R., *The Church in an Age of Revolution*, Harmondsworth, Penguin, 1961

Waddilove, A., *Digest of Cases decided in the Court of Arches*, London, W. Benning & Co., 1849

Wallas, G., *The Life of Francis Place*, London, Longman & Co., 1898

Wallbridge, E. A., *Martyr of Demerara. Memoirs of the Rev. John Smith, Missionary to Demerara*, London, 1848

Walpole, S., *History of England from the Conclusion of the Great War in 1815*, London, Longman, Green, 1879

Walsh, W., *The Secret History of the Oxford Movement*, 3rd edn, London, Swan, Saben and Sonnenschein, 1898

Walvin, J., *England, Slaves and Freedom, 1776–1838*, Basingstoke, Macmillan, 1986

Ward, M. A., *A Writer's Recollections*, New York, Harper, 1918

Webb, R. K., *The British Working-class Reader, 1790–1868: Literacy and Social Tension*, London, Allen and Unwin, 1955

Wheaton, H., *Elements of International Law*, 1st English edn, London, Stevens, 1878

Wilberforce, R. I. and S., *Life of Wilberforce*, London, John Murray, 1838

Wilberforce, Samuel, *Quarterly Review* 109 (1861), 248–305

Williams, E., *Capitalism and Slavery*, 1944; reprinted London, A. Deutsch, 1964

Williams, E. V., *Treatise on the Law of Executors and Administrators*, London, 1832

Williams, R., *Life and Letters*, edited by his wife, London, 1874

Persecution for the Word, with a Postscript on the Interlocutory Judgment and the Present State of the Case, London, 1862

Wilson, H. B., *Speech of H. B. Wilson before the Judicial Committee*, 1863

Wiswall, F. L., *The Development of Admiralty Jurisdiction and Practice since 1800: an English study with American Comparisons*, Cambridge, Cambridge University Press, 1970

Wolfram, S., 'Divorce in England 1700–1857', *Oxford Journal of Legal Studies* 5 (1985), 155

Wood, A., *Nineteenth-Century Britain, 1815–1914*, London, Longman, 1967

Woodward, E. L., *The Age of Reform: 1815–1870*, Oxford, Clarendon Press, 1938

Wright, R. A., *Legal Essays and Addresses*, Cambridge, Cambridge University Press, 1939

Yale, D. E. C., 'The Third Lord in *Rylands* v. *Fletcher*', *Law Quarterly Review* 86 (1970), 311

THESES

Ellens, J. P., 'The Church Rate Conflict in England and Wales 1832–1868', PhD thesis, University of Toronto, 1983

Hayes, B. D., 'Politics in Norfolk', PhD thesis, Cambridge University, 1957

INDEX

Aberdeen, Lord (G. H. Gordon), 65
Adams, J. (Dr), 108, 119
Admiralty Court, 7, 10, 18, 21, 25,
  41–2, 46–7, 50, 65, 182–3, 194–237
adultery, 103, 163, 167, 174–6, 178–9,
  187–8
advocates, 16–17, 19, 20
advowsons, 18
Africa, 85, 87–9
African Institution, 81
alimony, 6, 131, 168, 181–3
All Souls College, 1–2
altar, 289–93
Althorp, Viscount (J. C. Spencer), 38,
  75
American Civil War, 227–30
Anderson, J., 89–90
Anglo-catholics, 55
Anti-slavery Society, 68, 75–8, 81–3,
  90–1
apprenticeship, 74
archdeacons, 18
Arches, Court of, 5, 7, 9, 268, 315–42,
  346
Articles of Religion, 59, 274–5, 280–3,
  287–8, 321–5, 327–30, 333, 338,
  340
Austin, Mr (Revd), 97

Badeley, E., 273, 276–8
Baillie, Dr, 132
ballot, secret, 41, 317
baptism, 271–80, 333
Baptists, 95
Barret, Mr, 70
Bathurst, H. A., 107, 114, 134
Bedford, P., 28
Bergami, T., 136
Black Act, 27
Blackstone, W., 168

blasphemy, 31
Blomfield, C. J., 273, 277–9
booty, law of, 8, 12, 230–7
Boyce, Susan, 109, 111
brawling, 13, 161–2, 170–1
Brazil, 79
Bridges, G. W., 96
broad church, 55–6, 303–47
Brougham, H. P. (Lord), 8, 13, 15–17,
  20–2, 34, 36, 42, 46, 49, 50–1, 54,
  67, 72, 75, 81, 86, 98, 125, 135–8,
  145, 147–8, 152, 159, 163, 190,
  238–43, 252, 266–7, 280, 304, 316
Brunswick, 153, 157–8
Bunsen, Baron, 325–6
Burder, J., 259–62
burial, 250
Burnaby, Dr, 305–6
Buxton, Charles, 86
Buxton, Priscilla, 52, 83
Buxton, Sarah, 85
Buxton, T. F., 2, 8, 25, 28, 51–2, 65,
  71–89, 91, 97–8, 247
Byron, A. I. (Lady), 3, 6, 50, 100–33,
  177, 181
Byron, Ada, 100, 114, 124–8, 134
Byron, Captain, 119
Byron, G. (Lord), 100–33

Cambridge University, 59, 347
Campbell, Lord, 49, 240, 277
candles, 289
Canterbury Cathedral, 56
Cape of Good Hope, 76
capital punishment, 26–30
Caroline of Brunswick, Queen, 6, 24,
  50, 135–59, 181, 267
Carr, Frances, 2, 56–7, 159
Carr, Laura, 49
Carr, Sarah, see Lushington, Sarah

Catholic education, 37
Catholic emancipation, 3, 24–5, 35, 57–60, 344
Cato Street conspiracy, 149
Chancellorship (London), 9
Chancery, Court of, 105–6
Chelmsford, Lord, 242, 343
child custody law, 105–6, 114, 124–7, 183
child labour, 39–40
chimney-sweeps, 39
Church Building Commission, 22
Church, R. W., 303
church rates, 7, 13, 17, 44, 58, 161–2, 172, 249–69
civil law, 1, 15, 17
Clarendon, Lord, 222–3
Clarkson, T., 63, 86
clergy discipline, 17
Clermont, Mrs, 121, 126
Cleveland, Lord, 22
Cockburn, G. (Sir), 153
Coke, Lord, 60
Colenso, J. W., 339
Coleridge, J. D., 300, 319–20, 328, 334, 339
compensation to slave owners, 63, 74–6
condonation, 104, 120, 179–80
confession, 297–302
confirmation of bishops, 304–8
connivance, 139, 141, 179–80
Consistory Court (London) 5, 6, 9, 10, 160–93, 255–65, 290
Constitutional Association, 31
contract law, 212–17
corporal punishment, 30
Corporation Act, 57, 249, 253
correction of clerks, *see* clergy discipline
costs, 168, 207–8
Cottenham, Lord (C. C. Pepys), 240
counsel for prisoners, 32–3
Cranworth, Lord (R. M. Rolfe), 49, 242, 266, 309, 343
Crawford, W., 28
Creevey, T., 139, 149, 152
Crimean War, 219–30
criminal jurisdiction of ecclesiastical courts, 14, 17
criminal law, 25–34
criminal libel, 31
Croker, J. W., 45
crosses, 289–93
cruelty, 103, 114, 120, 163, 167, 174, 177–8, 182

Cuba, 79

damages, law of, 7
Darlington, Lord, 22
Darwin, C., 312–13
Davies, S. B., 119
de Clifford, Lord, 146
defamation, 13, 17–18, 161–2, 168–70
Delegates, High Court of, 8, 16, 201, 238, 279
Demerara, 31, 66–7, 97
Denison, G. A., 276, 280–8
Denman, T., 135–6, 144, 159
desertion, 139, 179
Dickens, Charles, 4, 10, 13, 170–1, 196
dilapidations, 17–18
Disraeli, B., 24
Dissenters, 35–7, 52–4, 57–9, 95, 249–69, 303, 344
Ditcher, J., 281
divorce, 6, 21, 102–4, 161–7, 172–88
Doctors' Commons, 5, 6, 10, 12–13, 15, 227, 248, 265, 305
Dodson, J. (Sir), 191, 305–6
donatives, 18
Doyle, Colonel, 116, 129
Doyle, Selina, 122, 124
duplex querela, 18

Easter offerings, 18
Ecclesiastical Commission, 22
Ecclesiastical Courts Commission, 9, 14–22, 50–1, 171, 189–90, 260, 268, 279
Ecclesiastical Revenue Commission, 22
education, 26, 34–8
Eldon, Lord, 159, 241
erastianism, 56, 306
Escoffery, J., 68–70, 97
Essays and Reviews, 56, 310–47
eucharist, 280–8
evangelicals, 52–5, 312
evidence
    law of, 32, 66, 107, 114, 120, 187
    oral, 13, 14, 15, 17, 20, 106, 143, 165, 199–200, 226
excommunication, 13, 258
extradition, 89–90

faculties, 161–2, 172
Faculties, Master of the, 9
Falmouth, Lord, 146
Farquhar, J., 119
Farrar, Dean, 341

Fletcher, Ann, 122
Forster, J., 77
free coloured people, 68–71, 92–3
free labour, 96
free trade, 79–81, 220–1

George IV, King, 135–55
Gladstone, J., 67
Gladstone, W. E., 37, 79, 280–1,
  283–4, 286, 297, 344
Gorham, G. C., 271–80
Gosling, J., 263–6
Gothic revival, 289–90
Granville, Lord (G. G. Leveson-
  Gower), 8, 44–5, 48–50, 220–2
Greville, C. C. H., 8, 46, 49, 99,
  220–1, 238, 273, 276–7, 307
Grey, C. (Earl), 8, 97, 138, 145, 149
Grey, G. (Sir), 228
Grote, G., 317
Grote, J., 317, 322, 340
Gurney, A., 85
Gurney, J. J., 84
Guy's Hospital, 36

habeas corpus, 89–90, 105, 125, 183
Hampden, R. D., 303–8
Hanbury, R., 25
Hanson, J., 102, 108, 131–2
Harding, J., 220, 222
Harewood, Lord, 73
Harrison, F., 311–14
Harrowby, Earl of, 146
Heath, D. I., 308–10, 334–6
hell, 34, 319, 330–1, 346
Heywood, Serjeant, 108
high church, 55, 270–302, 307
High Court of Admiralty, *see* Admiralty
  Court
High Court of Delegates, *see* Delegates
Hoare, S., 28
Hobhouse, J. C. (Lord Broughton),
  101–2, 115–16, 118–19, 131–3
Hodgson, F. (Revd), 118
Holland, Lord, 130–1
Home Missionary Society, 53, 55
Honduras, 70
Houghton, Baron (R. M. Milnes), 3
House of Lords, 43–50, 267
Hume, J., 43

Ilchester, 22
incarnation, 333
incest, 161–2, 171, 179

India, 8, 79, 85, 238, 246–7
international law, 8, 17–18, 24, 218,
  223–5, 228–30
Ireland, 60

jactitation of marriage, 161–2
Jamaica, 31, 63, 68–70, 76–9
James, Lord Justice, 347
Jenkins, R., 341
Jenner Fust, *see* Jenner
Jenner, H., 13, 21, 108, 119, 191,
  240–1, 265–6
Jeremie, J. (Sir), 83–4
Jeremie, Miss, 84
Jews, civil disabilities of, 57–61, 344
Jowett, B., 31, 343–4
judges, exclusion from Parliament, 41–3
jury trials, 17
justification, 329

Keble, J., 284, 295
Kingsdown, Lord, 242, 317, 326–7, 343
Kingsley, C., 340
Kinnaird, D., 111, 132
Knight Bruce, J. L., 240–1, 282
Knight, W., 28

laissez faire, 38
Lamb, C., Lady (Caroline Ponsonby),
  115
Lamb, C. (Mrs George Lamb), 127
Langdale, Lord, 274, 277
law reports, 10, 12–13
Lecesne, L. E., 68–70, 97
Lee, Dr S., 5
Leigh, Augusta, 107, 109–10, 117–20,
  125, 127–8
Liddell, R., 288–97
life peerage, 9, 43–50
Lincoln, A., 228
Liverpool, Lord (R. B. Jenkinson),
  146–9, 151, 155–7, 159
London University, 35–7, 50, 267
Lovelace, Lord, 134
low church, 55, 307
Lushington, Alice, 39, 283–4, 315
Lushington, Charles, 87
Lushington, Edward H., 2, 247
Lushington, Fanny (Lady), 63
Lushington, Godfrey, 3
Lushington, Henry (Sir), 63
Lushington, Hester (Lady), 3
Lushington, Sarah, 2, 107, 113, 134
Lushington, Stephen: character, 1–2;

death, 9, 346–7; education, 1; judicial style, 11–12, 186–7, 196–7, 204–5, 230–7; life peerage, 443–50; marriage, 1–2, 152; religious views, 55–7, 61–2; retirement, 9
Lushington, Susan, 101, 158
Lushington, Vernon, 3, 347
Lyall, W. R., 266
Lyndhurst, Lord, 45, 48, 49

Macaulay, T. B., 75
Macaulay, Z., 78, 84–5, 86
Majoochi, 143
Manning, H. E., 272, 281
marriage, form of, 58, 250
married women's property law, 104, 179
Marsh, W., 55
Mason, J. M., 227
Matrimonial Causes Act, 172
matrimonial law, 6, 15, 17, 21, 100–33, 160–8, 172–88
Maurice, F. D., 57, 307–8, 310, 337, 340–1
Mauritius, 75–6, 84
May, E., 149
Melbourne, Lord (W. Lamb), 42, 46, 76, 78–9, 303
Melville, Lord (H. Dundas), 3
Methodists, 53, 95–6
Mico Charity, 83
Mill, J. S., 338
Missouri, 89
Moore, T., 112, 123
Moravians, 95
Musgrave, T., 278

Newcastle, Duke of, 90
Nicholl, Sir John, 14, 16, 21, 190
Noel, Lady, 100–1, 107–13, 124–6, 130–2
Noel, R. (Sir), 100, 123
nomination boroughs, 40
Normanby, Lord, 88
nullity of marriage, 161, 167–8, 183–6

oaths, form of, 57, 60
obscenity, 31, 298
Ockham, 39, 56–7, 134, 290, 346–7
O'Connell, D., 44
ornaments 296–7
Owen, R., 38
Oxford Movement, 54–5, 291, 295
Oxford University, 1, 59, 303–4, 346–7

pacifism, 81

Palmer, R., 267
Palmerston, Viscount (H. J. Temple), 31, 228–30
Parke, J., see Wensleydale
Parliament, length of, 41
Peel, Sir R., 24–5, 92, 97
peerage for life, see Life peerage
penance, 13, 170–2
Penn, W., 87
Peterloo, 31, 149
pews, 17–18, 161–2, 172, 253–4, 289–90
Phillimore, J., 136, 146
Phillimore, R. J. (Sir), 9, 10, 14, 283, 286, 328, 342
Phillpotts, H., 271–80, 283, 287, 295
pin money, 130
Poland, 24
police, 26
Pollock, F. (Sir), 10, 21, 240
Poole, A., 297–302
Poor Law, 38–9
praemunire, 305
preconization, 304–8
Prerogative Court (Canterbury), 5, 6, 16
prisons, 26, 30
Privy Council
    Appeals Committee of, 8
    Judicial Committee of, 6, 9, 16, 46, 50, 160, 191, 201–2, 225, 238–48, 270–80, 295–7, 308–11, 327–8, 331, 342–4
prize law, 8, 219–30, 232–4
probate, 5, 6, 13, 15–17, 20, 21, 160–2, 168, 189–93
proctors, 16, 20
propitiation, 328–9, 333
prosecution societies, 31
punishment, see criminal law
Pusey, E. B., 284

Quakers, 81, 88, 250, 254

radicals, 24
Reading, 22
Real Property Commission (1833), 16
recrimination, 139, 142, 167, 179–81
Reeve, H., 328
Reform Act (1832), 22, 40–1, 73
reformers, 24–5
registration of births and deaths, 58–9, 250
restitution, law of, 217
restitution of conjugal rights, 6, 102, 161–7

ritualists, 55, 296–7
Robinson, C. (Dr), 108, 119
Robinson, J. B. (Sir), 89
Robison, Captain, 31
Romilly, S. (Sir), 125–6, 132
rood screen, 292
Rose, H. (Sir), 231–6
Rothery, H. C., 270, 347
rotten boroughs, *see* nomination
    boroughs
Russell, Lord John, 41–2, 46, 48, 57,
    78, 80, 151, 304
Russia, 24

sabbath observance, 31, 53, 55
St Barnabas' Church, 289–98
St Leonards, Lord, 45, 49
Salisbury, Bishop of, (W. K.
    Hamilton), 335
salvage, 8, 194–219
Sandon, Lord (Earl of Harrowby), 92
sati, 8
Scoble, J., 65, 80, 81
Scots law, 44, 47
Scott, W. (Sir), *see* Stowell
scripture, 320–8, 332–3, 343
sedition, 31
sequestrations, 17–18
Shephard, J., 160
Shepherd, S. (Sir), 131–2
Sibthorpe, Col., 25
simony, 18
sinecures, 14
slave trade, 3, 24, 63–6, 75, 79–80
slavery, 25, 31, 35, 50–4, 63–99, 230,
    347
Slidell, J., 227
Smith, John (Revd), 31–2, 66–7, 97
Smith, L. (Sir), 78
Smith, Vance, 346
Society for the Diffusion of Useful
    Knowledge, 34–5, 50, 267
Society for the Suppression of Vice, 31,
    55
Somerset, Duke of, 228
South America, 24
Stanley, A. P., 313–14, 320, 332, 340,
    344, 346–7
Stanley, Lord, 249, 268
Stephen, G. (Sir), 43, 65, 75–6, 84, 86
Stephen, J. F., 27, 319, 326, 335, 344–5
Stowell, Lord (W. Scott), 73–4, 102–3,
    111, 115, 142, 177, 202, 224–5,
    227, 229

street improvements, 40
Sturge, J., 77
Suffield, Lord (H. Harbord), 3
suffrage, 41
sugar duties, 22, 79–81, 95
Sumner, J. B., 9, 273, 278, 281–2, 286,
    295, 298–300, 331
suttee, see sati

Tait, A. C., 242, 270, 295, 298–301,
    307, 324, 328, 341, 344
Temple, F., 310, 344
Test Act, 57, 249, 253
Thorogood, J., 249–50, 254–7, 262
Tindal, N. C. (Sir), 135
tithes, 18
Tower Hamlets, 22, 54
Tractarians, 55, 272, 276, 278, 303,
    312, 316
Tregony, 22
Trent, The, 227–30
Trinidad, 71
Trinity House, 200
Trollope, Anthony, 56, 228, 284,
    313–14
Trotter, H. D., 84
Truro, Lord (T. Wilde), 135, 266–7

universalism, 329–30
universities, 35–7, 50, 58–9

vestments, 296–7
Victoria, Queen, 46, 79, 80
Villiers, Mrs, 111
Voysey, C., 346

Walpole, S., 135, 151
war, 221–2
Wellington, Duke of (A. Wellesley), 25,
    97
Wensleydale, Lord (J. Parke), 49, 241
West Indies, 25
Westbury, Lord (R. Bethell), 44, 48,
    331, 343
Wharncliffe, Lord, 241
Wharton, G. B., 126
Whigs, 22, 24, 35, 56, 78, 151
Whitlock, General, 231–6
Wigram, J. (Sir), 240
Wilberforce, S., 311–12, 314
Wilberforce, W., 31, 51, 70, 86
Wilbraham, G., 57
Wilde, T., *see* Truro
William IV, King, 159

Index

Williams, J. (Sir), 135
Williams, Lt-Gen., 90
Williams, R. (Revd), 311–47
Wills *see* probate
Wills Act, 1837, 190–3
Wilmot, R. J., 118–19, 129, 131
Wilson, D. (Bishop of Calcutta), 85

Wilson, H. B. (Revd), 311–47
Winchelsea, 22
Windham, W., 3
Wood, Alderman, 153

Yarnall, E., 339

DATE DUE

HIGHSMITH 45-220